Open Source Software Dynamics, Processes, and Applications

Stefan Koch
Bogazici University, Turkey

Managing Director:	Lindsay Johnston
Editorial Director:	Joel Gamon
Book Production Manager:	Jennifer Yoder
Publishing Systems Analyst:	Adrienne Freeland
Development Editor:	Joel Gamon
Assistant Acquisitions Editor:	Kayla Wolfe
Typesetter:	Lisandro Gonzalez
Cover Design:	Jason Mull

Published in the United States of America by
Information Science Reference (an imprint of IGI Global)
701 E. Chocolate Avenue
Hershey PA 17033
Tel: 717-533-8845
Fax: 717-533-8661
E-mail: cust@igi-global.com
Web site: http://www.igi-global.com

Library of Congress Cataloging-in-Publication Data

Open source software dynamics, processes, and applications / Stefan Koch, editor.
    p. cm.
  Includes bibliographical references and index.
  Summary: "This book is a multidisciplinary collection of research and approaches on the applications and processes of open source software, highlighting the development processes performed by software programmers, the motivations of its participants, and the legal and economic issues that have been raised"--Provided by publisher.
  ISBN 978-1-4666-2937-0 (hardcover) -- ISBN 978-1-4666-2938-7 (ebook) -- ISBN 978-1-4666-2939-4 (print & perpetual access) 1. Open source software. 2. Computer software--Development. I. Koch, Stefan, 1974-
  QA76.76.S46O628 2013
  005.3--dc23
                        2012039285

British Cataloguing in Publication Data
A Cataloguing in Publication record for this book is available from the British Library.

The views expressed in this book are those of the authors, but not necessarily of the publisher.

Table of Contents

Detailed Table of Contents

Chapter 1

    Arif Raza, University of Western Ontario, Canada
    Luiz Fernando Capretz, University of Western Ontario, Canada
    Faheem Ahmed, United Arab Emirates University, UAE

Recent years have seen a sharp increase in the use of open source projects by common novice users; Open Source Software (OSS) is thus no longer a reserved arena for software developers and computer gurus. Although user-centered designs are gaining popularity in OSS, usability is still not considered one of the prime objectives in many design scenarios. This paper analyzes industry users' perception of usability factors, including understandability, learnability, operability, and attractiveness on OSS usability. The research model of this empirical study establishes the relationship between the key usability factors and OSS usability from industrial perspective. In order to conduct the study, a data set of 105 industry users is included. The results of the empirical investigation indicate the significance of the key factors for OSS usability.

Chapter 2

    Kris Ven, University of Antwerp, Belgium
    Peter De Bruyn, University of Antwerp, Belgium

Previous research has shown that the knowledge that is available to an organization is an important factor influencing the adoption of open source software (OSS). Hence, it is important that organizations develop their absorptive capacity in order to successfully adopt OSS. Absorptive capacity refers to the ability of an organization to acquire, assimilate, and exploit new knowledge. However, no study has specifically investigated how organizations can develop their absorptive capacity by acquiring knowledge about OSS. This paper addresses this gap in research by investigating the organizational knowledge assimilation process within the context of the adoption of OSS. Based on a case study conducted at the Flemish government, a framework that is grounded in literature and that illustrates which contextual factors influence the development of absorptive capacity in the context of the adoption of OSS was developed.

Chapter 3

Spyridoula Lakka, University of Athens, Greece

Teta Stamati, University of Athens, Greece

Christos Michalakelis, University of Athens, Greece

Dracoulis Martakos, University of Athens, Greece

This study focuses on theory building providing a holistic conceptual framework that consists of an ontology based OSS business model and an OSS business model taxonomy. The study extends existing theory in OSS business models and corresponding taxonomies, based on the structured-case methodological approach. An exploratory study is conducted in two research cycles, for the identification, validation, and evaluation of the critical constructs of an OSS business model. Results reveal that OSS business models differ from traditional software business models, having specific features that affect the software value chain, the infrastructure, and the revenue model of an OSS oriented firm.

Chapter 4

Sandro Morasca, Università degli Studi dell'Insubria, Italy

Davide Taibi, Università degli Studi dell'Insubria, Italy

Davide Tosi, Università degli Studi dell'Insubria, Italy

Open Source Software (OSS) products do not usually follow traditional software engineering development paradigms. Specifically, testing activities in OSS development may be quite different from those carried out in Closed Source Software (CSS) development. As testing and verification require a good deal of resources in OSS, it is necessary to have ways to assess and improve OSS testing processes. This paper provides a set of testing guidelines and issues that OSS developers can use to decide which testing techniques make most sense for their OSS products. This paper 1) provides a checklist that helps OSS developers identify the most useful testing techniques according to the main characteristics of their products, and 2) outlines a proposal for a method that helps assess the maturity of OSS testing processes. The method is a proposal of a Maturity Model for testing processes (called OSS-TMM). To show its usefulness, the authors apply the method to seven real-life projects. Specifically, the authors apply the method to BusyBox, Apache Httpd, and Eclipse Test & Performance Tools Platform to show how the checklist supports and guides the testing process of these OSS products.

Chapter 5

Daniel Izquierdo-Cortazar, Universidad Rey Juan Carlos, Spain

Andrea Capiluppi, University of East London, UK

Jesus M. Gonzalez-Barahona, Universidad Rey Juan Carlos, Spain

The process of fixing software bugs plays a key role in the maintenance activities of a software project. Ideally, code ownership and responsibility should be enforced among developers working on the same artifacts, so that those introducing buggy code could also contribute to its fix. However, especially in FLOSS projects, this mechanism is not clearly understood: in particular, it is not known whether those contributors fixing a bug are the same introducing and seeding it in the first place. This paper analyzes the comm-central FLOSS project, which hosts part of the Thunderbird, SeaMonkey, Lightning extensions and Sunbird projects from the Mozilla community. The analysis is focused at the level of lines of code and it uses the information stored in the source code management system. The results of this study show that in 80% of the cases, the bug-fixing activity involves source code modified by at most two developers. It also emerges that the developers fixing the bug are only responsible for 3.5% of the previous modifications to the lines affected; this implies that the other developers making changes to those lines could have made that fix. In most of the cases the bug fixing process in comm-central is not carried out by the same developers than those who seeded the buggy code.

Chapter 6

M.M. Mahbubul Syeed, Tampere University of Technology, Finland

Timo Aaltonen, Nokia Research Center, Finland

Imed Hammouda, Tampere University of Technology, Finland

Tarja Systä, Tampere University of Technology, Finland

Open Source Software (OSS) is currently a widely adopted approach to developing and distributing software. OSS code adoption requires an understanding of the structure of the code base. For a deeper understanding of the maintenance, bug fixing and development activities, the structure of the developer community also needs to be understood, especially the relations between the code and community structures. This, in turn, is essential for the development and maintenance of software containing OSS code. This paper proposes a method and support tool for exploring the relations of the code base and community structures of OSS projects. The method and proposed tool, Binoculars, rely on generic and reusable query operations, formal definitions of which are given in the paper. The authors demonstrate the applicability of Binoculars with two examples. The authors analyze a well-known and active open source project, FFMpeg, and the open source version of the IaaS cloud computing project Eucalyptus.

Chapter 7

Linus Nyman, Hanken School of Economics, Finland

Tommi Mikkonen, Tampere University of Technology, Finland

A project fork occurs when software developers take a copy of source code from one software package and use it to begin an independent development work that is maintained separately. Although forking in open source software does not require the permission of the original authors, the new version competes for the attention of the same developers that have worked on the original version. The motivations developers have for performing forks are many, but in general they have received little attention. The authors present the results of a study of forks performed in SourceForge (http://sourceforge.net/) and list the developers' motivations for their actions.

Chapter 8

Andrea Capiluppi, Brunel University, UK

Klaas-Jan Stol, Lero (The Irish Software Engineering Research Centre), University of Limerick, Ireland

Cornelia Boldyreff, University of East London, UK

A promising way to support software reuse is based on Component-Based Software Development (CBSD). Open Source Software (OSS) products are increasingly available that can be freely used in product development. However, OSS communities still face several challenges before taking full advantage of the "reuse mechanism": many OSS projects duplicate effort, for instance when many projects implement a similar system in the same application domain and in the same topic. One successful counter-example is the FFmpeg multimedia project; several of its components are widely and consistently reused in other

OSS projects. Documented is the evolutionary history of the various libraries of components within the FFmpeg project, which presently are reused in more than 140 OSS projects. Most use them as black-box components; although a number of OSS projects keep a localized copy in their repositories, eventually modifying them as needed (white-box reuse). In both cases, the authors argue that FFmpeg is a successful project that provides an excellent exemplar of a reusable library of OSS components.

Chapter 9

This paper examines what is known about the role of open source software development within the world of game mods and modding practices. Game modding has become a leading method for developing games by customizing or creating Open Source Software extensions to game software in general, and particularly to proprietary closed source software games. What, why, and how OSS and closed source software come together within an application system is the subject for this study. Observational and qualitative is used to highlight current practices and issues that can be associated with software engineering and game studies foundations with multiple examples of different game mods and modding practices are identified throughout this study.

Chapter 10

There is an ample debate over the quality of Free/Libre Open Source Software (FLOSS) with mixed research results. The authors show that a reason for these mixed results is that quality is being defined, measured, and evaluated differently. They report the most popular approaches including software structure measures, process measures, and maturity assessment models. The way researchers have built their samples has also contributed to the mixed results with different project properties being considered and ignored. Because FLOSS projects evolve with each release, their quality does too, and it must be measured using metrics that take into account their communities' commitment to quality rather than just the structure of the resulting code. Challenges exist in defining what constitutes a defect or bug, and the role of modularity in affecting FLOSS quality. The authors suggest three considerations for future research on FLOSS quality models: (1) defect resolution rate, (2) kind of software product, and (3) modularity—both technical and organizational.

Stakeholders in Open Source Software (OSS) projects need to determine whether a project is likely to sustain for a sufficient period of time in order to justify their investments into this project. In an OSS project context, there are typically several data sources and OSS processes relevant for determining project health indicators. However, even within one project these data sources often are technically and/or semantically heterogeneous, which makes data collection and analysis tedious and error prone.

In this paper, the authors propose and evaluate a framework for OSS data analysis (FOSSDA), which enables the efficient collection, integration, and analysis of data from heterogeneous sources. Major results of the empirical studies are: (a) the framework is useful for integrating data from heterogeneous data sources effectively and (b) project health indicators based on integrated data analyses were found to be more accurate than analyses based on individual non-integrated data sources.

This study differs from previous studies on open source software (OSS) developer motivation by drawing upon theories of volunteerism and work motivation to investigate the motives and attitudes of OSS volunteer developers. The role of commitment is specifically interesting, which is well established in the volunteerism and work motivation literature as a predictor of turnover and positively related to work performance, but has been overlooked by OSS researchers. The authors have developed a research model relating motivations, commitment, satisfaction, and length of service to intention to contribute to OSS projects in the future. The research model is evaluated using data from an online survey of 181 OSS volunteer developers. The research results and more discussion of these areas of interest will be evaluated and discussed further in the chapter.

An important component of Early Warning Systems (EWS) for man-made and natural hazards is the command and control unit's Graphical User Interface (GUI). All relevant information of an EWS is concentrated in this GUI and offered to human operators. However, when designing the GUI, not only the user experience and the GUI's screens are relevant, but also the frameworks and technologies that the GUI is built on and the implementation of the GUI itself are of great importance. Implementations differ based on their applications in different domains but the design and approaches to implement the GUIs of different EWS often show analogies. The design and development of such GUIs are performed repeatedly on some parts of the system for each EWS. Thus, the generic GUI framework of a geospatial EWS for tsunamis is introduced to enable possible synergistic effects on the development of other new related technology. The results presented here could be adopted and reused in other EWS for man-made and natural hazards.

Preface

EVALUATION AND SELECTION OF FREE AND OPEN SOURCE SOFTWARE: A REVIEW AND PORTFOLIO PLANNING PROPOSAL

ABSTRACT

This preface reviews the importance of and approaches for arriving at an assessment and evaluation of open source projects. It then proposes a solution based on an analysis of their growth rates in several aspects. These include: code base, developer number, bug reports, and downloads. Based on this analysis and assessment, a well-known portfolio planning method, the BCG matrix, is employed for arriving at a very broad classification of open source projects. While this approach naturally results in a loss of detailed information, a top-level categorization is in some domains necessary and of interest.

INTRODUCTION

The adoption and evaluation of free (Stallmann, 2002) and open source (Perens, 1999) projects has gained increasing interest, both from an academic and business perspective (Norris and Kamp, 2004). In the context of several business model and approaches based on the idea of open innovation, organizations increasingly seek to get outside assistance and knowledge as embodied in software in preparing their own products or services. Due to the importance that such use together with sometimes continued collaboration has gained, it becomes a vital task and skill to choose the correct project and community.

This has led to the development of assessment schemes like OpenBRR (Open Business Readiness Rating) (Wassermann et al., 2005), Open Source Maturity Model (Petrinja et al. 2010a), QSOS by Atos Origin (2009), OpenBQR (Taibi et al., 2007), and similar achievements (Petrinja et al., 2010). Most of these approaches are based on detailed scoring of open source products, and aggregation using some form of weightings. While some consider that features of the underlying community form an important part of an evaluation (Robles et al., 2006), this is not generally acknowledged. In addition, while in some approaches the use of real data, both on community and the software product itself is planned, some rely on personal rating or data entry of many features. Some of the approaches are also overly complex for the context of managerial decision-making, or the aggregation of different aspects to higher levels of abstraction is poorly and problematically handled.

The approach first proposed by Koch and Stix (2008) tries to both rely on actual data, and to provide a top-level, aggregate classification scheme. They proposed to base such an effort on well-known portfolio planning techniques, especially the BCG matrix, and use growth rate analysis as axis of such a matrix.

DATA GATHERING AND ANALYSIS

For any evaluation and assessment based on actual data and not expert opinions, the information contained in software development repositories will be used. Software development repositories contain a plethora of information on software and underlying, associated development processes (Cook et al., 1998; Atkins et al., 1999). Studying software systems and development processes using these sources of data offers several advantages (Cook et al., 1998): It is very cost-effective, as no additional instrumentation is necessary, and does not influence the process under consideration. In addition, longitudinal data are available, allowing for analyses that consider the whole project history. Depending on the tools used in a project, possible repositories available for analysis include source code versioning systems (Atkins et al., 1999; Kemerer and Slaughter, 1999), bug reporting systems, and mailing lists.

In open source software development projects, repositories in several forms are also in use, in fact form the most important communication and coordination channels. Therefore only a small amount of information cannot be captured by repository analyses because it is transmitted inter-personally. As a side effect, the repositories in use must be available openly and publicly. Therefore open source software development repositories form an optimal data source for studying the associated type of software development.

Prior studies have included both in-depth analyses of small numbers of successful (Crowston et al., 2006) projects (Gallivan, 2001) like Apache and Mozilla (Mockus et al., 2002), GNOME (Koch and Schneider, 2002), or FreeBSD (Dinh-Tong and Bieman, 2005), and also large data samples, such of those derived from Sourceforge.net (Koch, 2004; Long & Siau, 2007). Primarily, information provided by version control systems has been used, but also aggregated data provided by software repositories (Crowston and Scozzi, 2002; Hunt and Johnson, 2002; Krishnamurthy, 2002), meta-information included in Linux Software Map entries (Dempsey et al., 2002), or data retrieved directly from the source code itself (Ghosh & Prakash, 2000).

Although this data is available, the task is made more complicated by the large size and scope of the project repositories or code forges, and the heterogeneity of the projects being studied (Howison and Crowston, 2004; Robles et al., 2009; Syeed et al., 2011; Sunindyo et al., 2011). Therefore, in the last years RoRs ("repository of repositories") have been developed, which collect, aggregate, and clean the targeted repository data (Sowe et al., 2007; Berger et al., 2010). Two examples are FLOSSMetrics and FLOSSmole. These RoRs usually hold data collected from project repositories, and some of them also store some analysis and metrics calculated on the retrieved data. The results (raw data, summary data, and/or analyses) will be stored in a database and accessible to the rest of the research community. The researcher therefore does not need to collect data independently.

For characterising the past development, and also gain an understanding of possible future developments, growth rates can be computed for several aspects like source code, contributors, bug reports, mailing list postings or downloads. All of these might give some insight, while of course the growth in size (of source code) is most often cited (and normally understood under the term software evolution). It should be noted that there are some interrelations between these aspects, for example quality of open source projects (Dinh-Trong & Bieman, 2005; Stamelos et al., 2002; Zhao & Elbaum, 2000; Ruiz & Robinson, 2011) and community. Prior research used characteristics of quality for which diverse metrics from software engineering like McCabe's cyclomatic complexity (McCabe, 1976) or Chidamber and Kemerer's object-oriented metrics suite (Chidamber & Kemerer, 1994) can be employed. Koch and Neumann (2008) have attempted such an analysis using Java frameworks, and found that a high number of programmers and commits, as well as a high concentration is associated with problems in quality on class level, mostly to violations of size and design guidelines. This underlines the results of Koru and Tian (2005), who have found that modules with many changes rate quite high on structural measures like size or inheritance. If the architecture is not modular enough, a high concentration might show up as a result of this, as it can preclude more diverse participation. The other explanation is that classes that are programmed and or maintained by a small core team are more complex due to the fact that these programmers 'know' their own code and don't see the need for splitting large and complex methods. One possibility in this case is a refactoring (Fowler, 1999) for a more modular architecture with smaller classes and more pronounced use of inheritance. This would increase the possible participation, thus maybe in turn leading to lower concentration, and maintainability together with other quality aspects. Underlining these results, MacCormack et al. (2006) have in a similar study used design structure matrices to study the difference between open source and proprietary developed software, without further discrimination in development practices. They find significant differences between Linux, which is more modular, and the first version of Mozilla. The evolution of Mozilla then shows purposeful redesign aiming for a more modular architecture, which resulted in modularity even higher than Linux. They conclude that a product's design mirrors the organization developing it, in that a product developed by a distributed team such as Linux was more modular compared to Mozilla developed by a collocated team. Alternatively, the design also reflects purposeful choices made by the developers based on contextual challenges, in that Mozilla was successfully redesigned for higher modularity at a later stage. On project level, research found a distinct difference: Those projects with high overall quality ranking have more authors and commits, but a smaller concentration than those ranking poorly. Thus, on class level a negative impact of more programmers was found, while on project level a positive effect. This underlines a central statement of open source software development on a general level, that as many people as possible should be attracted to a project. On the other hand, these resources should, from the viewpoint of product quality, be organized in small teams. Ideally, on both levels, the effort is not concentrated on too few of the relevant participants.

For computing and characterising the growth rates to capture these effects, the following methodology will be adopted. This is taken from a prior study of one of the project participants (Koch, 2007) on growth in size. The first step is to analyse whether a linear or other growth pattern is present in the data. To this end, both a linear and a quadratic model are computed for each project, taking the size in lines-of-code S as a function of the time in days since the first commit t, which is used as project start date, and using one month as time window. Therefore model A is formulated simply as $S_A(t) = a * t + b$ and model B as $S_B(t) = a * t^2 + t * b + c$. The necessary parameters are to be estimated using regression techniques. As a next step, it is necessary to explore whether the growth rate is decreasing over time. This can be done by analysing the second derivative of the quadratic model $S_B(t)'$, or directly the coefficient of the quadratic term a.

The sharp distinction between two groups of projects might prove too inflexible. A new group is therefore introduced representing linear growth in contrast to sub- and super-linear rates. This group is defined as those projects having either a better fit for the linear than the quadratic model, or a coefficient of the quadratic term between -0.1 and 0.1, thus being very near to zero. This allows for arriving, for each project and each aspect of interest, at a classification for the evolutionary behavior as being either sub-linear, linear, or super-linear.

THE BCG MATRIX AS A PORTFOLIO PLANNING TOOL

Portfolio planning methods have been applied in strategic decision making for over 20 years (Armstrong and Brody, 1994; Wind and Mahajan, 1981), although they have little theoretical support. They are presented in the literature as diagnostic aids and as prescriptive guides for selecting strategic options (Kotler, 1984). The general idea is to classify positions of products along two dimensions to form a matrix: attractiveness of the market and ability of the product to compete within that market, and to derive insights into strategic actions in this way. Managers often neglect to use a rational economic approach, instead applying unstructured judgmental processes. They may base their decisions on power or emotional factors, which might lead to many of their decisions as being irrational. Thus, portfolio planning methods, such as the BCG matrix, may lead managers to make decisions that are less irrational.

Maybe the most well-known portfolio planning method is the Boston Consulting Group (BCG) method (Day, 1986), the most widely used portfolio method in US firms (Armstrong & Brody, 1994). It is based on measuring market attractiveness by market growth rate, and it assesses the firm's ability to compete by its relative market share. The BCG matrix assumes a causal relationship between market share and profitability. It is based on product life cycle theory that can be used to determine what priorities should be given to different products. To ensure long-term value creation, a company should construct a portfolio using products that contains both high-growth products in need of cash inputs and low-growth products that generate cash. Each of the two axes is normally divided into a high and a low portion, resulting in four different quadrants. Each quadrant is assigned both a catching name and a general strategy (see also Figure 1).

Stars are located in the high growth and high market share area. Normally, the cash flow is rather balanced or even, but a position in stars should be maintained. Cash Cows are placed in low growth area coupled with high market share. Profits and cash generation will generally be high, with relatively small investment due to low growth, translating into a very desirable type. Dogs are placed in

Figure 1. BCG matrix

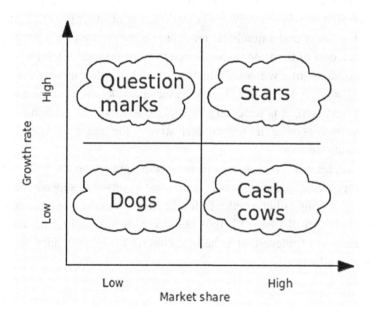

low growth and low market share quadrant, which are normally associated with a de-invest strategy. Question Marks are enjoying high growth but low market share, resulting in demand for cash but low profits. This kind of product over time might turn into either star or dog, so careful considerations is advised to invest or liquidate.

A review of previously published evaluations of the BCG matrix can be found in (Morrison & Wensley, 1991). Actual practical use of the BCG matrix is often found to be inhibited by difficulties in measurement of market growth rates and relative market shares. The results are highly sensitive on these measurements. As a result, different matrix methods are likely to yield different recommendations for the same situation.

OPEN SOURCE MATRIX AND CLASSIFICATION

We propose to adopt the BCG matrix approach for classifying open source projects. There are two main aspects to discuss and decide: The construction of the axes, and results of the classification. For constructing and measuring the axes, we propose to use the results of a growth rate analysis. The growth rate of an open source project is constructed using the growth rate in source code (which equals the software evolution viewpoint of software engineering research) and the growth rate of developers. For market share, we propose to use growth rates of bug reports and downloads. Bug reports normally are associated with usage of a product, especially by interested individuals, but might also signal a product with problems.

As each growth rate of the four types used here is classified in one of three steps, conversion into a single measure needed. We propose to use the mean of both rates, with source code respectively downloads taking priority in ties. Using this approach, an open source project matrix can be constructed, with the standard names having been replaced by possible representative release numbers (see Figure 2). Release numbers are usually coded based on major.minor release, with release 1.0 being a first fully functional release.

Figure 2. Open source project matrix

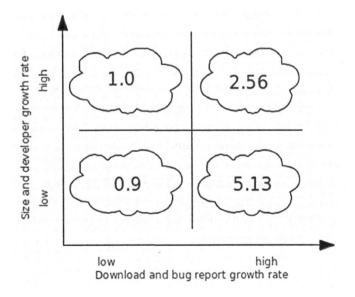

As can be seen, the classification results in four possible types of projects. This has to be translated into strategies. We need to differentiate between two possible uses, the first one being simple adoption, in which a company or individual wants to decide on which project within a given domain to adopt for a certain task. In the second case, a company wants to build a portfolio of projects. Possible reasons for this include a business model based on a range of software, cooperation with the open source world within a given area, or an application in marketing. Also a company that might pursue a development based on open source, but wants to keep open to several projects might pursue this idea. This leads to the following strategies assigned to the different types of projects.

1.0 (Question Marks) projects currently enjoy huge growth in size and participants, but have not achieved widespread adoption yet. Therefore they might become quite successful, but might fail. For a separate adoption decision, these projects pose considerable risk, while adding 1.0 projects to a portfolio might be interesting.

2.56 (Stars) projects enjoy both considerable growth and adoption. This makes them interesting candidates for any portfolio selection decision, and candidates for a singular adoption consideration.

5.13 (Cash Cows) projects have somewhat stabilized in their code and developer growth, but have achieved widespread adoption. This means that normally a mature solution has been found, with less emphasis on introducing new functionalities. This makes these projects prime candidates for consideration for a single adoption decision, and an interesting candidate for portfolio selection. On the other hand, there might be the need for maintenance at a later stage, maybe due to technological changes, but the community is not that active any more.

0.9 (Dogs) projects have neither huge growth nor adoption, meaning that they prove to be of interest to neither adoption or portfolio considerations. These projects could be termed as failed.

CONCLUSION AND FUTURE RESEARCH

This preface discussed the evaluation and selection of free and open source software projects. It also summarized an approach for constructing a top-level open source project classification based on growth rate analyses of several project aspects, and using portfolio planning techniques, especially the BCG matrix. Given current efforts of constructing the databases necessary to support the kind of analyses that form the basis of this approach, pursuing this road seems worthwhile. Portfolio planning approaches have been in business use for several decades, and despite some shortcomings, have provided value and are in wide-spread use. Given that software adoption decisions on organisational levels are often decisions made on a management level, adopting these common approaches might prove beneficial for communication between technical evaluation level and decision authorities.

In future research, an empirical evaluation of all possible approaches would be very important. This would include performing the necessary analyses based on a database, and presenting the results of categorization to decision-makers. The different approaches like OpenBQR or BRR etc. could then be evaluated according to effort needed, ease of use, understandability, or comprehensiveness. For the portfolio approach presented here, there are several possible ways of refinement of the approach that could be pursued: On the one hand, the construction of the axes could be discussed by adding or substituting aspects of projects or communities. On the other hand, there are other portfolio planning approaches besides the BCG matrix that could be explored.

Stefan Koch
Bogazici University, Turkey

REFERENCES

Armstrong, J. S., & Brodie, R. J. (1994). Effects of portfolio planning methods on decision making: experimental results. *International Journal of Research in Marketing, 11*(1), 73–84. doi:10.1016/0167-8116(94)90035-3

Atkins, D., Ball, T., Graves, T., & Mockus, A. (1999). Using version control data to evaluate the impact of software tools. In *Proceedings of the 21ˢᵗ International Conference on Software Engineering.* Los Angeles, CA, (pp. 324-333).

Atos Origin. (2009). *Method for qualification and selection of open source software (QSOS).* Retrieved from http://www.qsos.org

Berger, O., Vlasceanu, V., Bac, C., Dang, Q. V., & Lauriere, S. (2010). Weaving a Semantic Web across OSS repositories: Unleashing a new potential for academia and practice. *International Journal of Open Source Software and Processes, 2*(2), 29–40. doi:10.4018/jossp.2010040103

Chidamber, S., & Kemerer, C. F. (1994). A metrics suite for object oriented design. *IEEE Transactions on Software Engineering, 20*(6), 476–493. doi:10.1109/32.295895

Cook, J. E., Votta, L. G., & Wolf, A. L. (1998). Cost-effective analysis of in-place software processes. *IEEE Transactions on Software Engineering, 24*(8), 650–663. doi:10.1109/32.707700

Crowston, K., & Scozzi, B. (2002). Open source software projects as virtual organizations: Competency rallying for software development. *IEE Proceedings. Software Engineering, 149*(1), 3–17. doi:10.1049/ip-sen:20020197

Crowston, K., Howison, J., & Annabi, H. (2006). Information systems success in free and open source software development: Theory and measures. *Software Process Improvement and Practice, 11*(2), 123–148. doi:10.1002/spip.259

Day, G. (1986). *Analysis for strategic market decisions.* St. Paul, MN: West.

Dempsey, B. J., Weiss, D., Jones, P., & Greenberg, J. (2002). Who is an open source software developer? *Communications of the ACM, 45*(2), 67–72. doi:10.1145/503124.503125

Dinh-Trong, T. T., & Bieman, J. M. (2005). The FreeBSD project: A replication case study of open source development. *IEEE Transactions on Software Engineering, 31*(6), 481–494. doi:10.1109/TSE.2005.73

Fowler, M. (1999). *Refactoring: Improving the design of existing code.* Boston, MA: Addison-Wesley. doi:10.1007/3-540-45672-4_31

Gallivan, M. J. (2002). Striking a balance between trust and control in a virtual organization: A content analysis of open source software case studies. *Information Systems Journal, 11*(4), 277–304. doi:10.1046/j.1365-2575.2001.00108.x

Ghosh, R., & Prakash, V. V. (2000). The Orbiten free software survey. *First Monday, 5*(7).

Howison, J., & Crowston, K. (2004). The perils and pitfalls of mining SourceForge. In *Proceedings of the International Workshop on Mining Software Repositories,* Edinburgh, Scotland, (pp. 7-11).

Hunt, F., & Johnson, P. (2002). On the pareto distribution of sourceforge projects. In *Proceedings of the Open Source Software Development Workshop,* Newcastle, UK, (pp. 122-129).

Kemerer, C. F., & Slaughter, S. (1999). An empirical approach to studying software evolution. *IEEE Transactions on Software Engineering, 25*(4), 493–509. doi:10.1109/32.799945

Koch, S. (2004). Profiling an open source project ecology and its programmers. *Electronic Markets, 14*(2), 77–88. doi:10.1080/10196780410001675031

Koch, S. (2007). Software evolution in open source projects - A large-scale investigation. *Journal of Software Maintenance and Evolution, 19*(6), 361–382. doi:10.1002/smr.348

Koch, S., & Neumann, C. (2008). Exploring the effects of process characteristics on product quality in open source software development. *Journal of Database Management, 19*(2), 31–57. doi:10.4018/jdm.2008040102

Koch, S., & Schneider, G. (2002). Effort, cooperation and coordination in an open source software project: Gnome. *Information Systems Journal, 12*(1), 27–42. doi:10.1046/j.1365-2575.2002.00110.x

Koch, S., & Stix, V. (2008). Open source project categorization based on growth rate analysis and portfolio planning methods. *The 4th International Conference on Open Source Systems, IFIP Working Group 2.13 on Open Source Software, IFIP International Federation for Information Processing Series,* Vol. 275, (pp. 375-380). Milan, Italy: Springer Verlag.

Koru, A. G., & Tian, J. (2005). Comparing high-change modules and modules with the highest measurement values in two large-scale open-source products. *IEEE Transactions on Software Engineering, 31*(8), 625–642. doi:10.1109/TSE.2005.89

Kotler, P. (1984). *Marketing management* (5th ed.). Englewood Cliffs, NJ: Prentice-Hall.

Krishnamurthy, S. (2002). Cave or community? An empirical investigation of 100 mature open source projects. *First Monday, 7*(6).

Long, Y., & Siau, K. (2007). Social network structures in open source software development teams. *Journal of Database Management, 18*(2), 25–40. doi:10.4018/jdm.2007040102

MacCormack, A., Rusnak, J., & Baldwin, C. Y. (2006). Exploring the structure of complex software designs: An empirical study of open source and proprietary code. *Management Science, 52*(7), 1015–1030. doi:10.1287/mnsc.1060.0552

McCabe, T. (1976). A complexity measure. *IEEE Transactions on Software Engineering, 2*(4), 308–320. doi:10.1109/TSE.1976.233837

Mockus, A., Fielding, R., & Herbsleb, J. (2002). Two case studies of open source software development: Apache and Mozilla. *ACM Transactions on Software Engineering and Methodology, 11*(3), 309–346. doi:10.1145/567793.567795

Morrison, A., & Wensley, R. (1991). Boxing up or boxed in? A short history of the Boston Consulting Group share/growth matrix. *Journal of Marketing Management, 7,* 105–129. doi:10.1080/0267257X.1991.9964145

Norris, J. S., & Kamp, P.-H. (2004). Mission-critical development with open source software: Lessons learned. *IEEE Software, 21*(1), 42–49. doi:10.1109/MS.2004.1259211

Perens, B. (1999). The open source definition. In DiBona, C. (Eds.), *Open sources: Voices from the open source revolution.* Cambridge, MA: O'Reilly & Associates.

Petrinja, E., Sillitti, A., Wittmann, M., Nambakam, R., Oltolina, S., Ortega, F., ... Pares, J. (2010a). *Technical report: WD6.5.3 - Experimentation results, quality platform for open source software.* (IST-FP6-IP-034763).

Petrinja, E., Sillitti, A., & Succi, G. (2010). Comparing OpenBRR, QSOS, and OMM assessment models. In *Proceedings of the 6th International Conference on Open Source Systems (OSS 2010),* (pp. 224-238).

Robles, G., Gonzalez-Barahona, J. M., & Merelo, J. J. (2006). Beyond source code: The importance of other artifacts in software development (a case study). *Journal of Systems and Software, 79*(9), 1233–1248. doi:10.1016/j.jss.2006.02.048

Robles, G., González-Barahona, J. M., Izquierdo-Cortazar, D., & Herraiz, I. (2009). Tools for the study of the usual data sources found in libre software projects. *International Journal of Open Source Software and Processes, 1*(1), 24–45. doi:10.4018/jossp.2009010102

Ruiz, C., & Robinson, W. N. (2011). Measuring open source quality: A literature review. *International Journal of Open Source Software and Processes, 3*(3), 48–65.

Sowe, S. K., Angelis, L., Stamelos, I., & Manolopoulos, Y. (2007). Using repository of repositories (RoRs) to study the growth of F/OSS projects: A meta-analysis research approach. *OSS, 2007,* 147–160.

Stallman, R. M. (2002). *Free software, free society: Selected essays of Richard M. Stallman.* Boston, MA: GNU Press.

Stamelos, I., Angelis, L., Oikonomou, A., & Bleris, G. L. (2002). Code quality analysis in open source software development. *Information Systems Journal, 12,* 43–60. doi:10.1046/j.1365-2575.2002.00117.x

Sunindyo, W. D., Moser, T., Winkler, D., & Biffl, S. (2011). Analyzing OSS project health with heterogeneous data sources. *International Journal of Open Source Software and Processes, 3*(4), 1–23. doi:10.4018/jossp.2011100101

Syeed, M. M. M., Hammouda, I., & Systä, T. (2011). Tool assisted analysis of open source projects: A multi-faceted challenge. *International Journal of Open Source Software and Processes, 3*(2), 43–78. doi:10.4018/IJOSSP.2011040103

Taibi, D., Lavazza, L., & Morasca, S. (2007). OpenBQR: A framework for the assessment of OSS. In Feller, J., Fitzgerald, B., Scacchi, W., & Sillitti, A. (Eds.), *Open Source development, adoption and innovation* (pp. 173–186). Boston, MA: Springer. doi:10.1007/978-0-387-72486-7_14

Wasserman, A., Pal, M., & Chan, C. (2005). *Business readiness rating project.* BRR Whitepaper 2005 RFC. Retrieved from http://www.openbrr.org/wiki/images/d/da/BRR_whitepaper_2005RFC1.pdf

Wind, Y., & Mahajan, V. (1981). Designing product and business portfolios. *Harvard Business Review, 59*(1), 155–165.

Zhao, L., & Elbaum, S. (2000). A survey on quality related activities in open source. *Software Engineering Notes, 25*(3), 54–57. doi:10.1145/505863.505878

Chapter 1
An Empirical Study of Open Source Software Usability
The Industrial Perspective

Arif Raza
University of Western Ontario, Canada

Luiz Fernando Capretz
University of Western Ontario, Canada

Faheem Ahmed
United Arab Emirates University, UAE

ABSTRACT

Recent years have seen a sharp increase in the use of open source projects by common novice users; Open Source Software (OSS) is thus no longer a reserved arena for software developers and computer gurus. Although user-centered designs are gaining popularity in OSS, usability is still not considered one of the prime objectives in many design scenarios. This paper analyzes industry users' perception of usability factors, including understandability, learnability, operability, and attractiveness on OSS usability. The research model of this empirical study establishes the relationship between the key usability factors and OSS usability from industrial perspective. In order to conduct the study, a data set of 105 industry users is included. The results of the empirical investigation indicate the significance of the key factors for OSS usability.

INTRODUCTION

In the ISO 9241-11 (1998) standard, usability is defined as "the extent to which a product can be used by specified users to achieve specified goals with effectiveness, efficiency and satisfaction in a specified context of use." However, The International Organization for Standardization and The International Electro technical Commis-

sion ISO/IEC 9126-1 (International Organization for Standardization, 2001) categorizes software quality attributes into six categories: namely functionality, reliability, usability, efficiency, maintainability and portability. In the standard, usability is defined as "the capability of the software product to be understood, learned, used and attractive to the user, when used under specified conditions." Here, usability is further subdivided into understandability, learnability, operability and attractiveness.

DOI: 10.4018/978-1-4666-2937-0.ch001

While studying GNOME project, Koch and Schneider (2002) observe that in general, the number of people involved in OSS development are more than in traditional organizations, *"but the data show the existence of a relatively small 'inner circle' of programmers responsible for most of the output."* OSS users, however, come from every corner of the world having all sort of cultural, technical and non-technical backgrounds, requirements and expectations. They have free access as well as the ability to modify the source code (Aberdour, 2007). OSS is no longer reserved for computer developers alone, since a number of non-technical and novice computer users are growing at a fast pace, underscoring the need to understand and address their requirements and expectations (Iivari, 2009a). Although Laplante et al. (2007) believe that OSS has more potential to achieve higher software quality as compared to closed proprietary software; they observe the reluctance shown by many organizations in using OSS primarily due to "an inherent distrust of OSS quality." Nichols and Twidale (2006) state, "it is unfair to compare imperfect but public OSS processes with imagined but concealed commercial processes." They believe that due to the OSS environment, the software development process has become accessible that has been kept concealed in proprietary software. Referring much of the commercial software that failed to address usability issues properly, the authors do not consider usability a resolved issue in closed software projects either. They believe that research in the domain of OSS usability would be beneficial to both OSS as well as closed proprietary software products. Hedberg et al. (2007) observe that with the rapid increase in the non technical users of OSS, expectations related to higher software quality will grow as well. According to them, unlike the typical OSS approach, users will not be the co-developers who are competent enough to locate and fix the bugs; thus the quality assurance would need to be done before the software is delivered. They stress the need of having empirical research dealing with usability and quality assurance in OSS. de Groot

et al. (2006) maintain that *"many OSS projects, such as KDE, have established processes for the maintenance of software quality. However, these can only be of limited use when the actual quality of the product is still unknown."* While carrying out a study on the evolution metrics of OSS, Wang et al. (2007) propose a new set of metrics. Furthermore, their case study on Ubuntu – a popular Linux distribution, confirms the essential role of open source community and its members in OSS evolution.

Winter et al. (2007) consider the improvement of "the usage of a system" to support user activities as the main aim of usability engineering. Bodker et al. (2007) highlight that OSS developers need to have a full understanding, motivation and determination to address users' demands to avoid ending up with products that lack user friendliness, which could be a serious threat to its popularity and adoption. Ahmed (2008) refers to questionnaires that have long been used to gather users' assessment regarding subjective matters such as interfaces. However he realizes the need of more resources for usability testing as its success relies upon the test quality and coverage. Zaharias and Poylymenakou (2009) also consider usability questionnaires as a fast, cost effective way to collect users' feedback that can also be used to confirm target users.

We have already conducted three studies to empirically investigate the significance of certain key factors on OSS usability from OSS developers, users and contributors (that include users, developers, testers, systems analysts) points of view. This research work is the last of the series in which we analyze the industry users' perception regarding impact of the sub-factors of usability (understandability, learnability, operability and attractiveness) upon OSS usability. This study contributes to understanding the effects of the stated key factors which play a vital role in OSS usability.

We present the literature review regarding software usability issues in the open source software industry, in general and related to the key factors considered in this study, in particular. The research model and the hypotheses of this study are presented. The research methodology, data collection process, and the experimental setup are explained along with reliability and validity analysis of the measuring instrument and data analysis procedures. Hypotheses testing and the analysis of the results are presented, followed by the discussion that also includes the limitations of the study. Finally we conclude the paper.

LITERATURE REVIEW

Usability Issues: In General

Golden (2009) observes that "systems continue to be built and released with glaring usability flaws that are costly and difficult to fix after the system has been designed and/or built." He stresses that addressing usability issues at a software architecture design level makes it cost effective for software developers.

Cox (2005) identifies the fact that although issues related to human factors and usability are considered, they are too late in the software life cycles to have any useful impact. Juristo (2009) also believes in considering usability earlier in the life cycle. She has also come up with an approach to incorporate usability features as functional requirements.

Fitzpatrick and Higgins (1998) have considered usable software in compliance with the latest legislation as the one that is demanded by end users. They stress the need of having clear attribute listing of usable software along with the applicable measuring procedures.

Chrusch (2000) refers to and negates the seven myths of usability such as software development cost and time both increase due to usability, user-interface is just about addition of graphics to make it attractive, usability is about the interface design alone or it is only about common sense, for good user interface design developer's familiarity with

the standard guidelines is the only requirement, there is no need to do usability testing as long as developers have been working with the users long enough, and the final myth that usability issues will be addressed during help/documentation and training.

Te'eni (2007) believes that how useful and easy to use a system is, has a major role in determining user's intentions to make use of it.

Lewis (2006) stresses the designing systems for a wide range of users by stating that *"while public attitudes are improving, and integration into society of people with cognitive disabilities is increasing, there is still widespread ignorance about them and how technology can be of value to them."*

Seffah (2003) believes that software developers' knowledge regarding user interface design need to be enhanced to the level that they could be able to integrate such usability techniques in their design and development processes. In another work, Seffah and Metzker (2004) identify that due to the inconsistency in defining usability by standardization organizations and the software development industry, usability has different interpretations by different researchers. They stress the increase of communication between the software developers and the usability experts.

Advocating the concept of "Universal Usability", Shneiderman (2000) observes that to accommodate a wide variety of users, researchers and designers have to come up with such innovative designs that could be beneficial to all sections of users. He stresses the development, testing and refinement of such universal software to address usability issues related to diverse set of users. According to him, *"reaching a broad audience is more than a democratic ideal; it makes good business sense."*

Usability in Open Source Software

Considering usability as a research area in OSS that needs to be examined, Hedberg et al. (2007)

state *"u*ser feedback should be sought early, and the design solution should be iterated based on the user feedback." They see a great potential for usability experts to contribute towards OSS development.

According to Nichols and Twidale (2006), *"re*search in open source usability has the potential to be valuable to all kinds of software development, not just OSS." They emphasize on finding ways to ease usability bug reporting as well as involving usability experts during software analysis and design phases.

Nichols et al. (2001) identify the inability of many OSS users to do debugging of source code and their need of support even in bug reporting. They maintain that "as work on open-source projects is voluntary then developers work on the topics that interest them and this may well not include features for novice users."

Iivari and Iivari (2006) realize that in most of the cases, neither the prospective users of a software product are known nor can they be involved individually, particularly if the users are geographically and organizationally distributed; as a result "user focus can be limited to focus on typical, average or fictive user."

In their empirical study, Andreasen et al. (2006) found that although OSS developers realize the importance of end users, usability related issues do not get top position in their priority list. They identify that "currently, most developers have a very limited understanding of usability. Moreover, there is a lack of resources and evaluation methods fitting into the OSS paradigm."

Çetin and Göktürk (2008) believe that high usability of an OSS project can only be achieved through its measurement and analysis. They propose a measurement framework to assess OSS projects, which is required for their self evaluation.

Referring to the structured defect handling processes, significant use of configuration and bug tracking tools, Otte et al.(2008) highlight high rate of user participation, user testing and peer reviews in OSS projects.

Lee et al. (2009) recommend in their empirical study that "usefulness, ease of use, and reliability" are some of the major factors that OSS practitioners shall pay attention to, for improving OSS quality.

Literature Review of Key Factors

Referring to the difficulties in usability testing, Lindgaard (2006) states that "it is impossible to know whether all usability problems have been identified in a particular test or type of evaluation unless testing is repeated until it reaches an asymptote, a point at which no new problems emerge in a test" Iivari (2009b) empirically studies user participation in an OSS project and acknowledges "informative, consultative and participative roles for users" Viorres et al. (2007) believe in the end-users involvement during software design and development. They recognize the need of applying human-computer interaction (HCI) principles in the design processes of OSS to make use of their full potential. According to Seffah et al. (2006), failure of most interactive systems is mainly due to the unusable user interfaces. Referring to the difficulties in measuring software usability, they highlight the need to know the characteristics of users, their intended tasks, and identify that the lacking of either of the factors would end up in unrealistic results.

In ISO/IEC 9126-1 (International Organization for Standardization, 2001), understandability is defined as "the capability of the software product to enable the user to understand whether the software is suitable, and how it can be used for particular tasks and conditions of use." According to Seffah and Metzker (2004), software developers and usability experts can both be benefited, if they understand culture and practices of HCI and software engineering (SE), and learn techniques to improve communication between the two disciplines. Mørch et al. (2004) realize that understandability of end users can be increased, if developers could understand the semantics of integrating different user interface components.

Highlighting the diversity, different intelligence levels, and approaches of end users; Shneiderman (2000) states that some need less and some need more time to understand and acquire knowledge about new tools and user interface. Hedberg et al. (2007) refer to multiple meanings of user centered design (UCD) methodology; they argue that all of them "emphasize the importance of understanding the user, his/her tasks or work practices and the context of use."

Learnability is defined in ISO/IEC 9126-1 (International Organization for Standardization, 2001) as "the capability of the software product to enable the user to learn its application." Seffah et al. (2006) identify the need of more comprehensive guidelines to "account for the degree of influence of individual quality factors, such as the role of learnability versus understandability in usability problems." Mishra and Hershey (2004) stress that the understanding of requirements and knowledge background of users, can develop better learning tools. Yunwen and Kishida (2003) consider learning as one of the main motivational forces, which results in the participation of both users as well as software developers, in OSS culture. They believe that new members and users are attracted to OSS because of its high quality; as one of their own problems could be solved by the system whereas developers are attracted to OSS due to its learning opportunities.

Operability is defined in ISO/IEC 9126-1 (International Organization for Standardization, 2001) as "the capability of the software product to enable the user to operate and control it." Henderson (2005) emphasizes that developers should produce software having usable interface, which could meet user needs, and provide them the value they expect. Iivari and Iivari (2006) state that ideally an individual's needs should be supported by a system; they, however, realize that in real world each and every user cannot be accessed while designing, plus users should be prepared to make some compromises to have a uniform and a compatible system. The authors state

that "in certain situations the prospective users can all participate directly in the process, but in many cases only selected user representatives are involved." Crowston et al. (2003), while discussing the success of open source software projects, identify the contrasting features of proprietary software and OSS. They agree that in either case, system's success is measured through user satisfaction, most OSS projects are globally distributed with unknown population of users, which makes it hard to have true sample of users.

ISO/IEC 9126-1 (International Organization for Standardization, 2001) defines attractiveness as "the capability of the software product to be attractive to the user." Chrusch (2000) believes that proper application of usability techniques results in a good user interface. He observes that "many people misinterpret the visual design of an interface as the interface itself, but doing so ignores the entire interaction sequence needed to complete a task." Juristo (2009) identifies a flaw in the approach of development team, when they think that a system can be made usable by incurring right font, color, and nice set of controls. Markov (2003) states that usability is not about making a user interface attractive, rather it is about "total user experience."

RESEARCH MODEL AND THE HYPOTHESES

In this study we present a research model to analyze and empirically investigate the relationship between the key usability factors and the open source software usability. The theoretical model to be empirically tested in this study is shown in Figure 1.

We will examine the relationship of four independent variables and the OSS usability, which is the dependent variable in this model. Our aim is to investigate the answer to the following research question:

Figure 1. Research model

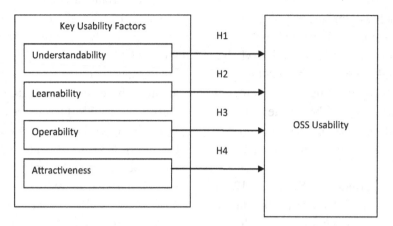

- **Research Question:** How do usability components (understandability, learnability, operability and attractiveness) affect usability from the industry users' perspective?

There are four independent and one dependent variable in this research model. The four independent variables are called "Usability Factors" in the rest of the paper. They include Understandability, Learnability, Operability and Attractiveness. The dependent variable of this study is the OSS usability. The multiple linear regression equation of the model is as follows:

$$\text{OSS Usability} = f_0 + f_1 v_1 + f_2 v_2 + f_3 v_3 + f_4 v_4 \qquad (1)$$

where f_0, f_1, f_2, f_3 and f_4 are the coefficients and v_1, v_2, v_3 and v_4 are the four independent variables. In order to empirically investigate the research question, we hypothesize the following:

- **H1. Understandability:** Is positively related with OSS usability.
- **H2. Learnability:** Has a positive impact on OSS usability.
- **H3. Operability:** Plays a positive role towards usability in OSS.
- **H4. Attractiveness:** Is positively related with OSS usability.

RESEARCH METHODOLOGY

The research conducted and presented in this paper includes the empirical results of a survey. In this study, the target population includes multinational companies whose employees are OSS users. Thirty companies consented to participate in this study, with the assurance of confidentiality for both the organization and the individuals. The participating organizations are involved in a wide range of operations, such as pharmaceuticals, telecommunications, automobile manufacturing, information technology, and consumer electronics. Specifically, these organizations include North American and European multinational companies, and they vary in size from small to large scale. We requested that the companies in the study distribute the questionnaires within their various departments, so that we have several responses from within the same organization. In particular, we required that the respondents possessed the minimum educational qualification of an undergraduate degree.

The survey was implemented by using the survey tool *"kwiksurveys"*. It was started in the last week of March 2010, and it was closed after three weeks, with 105 responses. We assured the participants that our survey neither required their identity nor would be recorded. However, to support our data analysis of the respondents' experience, we asked them, *"Do you agree that applying one of the concepts/techniques expressed by the above key factors, usability will, in your opinion, improve the product you are working on?"* Out of 105 total responses, 81% agreed that in their experience, the application of our key factors will improve the usability of their application; of the remaining participants, 16% were neutral and 3% disagreed with this statement, as reflected in Figure 2.

Data Collection and the Measuring Instrument

In this study, the questionnaires presented in the Appendix were used to learn, up to what extent these usability factors were important towards OSS usability, for the respondents of the survey. The questionnaires required the respondents to indicate the extent of their agreement, or disagreement with statements using a five-point Likert scale. We used sixteen separate items to measure the independent variables, and four items to measure respondents' points of view regarding OSS usability. We reviewed previous researches on the subject of OSS usability, so that a comprehensive list of measuring factors could be constructed. To measure the extent to which each of these usability factors have been

practiced in their projects, we made use of five-point Likert scale. The Likert scale ranged from "Strongly Agree" (1) to "Strongly Dis-agree" (5), for all items associated with each variable. The items for all the four usability factors are labeled sequentially in the Appendix and are numbered 1 through 16. We measured the dependent variable, i.e. OSS Usability on the multi-item, five-point Likert scale too. The items were specifically designed, for collecting measures for this variable, and are labeled sequentially from 1 through 4 in the Appendix.

Reliability and Validity Analysis of Measuring Instrument

The two integral features of any empirical study are reliability, which refers to the consistency of the measurement; and the validity, which is the strength of the inference between the true value and the value of a measurement. For this empirical investigation, we used the most commonly used approaches in empirical studies, to conduct reliability and validity analysis of the measuring instruments. The reliability of the multiple-item measurement scales of the four usability factors was evaluated by using internal-consistency analysis, which was performed using coefficient alpha (Cronbach, 1951). In our analysis, the coefficient

Figure 2. Application of usability factors in respondents' products

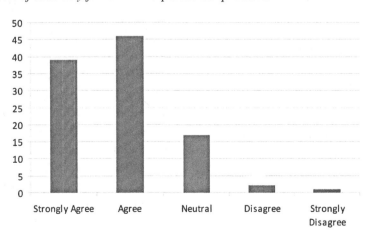

alpha ranged from 0.70 to 0.73 as shown in Table 1. Nunnally and Bernste (1994) find that a reliability coefficient of 0.70 or higher for a measuring instrument is satisfactory. van de Ven and Ferry (1980) state that a reliability coefficient of 0.55 or higher is satisfactory, and Osterhof (2001) suggests that 0.60 or higher is satisfactory. Therefore, we concluded that the variable items developed for this empirical investigation were reliable.

Comrey and Lee's (1992) Principal Component Analysis (PCA) was performed for all the four key usability factors, and reported in Table 1. We used Eigen value (Kaiser, 1970) as a reference point, to observe the construct validity, using principal component analysis. In this study, we used Eigen value-one-criterion, also known as Kaiser Criterion (Kaiser, 1960; Stevens, 1986), which means any component having an Eigen value greater than one was retained. Eigen value analysis revealed that all the four variables completely formed a single factor. Therefore we concluded that the convergent validity, sufficient for the data.

Data Analysis Procedure

We analyzed the research model, and the significance of hypotheses H1-H4, through different statistical techniques in three phases. In phase-I we used normal distribution tests and parametric statistics, whereas in phase II we used non-parametric statistics. Due to the relatively small sample

Table 1. Coefficient alpha and Principal Component Analysis (PCA) of variables

Usability Factors	Item no.	Coefficient α	PCA Eigen value
Understandability	1 - 4	0.73	1.86
Learnability	5 - 8	0.72	1.48
Operability	9 - 12	0.70	1.01
Attractiveness	13 - 16	0.71	1.06

size, both parametric as well as non-parametric statistical approaches were used, to reduce the threats to external validity. As our measuring instrument had multiple items for all the four independent variables as well as the dependent variable (refer to Appendix), their ratings by the respondents were summed up, to get a composite value for each of them. Tests were conducted for the hypotheses H1-H4, using parametric statistics by determining the Pearson correlation coefficient. For non-parametric statistics, tests were conducted for the hypotheses H1-H4, by determining the Spearman correlation coefficient. To deal with the limitations of the relatively small sample size and to increase the reliability of the results, the hypotheses H1-H4 of the research model were tested, using Partial Least Square (PLS) technique in Phase-III. According to Fornell and Bookstein (1982) and Joreskog and Wold (1982), the PLS technique is helpful in dealing with issues such as complexity, non-normal distribution, low theoretical information, and small sample size. The statistical calculations were performed using minitab- 15.

HYPOTHESES TESTING AND RESULTS

Phase I

To test the hypotheses H1-H4 of the research model (shown in Figure 1), parametric statistics were used in this phase by examining the Pearson correlation coefficient between individual independent variables (key usability factors) and the dependent variable (OSS usability). The results of the statistical calculations for the Pearson correlation coefficients are displayed in Table 2. The Pearson correlation coefficient between Understandability and OSS usability was found positive (0.42) at P < 0.05, and hence justified the hypothesis H1. The Pearson correlation coefficient of 0.42 was also observed at P < 0.05 between Learnability

Table 2. Hypotheses testing using parametric and non-parametric correlation coefficients

Hypothesis	Usability Factor	Pearson Correlation coefficient	Spearman Correlation coefficient
H1	Understandability	0.42*	0.40*
H2	Learnability	0.42*	0.41*
H3	Operability	0.51*	0.51*
H4	Attractiveness	0.40*	0.37*

* Significant at P < 0.05.

and OSS usability, and hence found significant at P < 0.05, as well. The hypothesis H3 was accepted based on the Pearson correlation coefficient (0.51) at P < 0.05, between Operability and OSS usability. The positive correlation coefficient of 0.40 at P < 0.05 was also observed between the OSS usability and Attractiveness, which meant that H4 was accepted too.

Hence, as observed and reported above all the hypotheses H1, H3 and H4 were found statistically significant and were accepted.

Phase II

Non-parametric statistical testing was conducted in this phase by examining Spearman correlation coefficients between individual independent variables (key usability factors) and the dependent variable (OSS usability). The results of the statistical calculations for the Spearman correlation coefficients are also displayed in Table 2. The Spearman correlation coefficient between

Understandability and OSS usability was found positive (0.40) at P < 0.05, and hence justified the hypothesis H1. For hypothesis H2, the Spearman correlation coefficient of 0.41 was observed at P < 0.05, hence significant relationship was found between Learnability and OSS usability in this test. The hypothesis H3 was accepted, based on the Spearman correlation coefficient (0.51) at P < 0.05, between Operability and OSS usability. The positive Spearman correlation coefficient of 0.37 at P < 0.05 was also observed between the OSS usability and Attractiveness which meant that H4 was accepted too.

Hence, as observed and presented above all the hypotheses H1, H2, H3 and H4 were found statistically significant and were accepted in the non-parametric analysis as well.

Phase III

In order to do the cross-validation of the results obtained in Phase I and Phase II, Partial Least Square (PLS) technique was used in this phase of hypotheses testing. The direction and significance of hypotheses H1–H4 were examined. In PLS, the dependent variable of our research model, OSS usability was placed as the response variable and the independent key usability factors as the predicate. The test results containing observed values of path coefficient, R^2 and F-ratio have been shown in Table 3. Understandability was observed to be significant at P < 0.05, with path coefficient 0.63, R^2: 24.9% and F-ratio as 27.54. Learnability had path coefficient of 0.85 with R^2: 65.3% and

Table 3. Hypotheses Testing using Partial Least Square (PLS) regression

Hypothesis	Usability Factor	Path Coefficient	R^2	F- Ratio
H1	Understandability	0.63	0.249	27.54*
H2	Learnability	0.85	0.653	156.44*
H3	Operability	0.80	0.556	103.9*
H4	Attractiveness	1. 08	0.607	128.35*

* Significant at P < 0.05.

F-ratio of 156.44 and found significant at P < 0.05 as well. Operability was observed to have the same direction as proposed in the hypothesis H3, with path coefficient: 0.80, R^2: 55.6% and F-ratio: 103.9 at P < 0.05. And finally Attractiveness with the path coefficient: 1.08, R^2: 60.7% and F-ratio: 128.35 at P < 0.05, was also found in accordance with the hypothesis H4.

Testing of the Research Model

The multiple linear regression equation of our research model is depicted by Equation-1. The purpose of research model testing was to provide empirical evidence that our key factors play a significant role towards open source software usability. The testing process consists of conducting regression analysis, and reporting the values of the model coefficients, and their direction of association. We placed OSS usability as response variable and key factors as predicators. Table 4 displays the regression analysis results of the research model. The path coefficients of the four variables: understandability, learnability, operability and attractiveness were found positive, and their t-statistics were also observed statistically significant at P < 0.05. R^2 and adjusted R^2 of overall research model were observed as 0.40 and 0.373 with F-ratio of 14.97, significant at P < 0.05.

Table 4. Multiple linear regression analysis of the research model

Model coefficient Name	Model coefficient	Coefficient value	t-value
Understandability	f_1	0.180	2.73*
Learnability	f_2	0.150	1.72*
Operability	f_3	0.154	2.12*
Attractiveness	f_4	0.238	2.85*
Constant	f_0	2.72	2.77*

* Significant at P < 0.05.

DISCUSSION: QUESTIONNAIRES AND RESPONSES

It is generally believed that testing procedures, in particular usability testing are conducted in different manners in closed proprietary software and in OSS projects. However many issues remain common in both. That is the reason some of the questions in our survey are specifically related to OSS and others are not, as we believe they are equally applicable to usability assessment in proprietary organizations as well as OSS projects. We have tried our level best to come up with open questions and avoid leading questions. As already mentioned, we have designed four items for each independent variable to collect measures on the extent to which the variable is practiced within each project.

In questions related to understandability, we have asked respondents' opinions about the relationship between understandability and functionality as well as about consistency and understandability. One of the statement related to Understandability (refer to Appendix) *"Easy to understand software would encourage user's involvement"* we believe, is beyond the categorization of OSS or proprietary software users, however equally important for both. When we asked whether software functionality needs to be compromised in order to increase understandability, 72% of the respondents disagreed (either disagreed or strongly disagreed), 12% agreed (either agreed or strongly agreed) and 16% remained neutral. 79% agreed that consistency in software design would increase understandability and hence usability; 16% remained neutral and only 5% disagreed with the statement. When we asked respondents' opinion about the statement *"Easy to understand software would encourage user's involvement,"* 81% agreed, 13% remained neutral and 6% disagreed. And finally about the *"Inconsistency in software is due to a lack of understanding user's expectations"* (Chrusch, 2000), 37% agreed, 40% disagreed and the rest

23% chose to remain neutral. Thus, overall, as our statistical analysis indicates, our hypothesis *"H1: Understandability is positively related with OSS usability,"* is found significant and has been accepted in the analysis.

Regarding learnabilty, we have asked our respondents about the relationship between learnability, accessibility and usability. We also inquired about whether OSS developers compromise learnability for efficiency and whether learnability being considered impracticable in the OSS environment. Our final question about learnability was related to the realization of the fact that a system could be made learnable only if its developer understands the needs and limitations of its users. 83% agreed that learnability increases accessibility and hence usability, 14% remained neutral and 3% disagreed. We have also asked the respondents to opine whether learnability may be compromised by developers to produce efficient products in OSS environment; 34% agreed, 42% remained neutral and 24% disagreed with the statement. 76% disagreed on considering learnability as a cognitive issue that is not practicable in OSS, 18% were neutral and only 6% agreed. Regarding the statement that to make a system learnable, OSS developers must understand the limits of their target users 72% agreed, 14% remained neutral and 14% chose to disagree. On the basis of the statistical investigation, the hypothesis *"H2: Learnability has a positive impact on OSS usability"* has been accepted.

In order to keep our statements unbiased and open, we asked our respondents' opinion about whether they agree that more learnable software makes it more operable and usable. We also asked them to opine about gradual introduction of advanced features in software. Responding to our survey statements related to operability, 76% believed that more learnable software is more operable and hence usable, 13% remained neutral and the rest 11% disagreed. 63% agreed that introducing advanced features of software to users in an incremental way would give them more control

in using the software; 20% remained neutral and 17% disagreed. There was a mixed response about the statement *"Operability is directly proportional to user satisfaction"*; 45% agreed, 31% remained neutral and 24% disagreed. Similarly, regarding the statement: *"The modularized system design results in operable software such that users encounter the difficulty levels gradually and progressively"* (Yunwen & Kishida, 2003), 52% agreed, 31% were neutral and 17% disagreed with the statement. The hypothesis *"H3: Operability plays a positive towards usability in OSS,"* as supported by the statistical analysis of our survey, has been accepted in our study.

About the attractiveness of software, 70% respondents of our survey believed that *"attractive to user"* software may not necessarily be a usable one, however 20% disagreed and the rest remained neutral. 67% agreed, 21% remained neutral and 12% disagreed that the more pleasant a software to use, more usable it would be. With the statement, *"Good user interface design is the result of properly applied usability techniques and practices"* (Chrusch, 2000), 79% agreed, 18% remained neutral and only 3% disagreed. Similarly, 94% believed that Usability is about *"total user experience,"* not only about attractive user interface (Markov, 2003); the percentages of the respondents who remained neutral and disagreed were 4% and 2% respectively. Our statistical analysis supports the hypothesis *"H4: Attractiveness is positively related with OSS usability,"* and is thus accepted in the study.

Limitations of the Study and Threats to External Validity

Empirical investigations of software engineering processes and products are done through surveys, experiments, metrics, case studies and field studies (Singer & Vinson, 2002). Wohlin et al. (2000) identify the ways in which the threats to external validity limit the researcher's ability to generalize the results of his/her experiment to industrial practice. In our study, we needed to support the external validity of our random sampling technique. Accordingly, we made a considerable effort to receive responses from many industry users; however, the total number of respondents was only 105 individuals. Although the proposed approach has some potential to threaten external validity, we followed appropriate research procedures by conducting and reporting tests to improve the reliability and validity of the study, and certain measures were also taken to ensure the external validity.

The increased popularity of empirical methodology in software engineering has also raised concerns on the ethical issues (Faden et al., 1986; Katz, 1972). We have followed the recommended ethical principles to ensure that the empirical investigation conducted and reported here would not violate any form of recommended experimental ethics.

CONCLUSION

We have already conducted three studies to empirically investigate the significance of identified key factors on OSS usability from OSS developers, users and contributors' points of view. This research study is fourth of the series of our empirical investigations, in which we have analyzed the impact of the key usability factors (understandability, learnability, operability and attractiveness) on OSS usability based on industry users' perception. The key factors considered in the study (understandability, learnability, operability and attractiveness) have been taken from the standard ISO/IEC 9126-1 (International Organization for Standardization, 2001). Empirical results of this study strongly support the hypotheses that understandability, learnability, operability and attractiveness have a positive impact on the usability of OSS projects. The study conducted and reported here shall enable OSS designers and developers to better understand the effectiveness of the relationships of the stated

key factors and usability of their projects. Currently we are working on developing a maturity model to assess the usability of open source software projects. This empirical investigation provides us some justification to consider these key factors as measuring instruments.

REFERENCES

Aberdour, M. (2007). Achieving quality in open-source software. *IEEE Software*, *24*(1), 58–64. doi:10.1109/MS.2007.2

Ahmed, S. M. Z. (2008). A comparison of usability techniques for evaluating information retrieval system interfaces. *Performance Measurement and Metrics*, *9*(1), 48–58. doi:10.1108/14678040810869422

Andreasen, M., Nielsen, H., Schrøder, S., & Stage, J. (2006). Usability in open source software development: Opinions and practice. *Information Technology and Control*, *5*(3A), 303–312.

Bodker, M., Nielsen, L., & Orngreen, R. N. (2007). Enabling user centered design processes in open source communities, usability and internationalization, HCI and culture. In *Proceedings of the 2nd International Conference on Usability and Internationalization held as part of the HCI International Conference Part I* (pp. 10-18).

Çetin, G., & Göktürk, M. (2008). A measurement based framework for assessment of usability-centricness of open source software projects. In *Proceedings of the IEEE International Conference on Signal Image Technology and Internet Based Systems* (pp. 585-592).

Chrusch, M. (2000). The whiteboard: Seven great myths of usability. *Interaction*, *7*(5), 13–16. doi:10.1145/345242.345251

Comrey, A. L., & Lee, H. B. (1992). *A first course on factor analysis* (2nd ed.). Mahwah, NJ: Lawrence Erlbaum.

Cox, D. (2005). A pragmatic HCI approach: Engagement by reinforcing perception with functional design and programming. *SIGCSE Bulletin, 37*(3), 39–43. doi:10.1145/1151954.1067459

Cronbach, L. J. (1951). Coefficient alpha and the internal consistency of tests. *Psychometrica, 16,* 297–334. doi:10.1007/BF02310555

Crowston, K., Annabi, H., & Howison, J. (2003). Defining open source software project success. In *Proceedings of the 24th International Conference on Information Systems*, Seattle, WA.

de Groot, A., Kiigler, S., Adams, P. J., & Gousios, G. (2006). Call for quality: Open source software quality observation. *IFIP International Federation for Information Processing, 203,* 57–62. doi:10.1007/0-387-34226-5_6

Faden, R. R., Beauchamp, T. L., & King, N. M. P. (1986). *A history and theory of informed consent.* Oxford, UK: Oxford University Press.

Fitzpatrick, R., & Higgins, C. (1998). Usable software and its attributes: A synthesis of software quality. In *Proceedings of the European Community Law and Human-Computer Interaction in People and Computers XIII Conference*, London, UK (pp. 3-21).

Fornell, C., & Bookstein, F. L. (1982). Two structural equation models: LISREL and PLS applied to consumer exit voice theory. *JMR, Journal of Marketing Research, 19,* 440–452. doi:10.2307/3151718

Golden, E. (2009). Early-stage software design for usability. In *Proceedings of the 31ˢᵗ International Conference on Software Engineering*, Vancouver, BC, Canada.

Hedberg, H., Iivari, N., Rajanen, M., & Harjumaa, L. (2007). Assuring quality and usability in open source software development. In *Proceedings of the 1st International Workshop on Emerging Trends in FLOSS Research and Development* (p. 2).

Henderson, A. (2005). The innovation pipeline: Design collaborations between research and development. *Interaction, 12*(1), 24–29. doi:10.1145/1041280.1041295

Iivari, J., & Iivari, N. (2006). Varieties of user-centeredness. In *Proceedings of the 39th Annual Hawaii International Conference on System Sciences* (p. 8).

Iivari, N. (2009a). Empowering the users? A critical textual analysis of the role of users in open source software development. *AI & Society, 23*(4), 511–528. doi:10.1007/s00146-008-0182-1

Iivari, N. (2009b). Constructing the users in open source software development: An interpretive case study of user participation. *Information Technology & People, 22*(2), 132–156. doi:10.1108/09593840910962203

International Organization for Standardization. (1997). *ISO 9241: Ergonomics requirements for office with visual display terminals (VDTs).* Geneva, Switzerland: ISO/IEC.

International Organization for Standardization. (2001). *ISO/IEC 9126-1: Software engineering – product quality – Part 1: Quality model* (1st ed., pp. 9–10). Geneva, Switzerland: ISO/IEC.

Joreskog, K., & Wold, H. (1982). *Systems under indirect observation: causality, structure and prediction.* Amsterdam, The Netherlands: North-Holland.

Juristo, N. (2009). Impact of usability on software requirements and design. In A. De Lucia & F. Ferrucci (Eds.), *Proceedings of the International Summer Schools Tutorial on Software Engineering* (LNCS 5413, pp. 55-77).

Kaiser, H. F. (1960). The application of electronic computers to factor analysis. *Educational and Psychological Measurement, 20,* 141–151. doi:10.1177/001316446002000116

Kaiser, H. F. (1970). A second generation little jiffy. *Psychometrika*, *35*, 401–417. doi:10.1007/BF02291817

Katz, J. (1972). *Experimentation with human beings*. New York, NY: Russell Sage Foundation.

Koch, S., & Schneider, G. (2002). Effort, cooperation and co-ordination in an open source software project: GNOME. *Information Systems Journal*, *12*, 27–42. doi:10.1046/j.1365-2575.2002.00110.x

Koppelman, H., & Van Dijk, B. (2006). Creating a realistic context for team projects in HCI. *SIGCSE Bulletin*, *38*(3), 58–62. doi:10.1145/1140123.1140142

Laplante, P., Gold, A., & Costello, T. (2007). Open source software: Is it worth converting? *IT Professional*, *9*(4), 28–33. doi:10.1109/MITP.2007.72

Lee, S. Y. T., Kim, H. W., & Gupta, S. (2009). Measuring open source software success. *Omega*, *37*(2), 426–438. doi:10.1016/j.omega.2007.05.005

Lewis, C. (2006). HCI and cognitive disabilities. *Interaction*, *13*(3), 14–15. doi:10.1145/1125864.1125880

Lindgaard, G. (2006). Notions of thoroughness, efficiency, and validity: Are they valid in HCI practice? *International Journal of Industrial Ergonomics*, *36*, 1069–1074. doi:10.1016/j.ergon.2006.09.007

Markov, N. (2003). *An introduction to the UCD methodology in the current environment*. Paper presented at the CASCON Workshop.

Mishra, P., & Hershey, K. A. (2004). Etiquette and the design of educational technology. *Communications of the ACM*, *47*(4), 45–49. doi:10.1145/975817.975843

Mørch, A. I., Stevens, G., Won, M., Klann, M., Dittrich, Y., & Wulf, V. (2004). Component-based technologies for end-user development. *Communications of the ACM*, *47*(9), 59–62. doi:10.1145/1015864.1015890

Nichols, D. M., Thomson, K., & Yeates, S. A. (2001). Usability and open-source software development. In *Proceedings of the ACM SIGCHI Symposium on Computer Human Interaction*, Palmerston North, New Zealand (pp. 49-54).

Nichols, D. M., & Twidale, M. B. (2006). Usability processes in open source projects. *Software Process Improvement and Practice*, *11*(2), 149–162. doi:10.1002/spip.256

Nunnally, J. C., & Bernste, I. A. (1994). *Psychometric theory* (3rd ed.). New York, NY: McGraw-Hill.

Osterhof, A. (2001). *Classroom applications of educational measurement*. Upper Saddle River, NJ: Prentice Hall.

Otte, T., Moreton, R., & Knoell, H. D. (2008). Applied quality assurance methods under the open source development model. In *Proceedings of the IEEE 32nd International Computer Software and Applications Conference* (pp. 1247-1252).

Seffah, A. (2003). Learning the ropes: Human-centered design skills and patterns for software engineers' education. *Interaction*, *10*(5), 36–45. doi:10.1145/889692.889693

Seffah, A., Donyaee, M., Kline, R. B., & Padda, H. K. (2006). Usability measurement and metrics: A consolidated model. *Software Quality Journal*, *14*, 159–178. doi:10.1007/s11219-006-7600-8

Seffah, A., & Metzker, E. (2004). The obstacles and myths of usability and software engineering. *Communications of the ACM*, *47*(12), 71–76. doi:10.1145/1035134.1035136

Shneiderman, B. (2000). Universal usability. *Communications of the ACM, 43*(5), 84–91. doi:10.1145/332833.332843

Singer, J., & Vinson, N. G. (2002). Ethical issues in empirical studies of software engineering. *IEEE Transactions on Software Engineering, 28*(12), 1171–1180. doi:10.1109/TSE.2002.1158289

Stevens, J. (1986). *Applied multivariate statistics for the social sciences*. Mahwah, NJ: Lawrence Erlbaum.

Te'eni, D. (2007). HCI is in business---focusing on organizational tasks and management. *Interaction, 14*(4), 16–19. doi:10.1145/1273961.1273975

van de Ven, A. H., & Ferry, D. L. (1980). *Measuring and assessing organizations*. New York, NY: John Wiley & Sons.

Viorres, N., Xenofon, P., Stavrakis, M., Vlachogiannis, E., Koutsabasis, P., & Darzentas, J. (2007). Major HCI challenges for open source software adoption and development online communities and social computing. In *Proceedings of the 2nd International Conference OCSC held as part of HCI International* (pp. 455-464).

Wang, Y., Guo, D., & Shi, H. (2007). Measuring the evolution of open source software systems with their communities. *SIGSOFT Software Engineering Notes, 32*(6), 7. doi:10.1145/1317471.1317479

Winter, S., Wagner, S., & Deissenboeck, F. (2007). A comprehensive model of usability. In J. Gulliksen, M. Borup Harning, P. Palanque, G. C. van der Veer, & J. Wesson (Eds.), *Proceedings of the EIS Joint Working Conferences on Engineering Interactive Systems* (LNCS 4940, pp. 106-122).

Wohlin, C., Runeson, P., Host, M., Ohlsson, M. C., Regnell, B., & Wesslen, A. (2000). *Experimentation in software engineering*. Boston, MA: Kluwer Academic.

Yunwen, Y., & Kishida, K. (2003). Toward an understanding of the motivation of open source software developers. In *Proceedings of the 25th International Conference on Software Engineering* (pp. 419-429).

Zaharias, P., & Poylymenakou, A. (2009). Developing a usability evaluation method for e-learning applications: Beyond functional usability. *International Journal of Human-Computer Interaction, 25*(1), 75–98. doi:10.1080/10447310802546716

APPENDIX

Key Usability Factors from OSS Industry Perspective (Measuring Instrument)

- **Understandability:** *"The capability of the software product to enable the user to understand whether the software is suitable, and how it can be used for particular tasks and conditions of use"* (International Organization for Standardization, 2001).
  a. To increase understandability in software functionality would have to be compromised.
  b. Consistency in OSS design would increase understandability and hence usability.
  c. Easy to understand software would encourage user's involvement.
  d. Inconsistency in software is due to a lack of understanding user's expectations (Chrusch, 2000).

- **Learnability:** *"The capability of the software product to enable the user to learn its application"* (International Organization for Standardization, 2001).
  a. Learnability increases accessibility and hence usability.
  b. In OSS environment, learnability may be compromised by developers for efficient products.
  c. Learnability is a cognitive issue that needs users' mental analysis and is not practicable in OSS.
  d. OSS developers must understand the limits of their target users to make a system learnable.

- **Operability:** *"The capability of the software product to enable the user to operate and control it"* (International Organization for Standardization, 2001).
  a. More learnable software is more operable and hence usable.
  b. Introduction of advance features of software to users in an incremental way would give user more control in using the software.
  c. Operability is directly proportional to user satisfaction.
  d. The modularized system design results in operable software such that users encounter the difficulty levels gradually and progressively (Yunwen & Kishida, 2003).

- **Attractiveness:** *"The capability of the software product to be attractive to the user"* (International Organization for Standardization, 2001)
  a. *"Attractive to user"* software may not necessarily be a usable one.
  b. The more pleasant a software to use, more usable it would be.
  c. Good user interface design is the result of properly applied usability techniques and practices (Chrusch, 2000).
  d. Usability is about *"total user experience,"* not only about attractive user interface (Markov, 2003).

- **Usability:** *"The capability of the software product to be understood learned, used and attractive to the user, when used under specified conditions"* (International Organization for Standardization, 2001).
  a. In OSS environment, adhering to standards and guidelines will take away OSS developer's freedom.
  b. The adaptation of proven methods in OSS environment would ensure higher quality and address usability issues (Hedberg et al., 2007).

16

c.   In order to know end users' requirements and expectations, there is a need of more communication between the software developers and their target users, instead of relying on their instincts (Koppelman & Van Dijk, 2006).

d.   Usability increases development costs and lengthens development time (Chrusch, 2000).

Chapter 2
Factors Affecting the Development of Absorptive Capacity in the Adoption of Open Source Software

Kris Ven
University of Antwerp, Belgium

Peter De Bruyn
University of Antwerp, Belgium

ABSTRACT

Previous research has shown that the knowledge that is available to an organization is an important factor influencing the adoption of open source software (OSS). Hence, it is important that organizations develop their absorptive capacity in order to successfully adopt OSS. Absorptive capacity refers to the ability of an organization to acquire, assimilate, and exploit new knowledge. However, no study has specifically investigated how organizations can develop their absorptive capacity by acquiring knowledge about OSS. This paper addresses this gap in research by investigating the organizational knowledge assimilation process within the context of the adoption of OSS. Based on a case study conducted at the Flemish government, a framework that is grounded in literature and that illustrates which contextual factors influence the development of absorptive capacity in the context of the adoption of OSS was developed.

INTRODUCTION

In the past decade, open source software (OSS) has become a viable solution for organizations. Although organizations were initially rather reluctant to adopt OSS (Goode, 2005), several commercial software companies started to offer OSS-related support, services, and products (Fitzgerald, 2006; Feller, Finnegan, & Hayes, 2008). This increased commercial support for OSS products has had a positive effect on the adoption of OSS (Dedrick & West, 2003; Fitzgerald & Kenny, 2003; Morgan & Finnegan, 2010). As a result, OSS has become widely adopted by organizations.

An increasing number of studies on the adoption of OSS have appeared in recent years (Ven &

DOI: 10.4018/978-1-4666-2937-0.ch002

Verelst, in press; Hauge, Ayala, & Conradi, 2010). Some of these previous studies have shown that the existence of internal knowledge in an organization is a critical factor to the successful adoption and assimilation of OSS (Fitzgerald, 2009; Ven & Verelst, 2011). This means that there are knowledge barriers involved in the adoption of OSS and that OSS can be considered a knowledge-intensive technology. To overcome these knowledge barriers, organizations must engage in a process of organizational learning (Attewell, 1992). The ease with which organizations can learn about OSS is influenced by their absorptive capacity. Absorptive capacity refers to the ability of an organization to acquire, assimilate, and exploit new knowledge (Cohen & Levinthal, 1990). Previous research has indeed suggested that organizations need to develop their absorptive capacity in order to successfully adopt OSS (Fitzgerald, 2009). Hence, a number of studies have investigated how knowledge and absorptive capacity influence the adoption of OSS (Fitzgerald, 2009; Ven & Verelst, 2010, 2011). However, to our knowledge, no study has specifically investigated how organizations can develop their absorptive capacity by acquiring knowledge about OSS in order to adopt OSS.

In this paper, we address this gap in literature by investigating how organizations can develop their absorptive capacity within the context of the adoption of OSS. To this end, we describe the results of a case study conducted at the Flemish government. The use of OSS within the Flemish government was considered to be relatively limited. From a knowledge-based perspective, it is also interesting to note that most IT tasks of the organization were outsourced to an external service provider. This means that the assimilation of new knowledge may represent a challenge to the organization. We analyzed our data using theoretical frameworks on absorptive capacity. Our focus is on how various contextual factors influence the process of acquiring, assimilating and exploiting knowledge about OSS. More specifically, we will investigate whether entities within the Flemish

government that have a higher absorptive capacity concerning OSS are more likely to adopt OSS earlier and more extensively than other entities. Based on this, we propose a framework of how organizations develop their absorptive capacity within the context of the adoption of OSS.

The remainder of this paper is structured as follows. We start by providing the theoretical background of our study by elaborating on the concept of absorptive capacity. We subsequently describe the research methodology underlying our study. This is followed by the discussion of the main findings of our case study. Finally, we present our framework, our main conclusions, and implications for theory and practice.

THEORETICAL BACKGROUND

It has been noted in literature that an organization's ability to acquire the knowledge required to effectively use that technology may be an important consideration in the adoption process (Attewell, 1992; Fichman & Kemerer, 1997). Attewell (1992) even claimed that although a technology itself can be relatively easy to acquire, the technical knowledge associated with using the technology may be difficult to obtain. In that case, organizations are faced with *knowledge barriers*, which can limit the diffusion of the technology (Attewell, 1992). In order to overcome these knowledge barriers, organizations need to engage in a process of *organizational learning* (Attewell, 1992; Levitt & March, 1988). Organizational learning requires individual learning, during which individual members of the organization acquire skills and knowledge about a technology (Attewell, 1992; Levitt & March, 1988; Kim, 1998). Organizational learning is mainly dependent on the organization's *absorptive capacity* (Kim, 1998). Cohen and Levinthal defined absorptive capacity as "*the firm's ability to identify, assimilate, and exploit knowledge from the environment*" (Cohen & Levinthal, 1989, p. 569). The higher the organization's absorptive capacity, the greater the organization's ability to acquire and exploit new knowledge (Cohen & Levinthal, 1989, 1990). Organizations that engage in a learning process will further extend their absorptive capacity, which in turn will stimulate and facilitate future learning (Lane, Koka, & Pathak, 2006). This implies that absorptive capacity is conceptualized as a self-reinforcing construct. The development of absorptive capacity is therefore subject to path-dependencies since the new knowledge that can be acquired by an organization is dependent on the prior knowledge of that organization (Cohen & Levinthal, 1990; Todorova & Durisin, 2007). When organizations use an insufficiently broad scope in acquiring new knowledge, the organization may be confronted with *competence traps* as described in the organizational learning literature (Whetten, 1987; Levitt & March, 1988). Competence traps occur when organizations continue to develop experience with inferior technologies since they are unable to recognize the merits of other and better technologies (Levitt & March, 1988).

The single most important factor that influences the level of absorptive capacity is the *prior knowledge* available within an organization (Cohen & Levinthal, 1990). Another important factor is the presence of boundary spanners in the organization. Boundary spanners (also called gatekeepers) scan the external environment for new knowledge, technologies and opportunities and translate this information in a form that is useful to the organization (Tushman & Nadler, 1986; Tushman, 1977). Boundary spanners are especially important when there are significant knowledge barriers involved in adopting a technology, and when the internal knowledge differs significantly from the externally available knowledge (Cohen & Levinthal, 1990). In such cases, the presence of boundary spanners in the organization can be a very effective way for the organization to learn about new technologies.

Since the publication of Cohen and Levinthal (1990), the concept of absorptive capacity has been used extensively in organizational and management research (Lane et al., 2006). Within information systems research, several authors have used the concept of absorptive capacity in an IT context. Boynton, Zmud, and Jacobs (1994), for example, operationalized IT absorptive capacity as consisting of two concepts: (1) *managerial IT knowledge*, or the extent to which there is a knowledge overlap between business and IT employees; and (2) *IT management-process effectiveness*, or an organization's maturity in implementing best-practice IT processes. Their results show that both components have a positive impact on the use of IT by organizations. Harrington and Guimaraes (2005) similarly proposed a measure of absorptive capacity that includes managerial IT knowledge and communication channels. They further show that both factors contribute to the success of the use of IT. In a study on the adoption of software process innovations, Fichman and Kemerer (1997) also found support for the fact that the use of a technology may be influenced by the ability of organizations to overcome knowledge barriers involved in the adoption.

Within the context of the adoption of OSS, Fitzgerald (2009) and Ven and Verelst (2011) have recognized the importance for an organization to acquire the required knowledge in order to successfully deploy OSS. Fitzgerald (2009) concluded that preexisting knowledge of and experience with OSS is an important organizational attribute and facilitating condition in explaining the assimilation of OSS. He further noted that a higher level of absorptive capacity can assist in the selection, integration, implementation, and successful adoption of OSS (Fitzgerald, 2009). The study of Ven and Verelst (2011) even suggested that the ability of organizations to acquire the required knowledge about OSS may be more important than the concrete technical advantages offered by OSS when making a decision on whether to adopt OSS. Hence, both studies concluded that knowledge about OSS is an important factor in the adoption decision and that the availability of OSS-related knowledge has a positive impact on the adoption of OSS. The study of Ven and Verelst (2010) investigated which factors influence the use of knowledge sources in the adoption of OSS. The knowledge sources considered by the authors included the use of vendor support, the use of a service provider, and the use of the open source community. The independent variables were based on the absorptive capacity theory and included current and prior use and experience with Unix and Microsoft Windows, the use of OSS, and characteristics of the IT department. The authors conducted an exploratory, quantitative study to explore the various relationships between these factors. Their results provided more insight regarding the situations in which organizations opt for specific knowledge sources in the adoption of OSS and illustrated that the absorptive capacity theory may assist in explaining the reliance on specific knowledge sources in the adoption of OSS.

These previous three studies all share the idea that absorptive capacity is an important factor that influences the adoption of OSS. However, no prior study has investigated in detail how organizations can actually develop their absorptive capacity in order to facilitate the adoption of OSS. Hence, we are concerned in this study with determining how the development of OSS-related knowledge can take place, and which factors determine the level of absorptive capacity in the context of the adoption of OSS.

METHODOLOGY

In order to study the knowledge assimilation process in the adoption of OSS, we conducted a qualitative study using the descriptive case study research method (Yin, 2003). This approach allowed us to study the phenomenon in its real-life context, and is appropriate to study "*why*" and

"*how*" research questions (Benbasat, Goldstein, & Mead, 1987; Dubé & Paré, 2003; Miles & Huberman, 1994; Marshall & Rossman, 2006). We chose to conduct a detailed investigation regarding the use of OSS by the Flemish government. The Flemish government refers to all government agencies related to the Flemish Region and Flemish Community and employs more than 45,000 civil servants. This organization was a particularly interesting research subject for several reasons. A first reason is that the Flemish government decided to handle its IT infrastructure and policy in a very decentralized way. Since a reorganization in 2006, the Flemish government consists of 13 policy domains. Each policy domain further consists of one department and one or more independent agencies (in the remainder of this paper, both departments and agencies will be referred to as entities within the Flemish government). One of the main goals of the restructuring was to assign more authority and autonomy to each entity, thereby creating a tendency towards a high level of decentralization. Each entity is responsible for deciding on how it will organize its IT function. Some entities prefer to primarily rely on a central outsourcing contract for their IT needs, while other entities—especially those agencies that are rather independent from the Flemish government—prefer to have most IT needs covered by their internal IT staff. It was therefore very interesting to study how the different entities possibly influenced each other in their attitudes towards OSS and—more importantly—to which extent they exchanged information and knowledge regarding IT in general and OSS in particular. A second interesting characteristic of the Flemish government is that it did not have a formal policy or uniform point of view regarding the use of OSS. In addition, although the interest in the use of OSS seemed to be gradually increasing, there was no clear overview of which entities were using OSS at the moment we started our case study. In fact, the overall opinion was that the use of OSS was very limited. A final reason that makes the Flemish government an interesting case is that it has entered into a major outsourc-ing agreement since 1998 with respect to the provisioning of all its IT services. Prior to 1998, the Flemish government handled the majority of IT tasks internally. Following the agreement with the service provider, a large proportion of internal IT staff members left the Flemish government to be employed by the service provider. Some of these employees still remained working within the Flemish government. After a number of years, the Flemish government awarded the outsourcing contract to a different service provider. Much IT-related knowledge therefore left the organization. Coinciding with the switch of service providers was that the various entities could now choose between relying on the external service provider and performing certain tasks by the internal IT staff. A consequence of this outsourcing agreement

is that the acquisition and assimilation of new IT knowledge may represent a significant challenge to the organization.

As part of our case study, we selected seven entities of the Flemish government that are dis-persed over 5 of the 13 policy domains. Since our aim was to study the knowledge assimilation process on OSS, we only considered including those entities that was either using OSS to at least some extent or those entities that were seriously considering using OSS in the near future. Since there was initially no clear overview of which entities were using OSS within the Flemish govern-ment, the majority of the entities were approached through informal contacts. The snowball sampling procedure was followed, since all informants were asked if they knew of other entities that used OSS. Table 1 provides a brief overview of the most

Table 1. Entities included in the case study

Entity	Assimilation stage	Description
1	General deployment (stage 6)	This entity had been using OSS for several years. The entity used OSS for most of its software needs (including (web)server software, programming languages and tools, content and document manage-ment systems, and office suites). An exception were its operating system and virtualization software. In addition, this entity was experimenting with an OSS GIS (Geographical Information System) ap-plication, as well as migrating its DBMS to an OSS alternative.
2	General deployment (stage 6)	This entity indicated to primarily use OSS from the PHP "family". As in Entity 1, this unit employed OSS for most of its needs (server software, DBMS, programming tools, content and document man-agement systems and office suites), with the notable exception of its operating systems. This entity was also experimenting with several OSS GIS applications.
3	Limited deployment (stage 5)	This entity applied primarily the WAMP (Windows, Apache, Mysql, PHP) stack in order to build its own applications. Apart from programming languages and tools, they sporadically used OSS for wiki's and ontology tools. In the past, they also employed an OSS document management system.
4	Commitment (stage 4)	This entity was using an OSS GIS application. The development of this GIS application was com-missioned by the Flemish government. The programming activities were outsourced to an external company (which was a different company than the service provider that was awarded the general outsourcing contract), and the application was published under the GPLv2 license.
5	Limited deployment (stage 5)	This entity introduced several OSS applications since its major restructuring several years ago (e.g., operating systems, webserver software, content management systems). However, several mission criti-cal systems were supported by proprietary software (such as DBMS, ERP software, and virtualization software).
6	General deployment (stage 6)	This entity had the purpose of using open standards for all its software in the long run. As such, most of the server applications were supported by OSS, including operating systems, webserver software, DBMS and mail servers. At the moment the case study was performed, the entity was also implement-ing an OSS office suite.
7	Evaluation / trial (stage 3)	This entity only used a very limited amount of OSS (i.e., some PHP applications and MySQL). How-ever, mainly due to its limited budget, this entity was since recently intensively looking and evaluating possible OSS alternatives for business intelligence and data warehousing, office suite, mail client and document management system purposes.

important OSS products that were used by each entity. Table 1 also provides an indication of the extent to which each entity had assimilated OSS at the time our case study was conducted. We applied the categorization of Fichman and Kemerer (1997) who distinguished between 6 assimilation stages, ranging from awareness to general deployment. The classification of entities in a specific assimilation stage is based on the number of different OSS products that were used, the extent to which the entity relied on each of these OSS products, and the extent to which the entity had developed knowledge about these OSS products. It is interesting to observe that—in contrast to the common perception of several actors within the Flemish government—several entities of the Flemish government did already use OSS rather extensively and successfully.

The data for our study was collected between October 2009 and May 2010. The primary mode of data collection consisted of semi-structured interviews with one or more informants at each entity. When possible, multiple persons within each entity were interviewed in order to increase validity (Benbasat et al., 1987). In total, interviews were held with 15 informants. All informants were well-informed about the use of OSS in their respective entity. An overview of our informants within each entity is shown in Table 2. Apart from the interviews conducted with members of the 7 entities in our sample, we also conducted interviews with informants at the management or policy level within the Flemish government. The aim of these interviews was to obtain a more profound view on the general IT strategy and policy of the Flemish government. With the exception of Entity 1 in which a single interview was conducted with two informants, all interviews were conducted with a single informant. Each interview was conducted at the business address of each respective entity. Interviews generally lasted between 60 and 120 minutes and were recorded for future reference.

Prior to the interviewing phase, a detailed questionnaire was designed. The questions were

Table 2. Overview of informants within each entity

Organizational Unit	Informants
Entity 1	Head of ICT department
	Database administrator
	Unix administrator
	Application manager
Entity 2	Head of ICT department
Entity 3	Head of ICT department
Entity 4	Project leader GIS applications
	Application manager
Entity 5	Head of ICT department
Entity 6	Head of ICT department
	Application manager
Entity 7	Head of ICT department
Management/ policy level	Head of ICT policy of the Flemish government
	Adviser to the Cabinet for Administrative Affairs
	Process manager for Agency for Government Officials

based on the academic literature on absorptive capacity (Cohen & Levinthal, 1989, 1990; Lane et al., 2006; Zahra & George, 2002; Todorova & Durisin, 2007). The aim of these questions was to translate the academic theory and concepts into concrete issues and topics in an OSS-related context. The questionnaire started with introductory questions concerning the mission and organization of the entity, the responsibilities of the informants, and the current use of OSS. The main part of the questionnaire consisted of exploring the various contextual factors that influence the absorptive capacity of each entity. All questions were open-ended, thereby inviting informants to offer any reactions related to the aforementioned factors. When necessary, additional follow-up was performed by e-mail conversations or phone calls.

During data analysis, we focused on describing the activities and perceptions related to the various contextual factors that influence the absorptive capacity of an organization. First, *within-case analysis* was performed to investigate the data from each entity (Yin, 2003). The data from each interview was analyzed shortly following each interview. We started our analysis by transcribing each interview. Next, a preliminary case report was written for each entity. This report contained an extensive summary of the information obtained during the interviews conducted in each entity. Second, we conducted a *cross-case analysis* to compare the findings across the various entities. In this phase, we identified commonalities and differences across the various cases and determined how differences in the absorptive capacity of—and the OSS assimilation stage achieved by—each entity could be explained. The within-case analysis was supported by a number of tables to visualize the data (Miles & Huberman, 1994). The main purpose of these tables was to summarize the data and to allow for cross-case analysis. Based on this analysis, a final case study report was written in which the detailed findings of our study were described. This case study report was sent to our informants to obtain corrections, additions and any other feedback to increase the validity of our findings.

FINDINGS

When presenting our findings, we will focus on the contextual factors that influence the development of absorptive capacity in the context of the adoption of OSS. In our analysis, we started from generally accepted frameworks on absorptive capacity that are described in literature (Cohen & Levinthal, 1990; Lane et al., 2006; Zahra & George, 2002; Todorova & Durisin, 2007). We applied, interpreted, and modified these frameworks to fit the OSS-related context by following an inductive approach by identifying manifestations of each of these constructs in the data obtained through our case study. We therefore investigated how these existing constructs apply to the context of the adoption of OSS, and if other relevant factors can be identified. The aim of this analysis is to

present an initial framework of how absorptive capacity can be developed, specifically within the context of the adoption of OSS. In addition, we will explore whether entities within the Flemish government that have a higher absorptive capacity concerning OSS (in terms of the factors discussed below) are more likely to adopt OSS earlier and more extensively than other entities.

Activation Triggers

Activation triggers are internal or external events that make an organization respond by looking for external knowledge to further develop the organization's absorptive capacity (Zahra & George, 2002; Lane et al., 2006). In the context of the adoption of OSS, this factor refers to the motivation of organizations to acquire knowledge about OSS. The reasons why the entities included in this study decided to further develop their OSS knowledge are displayed in Table 3. Given the scope of our study and since most factors are described in previous studies on the adoption of OSS (Morgan & Finnegan, 2010; Ven & Verelst, 2008, 2011, in press; Lundell, Lings, & Lindqvist, 2010; Benlian & Hess, 2010), we will focus on the two knowledge-related factors here, namely *prior internal knowledge* and *boundary spanners*.

Concerning *prior knowledge*, it has to be noticed that existing knowledge does not only facilitate the gathering of new related knowledge: it can also act as an independent decision factor when considering whether to adopt a certain technology. For example, Entity 2 and Entity 3 reported that their initial choice for starting to implement OSS in their entity was significantly influenced by the fact that one or more people in their department had already built up some knowledge or expertise in this area in the past. Additionally, informants of Entity 1, Entity 5 and Entity 6 stated that once they had actually implemented certain OSS products in their entity, they systematically tried to look for similar products or technologies in the future. This way, they were con-

Table 3. Motivations of the entities included in the study to adopt OSS or to build up knowledge about it

Trigger	Entity 1	Entity 2	Entity 3	Entity 4	Entity 5	Entity 6	Entity 7
Prior internal knowledge	□	●	●		□	□	
Boundary spanners	●	●	○		●	●	●
License costs	●	●	●		●	●	●
Available source code	○		●	□		○	○
Trialibility	●	○	●		●	●	●
Ideology	●				○	○	○
Functional match or superiority	○	○	●	●	●	○	○
External support	○	○		●	○	○	●
Use of open standards / Avoidance of vendor lock-in	●			●	○	●	●
Legend:							
●: important trigger for adoption and knowledge development							
○: relevant, but not decisive trigger for adoption and knowledge development							
□: trigger for adoption and knowledge development, but only in a secondary stage							

vinced that they could enjoy a kind of head start and lower learning cost. One informant explained this as follows: "*We do not always have a lot of time to finish a certain project [...] As we have a quite thorough knowledge regarding PHP tools, we systematically look for applications and tools in that direction. As such, we are prepared to sacrifice for example 5% of functionalities for an alternative which is actually PHP-based, but which we can understand and learn much faster.*" This illustrates the existence of *path dependencies*: the new knowledge that is acquired by organizations is dependent on the prior knowledge (Cohen & Levinthal, 1990). Organizations are therefore inclined to look for new technologies that require similar knowledge and have a tendency to avoid technologies that require the acquisition of completely new knowledge. This illustrates the existence of path dependencies and their manifestation during the development of absorptive capacity.

As shown in Table 3, *boundary spanners* played a crucial role in the adoption decision in the majority of the entities. For example, boundary spanners in Entity 1 and Entity 2 facilitated the experimentation (and evaluation) of OSS content and document management systems. Boundary spanners were also found to be useful in the subsequent assimilation phases. It was frequently mentioned by our informants that IT staff members that have access to external sources of information (e.g., books, websites, people with relevant experience) were useful when studying a new application. One informant, for example, mentioned: "*[The OSS products we use in our entity] are actually not that difficult and relatively easy to learn, you only have to know where to start.*"

Organizational Structures and Processes

In this section we will discuss the impact of three kinds of organizational structures and processes: *human resources policy*, *interdepartmental knowledge sharing* and *intradepartmental knowledge sharing*.

- **Human Resources Policy:** The human resources (HR) policy of a company has an important influence on the development of absorptive capacity since it impacts both the motivation and competences of employees (Minbaeva, Pedersen, Bjorkman, Fey, & Park, 2003). During the interviews each entity was asked (1) which criteria were used to recruit new IT employees; (2) to which extent (external) trainings were stimulated within their entity; and (3) whether the employees were evaluated on their job performance and/or their personal knowledge development. The responses of the various entities are summarized in Table 4.

Concerning the recruitment of IT personnel, all entities indicated to evaluate new applicants based on their prior IT experience and the possession of an IT or university degree. All entities acknowledged that prior (IT) experience was an advantage. Having a university degree was also considered to be advantageous by several entities. However, some entities valued interpersonal skills over purely technical knowledge—since people with a social science orientation were sometimes considered to be more communicative—and did not consider an IT degree to be the most important asset of applicants. This was explained by one of our informants as: *"I find the fact that applicants have the right people skills much more important than whether or not they have an official IT degree. It is important that those people are able to get from their desk and really talk to end users and other entities.".* Since prior knowledge is an important antecedent of absorptive capacity, the more diverse and broad the knowledge of employees, the easier it will be for these employees to acquire and assimilate new knowledge, and thus the higher their absorptive capacity.

All informants reported that they had sufficient opportunities to follow courses or allocate time for personal knowledge development. Entities that strongly encourage training allow employees to expand their knowledge base, which also helps to develop the absorptive capacity of the entity. As depicted in Table 4, some entities actively stimulated IT staff members to work on their personal development by encouraging or requiring IT staff members to follow additional training or education. These entities exhibited a higher OSS assimilation stage. One exception is Entity 7 that encouraged training, but had a lower assimilation stage. However, as explained in Table 1, this entity only recently started to explore the use of OSS, but was quite actively looking into various OSS solutions at the time of our study. Entities that strongly valued training also emphasized its importance in the evaluation of employees in addition to the job performance of their employees. As one informant mentioned: *"Every year, we hold an oral evaluation of each employee. During that conversation, I systematically ask them: how far*

Table 4. Overview of human resources policy

Entity	Assimilation stage	Recruitment			Training			Evaluation	
		Experience	IT degree	University degree	Voluntary	Encouraged	Required	Performance	Learning
Entity 1	6	●	●	●			●	●	●
Entity 2	6	●		●		●		●	●
Entity 3	5	●			●			●	
Entity 4	4	●			●			●	
Entity 5	5	●		●	●			●	
Entity 6	6	●	●	●		●		●	
Entity 7	3	●	●	●		●		●	●

have you proceeded with your personal training and development this year and what progress do you want to make next year? […] They also know that I find that extremely important. […] The absence of the willingness to learn of an employee is in my point of view not at all an acceptable attitude." As Table 4 illustrates, entities that were found to have a higher absorptive capacity in terms of HR policy (i.e., those that took an IT or university degree into account in recruitment, stimulated training, and also evaluated employees based on their training) were found to exhibit a higher assimilation of OSS.

Interdepartmental Knowledge Sharing

Another interesting issue to consider is whether entities communicated with each other in order to exchange knowledge. The case study provided an exceptional opportunity to study this phenomenon since each entity had the authority to decide on its own IT provisioning and since several entities were found to be using the same OSS products. This creates opportunities to share knowledge between entities by discussing practical problems that arise during the implementation of an OSS product or by asking for advice when considering to adopt a certain OSS product. Through knowledge sharing, entities can learn from the experiences of other entities, and thus acquire new knowledge, thereby increasing their absorptive capacity. We identified a number of formal and informal interdepartmental knowledge sharing initiatives. First, a number of working groups were identified that facilitated *formal interdepartmental knowledge sharing* concerning IT. The main goal of a first working group was the alignment of the large amount of independent IT strategies in the organization by exchanging information and by building common "ICT building blocks". A second working group was founded with the purpose of exchanging information at the managerial level, including on IT. A final working group was recently founded to explore and stimulate the use of open standards in

the organization. Notwithstanding the existence of these initiatives, the actual knowledge exchange (certainly within the first two working groups) was considered to be relatively limited by our informants. This could be partly explained by the fact that these initiatives were simply not known to several informants. Even when informants did know one or more of these formal initiatives, some of them decided not to join them (especially the first two) since experiences regarding similar initiatives in the past were not always positively evaluated. As one informant mentioned: "*At the Flemish government there are lots of working groups: in principle, I could place a full-time person on it to follow them all. Obviously, we do not have time for that, so I only participate when I'm extremely sure that something useful is done there and people are not just again losing their time in general and vague tittle-tattle*". Second, a number of initiatives concerning *informal interdepartmental knowledge exchange* were identified. The majority of our informants indicated that information sharing without any formal structure, procedures or arrangements was deemed to be more useful and efficient. Figure 1 schematically represents the interdepartmental knowledge sharing activities between the 7 entities. It could be observed that mainly Entity 1, Entity 6 and Entity 7 had multiple contacts with other units that were employing OSS. Entity 1 and Entity 2 also frequently exchanged relevant knowledge between each other. Employees from Entity 3, Entity 4 and Entity 5 were found to be slightly isolated from other entities using OSS. It further appeared that those entities with the highest OSS assimilation stage (i.e., Entity 1, Entity 2 and Entity 6) were more frequently and/or intensively exchanging knowledge with other entities. Entity 7 is again an exception since it started to investigate the use of OSS only recently. Since knowledge exchange is crucial to developing absorptive capacity in order to acquire new knowledge, a higher intensity of communication between entities indicates that those entities involved will be able to better develop

Figure 1. Interdepartmental knowledge sharing between entities

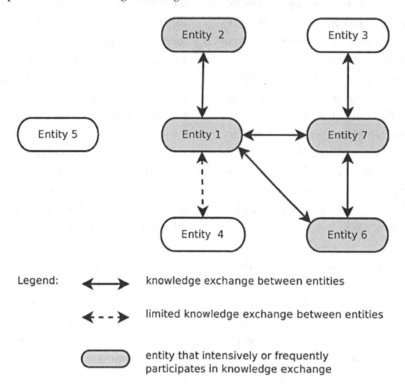

their absorptive capacity. The beneficial impact of informal communication was further illustrated by the fact that informants were generally pleasantly surprised to hear that other entities within the Flemish government were using the same OSS products as they did. Although IT staff members were not always aware of the software that was being used by other entities, it was considered an advantage to obtain this information in order to set up informal interdepartmental communication.

Intradepartmental Knowledge Sharing

Intradepartmental knowledge sharing refers to communication about the possibilities and use of OSS products within the same entity. In this case, knowledge is being shared between employees of the same entity. This ensures that this knowledge is translated into practices, procedures, and guidelines that remain within the entity when an employee leaves the entity. By avoiding that the

knowledge of employees is lost to the entity, the absorptive capacity of the entity increases, since the knowledge is then transferred from the individual to the entity. Intradepartmental knowledge sharing primarily took place via spontaneous and unplanned consultations and fixed (e.g., weekly) meetings, supplemented with explicit documentation (e.g., manuals) and documentation within the source code itself. When our informants were asked to give a self-report of the efficiency and effectiveness of that communication, no apparent relationship was found with their assimilation stage as shown in Table 5. Instead, it seemed that the feasibility of this intradepartmental knowledge sharing was correlated with the number of IT staff members. Entity 2, Entity 3, Entity 4 and Entity 7 each consisted out of three to four full-time employees and reported to succeed quite well in sharing each other's knowledge. Most of these entities also indicated to find it important that intradepartmental knowledge sharing took place.

Table 5. Overview of self-reported levels of inter-departmental knowledge sharing

Entity	Assimilation stage	Number of employees	Intradepartmental knowledge sharing
Entity 1	6	13	–
Entity 2	6	4	+ +
Entity 3	5	4	+ +
Entity 4	4	4	+
Entity 5	5	7	– –
Entity 6	6	13	–
Entity 7	3	3	+ +
Legend: + +: very good, +: good, –: moderately, – –: insufficient			

Table 6. Representation of the use of knowledge sources

Knowledge sources	Evaluation	Implementation	Use
Internet related sources	●	●	●
Source code	○	○	○
Professional magazines	●		
Academic literature	□		
Interdepartmental knowledge sharing	●	○	
Books		●	○
Training		●	○
Recruitment of new employees		□	□
Consulting		○	○
Intradepartmental knowledge sharing		○	●
Legend:			
●: extensively used knowledge source			
○: moderately used knowledge source			
□: knowledge source which was mentioned only by one entity			

One informant even mentioned that he once did not prolong the contract of a consultant who was not willing to follow the expected intradepartmental knowledge sharing practices such as writing the appropriate documentation. Entity 1, Entity 5 and Entity 6 indicated that although they definitely valued the benefits of intradepartmental communication, they were not always able to realize this due to the size of its IT department. One informant mentioned that it was *"increasingly difficult to share knowledge [intradepartmental] since our entity has grown"*.

Knowledge Sources

Another issue we considered was which knowledge sources were used to acquire the required knowledge about OSS and therefore to develop the entities' absorptive capacity. We identified 10 different knowledge sources in our case study. A summary of the knowledge sources used during evaluation, implementation and use of their OSS products is shown in Table 6.

A first observation is that Internet sources (such as forums and news sites) were consistently used throughout the evaluation, implementation and use of OSS. The source code was also used in all three phases, although not very frequently. During the evaluation of new applications, our informants indicated to rely primarily on professional magazines to keep up their general knowledge on the IT industry. One informant mentioned to occasionally consult academic sources for information. In the *implementation* and *use* phases, our informants mainly relied on books, external training, and consulting. One entity also considered the recruitment of new employees to be a source of new knowledge. Interdepartmental and intradepartmental knowledge sharing activities were also mentioned as knowledge sources. Interdepartmental knowledge sharing appeared to be more important in the early (i.e., evaluation and implementation) phases. In the later phases, the use of intradepartmental knowledge sharing became more important. The use of external support was also primarily located in the later phases. Some informants mentioned that they would like to rely on external support earlier in the adoption process, but that finding reliable support for some of these OSS products was still challenging.

The findings above suggest that some sequence exists in which the various knowledge sources are used. Some informants gave an explicit indication that such a recurring and systematic pattern may exist. One informant indeed noted: "*For me, the order is as follows: first, you do some surfing on the Internet and try out some available products without reading all too much. Then you look in the community for some problems you can't solve yourself. If necessary you can then buy a book or something and finally you can choose to optimize your advanced level through a real course*". These knowledge sources are used to develop the absorptive capacity of the entity since these knowledge sources allow employees to acquire new knowledge. This pattern further suggests that some knowledge sources may be more effective than others when developing absorptive capacity, depending on to which adoption phase the entity has progressed.

Prior Related Knowledge

Prior related knowledge is usually regarded as the single most important antecedent of absorptive capacity (Cohen & Levinthal, 1990). This prior knowledge helps individuals and the organization to acquire new knowledge that is related to, but different, from the already acquired knowledge. In general, all informants confirmed the expectation that prior IT knowledge facilitates the acquisition of future knowledge and allows this knowledge acquisition to occur more rapidly. We will now further elaborate on the aspect of internal knowledge by considering four distinct types of prior knowledge: *technical knowledge, domain*

knowledge, relative knowledge and *managerial knowledge*. These four types of prior knowledge all determine the level of absorptive capacity of each entity. We further explore how and to which extent each of these types contributes to developing absorptive capacity in the context of the adoption of OSS.

Technical Knowledge

Consistent with the generally accepted dimensions of *depth* and *breadth* of organizational knowledge, we further divide this aspect in *general IT education* (breadth), *OSS-specific knowledge* (depth), and *application-related knowledge* (depth). Concerning the *general IT education*, not all IT staff members possessed an IT degree. Several explanations for this observation were discovered during our case study: the decline of IT personnel as a consequence of the outsourcing deal, the high cost of certain IT profiles on the job market, and the preference for domain knowledge of applicants over purely technical IT knowledge. An IT degree was nevertheless considered by several informants to be useful in providing a background to acquire additional IT and OSS knowledge. This was illustrated by the fact that some IT staff members were pursuing an additional IT-related Master's degree. *OSS-specific knowledge* refers to knowledge that is specifically related to the characteristics and use of OSS. This OSS-specific knowledge was generally not considered by our informants to be the most important facilitator to acquire additional knowledge on OSS. Nevertheless, some exceptions could be observed. One informant claimed that he discerned a general "structure" within each OSS product that was useful when learning new OSS products. He explained this by the fact that "*lots of functionalities can be found in the same locations [...] also for example the log-files, they are systematically in the same folder and after some time you know where to find them*". Another person mentioned that it was important to learn how to interact with the OSS community by stating that "*[when I was trying to convince my colleagues of the possibilities with OSS], I had to really guide them in how they could efficiently use the online community*". In addition, several informants mentioned the convenience to be able to keep working with the same technology stacks when using OSS. The biggest advantage of prior experience with OSS was, however, attributed to the possibility to better evaluate the possibilities and maturity of other OSS products. As one informant for example noted: "*After some time you learn how to evaluate such a [OSS] product. [… for example:] to what extent is the product supported by the community?*". This prior knowledge therefore helped the entity to evaluate whether mature and suitable OSS was available, which facilitates the decision on whether or not to adopt OSS for a specific purpose. *Application-related knowledge* (i.e., knowledge related to a specific type of application) was generally considered to be the most important facilitator to acquire new knowledge. One informant who was a Unix administrator with many years of experience, mentioned that it was relatively easy for him to make the switch to another Unix-like operating system such as Linux, but that it was far more difficult for him to engage in a new DBMS, regardless of whether those applications were OSS or proprietary software. Similar reactions were noted from people employing DMBS, CMS and GIS applications. One person, for example, stated: "*[whether they are open source or not,] most GIS applications are essentially working in more or less the same way.*"

Domain Knowledge

Domain knowledge refers to the possession of knowledge regarding the functional domain that is being automated in the organization. This type of knowledge was valued by several ICT managers. Some entities mentioned that the domain knowledge concerning a policy domain of new ICT applicants was valuable in order for them to

be able to communicate with end users in their entity and to understand the organizational impact of the technology.

Relative Knowledge

The concept of relative knowledge refers to the knowledge one has about the presence of other persons and sources that can be useful in acquiring new knowledge (Cohen & Levinthal, 1990). Several informants confirmed that relative knowledge is a crucial dimension of prior knowledge. As one informant remarked: "*[…] it is clear that we do not always exactly know from each other [i.e., other entities] what we are doing, but that seems quite logical to me in such a large organization. On the other hand, I think it would be a huge advantage if we would have a more clear overview of that aspect in order to sometimes be able to make a kind of 'head start'*". The importance of relative knowledge also relates to the presence of inter- and intradepartmental knowledge sharing initiatives and the presence of boundary spanners.

Managerial IT Knowledge

Within the IT context, managerial IT knowledge can be considered an important component of absorptive capacity (Boynton et al., 1994; Harrington & Guimaraes, 2005). This component also proved to be relevant in our case study. Within the Flemish government, one entity is concerned with coordinating the e-government and IT services. This coordinating entity mainly monitors and provides advice and guidance regarding the services and IT solutions offered by the outsourcing partner to all requesting entities of the Flemish government and could be considered to be the central IT management level. Notwithstanding the existence of this coordinating entity, the distinct IT staff in all entities within the Flemish government have full decision authority on their IT use: they can decide to rely on the services of the coordinating entity and the associated outsourcing partner, or choose to support their own IT infrastructure. Some informants claimed that there was an insufficient overlap in the knowledge possessed by the IT staff and the higher management. This was considered to be a limiting factor to the opportunities of the organization to adopt new information technology in general and OSS in particular. Some informants suggested that more explicit communication and knowledge redundancy between management and IT staff members would facilitate the development of an official organizational policy about open standards and OSS. One informant mentioned that: "*[Most managers] are not fully aware of the possibilities and the options that [open standards and OSS] offer and maybe they would apply another policy in case they were more explicitly informed.*"

Organizational Strategies

Concerning the organizational strategy, both the outsourcing strategy and the decentralization strategy were found to have an impact on the development of absorptive capacity.

Outsourcing Strategy

The outsourcing strategy of the Flemish government seemed to be an important factor that impeded the development of OSS-related knowledge. Due to the outsourcing decision in 1998, the number of IT staff members within the organization decreased considerably. As a result, much general IT knowledge left the organization, which also means that the absorptive capacity of the organization decreased. One informant mentioned that this also led to a decrease in OSS-related knowledge since considerable OSS-related knowledge was available in-house prior to 1998. Our informants indicated that due to this decrease in knowledge, it was more difficult to negotiate with vendors or to take certain platform decisions. An example of this was the development of the open source GIS application that was used by Entity 4. Although the

agreement with the external firm that developed the application stipulated that the authority on all technology- and development-related choices rested with the Flemish government, many practical decisions were taken by the external firm instead. Another consequence was that some entities were less proactive in scanning the environment for useful new technologies and tended to rely on the service provider. This illustrates the presence of path dependencies in the technology choices made by the organization. Both observations are also consistent with the literature that suggests that outsourcing can have a negative effect on an organization's absorptive capacity (Cohen & Levinthal, 1990). In this specific case, much knowledge left the organization, which means that the various entities experienced more issues in acquiring and assimilating new knowledge (i.e., the entities were confronted with increased knowledge barriers).

Decentralization Strategy

The restructuring of the Flemish government in 2006 included a decentralization strategy that aimed to assign more authority to each entity within the organization, including on IT-related matters. This provided entities with the opportunity to initiate a number of OSS projects. However, this policy also made the knowledge sharing process between entities more difficult. Since each entity has decision authority on their IT provisioning, there is little (compelling) coordination at a higher level concerning IT usage. As a result, each entity has its own IT strategy, which also means that there is potentially little overlap in the IT products used and knowledge possessed by the various entities. This also limits the opportunities for mutual learning, which has a rather negative impact on absorptive capacity. These observations are consistent with the properties of a divisional structure as defined by Van Den Bosch, Volberda, and De Boer (1999). Although decentralization may increase flexibility, it has a limited positive influence on absorptive capacity. This can be explained by the low knowledge acquisition and sharing efficiency of decentralization (Van Den Bosch et al., 1999).

DISCUSSION AND CONCLUSION

Based on our observations described in the previous section, we developed a framework that graphically illustrates which contextual factors influence the development of absorptive capacity in the context of the adoption of OSS. This framework is shown in Figure 2 and is based on existing conceptual frameworks of absorptive capacity (Cohen & Levinthal, 1990; Lane et al., 2006; Zahra & George, 2002; Todorova & Durisin, 2007). We applied, interpreted, and modified these frameworks to fit the OSS-related context by identifying manifestations of each of these constructs in the data obtained through our

case study. The framework in Figure 2 therefore graphically illustrates how absorptive capacity can be developed within the context of the adoption of OSS. This framework extends existing frameworks on absorptive capacity by illustrating the process of developing absorptive capacity, specifically within the context of the adoption of OSS. In general, our findings are consistent with the literature on absorptive capacity. This provides additional support for the use of absorptive capacity as a theoretical framework to study the adoption and assimilation of OSS. Nevertheless, some additional comments can be made.

Our findings identified a number of factors that triggered the entities to explore the use of OSS. Although several studies have been conducted on the adoption of OSS, our findings suggest that it is interesting to consider these factors from a knowledge-based perspective. Several adoption factors that have previously been identified in literature were found to have knowl-

Figure 2. Factors influencing the development of absorptive capacity in the adoption of OSS (adapted from Cohen & Levinthal, 1990; Lane et al., 2006; Zahra & George, 2002; Todorova & Durisin, 2007)

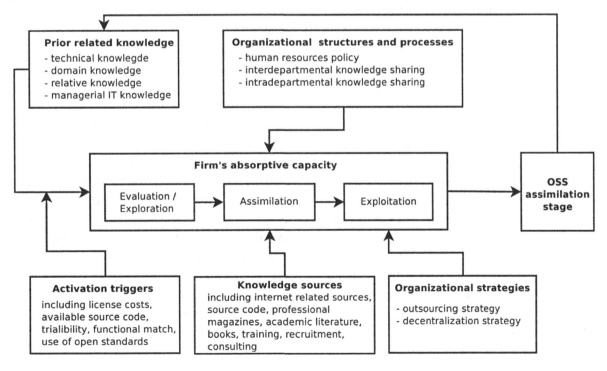

edge-related implications. The potential lower license cost of OSS can result in direct financial benefits for the organization, but can also allow the organization to invest more in internal knowledge assimilation (e.g., through training and education). Several informants also mentioned that the availability of the source code was a source of documentation and knowledge that assisted the learning process. The presence of boundary spanners was found to be very influential in facilitating the adoption of OSS, as well as in stimulating interdepartmental and intradepartmental knowledge sharing.

The academic literature generally considers prior related knowledge to be the most important antecedent of absorptive capacity. Our analysis showed, however, that some dimensions of prior related knowledge may be more pertinent than others regarding the development of absorptive capacity in the context of the adoption of OSS. As such, making an explicit distinction between different sorts of prior related knowledge seemed relevant. We distinguished between four different types of prior knowledge. It was noteworthy that technical knowledge (including general IT knowledge, OSS-specific knowledge, and application-related knowledge) proved to be less important than domain knowledge, relative knowledge and managerial IT knowledge. Although prior knowledge was found to be an antecedent of absorptive capacity as predicted by literature, we have found that organizational structures and processes played an even more important role in our case study. More specifically, we have found that a more proactive HR policy, participation in interdepartmental knowledge sharing, and intradepartmental knowledge sharing were positively related to the assimilation stage reached by each entity. The entities with the highest assimilation stage (Entity 1, Entity 2, and Entity 6) all exhibited a high absorptive capacity with respect to these factors. It therefore appears that entities with a high absorptive capacity were more likely to

adopt OSS earlier and more extensively than other entities. The importance of these organizational structures and processes may be explained by the fact that the Flemish government was still in the early OSS assimilation stages and made use of an outsourcing contract to cover most of its IT needs. Hence, relatively little prior internal knowledge was available in the organization. The importance of prior knowledge may therefore increase as the organization assimilates additional internal knowledge.

It was further observed that the various contextual factors that influence the development of absorptive capacity were only to a limited extent specific to OSS. Most informants did not consider learning about OSS to be fundamentally different than learning about other (proprietary) technologies. A notable exception was the fact that some informants indicated to experience certain knowledge-related advantages thanks to typical characteristics of OSS. This included the trialability of OSS that allowed to freely experiment with the product in advance, the availability of the source code that could serve as a knowledge source, and the recurring structure within each OSS product. One informant mentioned a negative consequence in that learning to interact with the OSS community required an additional learning effort.

There was a strong interest among our informants to be further informed about the results of the study in general and about the use of OSS in other entities of the Flemish government in particular. Among other reasons, this prompted the Flemish government to organize a seminar on the use of OSS in June 2010. During this seminar, a number of entities presented their use of OSS and provided practical advice to entities that wished to explore the use of OSS. The findings, conclusions and recommendations from our study were also presented during this seminar. This seminar could be considered a knowledge-sharing activity that could facilitate the further adoption of OSS. In fact, the conclusion of this seminar was that the Flemish government intended to further explore the potential of OSS. Based on our findings, we expect that a higher level of management commitment is required, as well as increased inter-departmental knowledge sharing. The latter will be especially important to sufficiently lower the knowledge barriers for entities that are unfamiliar with OSS. In addition, it will be important that a critical mass of OSS adopters within the Flemish government can be reached in order to guarantee the sustainability of the assimilation process.

Implications for Research

This study has made a number of contributions to academic literature. The results strongly support the importance of absorptive capacity in the adoption of OSS. Previous research on the adoption of IT has suggested that the ability of an organization to acquire the required knowledge is an important factor in the adoption of a new technology (Fichman & Kemerer, 1997; Attewell, 1992). It has therefore been suggested that the concept of absorptive capacity provides an interesting perspective to use within an IT context (Boynton et al., 1994; Harrington & Guimaraes, 2005). Some studies on the adoption of OSS have indeed suggested that the knowledge available within an organization is a crucial factor in the adoption decision and that a higher absorptive capacity facilitates the adoption of OSS (Fitzgerald, 2009; Ven & Verelst, 2011). Our study therefore supports the results of these previous studies. The complexity involved in assimilating new knowledge may imply that the internal knowledge of the organization can be a more important consideration in the adoption decision than the concrete advantages that OSS offers. As shown in our framework in Figure 2, there may be several triggers for an organization to consider the use of OSS. These triggers may refer to various advantages of OSS such as cost, trialability, and the availability of the source code.

However, the influence of these factors is situated in the beginning of the assimilation process when organizations become aware of, and interested in, OSS. Whether the organization is able to effectively assimilate OSS depends on the ability of the organization to acquire, assimilate, and exploit the required knowledge about OSS. Knowledge-related factors may therefore be more important in the subsequent assimilation stages.

To our knowledge, this study is the first to investigate in detail how organizations can develop their absorptive capacity in the context of the adoption of OSS. We strongly relied in our analysis on the prevalent frameworks and conceptualizations of absorptive capacity as described in literature (Cohen & Levinthal, 1990; Lane et al., 2006; Zahra & George, 2002; Todorova & Durisin, 2007). Based on the data obtained from our case study, we applied, interpreted and adapted these frameworks within the OSS-specific context. It is noteworthy that few contextual factors were found to be specific to OSS. This suggests that the adoption of OSS may be less different from the adoption of proprietary software than often assumed. Nevertheless, an important contribution of this study is that this framework provides an extension to the existing literature on absorptive capacity to illustrate how absorptive capacity can be developed, specifically within the context of the adoption of OSS.

By conducting an in-depth study on the development of absorptive capacity in the context of the adoption of OSS, we also contributed to the literature on absorptive capacity in two ways. First, it has been noted that although absorptive capacity is a complex construct, many quantitative studies use poor and shallow measures to operationalize the construct (Lane et al., 2006). We have used a qualitative approach to capture rich and in-depth insights to provide an initial identification and conceptualization of the contextual factors that influence the development of absorptive capacity in the adoption of OSS.

These results can be used by future studies on the adoption of OSS to develop quantitative measures. Second, it has been noted that several studies reduce the concept of absorptive capacity to the presence of prior knowledge (Lane et al., 2006). We used a more comprehensive approach in this study by considering a broad set of factors that influence the development of absorptive capacity. This study therefore addresses two shortcomings of the existing literature on absorptive capacity. Both aspects can also be seen as explicit efforts to avoid the *reification* of absorptive capacity (Lane et al., 2006).

Implications for Practice

This study also provides several useful insights for decision makers in organizations who are considering adopting OSS. Based on the results of this study, it is recommended that decision makers pay sufficient attention to the importance of knowledge in the assimilation of OSS. Professional literature—as well as several academic sources— tends to emphasize the various advantages that OSS may offer. Although these advantages may constitute valid reasons for considering adopting OSS, decision makers have to assess the ability of the organization to acquire the knowledge required for successfully adopting OSS. The introduction of OSS may require knowledge assimilation process if that knowledge is not available internally in the organization.

Our study further provides more insight into which factors facilitate this knowledge assimilation process. The identification of these contextual factors allows decision makers to evaluate the organization with respect to each of these factors in order to determine the ease with which the knowledge assimilation process can take place. It also allows decision makers to devise interventions to improve upon specific factors.

More generally, our results also underline the important role that employees in the organization play in trying out and experimenting with OSS. This is facilitated by the high trialability of OSS since OSS can be freely downloaded. This way, the organization acquires and assimilates knowledge that may be used (or exploited) at a later time. This is sometimes referred to as the *potential absorptive capacity* of an organization, which means that an organization assimilates knowledge that it may or may not exploit at a later time (Zahra & George, 2002). Although the knowledge may not be immediately used, this potential absorptive capacity helps IT staff members at a later time in identifying projects where OSS could provide an effective solution. It may also provide a way for an organization to avoid path dependencies (which may in the end lead to competence traps) since the organization learns about alternative technologies that the organization may otherwise not have considered.

Limitations

A first limitation of our study is that we studied the knowledge assimilation process in a single organization. However, this allowed us to perform an in-depth study of this phenomenon. We also studied the use of OSS by various entities in the Flemish government. Since it was difficult to obtain information on which entities were already using OSS, it is possible that we did not include all entities within the Flemish government that used OSS. The fact that we studied an organization from the public sector and that most of the IT needs were provided through an outsourcing contract may also limit the generalizability of our findings.

A second limitation is that we only included entities in our sample that were using OSS at the time of our study. It is, however, possible that other entities within the Flemish government have a high extent of OSS-related knowledge, but decided not to adopt OSS. Such extensive knowledge may, for example, allow the entity to realize that OSS may not be the best solution given the problem domain and available infrastructure. However, we were not able to collect any data on this in our study.

Another limitation is that our sample was limited to entities with a relatively small IT department (i.e., less than 15 employees). We selected the entities for our study based on the fact that they used OSS. This may indicate that the exploration and implementation of OSS was most likely to occur in entities with a small IT department. In smaller IT departments, it may be easier to convince colleagues about the potential and benefits of OSS. However, it would be interesting that future studies try to obtain more insight into this issue.

Finally, the OSS products that were adopted by the entities included in our study were primarily situated at the server or infrastructural level. This is consistent with observations in literature that the organizational adoption of OSS has primarily taken place at this level, and that the adoption of other types of OSS—such as desktop and enterprise software—is a much more recent phenomenon. However, the knowledge assimilation process concerning other types of OSS may be influenced by other factors. This could be another topic for future studies on the adoption of OSS.

REFERENCES

Attewell, P. (1992). Technology diffusion and organizational learning: The case of business computing. *Organization Science*, *3*(1), 1–19. doi:10.1287/orsc.3.1.1

Benbasat, I., Goldstein, D. K., & Mead, M. (1987). The case research strategy in studies of information systems. *Management Information Systems Quarterly*, *11*(3), 368–386. doi:10.2307/248684

Benlian, A., & Hess, T. (2010). Comparing the relative importance of evaluation criteria in proprietary and open-source enterprise application software selection a conjoint study of ERP and office systems. *Information Systems Journal*.

Boynton, A. C., Zmud, R. W., & Jacobs, G. C. (1994). The influence of IT management practice on IT use in large corporations. *Management Information Systems Quarterly*, *18*(3), 299–318. doi:10.2307/249620

Cohen, W. M., & Levinthal, D. A. (1989). Innovation and learning: The two faces of R & D. *The Economic Journal*, *99*(397), 569–596. doi:10.2307/2233763

Cohen, W. M., & Levinthal, D. A. (1990). Absorptive capacity: A new perspective on learning and innovation. *Administrative Science Quarterly*, *35*(1), 128–152. doi:10.2307/2393553

Dedrick, J., & West, J. (2003, December 12-14). Why firms adopt open source platforms: A grounded theory of innovation and standards adoption. In *Proceedings of the Workshop on Standard Making: A Critical Research Frontier for Information Systems*, Seattle, WA (pp. 236-257).

Dubé, L., & Paré, G. (2003). Rigor in information systems positivist case research: Current practices, trends, and recommendations. *Management Information Systems Quarterly*, *27*(4), 597–635.

Feller, J., Finnegan, P., & Hayes, J. (2008). Delivering the 'whole product': Business model impacts and agility challenges in a network of open source firms. *Journal of Database Management*, *19*(2), 95–108. doi:10.4018/jdm.2008040105

Fichman, R. G., & Kemerer, C. F. (1997). The assimilation of software process innovations: An organizational learning perspective. *Management Science*, *43*(10), 1345–1363. doi:10.1287/mnsc.43.10.1345

Fitzgerald, B. (2006). The transformation of open source software. *Management Information Systems Quarterly*, *30*(3), 587–598.

Fitzgerald, B. (2009). Open source software adoption: Anatomy of success and failure. *International Journal of Open Source Software and Processes*, *1*(1), 1–23. doi:10.4018/jossp.2009010101

Fitzgerald, B., & Kenny, T. (2003, December 14-17). Open source software in the trenches: Lessons from a large scale implementation. In *Proceedings of 24th International Conference on Information Systems*, Seattle, WA (pp. 316-326).

Goode, S. (2005). Something for nothing: Management rejection of open source software in Australia's top firms. *Information & Management, 42*(5), 669–681. doi:10.1016/j.im.2004.01.011

Harrington, S., & Guimaraes, T. (2005). Corporate culture, absorptive capacity and IT success. *Information and Organization, 15*(1), 39–63. doi:10.1016/j.infoandorg.2004.10.002

Hauge, O., Ayala, C., & Conradi, R. (2010). Adoption of open source software in software-intensive organizations - a systematic literature review. *Information and Software Technology, 52*(11), 1133–1154. doi:10.1016/j.infsof.2010.05.008

Kim, L. (1998). Crisis construction and organizational learning: Capability building in catching-up at Hyundai motor. *Organization Science, 9*(4), 506–521. doi:10.1287/orsc.9.4.506

Lane, P. J., Koka, B. R., & Pathak, S. (2006). The reification of absorptive capacity: A critical review and rejuvenation of the construct. *Academy of Management Review, 31*(4), 833–863. doi:10.5465/AMR.2006.22527456

Levitt, B., & March, J. G. (1988). Organizational learning. *Annual Review of Sociology, 14*, 319–340. doi:10.1146/annurev.so.14.080188.001535

Lundell, B., Lings, B., & Lindqvist, E. (2010). Open source in Swedish companies: Where are we? *Information Systems Journal, 20*(6), 519–535. doi:10.1111/j.1365-2575.2010.00348.x

Marshall, C., & Rossman, G. B. (2006). *Designing qualitative research* (4th ed.). Thousand Oaks, CA: Sage.

Miles, M. B., & Huberman, A. M. (1994). *Qualitative data analysis: An expanded sourcebook* (2nd ed.). Thousand Oaks, CA: Sage.

Minbaeva, D., Pedersen, T., Bjorkman, I., Fey, C., & Park, H. (2003). MNC knowledge transfer, subsidiary absorptive capacity, and HRM. *Journal of International Business Studies, 34*(6), 586–599. doi:10.1057/palgrave.jibs.8400056

Morgan, L., & Finnegan, P. (2010). Open innovation in secondary software firms: An exploration of managers' perceptions of open source software. *SIGMIS Database, 41*(1), 76–95.

Todorova, G., & Durisin, B. (2007). Absorptive capacity: Valuing a reconceptualization. *Academy of Management Review, 32*(3), 774–786. doi:10.5465/AMR.2007.25275513

Tushman, M. L. (1977). Special boundary roles in the innovation process. *Administrative Science Quarterly, 22*(4), 587–605. doi:10.2307/2392402

Tushman, M. L., & Nadler, D. (1986). Organizing for innovation. *California Management Review, 28*(3), 74–92.

Van Den Bosch, F. A. J., Volberda, H. W., & De Boer, M. (1999). Coevolution of firm absorptive capacity and knowledge environment: Organizational forms and combinative capabilities. *Organization Science, 10*(5), 551–568. doi:10.1287/orsc.10.5.551

Ven, K., & Verelst, J. (2008, June 9-11). The organizational adoption of open source server software: A quantitative study. In *Proceedings of the 16th European Conference on Information Systems*, Galway, Ireland (pp. 1430-1441).

Ven, K., & Verelst, J. (2010). Determinants of the use of knowledge sources in the adoption of open source server software: An absorptive capacity perspective. *International Journal of Technology Diffusion, 1*(4), 53–70. doi:10.4018/jtd.2010100105

Ven, K., & Verelst, J. (2011). An empirical investigation into the assimilation of open source server software. *Communications of the Association for Information Systems, 28*(1), 117–140.

Ven, K., & Verelst, J. (in press). A qualitative study on the organizational adoption of open source server software. *Information Systems Management*.

Whetten, D. A. (1987). Organizational growth and decline processes. *Annual Review of Sociology*, *13*, 335–358. doi:10.1146/annurev.so.13.080187.002003

Yin, R. K. (2003). *Case study research: Design and methods* (3rd ed.). Newbury Park, CA: Sage.

Zahra, S. A., & George, G. (2002). Absorptive capacity: A review, reconceptualization, and extension. *Academy of Management Review*, *27*(2), 185–203.

This work was previously published in the International Journal of Open Source Software and Processes, Volume 3, Issue 1, edited by Stefan Koch, pp. 17-38, copyright 2011 by IGI Publishing (an imprint of IGI Global).

Chapter 3
The Ontology of the OSS Business Model:
An Exploratory Study

Spyridoula Lakka
University of Athens, Greece

Christos Michalakelis
University of Athens, Greece

Teta Stamati
University of Athens, Greece

Dracoulis Martakos
University of Athens, Greece

ABSTRACT

This study focuses on theory building providing a holistic conceptual framework that consists of an ontology based OSS business model and an OSS business model taxonomy. The study extends existing theory in OSS business models and corresponding taxonomies, based on the structured-case methodological approach. An exploratory study is conducted in two research cycles, for the identification, validation, and evaluation of the critical constructs of an OSS business model. Results reveal that OSS business models differ from traditional software business models, having specific features that affect the software value chain, the infrastructure, and the revenue model of an OSS oriented firm.

INTRODUCTION

When Richard Stallman first set the Free Software (FS) definition, FS was considered more as an ideological movement against commercial exploitation of software (Stallman, 2002) stressed that free software was more a matter of liberty rather than price. The recasting of Free Software as Open Source Software (OSS) or Free/Libre Open Source Software (FLOSS), emphasized on the importance of making source code freely available implying that a company can choose to make source code freely available and still serve its own business interests as a for-profit organization. The increasing number of profitable activities around the OSS ecosystem (i.e. open communities, standards, and technologies) proves that OSS is not only an innovative model of production, but also a sustainable business model.

It has matured to a point where there are growing numbers of business solutions delivering real business value today. At the same time,

DOI: 10.4018/978-1-4666-2937-0.ch003

more and more IT and business decision-makers are identifying, pursuing, and succeeding with initiatives that employ elements of that ecosystem to achieve meaningful immediate and sustained business benefits. From a managerial perspective, there are still risks associated to the OSS adoption, revealing issues of whether, to what extent and when it is best to change a business' strategy towards an 'open source' approach. Related research (Ågerfalk et al., 2005; Goode, 2005; Ven et al., 2008) showed that the lack of strategic planning and clear business model are among the inhibitory factors that shape their decisions towards OSS.

Although a number of researchers have studied the different OSS Business Model (OSS BM) implementations recorded in industry (Daffara et al., 2007; Dahlander, 2007; Fitzgerald, 2006; Koenig, 2004; Krishnamurthy, 2003; Rajala et al., 2006), none of them have considered of its structural elements. The OSS BM domain knowledge is fragmented and the concept is rarely clarified explicitly. Such clarification is therefore required to unify the different points of view into one comprehensive framework providing a common understanding, language, and labeling, so as to leverage our communication in this context and our utilization of the concept.

Towards this gap in the literature, the objective of this paper is to provide with a comprehensive and generic OSS BM framework that explicitly defines its structural elements, describing the deeper structure of what firms adopting an OSS strategy, actually do. The study focuses on knowledge and theory building by providing answers to critical research questions regarding the critical constructs and common characteristics of an OSS BM, as a linkage between empirical data collected and conclusions drawn. The paper reports on the findings of the use of the structured-case approach and proposes a holistic conceptual framework composed of two models; the ontology-based OSS BM and the OSS BM taxonomy, which is derived as a vertical decomposition of the '*Value offered*' structural element. Finally, the opportunities and

threats stemming from the different OSS BM implementations are also discussed.

The rest of the paper is organized as follows: First, the theoretical background of the study and the research methodological approach are described. The next two sections report on the main findings of the two conducted research cycles. Finally, the conclusion section discusses the results and concluding remarks obtained from the study.

THEORETICAL BACKGROUND AND METHOD DESCRIPTION

The research focused on the key issues and challenges that affect a holistic OSS framework. In the spirit of the interpretivist school (Hussey et al., 1997; Lee et al., 2003; Myers, 1997; Orlikowksi et al., 1991; Remenyi, 1998; Walsham, 1995), the approach throughout the study was to understand existing OSS models and build a new theory, rather than to test established theories. This was achieved by studying a number of existing theories and OSS perspectives as different theoretical lenses through which a complex phenomenon might be viewed.

The research that has been undertaken proposes theory as a result of interconnected ideas that condense and organize knowledge (Neuman, 1991). The study involves a series of case studies of OSS oriented organizations by means of the structured-case research method (Carroll et al., 2000), which can be widely used to extend knowledge about existing theories in order to actually use them. The structured-case approach provides a focused but flexible methodological approach to the field research process, through outcomes integration allowing theory, knowledge and practice to emerge from the data collected; researchers guidance to follow and ensure accuracy; and ability to record the processes of knowledge and theory-building.

The method attempts to explain, predict and provide understanding, determining the relationships between concepts in order to build a knowledge guide with respect to various issues of OSS modelling. The development of conceptual frameworks namely, CF1, CF2... CFn is used to present the process of obtaining knowledge and theory building where CFn is the latest version of the theory built. The theory building process is interrelated with practice (Carroll, et al., 2000). Applied research can lead to theory building, which can lead to further field research and theory building. Thus, each research cycle can lead to updates of the existing CF. As part of the hermeneutic circle each new CF expresses the pre-understanding for the next cycle (Gummerson, 1998) following the natural human action of interpretation and world understanding (Carroll et al., 2000).

Essentially, a spiral towards understanding is enacted as current knowledge and theory foundations for yet another research cycle, which will enhance, revise or evaluate the research understanding. This is particularly appropriate for OSS, as it is an area distinguished by rapid changes, which suggests the need for theory and practice to become closely intertwined. The structured-case will enable theory to be developed that will reflect the concerns, problems and issues facing OSS oriented organizations (Carroll et al., 2000).

In the field of business models theory building, there is a diversity of definitions and approaches. Chesbrough and Rosenbloom (2002) emphasize on the connections between technical potential and the realization of economic value, Amit and Zott (2001) describe the design of the transactions of a firm in creating value, Linder and Cantrell (2000) focus on the firm's core logic for creating value, Malone et al. (2006) offer an operational definition and distinguish different types of business models, while Osterwalder (2004), Gordijn (2003) and Morris et al. (2005) emphasize on the model aspect following an ontology- based approach. Osterwalder et al. (2005) classified business models' researchers into three main categories: (1) those that study the business model as an "overarching concept" of all businesses (i.e. the structural elements of a business model); (2) those

that describe a number of different abstract types of business models with common characteristics (i.e. taxonomies); and (3) those presenting aspects of a particular real world business model (i.e. case studies). Considering Osterwalder's (2004) ontological approach for business models, the study aims at the identification of the structural parts of an OSS BM and the formation of an "overarching" ontological OSS BM as well as a taxonomy of the different types of OSS BMs.

Research Methodological Approach

In order to identify the structural parts of an OSS BM, two research cycles were applied. At the first cycle, a sample of 100 popular OSS related firms instances is considered as 'pilots' organizations, in order to explore the different possible business models cases. Appendix C presents the complete list of the selected samples and the market sector they occur.

The sample was chosen so as to reflect all three aspects of Information and Communication Technologies (ICT) markets, i.e. software, hardware and services market sectors. Thus, the instances concern sponsored OSS projects, or firms creating value out of OSS projects in terms of services, founded between 1984 and 2008. Projects not perceived by OSS developers as open source are excluded, e.g. Microsoft's 'shared source' projects, or other communities that use OSS development processes for a limited population without public release of intellectual property (Shah, 2006). Sample's instances were chosen according to their popularity in portals devoted to OSS technologies, such as SourceForge.net, Think Geek, LinuxDevices.com, DesktopLinux.com, as well as eWeek, CIOInsight and InfoWorld.

The second research cycle aims to validate, evaluate and further improve the initial findings. The data collection procedure followed the major prescriptions given by most textbooks in doing fieldwork research. A variety of secondary data sources, such as business reports and technical reports for standards and specifications, were used to collect data regarding the development of OSS models. All in all, a number of data sources, were used to derive the findings presented herein. These included workshops, interviews, illustrative materials such as newsletters and other publications of OSS oriented organizations.

A two-day workshop took place with the eighty two participants, experts from the Greek OSS market and Academia. The participants worked together in collecting all the information needed regarding the critical constructs of a holistic OSS framework. Protocols of procedures were defined beforehand in order to guide the group discussion and to document the OSS model scenario elements. Based on the workshops and the online consultation inputs the authors synthesized a set of key factors that are considered as important for the construction the OSS BM.

After the completion of the two-day workshop, short interviews were conducted on a one-to-one basis with the participants in order to stimulate conversation and breakdown any barriers that could otherwise have hindered the knowledge transfer between the interviewer and the interviewee. The authors acted as a neutral medium through which questions and answers were exchanged and therefore endeavoured to eliminate bias. Interviewers'

purpose were to obtain the definitely opinion of participants on OSS critical issues. Results are explicitly illustrated on Appendices A and B.

The overall methodological procedure is summarized in Figure 1. As it is shown, a pre-step of the first research cycle, is the construction of an initial conceptual framework CF1. CF1 is based on bibliographic input of previous research in the field of OSS BM (Bonaccorsi et al., 2006; Daffara & Gonzalez-Barahona, 2007; Dahlander, 2007; Fitzgerald, 2006; Ghosh, 2006; Hecker, 1999; Koenig, 2004; Kooths et al., 2003; Krishnamurthy, 2003; Rajala, et al., 2006; Raymond, 1999; Riehle, 2009). Literature concerning the organizational processes in sponsored OSS communities was also included, due to the fact that organization processes are considered as strategic decisions over the implementation of a successful OSS BM (Fleming et al., 2007; O' Mahony et al., 2007; Von Hippel et al., 2003; West et al., 2008). Four commonly cited elements were identified and placed in CF1 (Figure 2) as the main research issues revealed from our analysis, namely *(1)* the kind of OSS license adopted; *(2)* the offering or value of the OSS product and/or service; *(3)* the OSS community; *(4)* organization of production policy. CF1 will be further refined through the methodological process described in Figure 1.

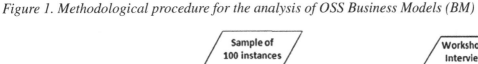

Figure 1. Methodological procedure for the analysis of OSS Business Models (BM)

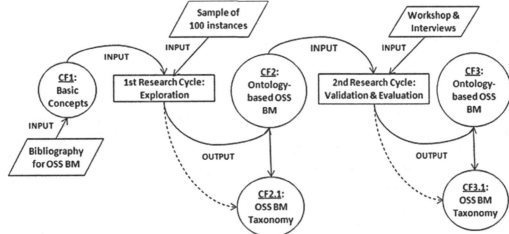

Figure 2. CF1: Basic Concepts for OSS BM

FIRST RESEARCH CYCLE

In the first research cycle, the sample of 100 OSS cases is explored in order to extract information for each of CF1 constructs. The results for each of these entities are presented in the following sections.

- **OSS Licenses:** OSS Licenses are used as a way for protecting the openness of the source code. There is a large number of OSS Licenses which can be classified in three major categories according to the level of restrictions they impose to users (Fitzgerald, 2006; Lerner et al., 2005; Rosen, 2004), as follows:

- **Reciprocal Licenses:** That are characterised by the fact that although source code may be modified, any distribution of a binary file must make available all changes to the source and remain under the same license. They are designed to effectively confront the "free riding" problem, i.e. utilisation of publicly created software for the creation of closed source software. Such licenses are the General Public License (GPL) which is the first FOSS li-

cense enacted, the Lesser GPL (LGPL), the Affero GPL, which are less strict by permitting linking with non-free modules etc. *Corporate type licenses* contain restrictions "inherited" to derivative products, yet these restrictions mainly aim to ensure that a specific firm retains control of derivative works, i.e. to allow OSS code to be mixed with proprietary, e.g. the Mozilla Public License (MPL), Eclipse Public License (EPL), etc. *Permissive licenses* place no restriction on the use of the code, requiring only a notice of the original copyright in any redistribution in source or binary form. Examples are the MIT License, Berkeley System Distribution (BSD) license, etc.

It can be deduced from the aforementioned classification that the choice of the OSS license is closely related to a firm's strategic approach towards the implementation of an OSS BM as it defines the level of risks a firm takes by opening the code to its competitors. Figure (3) presents the kinds of licenses adopted by the sample projects. Most of the instances have related their products to an OSS License[1]. Firms desire to avoid 'free-riding' problems by choosing the GPL (52%) and other reciprocal licenses like AGPL, LGPL, the Apache license, and the Common Public Attri-

Figure 3. OSS Licenses encountered in the sample

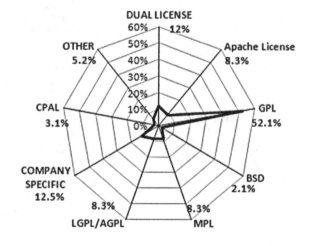

bute License (CPAL). These licenses also ensure good relationship with the OSS Community, as they are close to the FLOSS spirit. The second best choice is the Corporate type licenses (20.8% MPL included), which protect firms' Intellectual Property Rights (IPR) from being exploited by third parties. These licenses usually confer the firm's name, which is also a potential marketing strategy. Firms do not take the risk of leveraging permissive licenses (2.1%).

Finally, 12% of the firms in the sample prefer to apply two different licenses over the same product. The *dual license* approach is not an integrated license, or a different license type, but is rather a business strategy where a firm offers free use of open source code, or alternatively offers for a fee commercial distribution rights and a larger set of features for a product. Usually, the one of the two licenses is the GPL license, which prevents third parties from developing improvements that would rival the original software. Then the second license is an ordinary commercial license.

- **Value Offering:** Two clustering levels were applied in the sample instances, firstly according to the market sector they occur

and secondly according to their value offerings. At the first level, out of 100 cases, 73 were found in the software sector, 15 in the services sector and 12 are software designed for specific hardware and thus supported by hardware firms (Appendix C).

The different cases encountered in the *Software sector* are illustrated in *Figure (4a)*. The most popular strategy in the sample is the offering of different editions over the same product with additional features and functions. In this case there is the 'Community' edition, with the basic functioning offered free of charge. More features and functions are given in subsequent editions usually named 'Enterprise' and/or 'Professional' and which require some kind of payment. This may be either by annual subscriptions, or more scarcely, by a per unit price. (e.g Alfresco, Opsview, Compiere, Jaspersoft, etc.). Driven by these results, we define as '*Level of openness*' the extent to which a firm allows the customer to access specific parts of the code, as well as features and functions. The associated business model is named '*Added value editions*'. The 67% of the sample follows this strategy. In addition, although the 'Community' editions on all of these projects are offered with

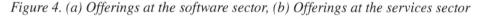

Figure 4. (a) Offerings at the software sector, (b) Offerings at the services sector

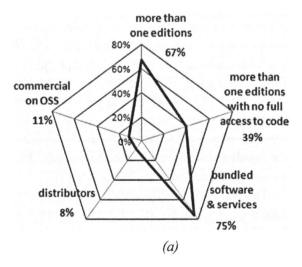

(a)

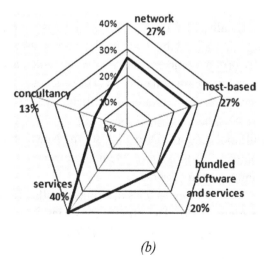

(b)

full access to code, the subsequent editions do not necessarily convey this feature. In particular, 39% of them were found to keep some part of the code closed on the subsequent editions.

- **Bundling Software with Services:** There is a high tendency (75% of the sample) to bundle products with services. Services vary from support, documentations, training, integration and migration offered for a particular software product. Pay method is not a per-unit-price, but in forms of subscription contracts. Contracts may present different levels of offerings in terms of the number of services and the duration of the time offered. Such cases are JBoss, Compiere, Alfresco, etc.

Distributors offer packaged distributions of OSS (usually the Linux operating system). Packages may include media distribution (e.g. CDs), installation upgrade and maintenance services and support. Firms adopting this model typically don't charge for the software but the rest of the package distribution in form of subscriptions. They may also capitalise on complementary software and applications that create on their own and that makes "best fit" with their distributions. This category accounted for 8% of the software cluster (e.g. Ubuntu by Canonical, Fedora and Linux by Red Hat, etc.).

Finally, 11% of the samples are cases offering commercial applications that run on an OSS platform or complementary software which adds more features or enhances an OSS product (*Commercial on OSS*). Examples of such instances are the Nusphere Corporations with the Nusphere PhP tools, Acquia Drupal. Also, the NoMachine company, a division of Medialogic S.p.A., is a Linux system integrator.

The *Services sector*'s offerings are illustrated in *Figure (4b)*. The cluster identifies 5 major categories. More particularly, 13% of the sample

offer *"Consultancy"* for the implementation of OSS solutions. The '*Services*' cluster which accounted for 40% of the services sample, included all the ordinary kinds of services met with the commercial software, yet adapted for the OSS case: OSS systems integration, migration from one system to another (i.e. from commercial to OSS), education and training, customization of OSS software, support, information systems outsourcing, remote server management, security and maintenance. In addition, an exclusively OSS related service was identified. This was "certification", which is actually an insurance that an OSS software package complies with a specified set of rules, and is legally liable for such compliance (e.g. OpenLogic). As a subset of the '*Services*' cluster the '*Bundling software and services*' cluster is identified, where service oriented firms may develop OSS and offer it for free, aspiring at attracting customers for their services offerings. In all cases the pay method is based on subscription contracts varying in price according to the number of services and duration of time provided. (e.g. Infrae, Zenoss, Cloud.com, etc.).

The *"Network"* of firms cluster, concerns an association of organizations from different locations around the world, doing custom software and related services in vertical markets. Successful paradigms of OSS network model are Orixo, Zea Partners and Infrae.

Finally, *"Host based service"* cluster creates value in a rather indirect way. It includes companies that use OSS as a cornerstone to their IT platforms for web based services and applications. Firms can reduce implementation costs and/or further customize the OSS platform to their specific needs. Google, eBay, Amazon, application service providers (ASPs) like Cloud.Com, EyeOS, for cloud computing, etc. make heavy use of OSS for delivering services to their customers.

The *Hardware sector* cluster of our sample, identified 8 instances of tools and drivers for specific *hardware manufacturer*s (e.g. software tools for SONY VAIO, drivers for Hewlett Packard printers, etc.) and 4 instances concerning *embedded software* for specific devices, e.g. the popular Android sponsored by the Open Handset Alliance, Denx' Embedded Linux Development Kit(ELDK). *Hardware manufacturers* typically create in-house software for the functioning of their products, such as drivers, configuration tools, etc. As their revenues stem from hardware and not software, writing code is an additional overhead and cost centre. Thus, many hardware manufacturers release their in-house code as OSS, or financially support OSS communities, so that to gain human resources for software development and maintenance. They also gain in popularity making this strategy an effective marketing practice. *Embedded open source software* is software adjusted for the functioning of embedded devices, i.e. devices processing computing capacity build for a specific purpose (e.g. mobile phones, machine controls). The most used OSS modified for embedded systems is the Linux operating system.

The 'value offering' clustering findings enables the specification of an initial OSS BM taxonomy CF2.1, illustrated in Figure 5. In addition to the 'value offering' clusters, the dual license strategy from the 'licenses' cluster was included as an OSS BM. This is a BM proposed in most of previous research in the field (Fitzgerald, 2006; Ghosh, 2006).

- **OSS Community:** All sample cases that develop OSS software have set up a community to interact with potential users and developers. The 'Community' element has a prominent place in the project's website, with considerable space and lots of functioning, revealing that all firms consider their relationship to the community of high importance. In such a community, potential users can find support, documentation, additional code or they can report requests for support and additional features. They can also take part in forums and actively participate with code development. Apparently, the firms devote additional effort and money to invest into a well structured and sufficiently strong community. This is an indication of the importance and necessity of firms to achieve the best partnership with the community, as this actually means a partnership with the users of a firm's product. The community can become a basic element of the firm's infrastructure, as it offers valuable resources of code, of developers and a continuous feedback from users (Lerner et al., 2000).

Feedback from OSS communities enables fast release cycles, which create the conditions for first mover advantages. Moreover, when the OSS

Figure 5. CF2.1: OSS BM Taxonomy

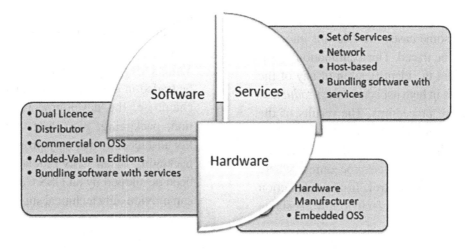

community is strong, it can serve as a marketing device for the diffusion of the product in a short period of time, which is an important feature for a market with network effects. Thus, all OSS BMs are community oriented, and firms are seeking the best possible ways of connecting their products to a sufficiently strong community. The latter is supported by a number of researchers such as (Ågerfalk et al., 2005; Ghosh, 2006; Lakhani et al., 2003).

- **Organization (Production and Governance):** Firms' practices on internal organization and relation to the corresponding OSS communities has been an objective of extensive research, (Baldwin et al., 2006; Capra et al., 2008; Dahlander, 2007; O' Mahony et al., 2007; West et al., 2008).

In terms of *production*, different working practices have been reported in the literature concerning the dispersion of project team's members, the access levels in code for inspection and validation to external participants, different levels of rights in the commit process, the rights for subprojects creation and the ability to observe or follow production processes. In terms of *governance* there are different working practices reported in the relevant literature, concerning the levels of access rights to community developers and formality imposed in processes such as becoming a community member, release authority and project leadership.

A subset of 20 instances of the sample was examined, excluding hardware and services sectors. Moreover, in some cases the relevant information could not be traced. The examination of our sample included the identification of any of the above practices in both aspects of the *production* and *governance* procedures. The results of the analysis are summarized in Table 1.

It can be shown that most restrictions are imposed in the governance procedures, where firms want to retain control. In the production procedures, most firms prefer to follow a scalable

Table 1. Results of the production and governance procedures analysis

Production	Percentage*	Governance	Percentage*
Scalable access levels to code	65%	Formality in processes for becoming a member	15%
Levels of rights in the commit process	65%	Project leadership to members	20%
Ability to observe the production process	75%	Give release authority	45%
* In a sample of 20 projects S/W sector			

access rights to users policy, however users have enough freedom to take part in the commit process.

CONCEPTUAL FRAMEWORK CF2

The findings of the first research cycle can be summarized as follows:

1. Choice of the *OSS license type*, according to the firms' strategy. Reciprocal licenses ensure good relationship to the community, corporate type license is best for a marketing strategy and finally the dual license strategy.
2. Creation and support of an *OSS Community*. Firms make use of community as it offers valuable resources of code, of developers and a continuous feedback from users, enabling fast release cycles. OSS community can also serve as a marketing device.
3. **Value Offering:** To potential customers can be traded in any part of the software value chain, i.e. the development, documentation, packaging, marketing and services. For instance, a firm may provide only the packaging of an OSS product which has been developed by an OSS Community, or can provide only technical support, or both.

The different kinds of trading are explicitly defined in the proposed OSS BM taxonomy of CF2.1.

4. Value comes also from the '*level of openness*' a firm imposes to a product, a feature that is not part of the proprietary software's value chain. The different 'levels of openness' are implemented with the creation of different editions of the same product, each of which has different value offerings in terms of functioning and code openness.

5. **Revenue Models:** Direct, mostly in terms of subscription contracts and indirect, in terms of cost savings and marketing strategies.

6. Configuration of the *organization* (production and governance), with different levels of restrictions.

In order to form an 'overarching' OSS BM, we will have to relate these basic OSS constructs to the constructs of an ontology-based business model as defined by Osterwalder (2004). Following this definition, we propose the ontology based OSS BM as the conceptual model CF2 (Figure 6).

Infrastructure comprises of three components: '*Capability*', which outlines the resources as well as the core competencies necessary to execute the company's infrastructure business model. '*Partner Network*', which portrays the network of cooperative agreements with other companies necessary to efficiently offer and commercialize value and finally '*Value Configuration*' which describes the arrangement of activities and resources. We extend the 'Infrastructure' construct to include the '*OSS Community*' construct, as explained in *(2)*. We also place '*Licence type*' and activities relevant to the organization model, namely the '*Production*' and the community '*Governance*', under the 'Value Configuration', as explained in *(2)*, *(6)*.

Value offered is mainly the utility of a software product gained by the use, or the kind of service related to that product. We place under this construct the '*Level of openness*' -as defined above- and all the parts of the software value chain. *Value offered* can be vertically decomposed to the CF2.1 OSS BM taxonomy.

- **Customer:** This part of the business model describes the segments of customers a company aims, the various means that a company employs to communicate with its customers and the kind of links a company establishes with its customers. No additional elements for OSS were found for this block.

- **Financial Aspects:** The 'Cost Structure' corresponds to the aggregate monetary consequences of the means employed in the business model. Contrary to the proprietary software, in an OSS BM, '*Revenue models*' do not stem from IPR fees, but as discussed in (5), may have direct and/or indirect profit centres.

Figure 6. CF2: Ontology-based OSS BM

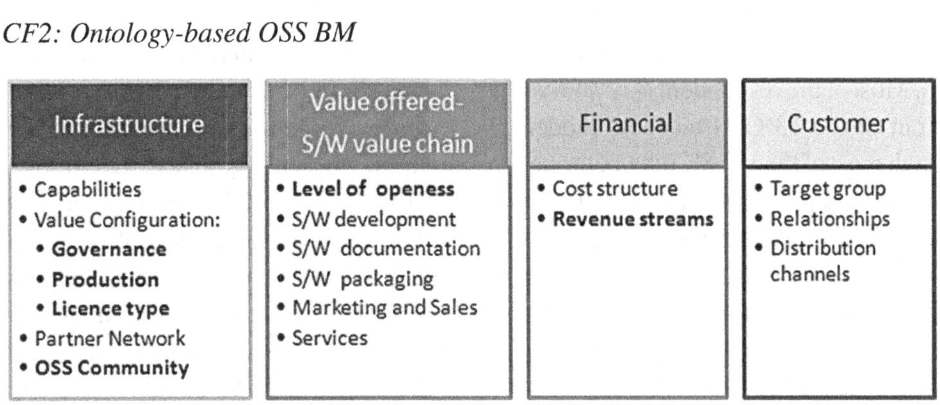

Infrastructure	Value offered-S/W value chain	Financial	Customer
• Capabilities • Value Configuration: 　• **Governance** 　• **Production** 　• **Licence type** • Partner Network • **OSS Community**	• **Level of openess** • S/W development • S/W documentation • S/W packaging • Marketing and Sales • Services	• Cost structure • **Revenue streams**	• Target group • Relationships • Distribution channels

SECOND RESEARCH CYCLE

As described in Figure 1, the second research cycle accepts the findings of the previous cycle, i.e. CF2.1, CF2 as inputs to be validated and evaluated with the methodological procedure described. It aims at the enhancing of the conceptual models with possible additional features or rejection of others that might have not been encountered and/ or omitted in the sample of the first research cycle.

Particularly, conceptual framework CF2.1 is firstly validated with comparison of results to the corresponding literature (Appendix A). Although validation was affirmative for all business models found in the sample, some differences were also revealed. Firstly, the *'Added value editions'* business model, is a new OSS BM proposed and was not found cited in the corresponding literature. Secondly, three more OSS BM was identified in the literature, which had not been encountered in our sample. These are *'Ancilliary market'* model, i.e. the capitalization of OSS related products, other than software, such as books, or other publications about OSS, and other physical items associated with OSS (e.g. O' Reilly publishing house.) and two indirect revenue models, i.e. the leverage of OSS as a *Marketing strategy* and as a means of *Cost savings for R&D*. The last two startegies can be applied by all three market sectors of ICT. The *'Ancilliary market'* business model is placed under the hardware sector cluster in accordance to the literature findings.

The above taxonomy CF2.1 including the OSS BM that turned up in the validation process, was further evaluated by the workshop and Interviews, as described. Most of the respondents (72%) were aware of 9 out of the 13 OSS business models listed, although most of them (65%) characterized them as 'business practices' or 'strategies' and not 'models'. All of the models of CF2.1 have been identified by the respondents, with the minimum occurrence *'Ancilliary market'*, with 28% and maximum occurrences the *'Added value editions'* and *'Distributor'* with 94%. Indirect OSS BM that stressed the value of OSS as a marketing policy to impose a *'Brand name'* (93%), and *'R&D cost savings'* (94%) were also identified. To the question 'what is their opinion about the advantages and disadvantages' of each of the models, there was a convergence of the opinions, the most cited of which are presented in Appendix A. Finally, there were reported interelations between sector clusters, i.e. the *'Bundling of software and services'* model, which is identified as a firm's practice in both software and services sectors and the *'Bundled OSS with a hardware'* resulting in a system of a much lower price. Taking into account these findings CF2.1 is refined to the CF3.1 OSS BM taxonomy (Figure 7).

As there is no previous attempt for the formation of an OSS ontology- based model and thus no relative literature for validation, the CF2 was only evaluated based on the workshop and Interview responses. The ontological approach of the OSS BM creation was explained to the respondents and they were asked to comment on the level of adequacy of the proposed constructs, i.e. weather these constructs should exist in the model, and if yes, whether they had been placed correctly. The results are analytically presented in Appendix B. The majority of the respondents agreed with the adequacy of the existence of these elements as OSS BM constructs. A small percentage found inadequacy of the constructs in *'Level of openness'* (18%), *'Governance'* (11%), while others were not sure of the adequacy of the *'Level of openness'*(5%) *and 'Production'* (12%).

For the placement evaluation, the process revealed a construct 'mismatch'. More particularly 79% of the respondents believed that *'License type'* should be under *'Value offered'* and not *'Value configuration'* construct. That was a correct output, as license type is more closely connected to the software value chain, than to the firm's infrastructure. For the rest of the constructs, the majority of the respondents agreed with their placement in the model. A small number were not sure with the placement of *'Level of openness'*(15%), and *'Production'* (12%). Finally, 20% of the respondents have suggested new constructs

Figure 7. CF3.1: OSS BM taxonomy

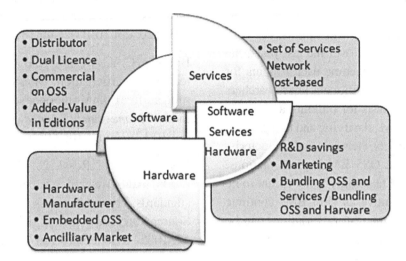

and their placements, which can be explored in a future research cycle. Taking into account these findings CF2 is revised to the CF3 ontology-based BM (Figure 8).

CONCLUSION

Following a specific methodological approach based on theory and experience about the OSS models, the research proceeds to propose an effective holistic framework for the OSS BMs that considers various parameters. It focuses on two main aspects of the business models literature, namely the formation of an ontology-based model that applies to OSS oriented firms and a taxonomy of the existing OSS BMs.

The outcomes from the data analysis of the case studies demonstrate that OSS BMs are influenced by a combination of technological and business elements. The authors follow the classification of OSS terminology, grouping the findings and allowing specific concepts to emerge within such groupings. The concepts revealed the structural elements of an ontology-based OSS BM. Furthermore, a vertical decomposition of the '*Value offered*' construct of the ontological OSS BM enabled the formation of a taxonomy for the different OSS BMs according to the market sector they occur. The taxonomy introduces a new OSS BM identified in the exploratory study, namely the '*Added-value editions*'.

Overall, the holistic framework provides with insights on the critical elements of an OSS BM

Figure 8. CF3: Ontology-based OSS BM

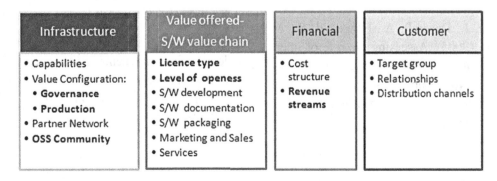

ontology, an explicit taxonomy regarding the different BM implementations and their corresponding opportunities and threats. As OSS has been highly diffused over the last years, the research findings can become useful inputs for both researchers and practitioners. For researchers it can become the basis for building a common ontological OSS BM, clarifying and unifying the ambiguous constructs, elements and characteristics of the different OSS BM implementations. Also, the proposed taxonomy is not meant to be exhaustive or definitive as OSS BMs continue to evolve and new interesting variations can be expected in the future. As there isn't a previous framework of the kind, this study aspires to create an efficient basis for future research in the field.

However, even in its current form, the framework can also become a useful tool for managers and decision makers that would think and anticipate the risks of adopting a new OSS BM, or adapting their existing BM towards OSS. The tool summarizes the architecture insights, structural elements of an OSS BM, the different implementations and the opportunities and threats of already practiced OSS BM in the market.

Revealing the limitation of the study, the number of our datasets and potential sample's inequality of proportion of each market sectors' instances are stressed. As a consequence, some of the results should be further improved in future research cycles. Further research may also focus on the identification of factors influencing the successful implementation of OSS BMs.

REFERENCES

Ågerfalk, P. J., Deverell, A., Fitzgerald, B., & Morgan, L. (2005). Assessing the role of open source software in the European secondary software sector: A voice from industry. In *Proceedings of the First International Conference on Open Source Systems*, Genova, Italy.

Amit, R., & Zott, C. (2001). Value creation in e-business. *Strategic Management Journal, 22*(6-7), 493–520. doi:10.1002/smj.187

Baldwin, C. Y., & Clark, K. B. (2006). The architecture of participation: Does code architecture mitigate free riding in the open source development model? *Management Science, 52*(7), 1116–1127. doi:10.1287/mnsc.1060.0546

Bonaccorsi, A., Rossi, C., & Giannangeli, S. (2006). Adaptive entry strategies under dominant standards: Hybrid business models in the Open Source Software Industry. *Management Science, 52*, 1085–1098. doi:10.1287/mnsc.1060.0547

Capra, E., & Wasserman, A. I. (2008). A framework for evaluating managerial styles in open source projects. *IFIP International Federation for Information Processing, 275*, 1–14. doi:10.1007/978-0-387-09684-1_1

Carroll, J., & Swatman, P. (2000). Structured-case: A methodological framework for building theory in information systems research. *European Journal of Information Systems, 9*, 235–242. doi:10.1057/palgrave/ejis/3000374

Chesbrough, H., & Rosenbloom, R. S. (2002). The role of the business model in capturing value from innovation: Evidence from Xerox Corporation's technology spin-off companies. *Industrial and Corporate Change, 11*(3), 529–555. doi:10.1093/icc/11.3.529

Daffara, C., & Gonzalez-Barahona, J. M. (2007). *Guide for SMEs (No. Deliverable D8.1.1)*. Retrieved from http://www.flossmetrics.org/sections/deliverables/docs/deliverables/WP8/D8.1.1-SMEs_Guide.pdf

Dahlander, L. (2007). Penguin in a new suit: A tale of how de novo entrants emerged to harness free and open source software communities. *Industrial and Corporate Change, 16*(5), 913–943. doi:10.1093/icc/dtm026

Fitzgerald, B. (2006). The transformation of open source software. *Management Information Systems Quarterly, 30*(3), 587–598.

Fleming, L., & David, M. W. (2007). Brokerage, boundary spanning and leadership in open innovation communities. *Organization Science, 18*(2), 165–180. doi:10.1287/orsc.1060.0242

Ghosh, R. A. (2006). *Economic impact of open source software on innovation and the competitiveness of the information and communication technologies (ICT) sector in the EU.* Maastricht, The Netherlands: United Nations University (UNU) MERIT.

Goode, S. (2005). Something for nothing: Management rejection of open source software in Australia's top firms. *Information & Management, 42*(5), 669–681. doi:10.1016/j.im.2004.01.011

Gordijn, J., & Akkermans, H. (2003). Value-based requirements engineering: Exploring innovative e-commerce ideas. *Requirements Engineering, 8*(2), 114–134. doi:10.1007/s00766-003-0169-x

Gruber, M., & Henkel, J. (2004). New ventures based on open innovation –an empirical analysis of start-up firms in embedded Linux. *International Journal of Technology Management, 33*(4), 356–372. doi:10.1504/IJTM.2006.009249

Gummerson, E. (1998). *Qualitative methods in management research.* Newbury Park, CA: Sage.

Hecker, F. (1999). Setting up a shop: The business of open source software. *IEEE Software, 16*(1), 45–51. doi:10.1109/52.744568

Hussey, J., & Hussey, R. (1997). *Business research: A practical guide for undergraduate and postgraduate students.* Basingstoke, UK: Macmillan Business.

Koenig, J. (2004). *Seven open source business strategies for competitive advantage.* Half Moon Bay, CA: Riseforth, Inc.

Kooths, S., Langenfurth, M., & Kalwey, N. (2003). Open-source software: An economic assessment. *MICE Economic Research Studies, 4,* 59.

Krishnamurthy, S. (2003). An analysis of open source business models. In Feller, J., Fitzgerald, B., Hissam, S. A., & Lakhani, K. (Eds.), *Perspectives on open source and free software.* Cambridge, MA: MIT Press.

Lakhani, K., & Von Hippel, E. (2003). How open source software works: "Free" user-to-user assistance. *Research Policy, 32*(6), 923–943. doi:10.1016/S0048-7333(02)00095-1

Lee, A., & Baskerville, R. (2003). Generalizing in information systems research. *Information Systems Research, 14*(3), 221–243. doi:10.1287/isre.14.3.221.16560

Lerner, J., & Tirole, J. (2000). The simple economics of the open source. *The Journal of Industrial Economics, 52*(2), 197–234.

Lerner, J., & Tirole, J. (2005). The scope of open source licensing. *Journal of Law Economics and Organization, 21*(1), 20–56. doi:10.1093/jleo/ewi002

Linder, J., & Cantrell, S. (2000). Changing business models: Surveying the landscape. *Accenture,* 1-13.

Malone, T. W., Weill, P., Lai, R. K., D'Urso, V. T., Herman, G., Apel, T. G., & Woerner, S. (2006). *Do some business models perform better than others?* SSRN eLibrary.

Morris, M., Schindehutte, M., & Allen, J. (2005). The entrepreneurs business model: Toward a unified perspective. *Journal of Business Research, 58,* 725–735. doi:10.1016/j.jbusres.2003.11.001

Myers, M. D. (1997). Qualitative research in information systems. *Management Information Systems Quarterly, 21*(2), 241–242. doi:10.2307/249422

Neuman, W. L. (1991). *Social research methods: Qualitative and quantitative approaches*. Boston, MA: Allyn and Bacon.

O' Mahony, S., & Ferraro, F. (2007). The emergence of governance in an open source community. *Academy of Management Journal, 50*(5), 1079–1106. doi:10.5465/AMJ.2007.27169153

Orlikowksi, W. J., & Baroudi, J. (1991). Studying information technology in organizations: Research approaches and assumptions. *Information Systems Research, 2*(1), 1–28. doi:10.1287/isre.2.1.1

Osterwalder, A. (2004). *The business model ontology - a proposition in a design science approach*. Lausanne, Switzerland: University of Lausanne.

Osterwalder, A., Pigneur, Y., & Tucci, C. L. (2005). Clarifying business models: Origins, present, and future of the concept. *Communications of the Association for Information Systems, 15*, 2–40.

Rajala, R., Nissila, J., & Westerlund, M. (2006). Determinants of OSS revenue model choices. In *Proceedings of the 14th European Conference of Information Systems*, Gothenburg, Sweden.

Raymond, E. S. (1999). *The magic cauldron*. Sebastopol, CA: O'Reilly Media.

Remenyi, D. (1998). *Doing research in business and management: An introduction to process and method*. Thousand Oaks, CA: Sage.

Riehle, D. (2009). *The commercial OSS business model*. Paper presented at the Americas Conference of Information Systems, San Francisco, CA.

Rosen, L. U. (2004). *Open source licensing: Software freedom and intellectual property law*. Upper Saddle River, NJ: Prentice Hall.

Shah, S. (2006). Motivation, governance and the viability of hybrid forms in open source software development. *Management Science, 52*(7), 1000–1014. doi:10.1287/mnsc.1060.0553

Stallman, R. (2002). *Free software, free society: Selected essays of Richard M. Stallman*. Boston, MA: GNU Press.

Ven, K., Verelst, J., & Mannaert, H. (2008). Should you adopt open source software. *IEEE Software, 25*(3), 54–59. doi:10.1109/MS.2008.73

Von Hippel, E., & Von Krogh, G. (2003). Open source software and the "private-collective" innovation model: Issues for organization science. *Organization Science, 14*(2), 209–223. doi:10.1287/orsc.14.2.209.14992

Walsham, G. (1995). The emergence of interpretivism in IS research. *Information Systems Research, 6*(4), 376–394. doi:10.1287/isre.6.4.376

West, J., & O' Mahony, S. (2008). The role of participation architecture in growing sponsored open source communities. *Industry and Innovation, 15*(2), 145–168. doi:10.1080/13662710801970142

APPENDIX A

Table 2. Evaluation and validation of CF2.1

Model	Validation/ Reference in Literature	Evaluation/Interview response		
		C1*	C2**	Comments of the respondents relevant to the OSS BM
distributor	(Fitzgerald, 2006), (Krishnamurthy, 2003), (Ghosh, 2006), (Kooths, et al., 2003)	90%	94%	• Linux is used, tested and implemented for years and thus is of proven quality. • Low entry costs for a firm as most of the software is developed within the OSS Community. • High levels of openness enable good relation with the OSS Community, which will continue to enhance the features of the software and release new versions. • Fast releases give the firm a first mover advantage, over commercial firms. • low entry barriers lead to proliferation of versions and high competition, thus is more difficult to establish a position in the market.
dual license	(Fitzgerald, 2006), (Koenig, 2004), (Krishnamurthy, 2003), (Kooths, et al., 2003), (Daffara & Gonzalez-Barahona, 2007), (Dahlander, 2007)	84%	88%	• The GPL version of the software is favoured by the OSS Community. As a result can attract developers and users and create a relative advantage to an unknown commercial product • difficulties in the management between the two license types. • software from external contributions require an explicit author acknowledgement of both licenses.
commercial on OSS	(Daffara & Gonzalez-Barahona, 2007), (Rajala, et al., 2006)	12%	45%	• low entry costs • no OSS license implications/ source code can be closed. • Careful choice of the OSS platform is recommended
Added value editions	no previous work found for this business model	92%	94%	• This is also a marketing strategy, as users get accustomed to the open and free version, thus they are more likely to choose the advanced product edition, if they need to. • Closed parts of source code is not favoured by the OSS community and thus a firm may not establish a good relation with it.
bundled software & services	(Koenig, 2004), (Rajala, et al., 2006), (Daffara & Gonzalez-Barahona, 2007)	95%	93%	• Subscriptions have no license implications. • Strategy favoured by both software and services firms.
services	(Hecker, 1999), (Koenig, 2004), (Rajala, et al., 2006), (Daffara & Gonzalez-Barahona, 2007), (Fitzgerald, 2006), (Ghosh, 2006)	67%	91%	• Services have no OSS license implications • no obligation in revealing their modifications in code development. • low entry costs • Human resources are the most important asset in the services market. With a proper policy, a part of these resources might be found in the OSS communities.
host-based	(Koenig, 2004)	78%	82%	Promising sector because of the high Internet and E-commerce adoption
network	(Ghosh, 2006)	14%	32%	• Collaboration nature of OSS, facilitates such business requires trust between actors as well as synchronization costs.
embedded	(Gruber et al., 2004), (Koenig, 2004)	25%	49%	• Value added by proven technological quality switching costs.
hardware manufacturers cited also as *'Widget Frosting'* model	(Hecker, 1999),(Raymond, 1999), (Fitzgerald, 2006), (Koenig, 2004),(Rajala, et al., 2006)	45%	72%	• bundled OSS with a hardware (e.g. server) resulting in a system of a much lower price. Strategy preferred by system manufacturers like IBM and Apple – • *INDIRECT OSS BM: 'bundled software &hardware'*

continued on following page

Table 2. Continued

Model	Validation/ Reference in Literature	Evaluation/Interview response		
Marketing cited also as *'Brand enabler'*	(Hecker, 1999),(Rajala, et al., 2006) (Fitzgerald, 2006), (Dahlander, 2007)	93%	93%	• Firms release code as a marketing strategy, so as to prove the quality of their products and create a brand name and consequently a position in the software market, where can easily sell its commercial software.
R&D cost savings	Not mentioned as a stand-alone BM	94%	82%	• Cost savings in experimenting with code reuse and support from OSS Community
Ancillary markets Cited also as *'Accessorizing'*	(Fitzgerald, 2006), (Hecker, 1999), (Raymond, 1999), (Fitzgerald, 2006),etc.	22%	28%	• These products can be books or other publications about OSS, and other physical items associated with OSS.
Note:	(*) **C1:** Percentage of respondents that mentioned this BM, in the questions *"what OSS Business Models are you aware of"*, *"what OSS BM would you suggest?"*. Respondents may have mentioned more than two OSS BM. (**)**C2:** Percentage of respondents that were aware of this OSS BM.			

APPENDIX B

Table 3. Evaluation of CF2

Construct:	should exist in the model			propose relevant construct		is at the correct place			propose new place/ other comments	
	Yes	No	Not Sure			Yes	No	Not Sure		
Governance	83%	11%	6%			89%	2%	9%	Under 'OSS Community'	6%
									At no place	4%
Production	84%	4%	12%	Development Model (DM):	7%	88%	0%	12%	(DM) under 'Value Configuration'	7%
				Modularity Level (ML)	5%				(ML) under 'value offering'	5%
OSS Community	98%	0%	2%			93%	0%	7%	Under 'Partner Network'	4%
Licence type	100%	0%	0%			12%	82%	6%	Under 'Value Offered'	79%
									At no place	5%
Level of openness	77%	18%	5%	code access	7%	82%	4%	15%	At no place	18%
S/W development	88%	2%	10%			88%	2%	10%	At no place	2%
S/W documentation	88%	2%	10%			88%	2%	10%	At no place	2%
S/W packaging	88%	2%	10%			88%	2%	10%	At no place	2%
Marketing &Sales	88%	2%	10%			88%	2%	10%	At no place	2%
Services	88%	2%	10%			88%	2%	10%	At no place	2%
Revenue streams	100%	0%	0%			100%	0%	0%		0%

Note: Results summarize both the workshop and interview responses

APPENDIX C

Table 4. List of OSS projects

	Company/OSS Project*	Sector		Company/OSS Project	Sector
1	1bizcom/bizcom	H/W	51	Openflows Networks ltd	Services
2	Acquia	Services	52	Openlogic	Services
3	Adaptive Planning	S/W	53	Openmoko/FreeRunner	H/W
4	Alfresco	S/W	54	OpenTerracotta	S/W
5	Alterpoint	S/W	55	Open-Xchange	S/W
6	Apache Foundation/Celtix/Apache CFX	S/W	56	Opsera/Opsview	S/W
7	Apache Software Foundation/OfBiz	S/W	57	Optaros	Services
8	Apple/Darwin	S/W	58	ORACLE/VirtualBox	S/W
9	Black Duck Software	Services	59	Orixo	Services
10	Canonical/Ubuntu	S/W	60	OSAF Chandler	S/W
11	CentraView	S/W	61	Pentaho/ Pentaho BI	S/W
12	CiviCRM	S/W	62	Progress S/W Corporation/Atrix	S/W
13	CleverSafe/Accesser	S/W	63	Real Networks/Helix	S/W
14	Cloud.com	Services	64	RedHat/ Linux	S/W
15	Colosa Inc./Process Maker BPM	S/W	65	RedHat/Fedora	S/W
16	Compiere	S/W	66	Redhat/Jboss	S/W
17	Denx/Embedded Linux Development Kit (ELDK)	H/W	67	rPath/Linux	S/W
18	EmuSoftware/Netdirector	S/W	68	Scalix	S/W
19	EnterpriseDB/Postgres Plus Standard Server	S/W	69	Sendmail	S/W
20	Exadel/JavaFX plugin	S/W	70	Sleepycat/Berkley DB	S/W
21	EyeOS	S/W	71	Smoothwall/Smoothwall Firewall	S/W
22	Funambol	S/W	72	Sonatype	Services
23	GreenPlum	S/W	73	Sony/ 'Sony Controls' for SonyVAIO	H/W
24	GroundWork	S/W	74	Sony/ 'Sony Vaio FX Library'	H/W
25	Hewlett Packard/ 'HP Linux Imaging and Printing'	H/W	75	Sony/ 'ksblc' for SonyVAIO	H/W
26	Hewlett Packard/ 'XPMap'	H/W	76	Sourcefire (SNORT)	S/W
27	Hewlett Packard/ 'Check_hp_print'	H/W	77	Sourcelabs/SWIK.net	Services
28	Hyperic/Hyperic Application & System Monitoring	S/W	78	SourceSense	Services
29	IBM/Eclipse	S/W	79	Splunk	S/W
30	IBM/Jikes	S/W	80	SSLExplorer	S/W
31	Infrae	Services	81	SugarCRM	S/W
32	Jasper wireless	H/W	82	SUN/ORACLE/ OpenOffice	S/W
33	Jbilling	S/W	83	SUN/ORACLE/Glassfish	S/W
34	Jitterbit	S/W	84	SUN/ORACLE/Netbeans	S/W

continued on following page

Table 4. Continued

	Company/OSS Project*	Sector		Company/OSS Project	Sector
35	KnowledgeTree	S/W	85	Symbiot/OpenSIMS	S/W
36	Lustre	S/W	86	Talend/ Open Studio.	S/W
37	ManyOne networks website	Services	87	TenderSystem	S/W
38	Mindquarry	S/W	88	Tetrain	Services
39	Mirth	S/W	89	UltimateEMR	S/W
40	MuleSource/Mule ESB	S/W	90	VirtualBox	S/W
41	Mysql	S/W	91	vTiger/vTiger CRM	S/W
42	Netscape/Mozilla	S/W	92	Vyatta	S/W
43	NightLabs GmbH/ Jfire	S/W	93	WSO2	S/W
44	NoMachine NX	S/W	94	XenSource (Xen)	H/W
45	Novell/ SUSE Linux	S/W	95	xTuple Norfolk USA	S/W
46	NuSphere Corp./Nusphere PhP Tools	S/W	96	Zea partners	Services
47	Open Handset Alliance/ Android	H/W	97	Zend (PHP)	S/W
48	OpenBravo/ OpenBravo ERP	S/W	98	Zenoss	Services
49	OpenClovis/ OpenClovis	S/W	99	Zimbra	S/W
50	OpenEMM	S/W	100	Zope/ERP5	S/W

* The name of the company is omitted when it coincides with the name of the OSS project.

1 Eight instances don't use any license, as they are services oriented firms. Although the sample consists of 15 services oriented firms, seven of them do produce some kind of software under the GPL.

This work was previously published in the International Journal of Open Source Software and Processes, Volume 3, Issue 1, edited by Stefan Koch, pp. 39-59, copyright 2011 by IGI Publishing (an imprint of IGI Global).

Chapter 4
OSS–TMM:
Guidelines for Improving the Testing Process of Open Source Software

Sandro Morasca
Università degli Studi dell'Insubria, Italy

Davide Taibi
Università degli Studi dell'Insubria, Italy

Davide Tosi
Università degli Studi dell'Insubria, Italy

ABSTRACT

Open Source Software (OSS) products do not usually follow traditional software engineering development paradigms. Specifically, testing activities in OSS development may be quite different from those carried out in Closed Source Software (CSS) development. As testing and verification require a good deal of resources in OSS, it is necessary to have ways to assess and improve OSS testing processes. This paper provides a set of testing guidelines and issues that OSS developers can use to decide which testing techniques make most sense for their OSS products. This paper 1) provides a checklist that helps OSS developers identify the most useful testing techniques according to the main characteristics of their products, and 2) outlines a proposal for a method that helps assess the maturity of OSS testing processes. The method is a proposal of a Maturity Model for testing processes (called OSS-TMM). To show its usefulness, the authors apply the method to seven real-life projects. Specifically, the authors apply the method to BusyBox, Apache Httpd, and Eclipse Test & Performance Tools Platform to show how the checklist supports and guides the testing process of these OSS products.

INTRODUCTION

Open Source Software (OSS) is currently enjoying increasing popularity and diffusion in industrial environments. However, verification and testing of OSS systems have not received the amount of attention they often have in Closed Source Software (CSS) (Zhao & Elbaum, 2003; Tosi & Tahir, 2010). Even very well-known OSS projects, such as Apache Httpd or the GCC compiler, do not seem to have mature testing processes and test suites defined inside their development process. This is probably due to a few mutually related reasons, which we outline.

DOI: 10.4018/978-1-4666-2937-0.ch004

1. Some testing techniques that are well established for CSS are not directly applicable to OSS systems, so a good deal of effort and cost is required for designing new testing solutions that are created *ad-hoc* for OSS systems.

2. OSS system development as a whole hardly ever follows the classic software engineering paradigms found in textbooks, so the execution of testing activities for OSS is less structured than for CSS.

3. The planning and the monitoring of the testing process of an OSS system hardly ever follow the guidelines used for CSS systems, so it is necessary to redefine some of the methods that are at the basis of the testing process.

4. OSS project testing often relies on the contributions from end-users, more than CSS does. This may occur via the distribution of testing or beta releases, or by using the feedback from users on stable releases. This allows OSS developers to shorten release cycles. In a way, this was stated by Linus Torvalds as "Given enough eyeballs, all bugs are shallow," which can be interpreted as referring to the importance of code review by peers, but also to the importance and power of testing by end-users contributing to OSS development with their feedback. The extent to which this occurs is larger than in CSS, and much larger than for products of other, more mature industrial sectors.

5. Often, OSS end-users independently test OSS products before using them. So, it is likely that the same kinds of tests are carried out over and over again by different users. This implies some wasted effort for end-users and lack of maturity of the testing process. In addition, this is against the very motivations of OSS, which implies sharing effort and reusing results, including those related to software verification and validation.

6. The lack of maturity of OSS testing processes is also indicated by the low coverage levels that are achieved by the test suites that are found along OSS products. Some results of the QualiPSo project show that the statement coverage levels of a number of well-known OSS projects do not exceed 25%. Clearly, this does not imply that at least 75% of source code statements have never been tested. Instead, this shows that a lot of the testing that is carried out goes undocumented, which is a symptom of low maturity.

Our experience in the context of OSS projects suggests that OSS communities do not usually view software testing as a primary software development activity. Also, most OSS projects do not fully integrate testing activities into their development process. In a survey, we asked 151 OSS stakeholders (developers, contributors, managers, end-users, etc.) to rate the importance of a number of factors that they take into account during the adoption of OSS components and products. The complete survey can be found in QualiPSo 1 (2010). It is worth noting that about 90% of the interviewees were actually involved in OSS projects as developers, contributors, integrators, managers, etc., and only 10% were end-users. Interviewees answered on average that the factor "existence of benchmarks / test suites that witness for the quality of OSS" has low importance. This may actually be a result of the fact that benchmarks and test suites are hardly ever available for OSS, more than the fact that benchmarks and test suites might not be important. So, OSS stakeholders do not use benchmarks and test suites simply because they often do not exist. We also analyzed the web portals of 33 well-known OSS products (Tosi & Tahir, 2010) and we discovered that, in the web portals

- Only 6% of the products provide the availability of a complete test suites
- 21% of the products provide performance benchmarks

- 3% show the usage of a testing framework to support testing activities
- 18% provide complete results about test suite executions
- 41% provide internal (or external) reports about the executions of benchmarks.

These somewhat discouraging data are in contrast with the trend followed by CSS products, for which software quality and consequently testing are considered very important during the development process. In CSS development, the testing process is much more rigorously defined and is considered a key factor for achieving high quality. In OSS development, bug detection and fixing depends much less on testing process rigor. OSS follows the "release early, release often" paradigm to have continual improvement and achieve high quality (Aberdour, 2007).

In Morasca et al. (2009) we thoroughly discussed some of the inherent characteristics of OSS products and a set of testing techniques that may address these characteristics. In this paper, we extend our preliminary work as follows.

1. We provide a set of testing guidelines that OSS developers may follow to decide which testing techniques make most sense for their OSS products. We introduce a checklist to help OSS developers optimize and improve the testing practices of their products, by identifying what needs to be checked to cause as many failures as possible by means of specific testing activities and test suites, according to the main characteristics of their products under test.

2. We merge these contributions in a proposal for a method for assessing the maturity of OSS testing processes, OSS-TMM (Open Source Software Testing Maturity Model). OSS-TMM is the first step towards the definition of a new Maturity Model specifically focused on OSS testing, whose final goal is the quality improvement of OSS products by supporting the planning, monitoring,

and execution of testing activities. Unlike existing models (Burnstein et al., 1996; Herbsleb et al., 1997; El Emam, 1997), which have been defined with CSS characteristics in mind, OSS-TMM takes into account the specific issues that characterize OSS from CSS systems.

3. To provide evidence of the usefulness of the checklist, we have applied OSS-TMM step-by-step to three real-life OSS projects: BusyBox, Apache Httpd and TPTP, and we compared the assessed scores with the density of reported bugs to understand whether a correlation exists between the two indicators. Moreover, we applied OSS-TMM to four additional representative OSS products, to assess the maturity of their testing process.

The paper is structured as follows. Section "Testing Guidelines for OSS" introduces the checklist and a set of testing guidelines for OSS products. Section "OSS-TMM Description" describes how to use the checklist and the guidelines for the assessment and the improvement of OSS testing processes. Section "OSS-TMM Evaluation" details our experience with BusyBox, Apache Httpd, and TPTP, and reports on the maturity of four additional OSS projects. Section "Related Work" discusses the state of the art in certifying software products. Section "Conclusions" draws our conclusions and future work.

TESTING GUIDELINES FOR OSS

We provide a set of testing guidelines and OSS-TMM to complement the testing mechanisms normally used in the OSS domain. Our goal is to help developers and contributors improve their testing process with relatively little effort. Specifically:

1. From a developers' point of view, OSS-TMM's goal is to simplify the internal process of testing OSS products by suggesting a rapid way for identifying a testing plan

that best fits the characteristics of the OSS product. Also, OSS-TMM aims at simplifying the assessment or certification process of OSS products by comparing available testing activities and the activities suggested by our guidelines. OSS-TMM may also speed up the testing activities by guiding developers in selecting testing strategies depending on the characteristics of their OSS product and may increase the quality and the trustworthiness perception of the OSS by improving the testing activity.

2. From the end-user's point of view, OSS-TMM aims at simplifying and speeding up the selection of an OSS product by evaluating the maturity of the testing process as a possible indicator about the whole quality of the product.

We have identified a comprehensive set of issues that characterize OSS systems and, correspondingly, a set of testing techniques that best fit the characteristics of OSS products (Morasca et al., 2009). In this section, these two sets are summarized and presented in a checklist that can be used by developers and end-user to identify the peculiarities of their OSS products, discover the level of compliance of the target OSS product with the typical OSS characteristics, and define the best testing practices for the target product. While some of them are not individually unique to OSS development, their ensemble characterizes OSS testing.

Checklist and Guidelines

Here, we report on the checklist, which is one of the improvements provided in this work. Table 1 shows the checklist. The checklist refers to the five main issues (I1 to I5) discussed in detail in our previous paper (Morasca et al., 2009).

The first issue (I1) addresses the full visibility of the logic and structure of the code. The second issue (I2) addresses all the aspects related to system analysis and product design activities, such as the definition of system requirements, risks, and quality assurance methodologies. The third issue (I3) addresses the way OSS products are developed and takes into account the concepts of collaborative and distributed development, virtual communities, and the idea of "unstructured companies" (Raymond, 2001). Issue I4 addresses the rapid growth that characterizes OSS systems (Mockus et al., 2000) and the creativity that characterizes the communities around OSS products (O'Reilly, 1999). Issue I5 addresses the way OSS products and projects are documented, and how these documents are disseminated.

The checklist itemizes a set of questions for each issue (see the left column of Table 1). Each question stresses a specific sub-issue that may (or may not) characterize the OSS project under concern.

The evaluator assesses the availability of each sub-issue by ticking the box "Y" if the sub-issue fully characterizes the system under analysis, "P" if the sub-issue partially characterizes the system under analysis, and "N" otherwise. Some sub-issues may not be applicable to the target system: if a sub-issue is not applicable, the testing guideline associated must be discarded. When the process is completed and all the checklist entries have been checked, the evaluator simply should take into account the testing techniques, which have a real impact on the system, by following the testing guidelines reported in Table 1 column <<*Guidelines*>>. Each testing technique is supplied with references to the literature. Questions and guidelines are formulated to limit subjectivity.

We will present how to use the checklist and how to apply it to real-life OSS projects.

OSS-TMM DESCRIPTION

In this section, we draw a step-by-step method (OSS-TMM) that developers and end-users can follow to assess the maturity level of a testing process.

Table 1. Checklist and guidelines for testing OSS products

	Y	P	N	Guidelines
I1 – Code Visibility				
I1.1 Is the source code available via Versioning Systems?				IF Y: regression testing is required for versioned projects to avoid the risk of introducing new bugs from a release to another; white-box unit and integration testing is required for projects structured in components, units of code, packages to test each unit of code in isolation or in integration and provide evidence that the functionality of each unit is implemented as specified. (IEEE Std 1008, 1986; Leung & White, 1990; Pezzè & Young, 2007)
I1.2 Is the project structured in folders: source, binary, libraries, docs?				
I1.3 Is information about releases (date, number, change-log) visible?				
I1.4 Is information about code revision (author, number, description) visible?				
I1.5 Are security issues meaningful for the product (private data, sensible data)?				IF Y: formal testing is required for functions that manipulate private / sensible data, penetration tests, dependencies tests, risk-based security tests (Howard, 2006; Dannenberg & Ernst, 1982; Arkin et al., 2005)
I1.6 Are the scripts of the test cases open source?				
I1.7 Does the project integrate third-party components and is it released under several OSI licenses[1] ?				IF Y: compatibility checks among the different licenses adopted by the project are needed to satisfy all the licenses dependencies and to avoid legal implications (http://sourceforge.net/projects/fossology/) (Tuunanen, 2009; Oksanen & Kupsu, 2008)
I1.8 Are log files about system executions available?		-		IF Y: dynamic analysis techniques are applicable to test at run-time the behavior of the system against the expected one (Ernst et al., 2001; Orso, 2010)
I2 - System Analysis and Product Design Activities				
I2.1 Is a project plan/roadmap available?		-		IF Y: the available system analysis should be exploited to design oracles and test cases for black box testing (category partition, catalogs, hw/sw requirements testing, acceptance testing) (Ostrand & Balcer, 1988; Pezzè & Young, 2007); IF N: evolutionary testing (Santelices et al., 2008)
I2.2 Is a risk analysis available?		-		
I2.3 Is a requirements analysis available?		-		
I2.4 Is a goal analysis available?		-		
I2.5 Are system designs available (in UML or other notations)?				IF Y: the available models should be used as starting point for model-based testing to derive test cases from the abstract representation of the system (Pretschner et al., 2005)
I2.6 Are standard protocols or patterns identified?		-		IF Y: conformance testing should be applied to verify the protocol behavior and to check the adherence of the source code to the identified standards (Bernhard, 1994)
I2.7 Are coding standards and conventions identified?		-		IF Y: style check and inspection should be used to verify the adherence to the identified conventions (http://pmd.sourceforge.net) (Fagan, 1986)
I2.8 Are performance requirements meaningful (real-time, normal constraints)?				IF Y: performance testing (load testing, stress testing, endurance testing) (IEEE Std 829, 2008; Weyuker & Vokolos, 2000; Pezzè & Young, 2007)
I2.9 Does the system follow a specific architectural style (e.g., SOA, peer-to-peer)?		-		IF Y: select the testing techniques specialized for the chosen architectural style (e.g., service-oriented architectures prefer on-line testing) (Mao et al., 2007)
I2.10 Is the system developed with a GUI?		-		IF Y: use capture&replay tools to automate the execution of GUI tests. Consider also usability aspects, and evaluate the product by testing it on users (http://jacareto.sourceforge.net) (Nielsen, 1999)
I2.11 Does the product use external libraries/plugins?		-		IF Y: check compliance among the target product version and the integrated modules through versioning compatibility checks and installation testing activities (Agruss, 2000)

continued on following page

Table 1. Continued

	Y	P	N	Guidelines
I3 - Development Process				
I3.1 Is a specific development process used (e.g., waterfall, continuous building)?		-		IF Y: verify whether the testing process is in line with the chosen development process to optimize the whole process and the use of available resources
I3.2 Are developers/contributors structured in teams?		-		IF I3.2 N and I3.3 Y: use the sand box as testing environment;
I3.3 Does the system provide a sand box environment?		-		
I3.4 Is a specific IDE used/recommended?		-		IF Y: make the most of the testing potentialities offered by the chosen IDE by exploiting external plugins or components that can support testing;
I3.5 Is a testing platform used/recommended?		-		IF N: select a testing framework (Open, 2010) to support and automate the testing process;
I3.6 Is a bug tracking system available?		-		IF Y: fault-based testing techniques to demonstrate the absence of a set of pre-specified and reported faults (Morell, 1990)
I4 - System Growth and Community Creativity				
I4.1 Is the number of code changes per release > 500 ?		-		Integration and regression testing activities should be improved proportionally to the size of the community and the vitality of the project. The same should happen for the automation of testing, the sharing of testing knowledge to increase the reusability of the test suites, the documentation of test-strategy/ tests-results, and the monitoring of testing activities. Also exploit *online built-in testing methodologies* to automatically collect input-output and interaction data. This facilitates the discover of functional and non-functional misbehavior (Mao et al., 2007)
I4.2 Is the number of developers/contributors > 100 ? (small community < 10; medium < 100; big > 100)		-		
I4.3 Does the system have different releases/system updates?		-		
I4.4 Is the number of open bugs/fixed bugs/... available?		-		
I4.5 Is the frequency of changes/updates/bug time solving recognizable? (to evaluate whether the project is active)		-		
I5 - Documentation and Dissemination				
I5.1 Is a system-level documentation available?		-		IF Y: exploit the documentation to simplify acceptance/system testing, usability testing, installation testing (IEEE Std 829, 2008)
I5.2 Is a library-level documentation available?		-		
I5.3 Is a feature-level documentation available?		-		
I5.4 Is a user manual available?		-		
I5.5 Are bugs reports available?		-		
I5.6 Is code documentation available (javadoc, etc.)?				
I5.7 Are docs disseminated via unstructured channels (forums, mailing lists)?		-		
I5.8 Are Installation requirements documented?				
I5.9 Are test-plans/test-designs/test-results not available?				IF Y: provide testing documentation through "test management tools" (such as TestLink, qaManager, etc.) that automate/simplify the generation of reports (Morasca et al., 2010; Open, 2010)

Process Assessment

The approach we propose is compliant with the ISO/IEC14598 standard (International Organization for Standardization, 2001), which gives guidance and requirements for evaluating software processes. OSS-TMM is based on five main steps (S1 – S5), as described next.

S1: Take the checklist of Table 1, sequentially scan each entry of the checklist, and inspect the target OSS product with reference to the issues reported in the checklist. Answer each question of the checklist and identify the testing guidelines that best fit the characteristics of your product by means of the testing guidelines provided in column <<*Guidelines*>> of Table 1.

S2: Define the Best Testing Practices (BTP) on the basis of the results of step S1. By "best testing practices," we mean the most mature process that can be theoretically achieved with reference to the inherent characteristics of the product. BTP will be a list of testing techniques that should be applied to the product under assessment to optimize its testing process. Of course, the definition of the BTP is not fully objective due to the huge number of testing techniques and practices that are potentially useful. Our intent is to suggest a survey of representative testing activities and technologies, and not a rigid model, due to the rapid evolution of the field, especially in the OSS world.

S3: Isolate and briefly analyze the currently Available Testing Practices (ATP) of the product in order to list the properties and the already used testing techniques. To do this, developers can for example ask the community whether (and which) testing activities have been performed on the product. End-users can for example surf the web portal of the product to collect data about testing activities.

S4: Verify the intersection degree between the activities of the testing process model derived in step S2 (BTP), with the ones analyzed in step S3 (ATP), and estimate the maturity level (ML) of the testing process referring to the four maturity levels identified in the next subsection.

S5: End-users can use the maturity level as an indicator that contributes to assessing the quality of the OSS product they are evaluating. Developers can use the maturity level to evaluate whether their ATP needs improvement. If this is the case, they can improve the testing process by following the recommendations and guidelines provided in the BTP.

Maturity Levels

In compliance with existing certification and maturity models, we identified four maturity levels (ML) that reflect the evolution of the testing process from one that is unstructured and undefined (ML 1) to one that is well planned, monitored, and optimized (ML 4).

Unlike in CMM and TMM (Herbsleb et al., 1997; Burnstein et al., 1996), our levels are not defined and structured as sets of predetermined maturity characteristics and goals, but they depend on the specific characteristics of the product under evaluation. Burnstein et al. (1996) define five maturity levels of a testing process starting from Level 1, in which the testing process is initial and not distinguishable from debugging, to Level 5 in which the testing process has a set of defined testing policies, a test life cycle, a test planning process, a test group, a test process improvement group, a set of test-related metrics, appropriate tools and equipments, controlling and tracking mechanisms, and finally a product quality control. Such a model is unsuitable in the OSS scenario where the testing process strongly depends on the inherent issues of the target product, where resources are limited for implementing such a testing process with several groups that work on testing, where developers are unstructured and are difficult to group in teams, where each developer/tester has the fully visibility of the code instead of a part of the product as often happen in closed-source projects, where system analysis and product design are usually not well planned activities thus making hard the definition of preplanned testing plans. In our experiments, we quickly applied Burnstein's Testing Maturity Model TMM to the 33 OSS products of our experiments, and we discovered that the vast majority of products fall into the first and second level. Therefore, TMM does not seem to be useful for differentiating the testing maturity levels of OSS products.

Hence, we identified four maturity levels with less stringent requirements than TMM, which are dynamically computed for each product by applying OSS-TMM. The fours maturity levels are defined as follows.

ML1: The activities performed by the ATP cover 25% of the activities suggested by BTP at the most. As a formula:

$$|ATP \cap BTP| < 25\%|BTP|$$

ML2: The activities performed by the ATP cover 25% to 50% of the activities suggested by the BTP. As a formula:

$$25\%|BTP| \leq |ATP \cap BTP| < 50\%|BTP|$$

ML3: The activities performed by the ATP cover 50% to 75% of the activities suggested by the BTP. As a formula:

$$50\%|BTP| \leq |ATP \cap BTP| < 75\%|BTP|$$

ML4: The activities performed by the ATP cover at least 75% of the activities suggested by the BTP. As a formula:

$$75\%|BTP| \leq |ATP \cap BTP| \leq 100\%|BTP|$$

We acknowledge that our proposal has a few subjective aspects, which will need to be minimized in the future. However, this is what happened to many successful proposals (e.g., in a different software subdiscipline, Function Points (Garmus & Herron, 2001)), whose initial proposal entailed a high degree of subjectivity that was reduced over the years.

The four maturity levels have a range of values that can be refined over time to normalize the values based on the results obtained from a more extensive industrial evaluation of OSS-TMM. For example, a unit of Siemens AG is experimenting OSS-TMM by assessing some internally used OSS products. Unfortunately, their results are not publicly available.

OSS-TMM EVALUATION

Here, we show how OSS-TMM can be used by applying it to BusyBox, Apache and TPTP. We show these three applications because of their popularity, maturity, and complexity. Also, these applications cover the most popular languages used to develop OSS, i.e., C, C/C++, and Java (http://langpop.com). The experimentation has been conducted by applying the OSS-TMM checklist both internally (i.e., in our labs) and also externally (i.e., thanks to the help of contributors of each project). In this way, we try to confirm the results we obtained internally.

BusyBox Case Study

BusyBox (http://www.busybox.net) is an OSS project, developed in C, which has some of the typical properties of OSS projects. BusyBox combines tiny versions of common UNIX utilities into a single small executable, providing minimalist replacements for the utilities usually found in Linux environments. BusyBox is a fairly large project with 177000 lines of code (LOC) and a medium size community of developers that contributes to its development (30 developers).

We applied OSS-TMM to BusyBox from the developer's point of view with the goals of:

Q1: Demonstrating the simple applicability of OSS-TMM to derive the ML of the product;
Q2: Verifying whether the suggestions provided by our model can actually be used to improve the testing process of BusyBox.

To answer the first research question *Q1*, we are interested in verifying that the computation of the maturity level can be accomplished by following the checklist suggestions (i.e., steps S1, S2, S3 and S4 are supported by the checklist) with a limited effort. To answer the second research question *Q2*, we fully implemented the BTP suggested by OSS-TMM to verify whether a well-designed testing process can actually improve the quality of BusyBox.

We sequentially applied all the steps of OSS-TMM. Thus, we analyzed BusyBox by scanning and answering each entry of the checklist, we identified the BTP in relation to the actual characteristics of BusyBox, we estimated the maturity level of the product, and finally we redefined the BusyBox ATP by following the suggestions provided by the identified BTP. For space reason, we are not able to report the complete checklist of BusyBox (Please refer to (http://qualipso. dscpi.uninsubria.it/web/oss-tmm/ to download the BusyBox's checklist).

Step S1: Analysis of Issues

In Table 2, we summarize all of BusyBox's characteristics derived from the analysis of the project through the checklist.

Step S2: BTP Derivation

The data collected during the previous step suggest that BusyBox is characterized by a high degree

Table 2. Step S1 outcome for BusyBox

Issue	BusyBox characteristic
I1.1	the whole project is managed via SVN
I1.2	the whole project is well structured in 28 folders
I1.3	information about releases are visible
I1.4	information about code revisions are visible
I1.5	sensible data are manipulated (e.g., username, pwd)
I1.6	all the scripts are open source to the community
I1.7	the popular GPLv2 license is used
I1.8	log files are not available
I2.1	the project plan/roadmap is unavailable
I2.2	the risk analysis is unavailable
I2.3	the requirements analysis is unavailable
I2.4	the goal analysis is unavailable
I2.5	UML diagrams are unavailable
I2.6	the standard "Shell and Utilities OGB" is used
I2.7	coding standards and conventions are not identified
I2.8	performance requirements are not meaningful
I2.9	BusyBox does not follow a specific architectural style
I2.10	BusyBox is designed without a GUI
I2.11	BusyBox does not integrate external libraries/plugins
I3.1	none specific development process is followed
I3.2	developers are unstructured
I3.3	a sandbox environment is not provided
I3.4	none specific IDE is used/recommended
I3.5	none specific testing platform is used/recommended
I3.6	the Bugzilla bug tracking system is integrated
I4.1	24110 revisions in total
I4.2	38 developers/contributors
I4.3	the analyzed release is: V1.14.0
I4.4	the number of new/resolved/closed bug is reported into Bugzilla
I4.5	BusyBox is a vital project
I5.1	the system-level documentation is unavailable
I5.2	the library-level documentation is unavailable
I5.3	a simple features-level documentation is available
I5.4	a short user manual is available (README file)
I5.5	bug reports are available
I5.6	the code documentation is unavailable
I5.7	documents are also disseminated via a mailing list
I5.8	installation requirements are not documented
I5.9	test documentation is unavailable

of visibility. The browsing of the source code is facilitated by the availability of a subversion system (SVN). Source files are packaged in 28 main directories and information is provided for each directory about the number of revisions, authors of the revisions, age of the latest revisions, and log entries. This facilitates the applicability of all the white-box testing techniques and a clear identification of the units that compose the entire system. The high level of modularity and the low level of interoperability among the features of BusyBox seem to suggest that developers should focus on unit testing activities.

Non-functional issues are not of primary importance for this kind of tool, due to its nature. BusyBox is a tool provided without a graphical interface, thus, approaches such as capture and replay are infeasible. The use of monitors that probe memory usage and execution/response time are not meaningful since the tool only provides calls to simple functions. Finally, since BusyBox provides replacements for most of the utilities usually found in GNU, developers should pay attention to testing security aspects. It is realistic to imagine a scenario in which a developer inserts malicious code into a BusyBox function to remotely control the operating system of an end-user that has installed BusyBox. This requires the execution of acceptance tests that check the main functionalities of the tool to allow only for trusted behaviors. For example, a test case should verify that the Unix command su (superuser) must not record the typed password.

As for issues I2, I3, I5, the BusyBox project is not supplied with project plans, documents that describe the system requirements analysis, risk analysis, technical documents that describe the use of standard protocols or patterns, architectural models, etc. The only standard to which developers pay attention, albeit without completely adhering to it, is the "Shell and Utilities" portion of the Open Group Base Standards. This strongly limits the applicability of all testing solutions that are based on project specifications such as

model-based and conformance testing techniques. However, the web portal of BusyBox provides a section that describes all the features and functionalities offered by BusyBox in a structured way. Each feature description reports the input and output parameters, the behavior the feature should have, and how to use the feature. This fosters the applicability of black-box techniques such as Category Partition and Catalog-based testing techniques in addition to white-box testing techniques. Moreover, developers and end-users should share testing knowledge with each other. Unit, system, and regression test results should be provided to the global community to favor and simplify BusyBox's integration testing.

As for I4, BusyBox is a vital and consolidated project (latest revisions are usually only a few days old and the release analyzed is V1.14.0) supported by a medium-size community of developers (currently, 38 accounts exist). It is characterized by a collaborative development process and rapid system growth. At the time of writing, the community performed 24,110 revisions, and forums and mailing lists are still alive and useful. Also, the bug tracking system seems to indicate an active community of developers (the mean time required to fix a bug is quite short: 3 to 4 days). All of these considerations seem to suggest the need for a strong regression testing activity during the whole development process of BusyBox, to avoid bugs introduced by excessive creativity.

Summarizing, the BTP for BusyBox should take into account the following activities: (1) unit testing; (2) integration testing; (3) regression testing; (4) security testing; (5) identification and use of test management tools; (6) fault-based testing techniques; (7) acceptance/system testing; (8) documentation of test results.

Step S3: ATP Analysis

Currently, BusyBox is released along with a test suite that can be executed by end-users and developers to identify problems and bugs when

BusyBox is installed on machines different from the tested ones. A quick look at the test suite suggests that developers have designed test cases to only stress each feature of BusyBox separately. Unfortunately, reports and documents that discuss the test cases and the execution results are not provided. The testing plan provided for BusyBox does not have the ability of automatically logging and collecting the test results, and users must manually signal potential bugs to the community.

Step S4: Maturity Level Evaluation

When comparing the BTP derived for BusyBox during step S2 and the one currently available, it is apparent that the testing activity of BusyBox is actually poor, and the huge number of bugs posted by the community may be a confirmation of this. The intersection between BTP and ATP does not exceed 25% (only 1 activity out of 8 is currently supported by the ATP), thus BusyBox has ML = 1. This suggests the need for applying all the testing techniques identified by OSS-TMM during step S2 to increase the quality of the product.

We contacted a contributor of BusyBox to have him also apply OSS-TMM to BusyBox. He derived a maturity level equal to the one we assessed (ML=1). This confirms the reliability of our evaluation.

Step S5: Testing Process Improvement

To improve the testing process of BusyBox, we followed the guidelines suggested by the outcome of step S2. We selected a test management tool (TestLink) to create and manage test cases and test plans, execute test cases, track test results dynamically, and generate reports. We planned integration, acceptance/system and regression testing activities, and then we generated a set of test cases for each activity. Then, we executed the test suites on a machine hosted in our lab with the following environment: Gentoo-r6 Linux distribution; Kernel 2.6.18; C compiler: gcc 4.1.2.

Table 3 reports the data collected during the execution of the test suites. Column <<*Busy-Box*>> reports the version of BusyBox under test; Columns <<*#ofTCs*>>, <<*PassedTCs*>>, <<*Failed TCs*>> report the total number of test cases for each test suite, the number of test cases that succeeded (i.e., that ended with no failures), and the number of test cases that failed (i.e., that resulted with the software having a failure), respectively. Acceptance and System testing has been performed by executing three different sets of test cases against three different versions of BusyBox (Table 3 (a)).

A simple example of test case is test (pwd) = (busybox pwd): this test case simply verifies that the working directory returned by the operating system is equal to the one returned by BusyBox. Regression testing has been performed by re-executing the 358 successful test cases, designed for BusyBox V1.12.1, against the new stable releases V1.12.4, V1.13.0 and V1.13.2 (Table 3 (b)). When executing the test suite against Busy-Box V1.12.4, none of the test cases failed. However, when executing the test suite against the

Table 3. Test cases results for BusyBox

Acceptance/System Testing			
BusyBox	**#of TCs**	**Passed TCs**	**Failed TCs**
V1.10.1	312	291	21
V1.12.1	387	358	29
V1.13.2	390	359	31
(a)			
Regression Testing			
BusyBox	**#of TCs**	**Passed TCs**	**Failed TCs**
V1.12.4	358	358	0
V1.13.0	358	354	1
V1.13.2	358	354	1
(b)			
Integration Testing			
BusyBox	**#of TCs**	**Passed TCs**	**Failed TCs**
V1.13.2	48	46	2
(c)			

BusyBox V1.13.0, three test cases which refer to the taskset command could not be executed because taskset has been removed from this version of BusyBox, and just one test case failed. The analysis of the test results allowed us to identify a new error introduced by a code change (related to the cpio command) in V1.13.0. The error even persisted in BusyBox V1.13.2.

Integration testing has been performed by executing 48 test cases that we designed to stress the interoperability between the BusyBox implementations of the most common UNIX utilities (e.g., cp command in combination with touch and cmp commands). Two test cases failed: the first one failed due to an unsupported option (-t) for the od command when piped with the echo command; the second one due to an unsupported option (--date=) for the touch command when piped with the mv command.

Experience Conclusions

This study shows evidence about the simplicity of OSS-TMM, as well as the real benefits introduced by a well planned testing process. Step S1 to Step S4 required a limited effort (one author of this paper worked two full days for this task), while Step S5 required a much more significant effort (one of the authors of this paper fully worked 1 month for this task due to the effort spent for implementing and executing the test cases). The restructured process provided the ability to detect three new errors in BusyBox with a real improvement of BusyBox's quality.

Apache Httpd Case Study

Here, we apply OSS-TMM to the Apache Httpd (http://httpd.apache.org/) project. Apache Httpd is an OSS HTTP server for operating systems such as UNIX and Windows, which provides HTTP services in sync with the current HTTP standards. Apache Httpd is a fairly large project with 135000

C/C++ lines of code (LOC) and a medium size community of developers that contributes to its development (60 developers).

We applied OSS-TMM to Apache Httpd from the end-user's point of view with the aim of demonstrating how a non-skilled user can derive the maturity level of the product he is evaluating. As in the previous case study, we sequentially applied all the steps of our OSS-TMM, with the exception that we focused on the steps followed by a end-user interested in evaluating the Apache Httpd product. A PhD student not involved directly in this work did the assessment. Hence, we first analyzed Apache Httpd through our checklist (step S1), we identified the BTP in relation to the actual characteristics of Apache Httpd (step S2), we analyzed the current testing activities for Apache Httpd (step S4), and we estimated the maturity level of the product by comparing the BTP and the Apache ATP (step S4). For space reason, we are not able to report the complete checklist of Apache Httpd. Please, refer to http://qualipso. dscpi.uninsubria.it/web/oss-tmm/ to download Apache's checklist.

Step S1: Analysis of Issues

In Table 4, we summarize all the Apache Httpd characteristics derived from the analysis of the project through the checklist.

Step S2: BTP Derivation

The data collected during the previous step show that Apache Httpd is managed via a historical archive well structured in packages and folders for each version of Apache Httpd (http://archive. apache.org/dist/httpd). For each directory the age of the latest revision, the size of the folder and a description is provided. This facilitates the applicability of all the white-box testing techniques and a clear identification of the units that compose the entire system. Due to the high number of

Table 4. Step S1 outcome for Apache Httpd

Issue	Apache Httpd characteristic
I1.1	Apache is managed via a Historical Archive
I1.2	the whole project is well structured
I1.3	information about releases are visible
I1.4	information about code revisions are visible
I1.5	SSI and AAA modules are security critical
I1.6	all the test scripts are open source to the community
I1.8	access log, error log files are collectable
I2.7	coding standards are specified in a style guide
I2.8	performance constraints: resource usage, latency, throughput, scalability
I2.11	external modules: mod python, mod ftp, mod mbox
I3.5	The Apache-Test Framework is recommended
I3.6	the Bugzilla bug tracking system is integrated
I4.1	the number of revisions is huge
I4.2	more than 60 developers/contributors (from: http://httpd.apache.org/contributors/)
I4.3	the analyzed release is: V2.2.11
I4.4	the number of new/resolved/closed bug is reported into Bugzilla
I5.8	installation requirements are documented (but not up-to-date)
I5.9	detailed test documentation is unavailable

packages and folders, testers should pay attention to unit, integration and regression testing activities. Apache Httpd exports two modules (SSI and AAA) that are security critical and thus require special attention when testing them. Apache Httpd provides the ability of collecting error log files, thus simplifying the applicability of Dynamic analysis techniques. Coding standards are defined in a style guide thus requiring code inspection to verify the adherence to (http://httpd.apache.org/dev/styleguide). Apache Httpd has a lot of performance constraints to take under control, such as the usage of resources, latency and throughput, thus requiring a strong activity for performance testing. Another important aspect

that characterizes the Apache Httpd project is the use of third-party modules (e.g., *mod_python, mod_ftp, mod_mbox*). It is important to

periodically verify the compliance of new Apache versions with the integrated modules. As for I4, Apache Httpd is a vital and consolidated project (latest revisions are usually only a few days old and the release we analyzed is V2.2.11) supported by a medium-size community of developers (currently, 60 contributors). It is characterized by a collaborative development process and rapid system growth, and forums and mailing lists (http://httpd.apache.org/lists) are still alive and useful. Also, the bug tracking system (http://httpd.apache.org/bug_report) seems to indicate an active community of developers. All of these considerations seem to suggest the need for a strong regression testing activity during the whole development process of the Apache Httpd server, to avoid bugs introduced by excessive creativity. The project is well documented and planned.

Summarizing, Apache Httpd's checklist suggests a BTP that takes into account the following testing aspects: (1) unit testing; (2) integration testing; (3) regression testing; (4) security testing; (5) dynamic analysis techniques; (6) source code inspection through checklists for C/C++; (7) performance testing; (8) versioning compatibility checks; (9) use of test management tools; (10) fault-based testing techniques; (11) acceptance/system testing and installation testing; (12) pay attention to documentation and sharing of test results.

Step S3: ATP Analysis

The end-user can surf the web portal of Apache Httpd to discover that Apache Httpd is currently released with a small test suite for testing the critical features of the project, and supports the *SPECWeb99* benchmark, *Flood* subproject, and the *Apache-test* framework. *SPECWeb99* and *Flood* can be used to gather important performance and security metrics for websites that use Apache Httpd. The *Apache-test* framework supports the definition of test suites for products running on the Apache Httpd, and can be used to run existing tests, setup a testing environment for a new project, and develop new tests. However, a complete test suite for integration and regression testing is not provided and source code inspection, and versioning compatibility checks are not yet performed.

Step S4: Maturity Level Evaluation

Comparing the BTP derived for Apache Httpd during step S2 and the one currently available ATP, it is clear that the testing activity of Apache Httpd is good and well planned. The testing aspects (1), (4), (7), (9), (11) and (12) of BTP are addressed by the ATP of Apache Httpd, thus implying an intersection between ATP and BTP equal to 50% and a ML = 3.

Experience Conclusions

Limited effort was required to accomplish all the steps (from S1 to S4): one PhD student, not directly involved in this work, took four days for this task. This case study demonstrates the support provided by the checklist, which greatly simplifies the analysis by suggesting step-by-step activities that non-skilled people can follow to determine the maturity level of the product under evaluation.

Moreover, we asked Apache contributors to fill in our checklist. A contributor of the Apache project applied OSS-TMM to Apache Httpd and he derived a maturity level equal to the one we assessed (ML=3) with a slightly different ATP/BTP ratio (67%). The contributor reported the availability of integration and regression test suites. The evaluation took 3 hours. The two evaluations confirmed the reliability of our experience.

TPTP Case Study

Here, we apply OSS-TMM to the TPTP (http://www.eclipse.org/tptp/) project. TPTP is an OSS platform that allows software developers to build test and performance tools that can be easily integrated with the platform. TPTP addresses the entire test life cycle, from early testing to production testing, including test editing and execution, monitoring, tracing and profiling, and log analysis capabilities.

TPTP is a large Java project with 200000 lines of code and a medium size community of developers that contributes to its development (60 developers).

Like in the previous case studies, we applied sequentially all the steps of OSS-TMM, from S1 to S4 and an author of this paper did the assessment. We first analyzed TPTP through our checklist (step S1), we identified the BTP in relation to the actual characteristics of TPTP (step S2), we analyzed the testing activities for TPTP to derive ATP (step S3), and we estimated the maturity level of the product by comparing the BTP and the TPTP ATP (step S4). For space reason, we are not able to report the complete checklist of TPTP. Please, refer to http://qualipso.dscpi.uninsubria.it/web/oss-tmm/ to download the TPTP's checklist. The TPTP characteristics derived from the analysis are summarized in Table 5, which only lists the issues that characterize TPTP and are useful to derive the BTP.

Starting from the TPTP characteristics highlighted in step S1, the best testing practices BTP for TPTP should take into account the following testing aspects: (1) unit testing; (2) integration testing; (3) regression testing; (4) licenses compatibility check; (5) black-box testing; (6) model-based testing; (7) conformance testing; (8) style check and inspection; (9) testing for architecture; (10) capture&replay; (11) usability testing; (12) versioning compatibility checks; (13) testing process check; (14) IDE potentialities exploitation; (15) fault-based testing; (16) improve integration/regression testing and test cases documentation; (17) documentation use for testing; (18) test management tool.

Analyzing TPTP's source code and the repository of the project, we found that TPTP is currently released with test suites for unit, integration, regression and performance testing. A complete list of the licenses used by the different components of

Table 5. Step S1 outcome for TPTP

Issue	TPTP characteristic
I1.1	TPTP is managed via CVS (http://dev. eclipse.org/viewcvs/)
I1.2	the whole project is well structured
I1.3	information about releases are visible
I1.4	information about code revisions are visible
I1.6	all the test scripts are open source to the community (see CVS)
I1.7	TPTP integrates several OSI licenses (www.eclipse.org/tptp/home/project_info/ releaseinfo/4.7/Open_Source.htm)
I2.1	the project roadmap is available (www.eclipse.org/projects/project-plan. php?projectid=tptp)
I2.5	system diagrams are available
I2.6	standard protocols are used (www.eclipse. org/tptp/platform/documents/)
I2.7	coding standards are specified (http://wiki.eclipse.org/index.php/Development_Conventions_and_Guidelines)
I2.9	TPTP uses a specific architectural style (www.eclipse.org/projects/dev_process/development_process_2010.php)
I2.10	TPTP provides a GUI
I2.11	a lot of external modules are used
I3.1	a specific development process is used
I3.2	developers are structured in teams
I3.5	the Eclipse IDE is used
I3.6	the Bugzilla bug tracking system is integrated
I4.1	the number of revisions is huge
I4.2	more than 60 developers/contributors (from: http://dash.eclipse.org)
I4.3	the analyzed release is: V4.7.0
I4.4	the number of new/resolved/closed bug is reported into Bugzilla
I5.1, I5.2, I5.3, I5.4, I5.5, I5.6, I5.8	TPTP documentation is available (www. eclipse.org/tptp/platform/documents/)
I5.9	test documentation is unavailable

TPTP can be found in the *project_info* section of the TPTP portal. A test suite that uses the *TPTP Automated Gui Recorder* is also available and attention is paid to versioning compatibility checks.

Test reports are available in the CVS repository and test cases are documented. Concluding, the testing aspects (1), (2), (3), (4), (10), (12), (13), (14) and (16) of BTP are addressed by the ATP of TPTP, thus implying an intersection between ATP and BTP equal to 50% and a ML = 3.

Experience Conclusions

The internal assessment took 4 hours. A contributor of TPTP was also asked to apply OSS-TMM to TPTP and he derived a maturity level equal to ML=3 with a slightly different ATP/BTP ratio (56%). The contributor reported the availability of a test management tool for testing documentation that we were not able to find during our analysis. The external assessment took 3 hours. At any rate, the two evaluations confirmed the reliability of this experiment.

Maturity Level vs. Bug Rate

We looked for correlation patterns between the maturity levels obtained and the quality of the three OSS projects, to comprehend whether high maturity of the testing process directly may imply high product quality, and low maturity low product quality. As for the dependent measure, we decided to select the bug rate (*BR*) of the product (i.e., the number of bugs divided by product size in thousands of lines of code), which is a sensible indicator of the overall product quality. Table 6 summarizes the results obtained. Bug data have been collected by analyzing the bug tracker system of each product with focus on *new*, *resolved* and *closed* bugs. Following the Bugzilla's documentation (http://www.bugzilla.org) the *new* status is for bugs that have been successfully reproduced by a member of the team; the *resolved* status is for bugs that are fixed by coding a solution that is released as an official patch; the *closed* status is for bugs that have been fixed and whose fixes have appeared in a release of the project. We selected the latest stable release of each product to avoid strange bug distributions related to newly released and unstable products, and we just considered the bugs that refer to the selected releases. We used SLOCCount (developed by D. Wheeler) for counting the physical source lines of code of each project (http://www.dwheeler.com/sloccount/). We limited this study to BusyBox, Apache Httpd and TPTP simply because the other projects we evaluated with OSS-TMM (Table 7) have bug tracker systems that are different from each other, thus introducing heterogeneity in the collected bug data. BusyBox, Apache Httpd, and TPTP use the Bugzilla V3.6 bug tracker system, thus ensuring homogeneity on the bug data reported. An analysis of Table 6 provides some evidence that a high maturity level impacts both on the ability of detecting new bugs (i.e., the bug rate value related to new bugs proportionally increases) and the ability of resolving and closing the newly discovered bugs (i.e., the resolved/closed bug value increases).

Table 6. OSS-TMM MLs vs bug rate

Project	ML (ATP/BTP)	Bug Rate
BusyBox v1.14.0	1	New: 0,006
	(14%)	Resolved: 0,19
		Closed: 0,00
TPTP v4.7.0	3 (50%)	New: 0,037
		Resolved: 0,07
		Closed: 0,83
Apache Httpd v.2.2.0	3 (55%)	New: 0,096
		Resolved: 0,93
		Closed: 0,06

Table 7. OSS-TMM MLs for four OSS projects

Project	OSS-TMM Maturity Level
DDD v3.3	ML=1
DebianOS v3.0	ML=1
PostgreSQL v8.3	ML=4
Xoops Core v2.3	ML=2

Other OSS-TMM Assessments

We also applied OSS-TMM to four additional OSS projects. We selected the projects by evaluating their size, organizational type (i.e., sponsored, foundation, spontaneous), and diffusion to identify a heterogeneous set of OSS projects. We selected: the Debian distribution (DebianOS) as a well-known, sponsored, and complex OSS product; the Data Display Debugger (DDD) as an unfamiliar, sponsored, and of reduced complexity project; the OSS database PostgreSQL as a specialized, sponsored, and complex product; the web content management system (Xoops) as a specialized, founded, and of reduced complexity project. In our evaluation, the four OSS projects obtained the maturity levels listed in Table 7. PostgreSQL has a very mature testing process with a complete test suite and an updated documentation, while the testing processes of the other projects are still in their infancy and need more attention.

RELATED WORK

Here, we compare our approach with what has been done in some related research areas that address software quality.

Software Process Improvement

Research in software process improvement focuses on certification models that deal with the quality of the software production process. The most important models are CMM and SPICE (Herbsleb et al., 1997; International Organization for Standardization, 2004). The Capability Maturity Model (CMM), and its extension CMMI, is a methodology that assists companies in understanding the capability maturity of their software processes. The maturity model involves several aspects related to five maturity levels (chaotic, repeatable, defined, managed, and optimizing), a cluster of Key Process Areas (KPA) (i.e., related activities that, when performed collectively, achieve a set of important goals), a set of goals (i.e., scope, boundaries, and intent of each key process area), common features (i.e., practices that implement a KPA), and finally key practices (i.e., the elements that effectively contribute to the implementation of the KPAs).

The Software Process Improvement and Capability dEtermination (SPICE / ISO15504) is a framework for the assessment of processes. The SPICE reference model focuses on a wider vision than CMM by taking into account five process and capability dimensions (customer-supplier, engineering, supporting, management, and organization). In compliance with CMM, they define a scale of capability levels, a cluster of process attributes (to measure capability of processes), a set of generic practices (i.e., indicators to aid assessment performance), and a process assessment guide.

Our approach is built upon the general ideas proposed by CMM and SPICE. However, OSS-TMM uses a simpler and less rigid maturity model than CMM and SPICE, because of its purpose and its focus on the testing dimension. Moreover, the OSS-TMM process assessment also suggests how to improve the available testing process of an OSS product by recommending the most suitable testing techniques.

Software Product Quality

The most important standard to ensure the quality of the product is ISO9126 (International Organization for Standardization, 2001). The ISO9126 standard takes into account several aspects of the internal, external, and in-use quality of a software product and it defines a quality model that includes a set of characteristics and sub-characteristics related to functionality, reliability, usability, maintainability, efficiency, and portability. In ISO9126, a wide set of complex measures are defined to assess product quality, while ISO14598 (International Organization for Standardization,

2001) provides, among other things, an explanation of how to apply the ISO9126 model.

Our approach focuses on the quality of the testing process instead of the whole product quality and it simplifies the evaluation of the process maturity by providing a checklist instead of a complex list of measures. The steps that compose the OSS-TMM process assessment are compliant with the guidance and requirements for software evaluation highlighted in ISO14598.

Testing Maturity Models

Research in testing maturity models complements CMM with the focus on testing aspects. The first work on this research area is provided by Burnstein et al. (1996). They defined a Testing Maturity Model (TMM) that helps evaluate the testing process of software products. TMM identifies five rigid maturity levels, a set of maturity goals and sub-goals (equivalent to KPAs of CMM), and a set of activities, tasks and responsibilities (ATR) for each maturity level.

Other CMM-based testing models have been proposed. For example, the Test Improvement Model (TIM) (Ericson et al., 1997) and the Test Process Improvement Model (TPI) (Koomen & Pol, 1999) suggest ways in which testers can improve their work. TIM and TPI identify key areas for the testing process starting from the organization and planning of testing activities to test cases generation, execution, and documentation review. While the previous approaches have been designed with CSS characteristics in mind, OSS-TMM exploits the inherent characteristics and issues typical of OSS products. Hence, OSS-TMM defines four maturity levels that are not structured as sets of predetermined maturity characteristics and goals, but they depend on the actual characteristics of the product under evaluation. Moreover, OSS-TMM supports both testers in improving the testing process and also companies and end-users in assessing the quality and the trustworthiness perception of the OSS product.

OSS Quality Assessment

Research in OSS quality assessment extends CMM and CMM-compliant models to identify, from the set of CMM goals, only the subset that is relevant for OSS products. The first CMM extension for OSS is the Open Source Maturity Model (OSMM) (Duijnhouwer & Widdows, 2009). OSMM defines a methodology and a set of OSS ad-hoc indicators to assess the global maturity of an OSS product, helping end-users to choose between equivalent OSS products. Since the definition of OSMM, several other models have been developed (e.g., Taibi et al., 2007). Recently, the Open Maturity Model (OMM) has been defined as an output of the QualiPSo project. OMM has been designed specifically for the Free/Libre Open Source software development process evaluation. The structure of the model resembles in many aspects the Capability Maturity Model (Petrinja et al., 2009) and OMM is compatible with CMM.

OSS-TMM does not provide a global assessment of the product quality but uses the testing process maturity level as an indicator of the process quality. This simplifies the applicability of the approach and the identification of weaknesses into testing processes.

CONCLUSION

In this paper, we have presented a set of testing guidelines that are *ad-hoc* for the inherent characteristics of OSS projects. The identification of the best testing technologies, which make most sense for the OSS products under test, is supported by a checklist of issues and testing guidelines. The usage of the guidelines and the checklist is merged in the OSS-TMM method that helps developers in assess and improve the testing process of their OSS products. Applications to BusyBox, Apache Httpd and TPTP show how the method comes into play on real-life projects. The method is currently under evaluation in Siemens AG to assess some

internally used OSS products. The results of this adoption will be the basis for refinement of OSS-TMM. We believe that continuous gathering and analysis of experiences will help pinpoint specific issues of OSS testing and better address the building of a more useful OSS-TMM. In addition, it will help reduce at least some of the subjectivity of OSS-TMM, in the same way as happened with other models in the past.

ACKNOWLEDGMENT

The research presented in this article was partially funded by the IST project QualiPSo (http://www.qualipso.org/), sponsored by the EU in the 6th FP (IST-034763); the FIRB project ARTDECO, sponsored by the Italian Ministry of Education and University; and the projects "Metodi e tecniche per la modellazione, lo sviluppo e la valutazione di sistemi software" and "La qualità nello sviluppo software," funded by the Università degli Studi dell'Insubria. We also acknowledge the developers of BusyBox, Apache Httpd and TPTP for their evaluations.

REFERENCES

Aberdour, M. (2007). Achieving Quality in Open Source Software. *IEEE Software*, *24*(1), 58–64. doi:10.1109/MS.2007.2

Agruss, C. (2000). Software installation testing - how to automate tests for smooth system installation. *Software Testing & Quality Engineering*, 32-37.

Arkin, B., Stender, S., & McGraw, G. (2005). Software penetration testing. *IEEE Security and Privacy*, *3*(1), 84–87. doi:10.1109/MSP.2005.23

Bernhard, P. J. (1994). A reduced test suite for protocol conformance testing. *ACM Transactions on Software Engineering and Methodology*, *3*(3), 201–220. doi:10.1145/196092.196088

Burnstein, I., Suwanassart, T., & Carlson, R. (1996). Developing a Testing Maturity Model for software test process evaluation and improvement. In *Proceedings of the IEEE International Test Conference* (pp. 581-589).

Dannenberg, R. B., & Ernst, G. W. (1982). Formal program verification using symbolic execution. *IEEE Transactions on Software Engineering, 8*(1), 43–52. doi:10.1109/TSE.1982.234773

Duijnhouwer, F. W., & Widdows, C. (2010). *Open Source Maturity Model*. Retrieved from http://www.osspartner.com

El Emam, K. (1997). *Spice: The Theory and Practice of Software Process Improvement and Capability determination*. Washington, DC: IEEE Computer Society.

Ericson, T., Subotic, A., & Ursing, S. (1997). TIM - a Test Improvement Model. *International Journal on Software Testing. Verification and Reliability, 7*(4), 229–246. doi:10.1002/(SICI)1099-1689(199712)7:4<229::AID-STVR149>3.0.CO;2-M

Ernst, M. D., Cockrell, J., Griswold, W. G., & Notkin, D. (2001). Dynamically discovering likely program invariants to support program evolution. *IEEE Transactions on Software Engineering, 27*(2), 99–123. doi:10.1109/32.908957

Fagan, M. E. (1986). Advances in Software Inspections. *IEEE Transactions on Software Engineering, 12*(7), 744–751.

Garmus, D., & Herron, D. (2001). *Function point analysis: measurement practices for successful software projects*. Reading, MA: Addison-Wesley.

Herbsleb, J., Zubrow, D., Goldenson, D., Hayes, W., & Paulk, M. (1997). Software quality and the Capability Maturity Model. *Communications of the ACM, 40*(6), 30–40. doi:10.1145/255656.255692

Howard, M. (2006). A process for performing security code reviews. *IEEE Security and Privacy, 4*(4), 74–79. doi:10.1109/MSP.2006.84

IEEE. (1986). *Std 1008-1987: IEEE standard for Software Unit Testing*. Washington, DC: IEEE Computer Society.

IEEE. (2008). *Std 829-2008: IEEE Standard for Software and System Test Documentation*. Washington, DC: IEEE Computer Society.

International Organization for Standardization. (2004). *ISO/IEC 15504-1 Information technology process assessment. Part 1: Concepts and vocabulary*. Geneva, Switzerland: ISO.

International Organization for Standardization (ISO). (2001). *ISO/IEC 14598-1 Information technology - software product evaluation. Part 1: General overview*. Geneva, Switzerland: ISO.

International Organization for Standardization (ISO). (2001). *ISO/IEC 9126-1 Software engineering - product quality. Part 1: Quality model*. Geneva, Switzerland: ISO.

Koomen, T., & Pol, M. (1999). *Test Process Improvement: a practical step-by-step guide to structured testing*. Reading, MA: Addison-Wesley.

Leung, H. K. N., & White, L. (1990). A study of integration testing and software regression at the integration level. In *Proceedings of the Conference on Software Maintenance* (pp. 290-301).

Mao, C., Lu, Y., & Zhang, J. (2007). Regression testing for component-based software via built-in test design. In *Proceedings of the ACM Symposium on Applied Computing* (pp. 1416-1421).

Morasca, S., Taibi, D., & Tosi, D. (2010). T-DOC: a Tool for the Automatic Generation of Testing Documentation for OSS Products. In *Proceedings of the IFIP International Conference on Open Source Software*.

Morasca, S., Taibi, T., & Tosi, D. (2009). Certifying the testing process of open source software: New challenges or old methodologies? In *Proceedings of the IEEE International Workshop on Free/Libre/Open Source Software Research and Development* (pp. 25-30).

Morell, L. J. (1990). A theory of fault-based testing. *IEEE Transactions on Software Engineering*, *16*(8), 844–857. doi:10.1109/32.57623

Nielsen, J. (1999). User Interface Directions for the Web. *Communications of the ACM*, *42*(1), 65–72. doi:10.1145/291469.291470

Oksanen, V., & Kupsu, M. (2008). *OSLC Open Source License Checker V3*. Retrieved from http://forge.ow2.org/projects/oslcv3/

Orso, A. (2010). Monitoring, analysis, and testing of deployed software. In *Proceedings of the FSE/SDP Workshop on Future of Software Engineering Research* (pp. 263-268).

Ostrand, T. J., & Balcer, M. J. (1988). The category-partition method for specifying and generating functional tests. *Communications of the ACM*, *31*(6), 676–686. doi:10.1145/62959.62964

Petrinja, E., Nambakam, R., & Sillitti, A. (2009). Introducing the OpenSource Maturity Model. In *Proceedings of the IEEE International Workshop on Free/Libre/Open Source Software Research and Development*.

Pezzè, M., & Young, M. (2007). *Software Testing and Analysis. Process, Principles, and Techniques*. New York, NY: John Wiley & Sons.

Pretschner, A., Prenninger, W., Wagner, S., Kuhnel, C., Baumgartner, M., Sostawa, B., & Zolch, R. (2005). One evaluation of model-based testing and its automation. In *Proceedings of the 27th International Conference on Software Engineering* (pp. 392-401).

Santelices, R. A., Chittimalli, P. K., Apiwattanapong, T., Orso, A., & Harrold, M. J. (2008). Test-suite augmentation for evolving software. In *Proceedings of the IEEE International Conference on Automated Software Engineering* (pp. 218-227).

Taibi, D., Lavazza, L., & Morasca, S. (2007). OpenBQR: a framework for the assessment of OSS. *International Journal on Open Source Development, Adoption and Innovation*, 173-186.

The Qualipso Project 1. (2010). *How European software industry perceives OSS trustworthiness and what are the specific criteria to establish trust in OSS*. Retrieved from http://www.qualipso.eu/node/45

Tosi, D., & Tahir, A. (2010). How developers test their Open Source Software Products. A survey of well-known OSS projects. In *Proceedings of the 5th International Conference on Software and Data Technologies*.

Tuunanen, T., Koskinen, J., & Kärkkäinen, T. (2009). Automated software license analysis. *International Journal on Automated Software Engineering*, *16*(3), 455–490. doi:10.1007/s10515-009-0054-z

Weyuker, E. J., & Vokolos, F. I. (2000). Experience with performance testing of software systems: issues, an approach, and case study. *IEEE Transactions on Software Engineering*, *26*(12), 1147–1156. doi:10.1109/32.888628

Zhao, L., & Elbaum, S. (2003). Quality assurance under the open source development model. *International Journal of Systems and Software*, *66*(1), 65–75.

ENDNOTES

[1] See http://www.opensource.org/licenses/ for an exhaustive list of licenses approved by the Open Source Initiative (OSI)

This work was previously published in the International Journal of Open Source Software and Processes, Volume 3, Issue 2, edited by Stefan Koch, pp. 1-22, copyright 2011 by IGI Publishing (an imprint of IGI Global).

Chapter 5
Are Developers Fixing Their Own Bugs?
Tracing Bug-Fixing and Bug-Seeding Committers

Daniel Izquierdo-Cortazar
Universidad Rey Juan Carlos, Spain

Andrea Capiluppi
University of East London, UK

Jesus M. Gonzalez-Barahona
Universidad Rey Juan Carlos, Spain

ABSTRACT

The process of fixing software bugs plays a key role in the maintenance activities of a software project. Ideally, code ownership and responsibility should be enforced among developers working on the same artifacts, so that those introducing buggy code could also contribute to its fix. However, especially in FLOSS projects, this mechanism is not clearly understood: in particular, it is not known whether those contributors fixing a bug are the same introducing and seeding it in the first place. This paper analyzes the comm-central FLOSS project, which hosts part of the Thunderbird, SeaMonkey, Lightning extensions and Sunbird projects from the Mozilla community. The analysis is focused at the level of lines of code and it uses the information stored in the source code management system. The results of this study show that in 80% of the cases, the bug-fixing activity involves source code modified by at most two developers. It also emerges that the developers fixing the bug are only responsible for 3.5% of the previous modifications to the lines affected; this implies that the other developers making changes to those lines could have made that fix. In most of the cases the bug fixing process in comm-central is not carried out by the same developers than those who seeded the buggy code.

DOI: 10.4018/978-1-4666-2937-0.ch005

1. INTRODUCTION

One of the most recognised advantages of the Free/Libre/Open Source Software (FLOSS) development model is its reliance on an open process: anyone is welcome to contribute; the majority of developers can focus on modularised, limited sections within a very large and complex system; and few core developers are generally experts in several areas of the source code, in a well accepted layered model (the "onion model" Mockus et al., 2002). These layers have been connected to actual responsibilities; core developers should focus on the main, more important features, while experimental versions should be implemented and tested by contributors on the development fringes (Goldman & Gabriel, 2004). Also, the layers of such model have been related to a shift in productivity: a recurring finding within FLOSS empirical research has shown that most of the development work is achieved by a small amount of developers, in a typical Pareto distribution (Koch, 2009).

The combinations of all the findings above have various, and not completely understood, effects. In some cases, a strong *territoriality* will emerge among developers "owning" certain parts of the code, and becoming more and more proficient in those (German, 2004; Robles et al., 2006). In other cases, the very nature of the FLOSS development implies that contributors join and then leave without necessarily halting the project (Robles & González-Barahona, 2006), but resulting in abandoned code and orphaned lines (Izquierdo-Cortazar et al., 2009).

Finally, certain developers will need to be active in maintenance activities: *corrective* maintenance fixing bugs in various parts of the code, for instance when source code is first introduced by developers with a low knowledge of the project (junior developers); *perfective* maintenance, for instance when new improved features are needed but the original developers have left the project and abandoned their contributions (Adams et al., 2009); *adaptive* maintenance, for instance

when adaptations are needed, but the source code has been contributed in a programming language different from the main one supported by the project, so the current developers do not have enough skills in that language. Although in specific FLOSS communities there is the shared expectation that the original contributor will support his/her modules (especially in highly modular FLOSS projects, as Moodle or Drupal, Capiluppi et al., 2010), the volatility of contributors and the process of bug-fixing need to be clarified with respect of who introduced a certain bug, and who contributed the code to fix it. Examining and determining the proportion of errors that are fixed by different developers than those who introduced the error could provide a first approach to better understand the bug-fixing process in the specific FLOSS communities being studied.

In order to tackle this problem, the present study analyses the code base contained within the *comm-central* project (http://hg.mozilla.org/comm-central), a Mercurial Software Configuration Management (SCM) repository of Mozilla components (Thunderbird, SeaMonkey, the Lightning extension and Sunbird). Given the number and ID of each fixed bug, this research evaluates which changes have been performed, and by who, in the process of fixing the specific bug. The objective of this research is to evaluate patterns of bug-fixing activities within this FLOSS community, in order to detect, if any, the most recurrent and relevant scenarios among developers fixing bugs and those seeding the problem in the first place.

This paper makes two main contributions:

1. **Identifying Bug-Fixing and Bug-Seeding Committers:** The detection of those commits that have fixed a bug is crucial to determine the previous changes that took place to *seed* that bug. Using the source code lines that were handled by committers and tracing their history back make possible to know who previously handled those lines. Thus, it is possible to trace the changes in

the SCM that made possible the birth of a potential bug. In addition, it has been detected the existence of exceptional large movements of lines in just one commit what may provoke distortions in the results and were left as open research questions.

2. **Characterization of Bug-Seeding Activity:** Once the bug-seeding commits have been detected, it is also interesting to know how many developers have been involved in those commits that later has been raised as a bug. With this approach, we are able to know the number of people that added or modified a piece of source code before it was detected as an issue by the community.

The paper is organized in the following sections: Section 2 analyzes the related work and the background for the study; Sections 3 and 4 introduce the technique used to extract data from the Mercurial SCM based on the *hg diff* tool. Section 5 presents the main results found after using the proposed method *comm-central*, while Section 6 raises a set of threats to validity. Finally Section 7 concludes the paper with pointers towards further work.

2. BACKGROUND AND RELATED WORK

This section reports on the related work and the existing tool-sets: it is reported here in order to show how this research builds on, compares to or complements existing approaches and results.

This paper uses the *diff* tool to identify changes between revisions: *diff* is provided by several source code management systems, and its basic algorithm has been theoretically and extensively explained (Ukkonen, 1985; Miller & Myers, 1985; Myers, 1986). This tool basically collects two revisions of a file (or revisions of the same directory) and it returns the differences found between them. Its main goal is to look for "plain" differences between two files: however, its implementation contains both a way to identify the "actual" differences between two files, and a facility to ignore "apparent" differences (e.g., spaces, indentations, newlines, etc). The GNU implementation of this algorithm is explained in MacKenzie et al. (2002): this paper uses the "unified" format of the *diff* algorithm to retrieve all the differences between each two revisions of the source code found at the Mercurial repository of the *comm-central* project. Other researchers used the *diff* tool in their approach when retrieving data from FLOSS repositories (specifically CVS and Subversion) (Canfora et al., 2007; Zimmermann et al., 2006).

Previous studies have made use both of SCM repositories and log messages left by developers, as a way to determine whether an observed activity is a bug-fixing process or not. Focus has been given to how developers should know precisely how this is being carried out (i.e., the process) and by whom (i.e., the responsibilities) (Guo et al., 2010). Some authors (Kim et al., 2008; Sliwerski et al., 2005) have worked at this level; however, it has to become clear that some FLOSS communities are more effective than others in documenting whether a commit is fixing an existing bug, or if it is a more generic maintenance activity. The present study is only based on the Mozilla Community, since within this community, it is relatively simple (compared to other communities) to determine if one of its commits is related to a bug in the Bug Tracking Systems. In this community, and within the SCM recorded activities, most of the commits dealing with bug fixes (or related to an open bug report) are tagged with an initial word "bug" or "Bug". In some rare occasions, these have been detected to be generic features and not real bugs. A cross-validation is performed below, in order to visualise the precision and recall of this approximation, and it is shown that the above mismatch represents a minor number of occurrences.

Similarly to previous studies (Kim et al., 2008; Śliwerski et al., 2005), this research is performed at the granularity level of source lines, which provides a way of handling the ambiguity of working with commits. When considering the committer A who fixes a certain bug, and the lines she modifies, some of these lines could have been introduced fully or partially by the same committer, or introduced by different committers without the participation of A (pictured in Figure 1). Extending these two basic scenarios, we could find further scenarios:

- The same set of lines was modified in a previous commit by the same developer a (only);
- The same set of lines was modified in a previous commit by a different developer b (only);
- The same set of lines was modified by more than one developer (a+b+c+...), including the same developer a fixing the bug;

- The same set of lines was modified by more than one developer (b+c+d+...), but excluding the developer fixing the bug;

In terms of relating the bug-fixing process and its responsibilities, some authors have dealt with the idea of who should be fixing a certain bug (Kagdi et al., 2008; Ma et al., 2009) based on previous changes of the same file, or at least slices of the changes introduced in a file. Another approach used to deal with the same problem has been adopted at the level of the bug tracking system. In a study based on the development of Microsoft Windows Vista and Windows 7, it has been found that the number of reports "opened" by one developer and initially "assigned" to her development team tend to be fixed more quickly than bugs that are assigned to another development team (Guo et al., 2010). Finally, it has also been reported that specific FLOSS communi-

Figure 1. Scenarios of committers and lines changed. Lines that are introduced in a given fix time (t-1) are later (t) detected as being part of a bug-fixing commit. Thus, the set of lines that are being handled in (t) could have been previously introduced by the same developer (A), partially introduced by the same developer or introduced by a different developer.

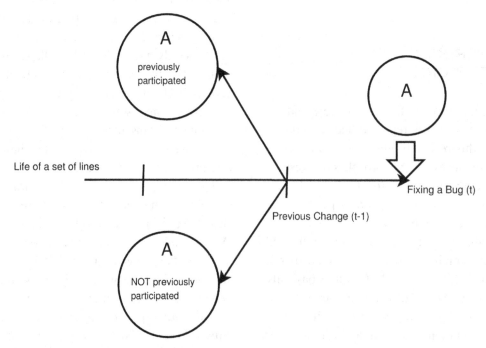

ties try and reinforce a per-contributor sense of responsibility: in highly modular projects (as for instance Moodle or Drupal), for example, it is a shared expectation within the community that the original contributor will support his/her modules (Capiluppi et al., 2010) and keep them in sync with the evolution of the core system (Hao-Yun Huang & Panchal, 2010). Finally, other authors have dealt with the idea of looking for bug-fixing patterns in the source code (Pan et al., 2009) analyzing the different revisions provided by a given SCM system, but focusing on the semantics of the source code. In other words, they are aware of several common fix patterns such as "addition of precondition check" or "different method call to a class instance". However, at the level of the source code, and to the best of our knowledge, no studies aiming to determine if developers that fixed the bug are the same than those who introduced the bug have been undertaken.

3. ASSUMPTIONS AND DEFINITIONS

3.1. Assumptions: SZZ Algorithm

This paper makes use of the SZZ algorithm (Śliwerski et al., 2005), whose main goal is to determine the origin of a bug, by identifying the bug-fixing commits, and by using a *diff* tool. The authors of this algorithm assume that the lines that have been *removed* of *modified* in the bug-fixing commit are the ones where the bug was located. Thus, tracing back the origins of those lines (by means of the *annotate* command in the SCM), the authors could reach the origins of those lines, and admittedly, the origins of the bug. Generally speaking, the first modification or the addition of those *modified* or *removed* lines can be accounted as the origin of that bug. The operationalization of the algorithm used in this paper is slightly different, but based on the same assumption: the lines affected in the process of fixing a bug are the same one that originated or *seeded* that bug.

3.2. Definitions

This study is based on (and could be extended to other) projects which make use of a distributed SCM system called *Mercurial*. For each of the analyzed projects, the log provided by each of the named SCMs was analysed. For this purpose, the definitions used in this empirical case study are the following:

- **Commit (or Revision):** Change to the source code submitted to the SCM system. This updates the current version of the tree directory with a new set of changes. Such changes are generally summarized in a *patch* which is a set of lines with specific information about the affected files, but also about the affected lines.

- **Committer:** Person who has rights to commit to a specific SCM repository, hence allowed to make changes. The Mercurial case presents some peculiarities: the developers working as maintainers and uploading changes to the main branch of the repository are not registered by the Mercurial SCM. Thus, all of the changes are initially considered as uploaded by the original author[1]. Thus, through this paper, the concept of developer, committer or author will be considered as synonyms. Nevertheless, depending on the SCM, those concepts are slightly different.

- **Bug-Fixing Commit:** This is a special type of commit where issues reported by other developers have been fixed. In the comm-central repository this is generally reported in the title of a commit by referencing a "bug" or a "Bug".

- **Line:** This is the basic piece of information of this study and they are generally handled by committers. These lines could be *added* - new line, *modified* - modification of some part of that line and *removed* - there is a deletion of that line.

- **Bug Seeding-Commit:** Given a commit, and the output of the *hg diff* command, it is possible to obtain a complete picture of the lines that were added, modified or removed, but also about the committer, the date and which files were handled. This is necessary both to track which lines have been changed for fixing a bug, and to track which committers have provided changes to the same set of lines in previous commits. Figure 2 shows how the latter identification has been achieved. In the example file (far right), three sets of lines can be recognised ("set of lines 1", "set of lines 2" and "set of lines 3"): the first two sets are affected by changes, the third has been unchanged throughout.

Tracking back the history of each set in the database, we are able to know that "set of lines 1" was added in commit number 1 and then modified in commit number 5. With respect to "set of lines 2", they were added in commit number 5 and later modified in commit number 7. With respect to the authorship, we know that the "set of lines 1" was added by a developer named A. The modification of "set of lines 1" and the addition of the "set of lines 2" was done by the same committer, named C and finally, in commit 7 changes were made on the "set of lines 2" by developer C. In this specific figure, other commits might have happened, but they have not modified or removed the set of lines we are interested in. Specifically, commit number 2, 3, 4 and 6 took place, but none of them modified the studied sets of lines.

4. EMPIRICAL APPROACH AND OPERATIONALIZATION

As the main goal of this research, this paper aims to identify and characterise the bug-fixing and bug-seeding activities in FLOSS communities. From a managerial perspective, the bug-seeding activity could be useful to clarify how and when the buggy source code has been introduced into the repository, how developers deal with this, and which effort needs to be applied and by who. In addition, specific sub-questions were formulated to achieve the main goal of the paper:

1. How are the bugs in *comm-central* recorded and referred to by developers? What is the accuracy and consistency of recording such bug-fixing information?
   - **Rationale:** From the maintenance point of view, it is necessary to study how the community records which issues have being fixed. The empirical approach used in this paper is based on the information provided by the log message left by the developers when fixing a bug. This information depends on the analysed community (i.e., Mozilla), and it could be recorded differently in other communities.
2. How can one define the *bug-fixing* and *bug-seeding* activities when tracking the same set of lines?
   - **Rationale:** This question is related to the detection of bug-seeding commits that later were classified as "buggy" by the community. And more specifically, how they are detected by means of the differences found between each pair of revisions in the source code.
3. Are there specific events in the activity log that could impede the correct tracking of such set of lines? How to avoid that such events interfere with the tracking of a given set of lines?
   - **Rationale:** Some events in the community could force to move huge quantities of source code to another repository (e.g., in case of migrations), refactoring (e.g., when changing loads of methods names), license requirements (e.g., when migrating to

another license) or others. These factors can cause large peaks to be visualised in the evolutionary trends, that could artificially skew the results.

4. Are there recurring patterns of bug-fixing among the developers of the *comm-central* community?

  ○ **Rationale:** This questions aims to study the behaviour of developers when fixing bugs and try to look for specific patterns of bug-seeding activity. It is still not well understood how bugs are being introduced in the source code and if those developers that usually introduce issues are the same ones in charge of fixing them. Another interesting question is the one related to how many people are usually introducing changes to the same piece of source code that later is found to be "buggy".

4.1. Understanding the *diff* Output

Past research studies have focused on source code lines in two ways, either by using the source code management system (SCM) hosting the project, or by first downloading the source code from the repository, and then using the *diff* tool provided by the operating systems. In the first case, it is necessary to download the SCM and later use the diff tool provided within, but most researchers avoid that mostly due to the bottleneck represented by the network. In the latter, one has to download the source code for all the revisions of all the files contained in a software system. Using a distributed SCM such as Git or Mercurial (instead of a traditional SCM, as CVS or SVN), the bottleneck of the network is removed and the corresponding analysis becomes much faster. As documented in Section 6, this approach still holds some limitations that have to be addressed in the threats to validity.

A diff is a summary of the changes undertaken between two files, and stored in a SCM system. The diff command compares the files line by line and summarizes the differences in a specific format. Below, the partial output of a unified diff format between two commits (12 and 13) in the *comm-central* repository is shown. This example is not specific from the source code since this is a special file to build the project, however it is simple enough to be easily understood.

The *hg diff* command, by default, shows the diff between two revisions using the unified format: the diff format starts with two-lines header where the original file name is preceded by −−− and the new file is preceded by +++. After this, there are one or more change hunks (usually named as *chunks*) which contain information related to the differences in the file. Those lines which were added starts with a + character, those removed starts with a − character and those which were neither added, nor removed starts with a space character " ". Finally, if a line is modified, this is

Box 1.

```
diff -r f1...1d -r 0b...f7 suite/
build.mk
--- a/suite/build.mk Fri Jul 25
11:32:27 2008
+++ b/suite/build.mk Fri Jul 25
11:51:57 2008
@@ -43,6 +43,10 @@

 TIERS += app

+ifdef MOZ_COMPOSER
+tier_app_dirs += editor/ui
+endif
+
 ifdef MOZ_CALENDAR
 MOZ_EXTENSIONS += webdav
 endif
```

represented as added and removed, so this changes will appear adjacent to one another. Thus, if a set of adjacent lines are modified, the old revision of the lines will show several lines beginning with −, adjacent to the new revision of the lines, and beginning with +. In the previous example, four lines have been added in a file called "build.mk". The values between "@ @" represents the position of those lines in that file before and after the change). For more information it is recommended to read the reference MacKenzie et al. (2002).

4.2. Retrieving Information from *diff* Files

A freely available tool has been used to retrieve information from consists of several steps that are specified in the following list:

1. **Downloading the SCM:** The BlameMe tool is specifically designed to work with Git or Mercurial repositories. These are distributed SCM and provide all of the change history locally. This is an advantage if compared to other centralized SCMs such as CVS or SVN since there is an actual and huge difference in terms of time (avoiding the bottleneck represented by the network access).
2. **Collecting Commits:** As seen above, the very *hg* command provides a special command to check differences between two revisions: *hg diff*. This has been used to interact between the program and their Mercurial repository.
3. **Parsing the Revisions:** The tool is launched using the previously downloaded repository and storing all the differences in a MySQL database. For this purpose, each of the lines is stored together with its reference to its file and the position in that file (specifically, there is a list per file, and each node is the position in that file for a given line). If a new set of lines are detected to be added or removed, those are directly added in the specified position (explained in Section 4.1).

4.3. Case Study

The proposed method has been applied to describe the bug-fixing process at the level of source lines using the *comm-central* project and its Mercurial repository. As mentioned, this repository contains the source code of Thunderbird, SeaMonkey, Lightning extension and Sunbird [2].

The use of the Mercurial repository (after the migration from CVS) started on the 22th of July, 2008 and it has been studied till the 20th of July, 2010 (i.e., two years of source code history). Considering the whole life of the project until the start of this study, 5,982 commits were studied and the differences between revisions have been stored in a MySQL database. In this database, we have stored information of 4,973,038 changes to the source code regarding added, modified and removed lines.

The case studies presented in this paper are based on the differences between two revisions of the source code, and specifically focused on the bug-fixing commits. The commits studied are 2,969 out of an overall 5,982 commits; the total amount of lines considered are 2,912,866.

5. RESULTS

This section provides the results of the empirical study performed on the comm-central repository, in three parts: first, the study of how to properly detect bug-fixing commits is reported, detailing on the precision and recall in such process. Second, the issue of dealing with large commits is presented and addressed. Third, the approach of detecting bug-fixing and bug-seeding committers is clustered in several scenarios, and finally the results on each scenarios are proposed.

5.1. Identifying Bug-Fixing Commits

This first part of the research aims to validate the log messages provided by the *comm-central* community, and to understand the consistency and reliability of their records with regards to bug-fixing activities. To achieve this purpose, we developed an empirical approach and then checked how many false positives and false negatives we obtained from applying it. The approach used is as follows:

1. Given 3,000 bug-fixing commits, and a confidence level of 95%, the random sample was sized in 100 commits. From each of those, the log message was retrieved and the log message inspected.
2. A simple heuristic, based on the observation of the log message and used by another paper analyzing the Mozilla community (Kim et al., 2008) was used. This heuristic consists of the selection, as commits fixing an issue, those fitting the following regular expression: . This regular expression will filter all of the commit messages which start with the key word "Bug" or "bug".
3. The log message of those random selections of commits was manually inspected to evaluate whether they refer to real bugs, either checking the underlying source code or by parsing the relative Bug Tracking System.

In order to evaluate the precision and recall of such approximation, the constituent parts are as follows:

- **(TP) True Positive:** 78
- **(FP) False Positive:** 7
- **(TN) True Negatives:** 6
- **(FN) False Negatives:** 9
- **Total Commits:** 100

Therefore we evaluated:

- **Positive Predictive Value:** $TP/(TP+FP)=$ 78/(78+7)=91,7%
- **Negative Predictive Value:** $TN/(FN+TN)$ =40%

- **Sensitivity:** $TP/(TP+FN)$=78/78+9=89,65%
- **Specificity:** $TN/(FP+TN)$=6/7+6=46,15%

Since the *Precision* actually coincides with the positive predictive, and the *Recall* coincides with the sensitivity, we conclude that *precision*=91,7% and *recall*=89,65%. One further aspect to notice is that out of 100 random commits, 85 have the word "Bug" or "bug" in their title, and 76 out of 100 are actually containing code that deals with a bug. The implications of this initial finding are discussed later.

5.2. Dealing with Very Large Commits

As reported in previous studies, software systems, and most noticeably FLOSS systems, display at times high (and isolated) peaks of activity. In some specific cases, it has been possible to detect a very large amount of source lines (e.g., more of 80% of the overall system) being moved within FLOSS projects (Canfora et al., 2007; Fernández-Ramil et al., 2009; MacLean et al., 2010; Hindle et al., 2008). This means that in some changes, one can detect huge changes reaching million of lines. From a maintenance or evolutionary point of view, this is hardly accountable as a maintenance activity. However, this problem has not been taken into account by Kim et al. (2008), whose analysis is one of the pillars for this study.

Also in the study of the *comm-central* repository, it has been found that a small number of commits (no more than 10% of the total set) handles several thousands (in some cases hundreds of thousands) of lines in just one commit. Apart from exceptional cases where developers indeed modified a vast amount of source lines, the peaks could also be caused by automatic bots, changes in the licenses, or by accidental removal and addition of source code. As an example of such distortions, Figure 3 shows the number of aggregated number of removed lines[3]. The figure depicts a situation of common removal of lines, but in some specific commits, we can see how suddenly a large set of lines is removed (for example, close to id 723 or 4,200).

In order to deal with such distortions, the commits fully or partially affected by those changes were removed from the sample: given an overall number of 2,912,866 lines and 2,969 commits detected in the bug-fixing process, the sample was therefore reduced to 731,941 lines and 1,747 commits. In summary, the four largest commits (IDs 0; 1,002; 817; 5,213 and 5,383[4]), and the lines affected, were removed from the sample.

5.3. Identifying *Bug-Fixing* and *Bug-Seeding* Committers

In order to detect the bug-fixing committers, and the developers dealing in the past with the same section of code (as per the scenarios in Figure 1), this paper uses the same assumption formulated

in Kim et al. (2008): in a bug-fixing commit, one has to consider only the "set of lines" removed or modified in that commit (Figure 2), instead of the whole file, or set of files, committed in the transaction.

This algorithm is named as the "*SZZ* algorithm" and fully detailed in Śliwerski et al. (2005): considering the set of lines modified in a bug-fixing commit, the algorithm focuses on the previous commit in time (i.e., "one step back") where all the lines in such set were modified: in this way, it is possible to obtain the latest commit where each line was previously modified (Figure 2), and correlating it with their actual committer (Figure 1). The assumption of the algorithm, also used in this paper, is that the bug was actually introduced in that previous commit.

Using this approach, the total number of developers dealing with either bug-fixing commits or bug-seeding commits were evaluated. Overall, 450 different committers have committed once

Figure 2. Identifying previous changes and committers

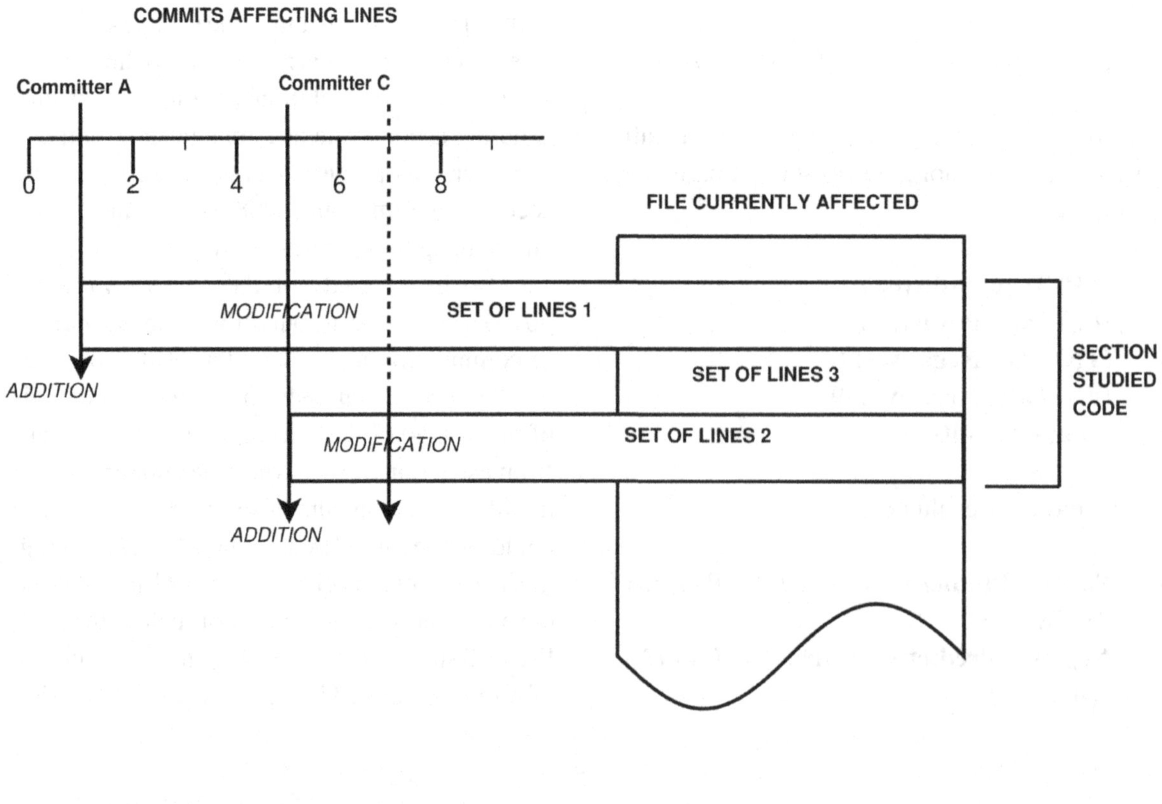

Figure 3. Aggregated number of removed lines detected in bug-fixing commits

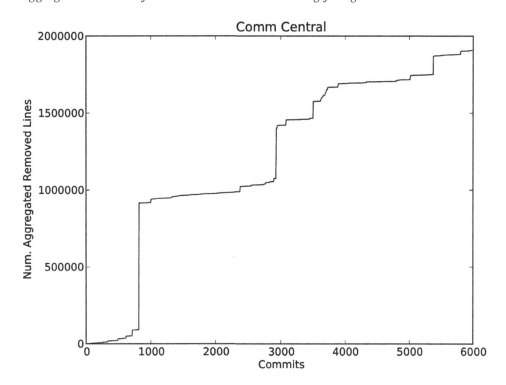

to the Mercurial repository: of those, 287 are authors of at least one bug-fixing commit, and 383 are authors of at least one bug-seeding commit. This seems to negate that specific developers are dedicated to fix bugs: in addition, it is worth to mention that the Mozilla community has identified the Thunderbird project as "core" project, in which senior developers will peer review the commits made by others. This may distort the dataset used in this paper and open another set of questions, for instance linking those policies with the outcomes of the project.

In order to visualise at first the summary of results, Figure 4 shows the density chart of the bug-seeding developers: since most of the values are located to the left-side of the chart, only 1 or 2 developers are involved in 80% of the cases (1,392 out of 1,747 commits overall). More specifically, 1,035 bug-fixing commits (60% of the overall sample) involve just one developer previously seeding the lines, but only 7% of the total seeded lines (50k out of 747k lines).

Based on this initial set of results, the two scenarios shown in Figure 1 were further divided into three more scenarios: one previous developer (covering a 60% of the sample), two previous developers (covering an additional 20% of the sample) and the rest of them (covering the rest of the 20% of the sample). This provides a final list of six scenarios:

S1: Bug-fixing and bug-seeding commits made by committer A;

S2: Bug-fixing commit made by A, bug-seeding commit made by B;

S3: Bug-fixing commit made by A, bug-seeding commit made by A and B only;

S4: Bug-fixing commit made by A, bug-seeding commit made by B and C only;

S5: Bug-fixing commit made by A, bug-seeding commit made by A, B and others;

S6: Bug-fixing commit made by A, bug-seeding commit made by B, C and others;

Figure 4. Density chart of number of committers involved in changes at (t-1) to lines bug-fixed at t

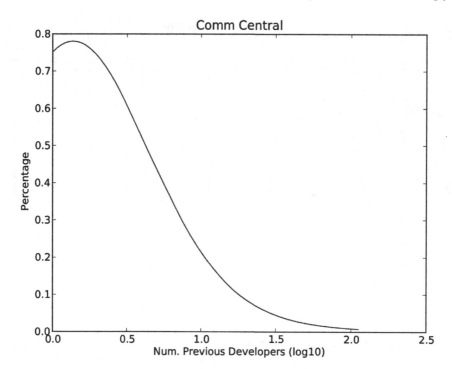

5.4. Analysis of Scenarios

Scenarios S1 and S2

Table 1 focuses the analysis on the bug-seeding commits by at most one committer, which correspond for some 60% of all the bug-fixing commits. The summary in the table distinguishes whether the author of the bug-fixing commit is the same committer (*Same Comm.* column, e.g., scenario S1) or a different one (*Diff. Dev.* column, e.g., scenario S2) who seeded those buggy lines. Results show that, in terms of developers involved, the bug-fixing process is performed by different

Table 1. One previous committer written down in the method part

	Overall	Same Comm.	Diff. Comm.
Commits	1,035	62	973
Lines	50,078	973	49,348

committers from those seeding the bug: for only 6% of these commits (62 out of 1,035) the bug-fixer is the same and the only one involved in the bug-seeding activity (e.g., scenario S1). In all the other cases, a different committer A is involved in the fixing of lines that were seeded by B (e.g., scenario S2).

Scenarios S3 and S4

When considering a maximum of two bug-seeding committers, it was found that only 357 commits comply with the requirements of Scenarios S3 and S4. Table 2 shows the results differentiated for S3 and S4: 43 out of 357 commits were seeded fully or partially by the same committer who finally fixed the bug. In terms of lines handled, 6,834 lines were co-changed with another committer and submitted by the same committer A, while 218 were co-changed with A but committed by another committer B. These results provide another point of view of the community: generally speaking, it

Table 2. Commits: two previous committers

	Overall	S3 (A+B)	S4 (B+C)
Commits	357	43	314
Lines	15,581	7,052 (6,834 + 218)	8,529

Table 3. Rest of the cases: from 3 to 10 previous committers

Num. Previous Committers	
S5 (A+B+...)	S6 (B+C+...)
3_27 (773 + 3,011)	128 (29,246)
4_11 (85 + 441)	59 (5,010)
5_9 (148 + 696)	24 (1,840)
6_3 (9 + 253)	21 (2,126)
7_3 (30 + 13,089)	12 (2,844)
8_3 (79 + 5,207)	4 (141)
9_5 (30 + 1,328)	8 (3,575)
10_2 (11 + 183)	6 (1,422)

seems that most of the commits where two people have previously participated were mostly handled by people different from those who fixed the bug. However, in 43 commits, the same committer was found to participate in the changes. This raises another question related to the quantity of source code handled by other committers than the one who fixed the bug. In that case, we realized that just a 3% of that source code (218 lines) was really handled by someone different: this shows similar results to the S1 and S2 scenarios, where just one committer was found.

As visible in the same table, most of the bug-seeding commits are by other two developers (B+C), but only half of the source code is handled in the process.

Scenarios S5 and S6

The last two scenarios comprise the commits with up to 10 previous committers handling the source code. Table 3 shows the number of committers found for each commit. For instance, for the first row, the values show that there are 27 commits where the same committer fixes and seeds the bug together with others (Scenario 5), while there are 128 commits where that committer did not participate at all (and different people seeded those lines). Albeit more committers could be possible, the threshold of 10 committers reaches 98% of the total sample of commits analyzed (1,717 out of 1,747 commits). Figure 5 (left and right) shows the absolute and relative number of commits for the values presented in Table 3. In Figure 5 left, the x-axis are divided by the number of previous developers involved in the set of lines that in the

current commit were modified or removed. The y-axis represents the number of absolute commits detected. We can see how Figure 5 (top) shows that most of the commits were previously handled by people totally different from the ones who were later dealing with the bug-fixing commit. Figure 5 (bottom) adds extra information in order to check the relative percentages of such values, and to conclude that, in all of the cases, more than a 60% of the total bug-seeding commits had a different committer than the one who made the bug-fixing commit. Using relative numbers, in eight out of ten combinations, the second set of data (commits fixed by A, but not seeded by A) is the most general.

5.5. Finer Granularity: Lines Affected

In order to study the results at a finer granularity, Figure 6 uses the lines to complement the above results. Depending on the number of bug-seeding committers, this figure shows the number of lines seeded in the various scenarios: for each number of previouscommitters detected (x-axis), the number of seeded lines by the same committer who fixed that bug is shown.

The notation "Same Commmit and Same Committers," represents the relative number of

Figure 5. Scenarios and their relevance: S5 refers to those commits where the same committer who is fixing the issue, previously participated. S6 refers to those commits where that committer did not previously participate

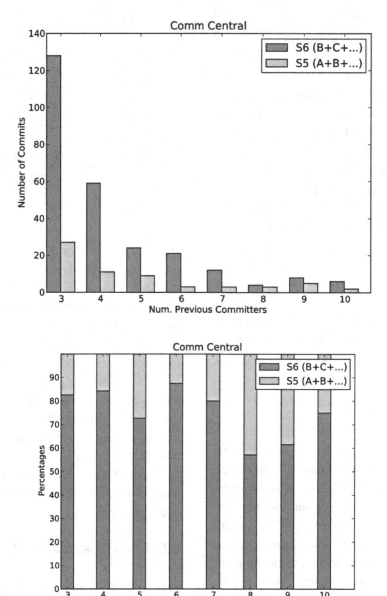

lines that were also previously handled by the same committer who fixed the issue (Scenarios S1, S3 and S5 - A also previously participated). With the notation "same Commit and Diff Committers" the figure shows the Scenarios S1, S3 and S5, but discarding the lines previously modified by the bug-fixing committer. Finally, the notation "Rest of them", is the aggregation of

the rest of Scenarios (S2, S4 and S6), where the committer who fixed the bug did not previously participate at all.

As a results from this figure, it can be seen how for all of the cases (except in two previous developers), the committer who has fixed a bug has not participated at all in seeding that bug.

Figure 6. Scenarios and their relevance – Lines affected

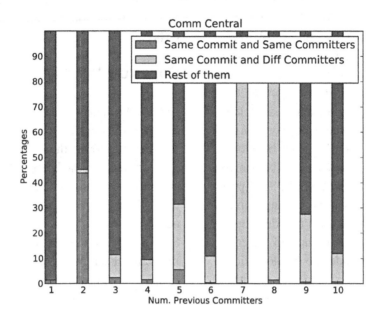

5.6. Discussion

The analysis of the Mozilla community, and of the *comm-central* project, has shown few interesting insights: given the specificity of this community, and the process that was put in place at the maintenance level, generalising such findings could be problematic. Nonetheless, these observations provide an initial set of results to characterise the bug-fixing and bug-seeding activities in the Mozilla community, to be used as a baseline to be compared against other FLOSS projects.

- **Overall Bug-Fixing Activity:** It has been found that some 50% of all the commits are detected as fixing bugs: considering that the precision of detecting bug-fixing commits proved substantially high, this is an impressive amount. Nonetheless, this value is largely dependent on the policy applied by the Mozilla community when submitting changes to the source code: this policy alone could lead to an overrating or underrating of the results.

- **Bug-Fixing and Territoriality:** The main result found, that bug-seeding committers are rarely also bug-fixing committers, somehow conflicts with what is found in the FLOSS literature: strong "territorial" developers, and specific responsibilities of the developers over their source code have been observed from previous works (German, 2004; Capiluppi et al., 2010). However, it seems that the concepts of "source code territoriality" [5] and "bug-fixing territoriality" are based on different assumptions: for the vast majority, bugs are fixed by other developers than the ones who introduced or seeded such bugs.

- **Bug-Fixing and Individual Roles:** Regarding the bug-seeding activity, it was found that each piece of source code modified in a bug-fixing commit is previously modified mostly by one developer. From a system perspective, this reflects the result that many frequency distributions in software are power-law (e.g., many changes are handled only once, and by one developer, while few changes are handled more often and by several developers); from a managerial perspective, this result shows that developers usually fix bugs that were introduced by other developers. This could either reflect the presence of specific bug-fixing developers, or a more shared activity of bug-fixing, where newcomers tend to fix bugs left open by other developers (Ye et al., 2004). Furthermore, focusing on Scenarios 3 or 4, there is a 80% of probability that a selected bug-fixing commit was introduced by at most two developers. This again shows that in most of the cases, pieces of source code are by definition a valuable piece of knowledge. Some authors have dealt with the idea of *concepts* when developing software, and it seems that working at the level of methods or functions is the best way to understand previous changes made by others. A possibility here is to match pieces of source code and methods to check this hypothesis.

- **Bug-Seeding and Movement of Code:** At the granularity of commits, Scenarios 5 and 6 have shown that bug-seeding commits were handled by several (even dozens of) committers. A possible explanation could be related to the observed huge movements of lines in bug-fixing commits: it could be found that for a given commit, several people previously participated in such a bug-seeding commit.

6. THREATS TO VALIDITY

Generally speaking, any empirical study like this is bound to many threats to their validity. It has been claimed that studying FLOSS projects from an empirical point of view could raise several threats that should be considered (Fernandez-Ramil et al.,

2008). Among them, we can find those related to the data extraction, the granularity of the study or how mature is the selected projects.

Construct Validity

At first, the heuristic used to obtain bugs from the SCM log messages is far from be perfect. As seen in Kim et al. (2008), the selection of bugs (even for those projects studied in the Mozilla community) are based in a corpus and some other semantic data which improve the data obtained. Also, as addressed by Chen et al. (2004), analyzing the SCM logs could be error prone. However, after manually checking 100 commits with the heuristic used, the percentages of error were very low. This is due to the selection of a project from the Mozilla community which generally shows good practices by precisely pointing to the bug tracking system for almost each change in the source code.

Second, most of the work is based on the analysis by the *diff* tool provided by the Mercurial SCM. Although this is a reliable tool, we have detected some limitations in the use of *diff* to retrieve the authorship and other related data. As addressed by Canfora et al. (2007) and Zimmermann et al. (2006), we could obtain wrong indications in the number of actual changes in the source code after a commit. One of the main reasons for those changes could be some movements of data from one directory to another, or some merges from different branches. In order to deal with them, most of the big spikes, as aforementioned, were removed.

Finally, it is worth to mention that the large additions of lines are an issue which has not been resolved in this paper. Future revisions following a commit affecting thousands of lines may lead to the wrong conclusions, by showing that most of the work was done by just one committer, although this could be just a distortion of few commits.

Internal Validity

The tools and script used could present some minor bugs that may affect the results. However, they have followed a validation process what makes the results reliable enough. After the initial development and after several tests, a final manual study of several commits was carried out and in all of the cases the comparison between the information in the database and the SCM matched in a 100% of the cases. However, the tools used could raise some errors in the future that could not have been taken into account yet.

External Validity

The selected project is not large enough to represent the overall number of FLOSS projects. However, we present a first initial step to describe the bug-fixing process based on the Mercurial SCM. As further work, the authors want to extend the analysis at least to the whole Mozilla community.

7. CONCLUSION AND FURTHER WORK

This paper has presented an empirical analysis of the *comm-central* FLOSS community, in order to detect whether the bug-fixing activity among developers could be modeled into patterns and recurring scenarios. This community was selected for the consistency and reliability of their messages into the SCM repository, in particular the messages dealing with the bug-fixing activities. With these characteristics, this community and their data can be leveraged to shed important hints on how FLOSS developers proceed to the very needed corrective maintenance, and more importantly, whether the bug-fixing committers are the same who contributed to introduce and seed the bug in the first place.

As a first result, we could confirm the reliability and consistency in referencing the bug-fixing commits within the *comm-central* community, with a precision larger than 90%: this produces very accurate results in terms of tracking the actual bug-fixing committers, and the lines that were modified in the process. It also forms a basis of good practices that will be leveraged in future works when studying the larger Mozilla community (an order of magnitude larger in terms of activity and committers).

Secondly, we proposed a method to define and track both the bug-fixing and the bug-seeding committers: given the set of lines affected by the bug-fixing commit, the set of previous revisions was studied in order to detect which committers were actually "seeding" such bug without contributing to its removal or fixing.

Thirdly, we proposed an approach to avoid the distortion of spurious data: it was observed that the *comm-central* community produces high peaks of activity (MacLean et al., 2010; Canfora et al., 2007; Fernandez-Ramil et al., 2008). This problem was been raised by Kim et al. (2008): what we did to tackle the issue was to remove the five largest commits, which alone were responsible of over 2M lines modified, added or removed. We proposed that researchers should remove at least three main cases: 1- Initial import of commits, 2- Huge removal followed by addition of lines of code, 3- Huge addition followed by removal of lines. In all of those cases, the results could be directly influenced.

Furthermore, we proposed to use the *diff* provided by the SCM as a way to let us know authorship at the granularity of a line: other works such as Canfora et al., (2007), Zimmermann et al. (2006), and Kim et al. (2008) have used another different approach to deal with the idea of following the life of a line. Several difficulties emerge when trying to track the whole lifecycle of these lines, but not at the level of going a step back in their history. Thus, using this tool could be a faster and more effective way of determining the authorship of each line.

Finally, with respect to the results, it was shown how the corrective maintenance is being carried out by people on the *comm-central* community. We have detected that less than 5% of the bug-fixing commits were handled by who first introduced the changes or "seeded" the bug. With respect to these results, in most of the cases the committers involved in the bug-fixing process are not the same as those initially seeding the bug. These results are vastly different and unexpected if compared with corporate software development, where developers "opening" a bug are most likely to also be responsible for its fixing and closure.

As further work, the authors would like to address two open questions (related to the GQM approach) that could be easily answered using the same dataset. First of all, the central idea of the paper is related to the fixing process and if the committers are fixing their own bugs. However, we have not studied if those committers are aware that in some cases they have been introducing errors in the source code, or at least the seed of a future bug. Checking how many of them have been working in a given time-window after the detection of a bug could provide another insight of the bug-fixing process.

Another similar idea is related to the seed of the bug. We have seen how given a commit fixing a bug we could trace when the involved source code was previously added or modified and, thus, who was the "bug-seeder". However we do not fully understand the causes. For instance, we could trace if that developer modified a piece of source where she usually does not work, if the commit modified a file that was lately several times modified, if a committer submitted a change in a programming language not usual to her or some other possibilities.

ACKNOWLEDGMENT

The authors would like to thank Prof Cornelia Boldyreff for the extensive comments on the paper. In addition, this work has been partially funded by the European Commission, under the ALERT project (ICT-258098).

REFERENCES

Adams, P. J., Capiluppi, A., & Boldyreff, C. (2009). Coordination and productivity issues in free software: The role of brooks' law. In *Proceedings of the International Conference on Software Maintenance* (pp. 319-328). Washington, DC: IEEE Computer Society.

Canfora, G., Cerulo, L., & Penta, M. D. (2007). Identifying changed source code lines from version repositories. In *Proceedings of the Fourth International Workshop on Mining Software Repositories* (p. 14). Washington, DC: IEEE Computer Society.

Capiluppi, A., Baravalle, A., & Heap, N. (2010). Open standards and e-learning: the role of open source software. In *Proceedings of the 6th International Conference on Open Source Systems,* Notre Dame, IN.

Chen, K., Schach, S. R., Yu, L., Offutt, J., & Heller, G. Z. (2004). Open-source change logs. *Empirical Software Engineering, 9,* 197–210. doi:10.1023/B:EMSE.0000027779.70556.d0

Fernández-Ramil, J., Izquierdo-Cortazar, D., & Mens, T. (2009). What does it take to develop a million lines of open source code? In *Proceedings of the 5th International Conference on Open Source Systems* (pp. 170-184).

Fernandez-Ramil, J., Lozano, A., Wermelinger, M., & Capiluppi, A. (2008). Empirical studies of open source evolution. In Mens, T., & Demeyer, S. (Eds.), *Software evolution: State-of-the-art and research advances* (pp. 263–288). Berlin, Germany: Springer-Verlag.

German, D. M. (2004). Using software trails to reconstruct the evolution of software: Research articles. *Journal of Software Maintenance and Evolution: Research and Practice—Analyzing the Evolution of Large-Scale Software, 16*(6), 367-384.

Goldman, R., & Gabriel, R. (2004). *Innovation happens elsewhere: How and why a company should participate in open source.* San Francisco, CA: Morgan Kaufmann.

Guo, P. J., Zimmermann, T., Nagappan, N., & Murphy, B. (2010). Characterizing and predicting which bugs get fixed: an empirical study of Microsoft windows. In *Proceedings of the 32nd ACM/IEEE International Conference on Software Engineering* (pp. 495-504). New York, NY: ACM.

Hao-Yun Huang, Q. L., & Panchal, J. H. (2010). Analysis of the structure and evolution of an open-source community. In *Proceedings of the ASME International Design Engineering Technical Conferences & Computers and Information in Engineering Conference.*

Hindle, A., German, D. M., & Holt, R. (2008). What do large commits tell us? A taxonomical study of large commits. In *Proceedings of the International Working Conference on Mining Software Repositories* (pp. 99-108). New York, NY: ACM.

Izquierdo-Cortazar, D., Robles, G., Ortega, F., & Gonzalez-Barahona, J. M. (2009). Using software archaeology to measure knowledge loss in software projects due to developer turnover. In *Proceedings of the Hawaii International Conference on System Sciences* (pp. 1-10). Washington, DC: IEEE Computer Society.

Kagdi, H. H., Hammad, M., & Maletic, J. I. (2008). Who can help me with this source code change? In *Proceedings of the 24th IEEE International Conference on Software Maintenance* (pp. 157-166). Washington, DC: IEEE Computer Society.

Kim, S., Whitehead, E. J., & Zhang, Y. (2008). Classifying software changes: Clean or buggy? *IEEE Transactions on Software Engineering, 34*(2), 181–196. doi:10.1109/TSE.2007.70773

Koch, S. (2009). Exploring the effects of source-forge.net coordination and communication tools on the efficiency of open source projects using data envelopment analysis. *Empirical Software Engineering, 14*(4), 397–417. doi:10.1007/s10664-008-9086-4

Ma, D., Schuler, D., Zimmermann, T., & Sillito, J. (2009). Expert recommendation with usage expertise. In *Proceedings of the International Conference on Software Maintenance* (pp. 535-538). Washington, DC: IEEE Computer Society.

MacKenzie, D., Eggert, P., & Stallman, R. (2002). *Comparing and merging files with GNU diff and patch.* London, UK: Network Theory.

MacLean, A. C., Pratt, L. J., Krein, J. L., & Knutson, C. D. (2010). Trends that affect temporal analysis using sourceforge data. In *Proceedings of the 5th International Workshop on Public Data about Software Development* (p. 6).

Miller, W., & Myers, E. W. (1985). A file comparison program. *Software, Practice & Experience, 15*(11), 1025–1040. doi:10.1002/spe.4380151102

Mockus, A., Fielding, R. T., & Herbsleb, J. D. (2002). Two case studies of open source software development: Apache and Mozilla. *ACM Transactions on Software Engineering and Methodology, 11*(3), 309–346. doi:10.1145/567793.567795

Myers, E. W. (1986). An o(nd) difference algorithm and its variations. *Algorithmica, 1,* 251–266. doi:10.1007/BF01840446

Pan, K., Kim, S., & Whitehead, E. J. Jr. (2009). Toward an understanding of bug fix patterns. *Empirical Software Engineering, 14*(3), 286–315. doi:10.1007/s10664-008-9077-5

Robles, G., & González-Barahona, J. M. (2006). Contributor turnover in libre software projects. In *Proceedings of the IFIP Open Source Software Conference* (Vol. 203, pp. 273-286).

Robles, G., González-Barahona, J. M., & Guervós, J. J. M. (2006). Beyond source code: The importance of other artifacts in software development (a case study). *Journal of Systems and Software, 79*(9), 1233–1248. doi:10.1016/j.jss.2006.02.048

Śliwerski, J., Zimmermann, T., & Zeller, A. (2005). When do changes induce fixes? In *Proceedings of the International Workshop on Mining Software Repositories* (pp. 1-5). New York, NY: ACM.

Ukkonen, E. (1985). Algorithms for approximate string matching. *Information and Control, 64*(1-3), 100–118. doi:10.1016/S0019-9958(85)80046-2

Ye, Y., Nakakoji, K., Yamamoto, Y., & Kishida, K. (2004). The co-evolution of systems and communities in Free and Open Source software development. In Koch, S. (Ed.), *Free/Open Source software development* (pp. 59–82). Hershey, PA: Idea Group. doi:10.4018/978-1-59140-369-2.ch003

Zimmermann, T., Kim, S., Zeller, A., & Whitehead, E. J., Jr. (2006). Mining version archives for co-changed lines. In *Proceedings of the International Workshop on Mining Software Repositories* (pp. 72-75). New York, NY: ACM.

ENDNOTES

[1] For more information regarding this issue, the Mercurial website offers a set of third part extensions where this issue could be solved: http://mercurial.selenic.com/wiki/UsingExtensions

[2] However, as addressed in https://developer.mozilla.org/en/comm-central, this only includes a subset of the code required to build those projects.

[3] This figure only shows those commits where at least one line was removed.

[4] It should be noticed that the commits listed here are real commits, while the aforementioned, 723 or 4,200 are ids and they do not correspond to real revision numbers in the SCM.

[5] Pieces of source code (i.e., methods or files) managed by only one developer.

This work was previously published in the International Journal of Open Source Software and Processes, Volume 3, Issue 2, edited by Stefan Koch, pp. 23-42, copyright 2011 by IGI Publishing (an imprint of IGI Global).

Chapter 6
Tool Assisted Analysis of Open Source Projects:
A Multi-Faceted Challenge

M.M. Mahbubul Syeed
Tampere University of Technology, Finland

Imed Hammouda
Tampere University of Technology, Finland

Timo Aaltonen
Nokia Research Center, Finland

Tarja Systä
Tampere University of Technology, Finland

ABSTRACT

Open Source Software (OSS) is currently a widely adopted approach to developing and distributing software. OSS code adoption requires an understanding of the structure of the code base. For a deeper understanding of the maintenance, bug fixing and development activities, the structure of the developer community also needs to be understood, especially the relations between the code and community structures. This, in turn, is essential for the development and maintenance of software containing OSS code. This paper proposes a method and support tool for exploring the relations of the code base and community structures of OSS projects. The method and proposed tool, Binoculars, rely on generic and reusable query operations, formal definitions of which are given in the paper. The authors demonstrate the applicability of Binoculars with two examples. The authors analyze a well-known and active open source project, FFMpeg, and the open source version of the IaaS cloud computing project Eucalyptus.

INTRODUCTION

Open Source Software (OSS) is currently a widely adopted approach to developing and distributing software. Successful open source projects are typically complex, both from the point of view of the code base and with respect to the developer and

user community. Such a project may consist of a wide range of components, coming with a large number of versions reflecting their development and evolution history. While it is a challenge to acquire knowledge from developers and users due to their distributed nature, open source development and user communities often produce a rich software repository as a byproduct. In addition to source code and other software artifacts, there

DOI: 10.4018/978-1-4666-2937-0.ch006

are repositories containing other sources of information such as bug reports, mailing lists, and revision history logs.

A variety of tools and techniques have been proposed to study open source projects. However, most of these techniques suffer from fragmentation and lack of synergies. For instance, many tools apply reverse engineering techniques to study the software side of OSS (Knab, Pinzger, & Bernstein, 2006; Zhou & Davis, 2005). Other works have considered social network analysis techniques to study the social model of OSS (Martinez-Romo, Robles, Ortuo-Perez, & Gonzalez-Barahona, 2008; Kamei, Matsumoto, Maeshima, Onishi, Ohira, & Matsumoto, 2008).

We argue that the separation between the two is artificial. The dimensions are complementary, not discrete categories. They can be used together to provide a lot of useful information. To make a decision about using OSS as a part of a software product to be developed, it is essential to be able to understand the role of the developer community in the development and maintenance of different parts of the OSS code base. This would also help in estimating and planning the future development and maintenance activities of the software product. For instance, understanding the relations of the code and developer community structures helps in understanding where the expertise lay within the developer community, which in turn helps in deciding who to contact concerning issues related to a specific part of the OSS code base.

In this paper we address such challenges as follows: first, a compact and extensible metamodel is proposed which captures both the code base and the community dimension of OSS projects; second, a set of reusable formal descriptions of operations are given, which allows the relationships between the code structure and the community structure to be queried and third, a tool, Binoculars, corresponding to both the metamodel and the defined operations is implemented to study the feasibility of our approach. The tool, Binoculars is able to (a) merge a community view with source code views; (b) provide different perspectives to view the data presented in the form of a graph. This feature can be used, for example, to identify and study the groups of developers working with the same (or related) code fragments, or to study whether communication structures of the developing community conform to the architecture of the software, or trace out the relationship between the developer and the user community in the context of the codebase; (c) render the graph information at different levels of abstraction; (d) provide query support for the graphs.

We also demonstrate the applicability of our approach and the tool with two examples. First, we analyze a well known and active open source project FFMpeg (FFmpeg, 2010) and show how to make queries essential from the point of view of development and maintenance of software relying on FFMpeg code. Then we analyze the open source version of the Eucalyptus project (Eucalyptus, 2011) and its community, due to its emerging impact in the field of cloud computing.

The paper is structured as follows. In Section TOWARDS A GENERIC OSS ANALYSIS TOOL we propose our approach. The tool, Binoculars, is described in Section TOOL SUPPORT. The applicability of Binoculars is discussed in Section CASE STUDY. We review known approaches and techniques for analyzing OSS projects in Section RELATED WORK and distinguish our work from that of existing ones. Finally, some concluding remarks and future development of the work are presented in Section DISCUSSION.

TOWARDS A GENERIC OSS ANALYSIS TOOL

Comprehension of a software project can be addressed at different abstraction levels (Rosso, 2006). At the lowest level, the file system (code base) can be analyzed and refactored by employing reverse engineering techniques to extract code dependency and the architecture of the system. At the next highest level of abstraction, the community structure and people's (developers and users) activities, communication, and social interaction can be analyzed. It should be noticed that dependency exists at each abstraction level as well as between the levels. For example, code level dependency arises due to interface dependency, inclusion, code dependency and so on. Also at the community level, interpersonal communication leads to social dependencies among people in the organization. Interlevel dependency arises due to the fact that developers work on the project artifacts, fixing reported bugs, incorporating new features whereas users often posts bug reports, asking for new features and so on.

Social network analysis (SNA) (Rosso, 2009) in this regard can be used to capture and effectively model these dependencies through graphs, where entities (e.g., developers, users, code files, bugs) are presented as vertices and the dependencies among the entities are modeled as edges (or arcs). For example, social networks can be dug from the model based on the persons working on the same files (or issues) or we can study who are working with the same bug reports. Different measures and metrics in SNA can be applied on these relation-

ship graphs to get an insight of the project. For instance, metrics like density, centrality, closeness, betweenness (Carrington, Scott, & Wasserman, 2005) can be applied on the resultant graphs.

We approach the goal of building a generic and customizable OSS analysis tool by starting from a relatively simple metamodel that can later be extended by the concepts needed to support the different data sources and purposes (see e.g., Table 2 in Section RELATED WORK). This is essential, since OSS projects like any software projects, vary significantly. We believe that a small metamodel that is widely applicable through extensions is more useful than a comprehensive and detailed one, the use of which can be either limited or unnecessarily cumbersome.

The Binoculars metamodel is divided into domain independent and domain specific models. In the former, everything is modeled as mathematical graphs, whereas the latter introduces the open source related aspects. The domain independent model consists of classes Node and Arc, which are depicted in the upper part of Figure 1.

Figure 1. The Binoculars metamodel

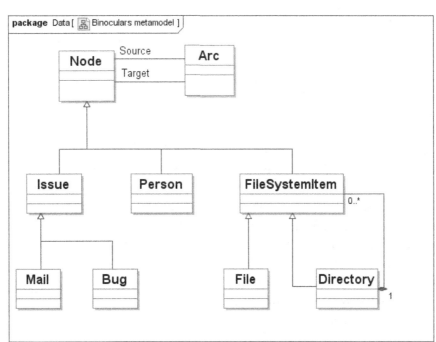

The domain specific model introduces concepts for modeling an open source project. The abstract class FileSystemItem (on the right hand side), whose concrete subclasses are File and Directory, is used for modeling the actual implementation. Introducing the composition relationship between Directory and FileSystemItem allows us to model the real file system of the implementation. Objects of the class Person (in the middle) form the open source community.

Finally, Issues (Mails and Bug reports) model the communication that takes place during development.

Due to the fact that these are all subclasses of the abstract class Node, they can have links (instance of Arc) with any other types of Nodes. This allows us to mine, combine and in particular refine the information available for the subject project. The domain specific model could be more detailed and it could include more aspects. For example, in many reverse engineering activities the actual implementation is modeled to the level of (member) functions, or even programming-language-level statements. Moreover, the class Issue has several obvious derivations, like chat messages. Open source development is often based on patches delivered by the developers. The model could be augmented with the class Patch. Then the class File would have a composition relation with the class Patch. For the purposes of this paper we have selected a high level of abstraction for our demonstration purposes. Finally, the other aspect of OSS projects, i.e., licensing, may introduce new node types to be added to the metamodel.

In order to instantiate the model we utilize all available sources of information, like the code base, mailing lists, bug tracking tools and meta information from the project's www pages. The sources are the ones that fix the domain specific model. In Binoculars each of these sources are represented as repositories, namely person, file and issue, corresponding to the three subclasses of Node and their substructures, depicted in Figure 1. The Binoculars Metamodel. Extracted

information is stored in these repositories and are interpreted and presented as graphs with nodes and edges. An edge may have a weight, showing the strength of a relationship. Also, an edge may be directed depending on the relationship. In such cases we denote edges as arcs.

We define a set of operations to operate on repositories for generating relationship graphs. The operations can also be performed on the generated graphs to derive other relationship graphs. To present these operations, we first define the repository structure, and then discuss the syntax of the operations which is followed by their description with illustrative examples. The formal definition of these operations with detailed discussion is provided in the appendix.

Repository Structure

Let,

$$\rho = \{R^1, R^2, \cdots, R^n\}$$

be the set of repositories. Where each repository,

$$R^i = \{r_1^i, r_2^i, \cdots, r_m^i\}$$

consists of repository elements r_j^i. Each repository element

$$r_j^i = \{c_{j1}^i, c_{j2}^i, \cdots, c_{jx}^i\}$$

consists of attributes c_{jk}^i describing it. Each attribute element $c_{jk}^i = \{c_{jkp}^i\}$ consists of a number of attribute values c_{jkp}^i as shown in Figure 2.

For example, consider a set of repositories,

$$\rho = \{File^F, \ Person^P, \ Issue^I\}$$

where the $File^F$ repository contains a description of the code files, the $Person^P$ repository contains

Figure 2. Graphical representation of the repository model

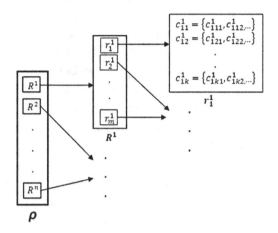

detail of each person (either user or developer) involved in the project and $Issue^I$ repository contains information about the issues (e.g., reported bugs, feature requests) raised by the project personnel. For this illustration consider only the $File^F$ repository. The repository

$$File^F = \{file_1^F, file_2^F, \cdots, file_m^F\}$$

consists of code files as repository elements. Each code file,

$$File_j^F = \{f_{name\,j1}^{\ F},\ path_{j2}^F,\ extension_{j3}^F,\ developer_{j4}^F,\ includes_{j5}^F,\ copyright_{j6}^F\}$$

Figure 3. An example of the file repository

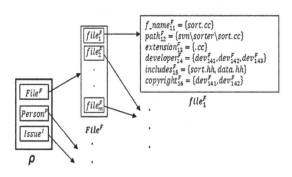

consists of six attributes referring to the name of the file, its path, extension, a list of the names of developers, included files and copyright information. This repository structure is shown in Figure 3.

Graph Operations

In this section the rationale and an abstract level discussion of the graph operations are presented. The syntax of these operations is presented in Figure 4. The syntax follows *Larch-like* notations (Guttag & Horning, 1993). As shown in Figure 4, we have four sorts, namely *repository*, *attributeName*, *graph* and *vertexSet* based on which graph operations are defined. Sort *repository* contains repository elements of a certain type, sort *attributeName* is the name of an attribute in a repository, sort *graph* represents a relationship graph, and finally sort *vertexSet* is a set of vertices in a given graph.

Operations are categorized in *repository operations* and *graph operations* (Figure 4). Repository operations are used to explore and combine information originating from different sources. Since we aim at an approach and a tool that can support studying both code and community dimensions of OSS projects, we need a

Figure 4. List of operations implemented in Binoculars

```
algebra BinocularsOperation
introduces
        sorts repository, attributeName, graph, vertexSet;
operations
        {Repository operation}
        interConnect: repository × attributeName → graph;

        {Graph Operation}
        intraConnect: graph × vertexSet → graph;
        intersection: graph × graph → graph;
        union: graph × graph → graph;
        difference: graph × graph → graph;
        symmetric difference: graph × graph → graph;

end BinocularsOperation.
```

Figure 5. 2-mode network showing relationship between developers and the code files

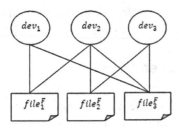

way to show relationships between elements in two distinct repositories. So, we use the concept of affiliation networks (Rosso, 2009) for showing relationships between two sets of components (or vertices). In an affiliation network one set is called "actors" and the other is called "events". Thus an affiliation network is called a "2-mode network" and represented as a bipartite graph. In the context of Binoculars, actors denote attribute values, and events represent the repository elements. The other types of operations, graph operations, are used to support more detailed analysis of the information included in the graphs.

Repository operations are applied directly to repositories. We have one such operation, called the *interConnect* operation, which accepts a repository and an attribute name as argument. For each repository element the attribute contains one or more attribute values. The *interConnect* operation creates relations between repository elements and each of the attribute values, thus generating an affiliation network. For example, consider the *File* repository presented in Figure 3. Each code file in this repository has an attribute called developer that consists of a list of developer names who contributed to that file. Thus, it is quite natural to have a relationship between that code file and it's developers. Applying *interConnect* operation in this case would generate a bipartite graph (Figure 5), which is a 2-mode affiliation network showing the relationship between two distinct sets of entities, as code files and their developers. Thus, one can easily study the relationship between

two components (actors and events) in a software project through such graphs. A formal definition of the *interConnect* operation is given in the appendix, section The interConnect operation.

The second category of operation is the graph operation. There are five operations belonging to this category, namely *intraConnect* operation and four set operations (Figure 4). The *intraConnect* operation is used to transform the 2-mode networks (generated by the *interConnect* operation) into two 1-mode networks. To do so, this operation accepts a graph generated by the *interConnect* operation and one of the vertex sets (either actors or events) in the input graph. Based on the vertex set, this operation generates relationships among the vertices in the other vertex set. Thus it is possible to investigate relationship from the perspective of the actors or the events. Let us consider the example graph above (Figure 5), which shows relationships between code files (events) and developers (actors). Application of the *intraConnect* operation on this graph could generate either a graph showing the relationship between developers (actors) based on common code file sharing (Figure 6) or a graph showing the relationship between code files (events) based on common developer involvement (Figure 7). Edge weights in these graphs show the relationship strength between pairs of nodes. For example, the edge weights in the graph shown in Figure 6 reveal how many code files are shared among the developers.

Here, the actors graph depicts collaboration among the members (developers) within the community based on common interest and responsi-

Figure 6. 1-mode network showing relationship among developers based on common code file sharing

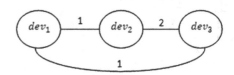

Figure 7. 1-mode network showing relationship among code files based on common developer involvement

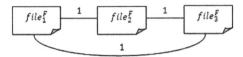

bilities (e.g., code file sharing). On the other hand, the events graph can be used to understand the degree of *interlocks* (Rosso, 2009) between events as created by actors. For example, a developer working on two code files simultaneously creates an interlock between them. An interlock between the files thus represents the working area of the person involved as well as revealing dependency among the code files evolved due to common developer interest. If multiple developers are involved, then the interlock gets even stronger. This information would be useful for a new developer working on some part of the project. For example, he can find out which developers previously worked on a certain part of the code base or what other files are significantly manipulated along with the file in question. The formal definition and weight calculation of the *intraConnect* operation are discussed in the appendix, section The intraConnect operation.

Set operations are commonly applied to graphs. Figure 4 lists four such set operations, namely intersection, union, difference and symmetric difference. These set operations have several implications for analyzing actors or events graphs, which include analyzing a community from multidimensional perspectives, identifying groups and their interrelationship based on a certain criterion. For example, one might wish to identify the group of people who work as developers as well as bug fixers in the community, or what are the groups in the developer community according to their responsibilities and how these groups are related to each other, or does the actual code file dependency match the dependency evolved due

to common developer interest (an application of Conways law (Conway, 1968)). Next, these set operations are presented with an example from the perspective of the developer community.

Consider the two actor graphs shown in Figure 8. The graph in Figure 8(a) shows the relationship among the developers due to common code base sharing and the graph in Figure 8(b) shows the developer relationship in the community due to common bug solving. The edge weight in both the graphs shows how many code files or bugs are shared among the developers.

The application of the intersection operation keeps the common section of the input graphs, showing the region having multidimensional exposure. For example, one might be interested in identifying the community of developers who work both as a developer as well as an issue or bug solver in an OSS project. An edge weight in the resultant graph is calculated by adding the edge weights between the corresponding actor nodes in the input graphs. The graph shown in Figure 9 is such a graph generated by applying the intersection operation on the graphs in Figure 8. This graph shows the developer community

Figure 8. (a) Relationship among developers based on common code file sharing (b) Relationship among developers due to common bug solving

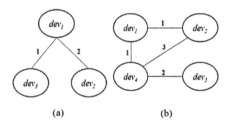

Figure 9. Intersection operation applied on graphs shown in Figure 8

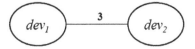

who contribute to the code base as well as in bug solving. Formal definition and weight calculation of the intersection operation is also given in the appendix, section Set operations.

Union operation retains both the input graphs, thus showing at most three regions, one that is common to both the input graphs (if any) and the two that are present in either of the input graphs. Hence this operation can be used to exhibit the entire community with their focus domains of activity in the project. For example, the graph shown in Figure 10 is generated by applying union operation on the graphs in Figure 8. In this graph, the relation shown with a thick solid line is involved in both code base developments as well as in bug solving, but the relations shown with the thin solid line and thin dashed lines are the relations involved in code development and bug solving, respectively. A formal definition of union operation with the weight calculation procedure is presented in the appendix, section Set operations.

Difference and Symmetric difference operations are only used for distinct regions in the input graphs, excluding the common region. Thus, these operations are most suitable for finding out about specialized regions in a community. For example, one might be interested in finding out the group of people in the developer community working only as bug fixers or as developers. Figure 11 shows the graph generated by applying difference operation on the graphs shown in Figure 8. This graph shows the part of the developer community that only takes part in bug fixing. The formal definition and weight calculation procedure for

Figure 10. Union operation applied on graphs shown in Figure 8

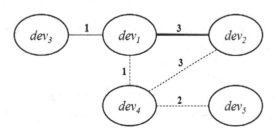

Figure 11. Difference operation applied on graphs shown in Figure 8

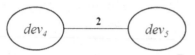

difference and symmetric difference operations are given in the appendix, section Set operations.

TOOL SUPPORT

Architecture

Binoculars supports visualization of information through graphical representation. Emphasis was given to extracting relevant information, deriving relationships information which is represented and rendered through graphs. Figure 12 shows the architecture of Binoculars.

Binoculars architecture is based on the Eclipse RCP (Rich Client Platform) (Eclipse, 2010) and MVC (Model-View-Controller) architecture. RCP provides a flexible means to implement desktop applications either as plugins or as standalone applications. One of the main characteristics of MVC architecture is its ability to separate the business logic and application data from its presentation. In this architecture, the model stores data and during the course of editing, undo, and redo, the model is the only thing that endures. Thus all operations are applied to the model data for manipulation. Whereas Views are the way to present the model data in different ways. Whenever the underlying model changes, it would be updated and reflected in the corresponding views. And the interaction and synchronization between the model and its view is maintained by the Controller. Thus a controller is responsible for intercepting the requests from view and passing it to the model for appropriate action, the result of which is then passed back to the view for necessary updates.

Figure 12. Overall architecture of Binoculars

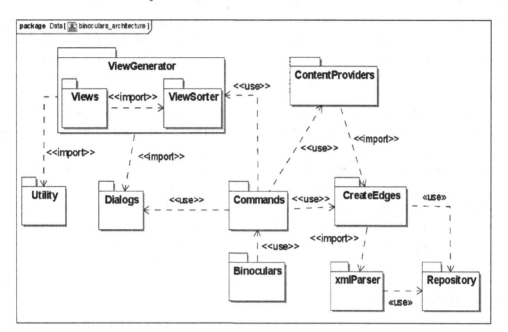

In Binoculars, models are implemented in the ContentProviders module, views are implemented and maintained in the ViewGenerator module, and the controller is implemented in the Commands module as shown in Figure 12.

The ContentProviders models the graph information that is generated and supplied by the CreateEdge module. The CreateEdge module digs up the repository information for generating graph data. The underlying graph generating methods (i.e., operations that are defined in section Graph Operations and in the appendix) are implemented in this module. Graph information is generated as XML data which contains the edge list, edge weight, details of the edge weight and associated node information. To help support mining the repositories and to generate XML data, the xmlParser module is used. This module uses the DOM XML parser (W3 Schools, 2010) to extract as well as to create new XML data for the graphs. The Repository module is the one which implements the metamodel presented in section TOWARDS A GENERIC OSS ANALYSIS TOOL and parses required information from different data sources.

The ViewGenerator module has two component modules, Views and ViewSorter. The Views module represents the data provided by the ContentProviders. Views can present model data in different ways, such as tabular, chart, tree and graphs. The ViewSorter module is utilized by the Views to organize its content when displaying. It is possible to open multiple instances of a view with customized data obtained from the same ContentProvider. This kind of customized visualization is handled by the Utility module.

There are many ways to customize a graph and to generate a new one based on user settings. For example, a graph can be customized by (a) selecting specific nodes or edges of the graph, (b) setting a weight range for the edges, (c) selecting attribute values for nodes, and (d) n-level nearest neighbor of a selected node. All these customizations of a graph are carried out by the commands implemented in the Commands module (in the middle of Figure 12). Required interfaces and a validation mechanism for the user inputs are implemented in the Dialogs module. Both Commands and ViewGenerator modules use these

107

interfaces for user interaction. Appropriate command accepts the verified user data and passes it to the ContentProvider. The ContentProvider module updates the model and returns it to the corresponding views. The views are then updated accordingly.

The module Binoculars in Figure 12 contains the basic components that are required to run an RCP application. The most important components are the RCP main application class which implements the interface IApplication, one Perspective which holds menus and three place holders called folders, and a Workbench Advisor which controls the appearance of the application (menus, toolbars, perspectives, etc).

Libraries and Platform Used

In what follows, the platform and libraries used to implement Binoculars are introduced.

- **Eclipse SDK:** Eclipse SDK (http://www.eclipse.org) is an open source, multi-language software development environment comprising an IDE and a plug-in system to extend it. Eclipse is used for developing Binoculars.
- The Java SE (version 6) Runtime Environment is used for developing the tool (Oracle, 2011).
- **Eclipse RCP (Rich Client Platform):** Eclipse RCP (Eclipse, 2010) allows the Eclipse platform to be used to create flexible and extensible desktop applications. Eclipse is built upon a plugin architecture, where a plugin is defined as the smallest deployable and installable software component of Eclipse. This architecture allows developers to use existing plugins, other third party extensions and own custom-built ones.
- **Zest:** ZEST is a graph visualization Toolkit built as an Eclipse plug-in. It provides a convenient set of API's for rendering and manipulating graphs (http://www.eclipse.org).

- **JFree chart:** JFreeChart (Gilbert & Morgner, 2010) is a Java chart library with a set of API's supporting a wide range of chart types. JFreeChart is open source and distributed under the terms of LGPL (GNU Lesser General Public License). To use JFreeChart, the libraries (.jar) of JFreeChart need to be added to the Java classpath.
- **Dom XML parser:** The XML DOM (W3 Schools, 2010) defines a standard way for accessing and manipulating XML documents. It provides a convenient set of API's in Java for creating and manipulating XML documents.
- **SWT (Standard Widget Toolkit):** SWT is an open source widget toolkit available as an Eclipse plug-in and used to design efficient, portable user-interfaces in Java.

Features

The features of Binoculars are implemented to support the analysis of open source projects from the perspective of both community and code base. Figure 13 shows the main interface of Binoculars.

As shown in Figure 13, Binoculars has three panels (left, top and bottom), each of which is used to hold and display multiple views. Views are used to hold and display different representations of the data upon request. Depending on the purposes, Binoculars has six views. They are, project views, tabular graph data view, graph view, tabular chart data view, chart view and project data view.

The left panel is used to hold and display the project view, the top panel is used to hold tabular graph data view, project data view and tabular chart data view, and the bottom view holds and displays the graph view and the chart view. What follows describes the functionalities of each of these views and their intercommunication.

- **Project View:** This view lists the projects and the graphs that are generated under

Figure 13. Binoculars user interface

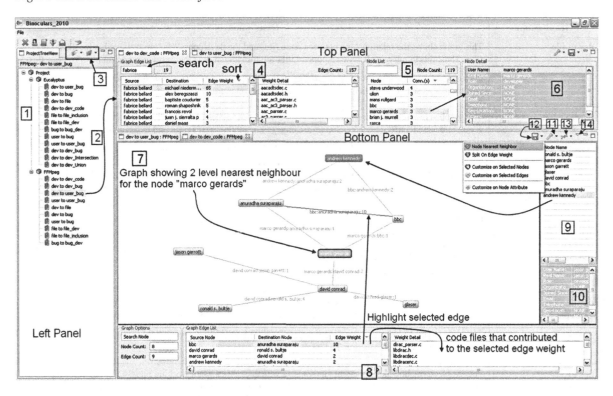

each project. This list is organized in a tree structure as shown in Figure 13, item 1. Clicking on a graph name under a project, would display the tabular representation of the graph in the top panel (Figure 13, item 2). Project view also has menu level commands (Figure 13, item 3) that allows users (a) to add new projects and graphs under existing projects and (b) to remove existing graphs and projects. The list of graphs that can be generated under a project are listed in Table 1. Each graph in this table is described by its unique name, purpose and graph operation that is applied to generate the graph.

- **Graph Data View [Tabular]:** This view displays graphs as a list of edges and nodes. It contains the following, (a) An edge list table consisting of graph edges. Each edge is described by source node, destination node, edge weight and weight detail. (b)

A node list table which lists all nodes in the graph with the number of connections for each node. (c) A node description table which shows information about a selected node (Figure 13, items 4, 5, 6 respectively). Table data can be searched and sorted based on a selected column. For example, the edge list table (Figure 13, item 4) is sorted in descending order based on edge weight and a search is made with the word *fabrice*.

- **Graph View:** This view displays graphs in a graphical way with detailed graph information. This view consists of the following components, (a) a graph display pane which displays the graphs consisting of nodes and edges. Edges might have weights depending on the graph; (b) an edge detail pane which consists of an edge list table, a weight detail table and a graph option table. The weight detail table displays

Table 1. Graph visualization supported by binoculars

Graph Name	Description
dev to file	This graph shows the relationships between code files and the developers who are responsible for those code files. Thus, this graph reveals how responsibilities are distributed over the developer community. To draw this graph, an $interConnect(File^F, developer)$ operation is performed. A detailed description of this operation is presented in the appendix, The interConnect operation.
Dev to issue	This graph shows relationships between developers and user issues answered by the developers. From this graph, one can identify which developers are engaged in solving user issues and to what extent. To draw this graph, an $interConnect(Issue^I, developer)$ operation is performed.
User to issue	This graph shows relationships between issues and the users who posted those issues. From this graph one can easily figure out the interest areas of users and their contributions, as subject areas of the issues should be related to the purpose of use. To draw this graph, an $interConnect(Issue^I, user)$ operation is performed.
file to file_inclusion	This graph shows relationships between code files of the project based on the inclusion structure. Thus it can reveal how code files are dependent on each other. To draw this graph, an $interConnect(File^F, inclFile)$ operation is performed.
dev to dev_code	This graph shows relationships between developers based on a common code file use. The edge weight between two developer nodes specifies how many code files they share in common. To draw this graph an $intraConnect(G_{File-Developer}, File)$ operation is performed. A detail description of this operation is presented in the appendix, section The intraConnect operation.
dev to dev_issue	This graph shows how developers are interacting with each other when working on issues. A relationship exists between two developers if they worked on a common issue. The edge weight between two nodes shows how many common issues exists between two developers. To draw this graph an $intraConnect(G_{Issue-Developer}, Issue)$ operation is performed.
user to user_issue	This graph shows relationships between users based on a common issue. Generally issues (such as bug reporting, feature request) are posted by users and it is quite common that many users have the same issue in common. Thus, there are relationships between them. The edge weight in this graph again shows the multiplicity of such occurrences. To draw this graph an $intraConnect(G_{Issue-User}, Issue)$ operation is performed.
file to file_dev	This graph shows relationships between code files based on a common developer involvement. That means if two code files are written or maintained by the same developer then there exists a relationship between them. To draw this graph an $intraConnect(G_{File-Developer}, Developer)$ operation is performed.
issue to issue_dev	This graph shows relationships among issues based on common developers' involvement, which in turn reveals what subject area of these issues actually motivates developers' in solving them. To draw this graph an $intraConnect(G_{Issue-Developer}, Developer)$ operation is performed.
dev to dev_Intersection	This graph shows the group of developers in the community who work as active developers as well as issue solvers. Edge weights in this graph shows how frequently two developers interact with each other while performing both the roles. To draw this graph an $intersection(G^F_{developer}, G^I_{developer})$ operation is performed. Details of this graph operation are presented in the appendix, section Set operations.
dev to user_issue	This graph shows relationships between developers and users of the software based on a common issue, as in a typical OSS project one of the major media of communication among the developers and users is the issue tracking system. To draw this graph an $intersection(G^F_{developer}, G^I_{developer})$ operation is performed.

continued on following page

Table 1. Continued

Graph Name	Description
file to file_Intersection	This graph shows to what extent the inclusion architecture of the code base matches that of the file relationship due to the developers' involvement. In other words it reveals whether the community structure matches that of the product architecture, an application of Conways law (Conway, 1968). To draw this graph an $intersection(G_{File}^{Dev}, G_{File}^{Inc})$ operation is performed.
dev to dev_Union	This graph shows relationships among all the developers in the community based on their working domain. So, this graph would answer questions like, who is doing what, to what extent and in doing their jobs who are the other people they are interacting with. To draw this graph a $union\left(G_{developer}^{F}, G_{developer}^{I}\right)$ operation is performed. Details of this graph operation are presented in the appendix, section Set operations.
dev to dev_Difference	This graph shows the relationships of that part of the developer community who work only as developers. To draw this graph a $difference(G_{developer}^{F}, G_{developer}^{I})$ operation is performed. Details of this graph operation are presented in the appendix, section Set operations.
file to file_Difference	This graph shows those parts of the code base that do not match with the file relationships due to community involvement. To draw this graph a $difference(G_{File}^{Inc}, G_{File}^{Dev})$ operation is performed.
dev to dev_SymmDiff	This graph portrays two groups (if exists) in the developer community, one of which performs specifically as developers and the other only as issue solvers. To draw this graph a s $ymmdifference(G_{developer}^{F}, G_{developer}^{I})$ operation is performed. Details of this graph operation are presented in the appendix, section Set operations.

weight detail when an edge in the graph is selected and the graph option provides the graph summary data and searching facility; (c) a node list pane which lists all the nodes of the displayed graph; and (d) a node detail pane which shows information about a node selected from the displayed graph. All these components are shown in Figure 13, items 7, 8, 9, 10 respectively.

Both graph data view and graph view consist of a comprehensive set of menu level options to customize graph data and its visualization. These options are discussed bellow.

- **Graph Customization:** Displayed graphs can be customized in five different ways (Figure 13, item 11). These options are as follows, (a) node nearest neighbor: *n* level nearest neighbor of a selected graph node can be viewed. For a given node this option shows all the nodes that are nearest to it by the selected level. The graph in Figure 13 shows the 2 level nearest neighbor for the selected node *marco gerards*; (b) split on edge weight: a graph can be customized based on a given range of edge weights. The edges satisfying the weight range are displayed; (c) customize on selected nodes: a list of nodes from the displayed graph can be selected to draw a customized graph with those nodes, provided they have relations in the original graph; (d) customize on selected edges: a customized graph can be constructed by selecting a list of edges from the original graph; (e) customize on node attributes: this option gives the opportunity to customize a graph based on a given attribute value. For example, the graph in Figure 14 shows those developers and their relationships in the Eucalyptus community who live in the United States of America. All the component panes in the graph view are updated according to the customization.

Table 2. A two dimensional classification of open source analysis tools

-	Software	Communication	Configuration	Knowledge	Statistics	Contribution
Code analysis	(Knab, Pinzger, & Bernstein, 2006; Sarma, Maccherone, Wagstrom, & Herbsleb, 2009) (Knab, Pinzger, & Bernstein, 2006; Sarma, Maccherone, Wagstrom, & Herbsleb, 2009)		(Sarma, Maccherone, Wagstrom, & Herbsleb, 2009; Zhou & Davis, 2005)(Sarma, Maccherone, Wagstrom, & Herbsleb, 2009; Zhou & Davis, 2005)			(Chacon, 2010)
SNA	(Martinez-Romo, Robles, Ortuo-Perez, & Gonzalez-Barahona, 2008; Sarma, Maccherone, Wagstrom, & Herbsleb, 2009)(Martinez-Romo, Robles, Ortuo-Perez, & Gonzalez-Barahona, 2008; Sarma, Maccherone, Wagstrom, & Herbsleb, 2009)	(Kamei, Matsumoto, Maeshima, Onishi, Ohira, & Matsumoto, 2008; Crowston & Howison, 2005)	(Porruvecchio, Uras, & Quaresima, 2008)	(Mller, Meuthrath, & Baumgra, 2008)	(Wiggins, Howison, & Crowston, 2009)	
Licensing	(Di Penta & German, 2009; Tuunanen, Koskinen, & Karkkainen, 2006)					
Prediction	(English, Exton, Rigon, & Cleary, 2009)	(Beaver, Cui, St Charles, & Potok, 2009)	(English, Exton, Rigon, & Cleary, 2009)	(Beaver, Cui, St Charles, & Potok, 2009)		
Evolution	(Bouktif, Antoniol, Merlo, & Neteler, 2006; Capiluppi & Fernandez-Ramil, 2007)	(Bouktif, Antoniol, Merlo, & Neteler, 2006)	(Bouktif, Antoniol, Merlo, & Neteler, 2006; Capiluppi & Fernandez-Ramil, 2007)		(Koch & Stix, 2008)	(Deshpande & Riehle, 2008)
Project Exploration	(Souza, Quirk, Trainer, & Redmiles, 2007; DeLine, Khella, Czerwinski, & Robertson, 2005)		(Mockus & Herbsleb, 2002; DeLine, Khella, Czerwinski, & Robertson, 2005)			(Mockus & Herbsleb, 2002)
Awareness	(Biehl, Czerwinski, Smith, & Robertson, 2007; Froehlich & Dourish, 2004)	(Froehlich & Dourish, 2004)				
Conflict management	(Sarma, Noroozi, & Van der Hoek. 2003; Schmmer & Haake, 2001)					

Figure 14. Graph customization on the attribute geo location with value "America"

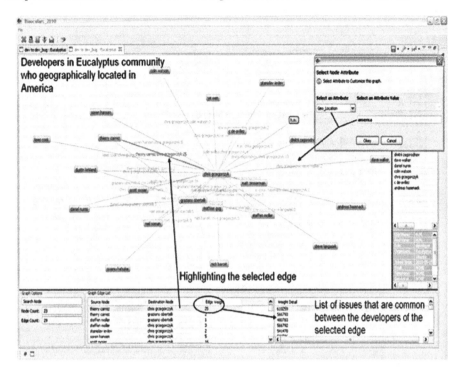

- **Save Graph:** The original graph or it's customized version can be saved in XML files (Figure 13, item 12). It is also possible to save the graph nodes and their associated detail in XML files.
- **Layout Change and Zooming:** Four layout options (namely, spring, grid, tree, radial) are provided for visualizing graphs (Figure 13, item 13). The displayed graph can also be zoomed between 50% and 400% (Figure 13, item 14).
- **Chart View:** Charts are used to show summary data of the project. Two charts are currently available, a pie chart and a bar chart. Charts can be generated based on selected attributes. For example, Figure 15 shows a pie chart revealing bugzilla distribution in the Eucalyptus project based on their priority level.

Apart from these, Binoculars has three more views for visualizing the project repositories.

These are the project personnel view which shows project personnel information under their respective projects. Similarly project code base view and project bugzilla view respectively provide codebase information and an issue history log of a project.

Feasibility and Scalability of Binoculars

Binoculars requires repository information to create a graph. Repository information is collected from projects data management systems as discussed in section Data Collection. Customized parsers are built to fully automate this data collection process. But due to the diverse nature of data management systems of OSS projects, it is really hard to have a generalized parser for all the projects. Thus parsers are not the part of Binoculars.

Both the repository information and the created graphs are stored in XML files as discussed

Figure 15. Pie chart showing bugzilla distribution according to their priority in Eucalyptus project

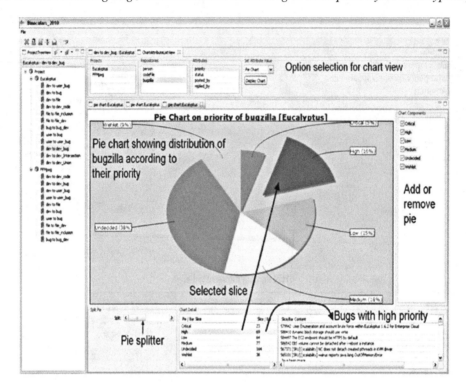

in section Architecture. For creating a new graph, Binoculars extract information from the related repositories and create and store the graph in a XML file. For rendering an existing graph, it simply uses the corresponding graph XML file. Thus creating and rendering a graph requires normal processing time.

One can extend an existing repository by simply adding information in the XML files with defined tags. Similarly, a new repository can be added using the existing XML template. Again, Binoculars operates on the repository information, thus it is not dependent on the programming language used in a project.

CASE STUDY

In this section, we demonstrate the use and applicability of our approach and the tool Binoculars

by analyzing the selected open source projects, FFMpeg (2010) and Eucalyptus (2011).

Short Description of FFMpeg

FFmpeg is a complete, cross-platform solution to record, convert and stream audio and video in numerous formats (FFmpeg, 2010). There are more than 140 projects listed in the FFMpeg official website which use programs from the FFMpeg project (FFmpeg, 2010).

The name of the project comes from the MPEG video standards group, together with "FF" for "fast forward" (Bellard, 2006). Fabrice Bellard is the originator of this project and FFmpeg is his trademark.

FFmpeg is written in C and developed under Linux. It is free software and is licensed under the GNU Lesser General Public License (LGPL) version 2.1 (FFmpeg, 2010) or later. FFmpeg also incorporates several optional parts and optimizations that are covered by the GNU General Public License (GPL) version 2 or later.

In the FFmpeg project, information is mainly maintained in a version control system, a bug reporting system and a registered user information system. These are the basic sources of information for the analysis.

Short Description of Eucalyptus

Eucalyptus is a software platform which implements scalable IaaS (Infrastructure as a Service) style private and hybrid cloud computing (Eucalyptus, 2011). The platform provides a single interface that lets users access computing infrastructure resources (e.g., machines, network, and storage). These resources are available in private clouds implemented by Eucalyptus inside an organization's existing data center as well as externally in public cloud services. The software is designed to be modular and the extensible web-services based architecture enables Eucalyptus to export a variety of APIs toward users via client tools. Currently Eucalyptus implements the Amazon Web Service (AWS) API (Eucalyptus, 2011), which allows interoperability with existing AWS-compatible services and tools.

There are the enterprise edition and the open-source edition of Eucalyptus. Version 1.5.2 was the first release as an open source. This open source version of Eucalyptus is currently available with most of the Linux distributions including Ubuntu, Red Hat Enterprise Linux (RHEL), CentOS, SUSE Linux Enterprise Server (SLES), OpenSUSE, Debian and Fedora.

As cloud computing is an emerging phenomenon and the Eucalyptus OSS community makes a large contribution in this field, we are thus particularly interested in the open source version of Eucalyptus. For our purposes we explore all the possible sources of information provided by the open source version of Eucalyptus. The sources are mainly available in the following categories: the user information system, the version control system and the bug reporting system.

Research Questions

Following are the queries that are investigated and answered using Binoculars. Primary focuses of these queries are the community aspects, the code base and their relationships in an OSS project.

Q1: Where does the expertise lay within the developer community?

Q2: Whom (developer) users should contact to solve an issue?

Q3: How many people work on each software component? Who are they?

Q4: Does the inclusion structure of the code base conform to the organizational structure (i.e., do Conway's law apply)?

Q5: What are the critical issues related to the performance of the software?

These queries are motivated by the fact that software development is no longer a single handed job (Rosso, 2009). Rather, it is a collaborative and distributed work in both form of software development (closed source and open source) process. Thus cultural, time zone, and language differences among the community members are obvious. Improving software development in this context requires better understanding and improved coordination and communication (Mockus & Herbsleb, 2003; Herbsleb, Moitra, & Lucent Technol., 2001). This coordination and collaboration issues for improving software knowledge are studied in software engineering for quite a long time (Cockburn, 2001; Schwaber & Beedle, 2001) and was empirically validated (Bellini, Canfora, Garcia, Piattini, & Visaggio, 2005). Likewise, exploiting and understanding this collaboration and coordination, and its relation with the underlying software architecture has profound impact both on software architecture evolution (CYB, MacCormack, & Rusnak, 2008) and on software quality (Ye, 2006; Herbsleb, 2007). The queries stated are derived from these needs. In Rosso (2009) some of these queries are explored and answered from community perspective using SNA measures and metrics. But, for in-depth understanding on this issue requires exploration of relationship between community and the code base of an OSS project.

In what follows, the data collection process and answer to the research questions using FFMpeg and Eucalyptus. In answering the queries, first a brief discussion on the context and focus of the query is given.

Data Collection

The main sources of information for the two projects, FFMpeg and Eucalyptus are, code repository, bug tracking system, registered user information system and mailing list. We take a snapshot of the SVN code repository of FFMpeg project on 20-09-2010 and use the code base of Eucalyptus-1.6.2. Other information sources (bug tracking system, user information system and mailing lists) are extracted from the first entry up to 20-09-2010. For extracting data from the information sources described above, we build parsers in java and represent the extracted data in XML files which constitute the repositories for Binoculars.

As discussed, Binoculars contains three repositories to store extracted information, namely, Person, File and Issue repositories. Person repository contains project personnel information including, unique user name; real name; role performed in the community (e.g., developer, user, active developer); date of joining to the project; project or part of the project working for; other detail such as, geographical location, email address, communication medium used, preferred language(s) and phone number. File repository contains information about the code files, which consists of file name; its path to the svn; extension of the file; developer(s) who implemented or maintain the file; inclusion information, and copyright

information. Finally, Issue repository contains information extracted from the bug repository as well as from the mailing list. This repository consists of issue id; title of the issue (subject of a mail or a bug report); its priority level, and current status; name of the persons who posted and replied to the issue along with date and time of posting, and the description of the issue.

To identify and distinguish personnel (either developer or user) in a project, we adopted the following approach; first we collected the person information from the code repository for each code file. Then we searched the registered user information system to identify personnel with their role defined as developer. These two sources provide the developers list in a project. Other personnel whose responsibility was mentioned as user in the registered user information system or who are not in the developer list were considered as users of the project. Also for code files, it might be possible that two files have the same name. To resolve this conflict, we used absolute path for each code file.

Case Study: 1 FFMpeg

In this section we discuss how selected queries are answered when analyzing an FFMpeg project using Binoculars.

Q1: Where does the expertise lay within the developer community?

- **Description:** Developers might have different areas of interest and expertise with respect to the code base and responsibilities should be distributed accordingly. Thus, it is obvious that developers having the same interest area would share knowledge more frequently and they are the main sources of information for that portion of the code base. The main focus of this query is to find out the expertise groups within the developer community.

To answer this query an

$$intraConnect\ (G_{File-Developer}, File)$$

operation is performed. The resultant graph is shown in Figure 16.

According to this graph, developers MN and FB share 65 code files between them. However, developer FB shares about 49 code files with 19 other developers. M.N. also shares 40 code files with another 15 developers. Thus, it is quite clear that both MN and FB are the central developers in FFMpeg and make a significant contribution to different areas of the code base.

Q2: Whom (developer) users should contact to solve an issue?

- **Description:** In an open source project developers play two types of roles: (a) de-

veloping and maintaining the software and (b) dealing with user issues, which may directly or indirectly relate to the product. Depending on the area of interest, developers may choose either or both of these roles. Developers playing both roles and exchanging ideas with each other form the core of the developer community. This community of developers has the in-depth knowledge of the software and the user community as they both deploy the software and solve user polled issues. A user having some problem in hand may find the proper person in the developer community whom he should contact. This question was also polled in Anvik, Hiew, and Murphy (2006) where a machine learning technique was used to suggest a small number of developers suitable to resolve a reported issue.

Figure 16. Developer relationship graph based on code file sharing in FFMpeg with top two developers communication domain

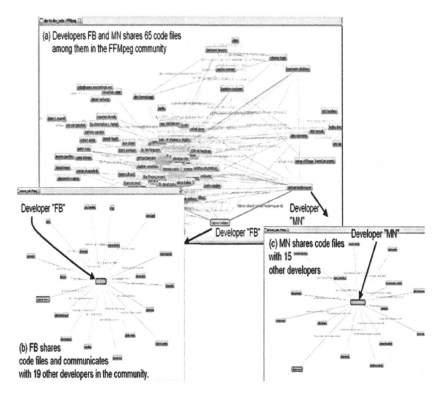

To answer this query an

$$intersection(G_{developer}^F, G_{developer}^I)$$

operation is performed. The resultant graph contains only 13 developers but they have no connection between them. This means that the communication network in the developer community which evolved due to the code development is not the same as the one evolved due to bug or issue solving. In other words, developers who are responsible for a particular portion of the code base are not necessarily the same group of developers who are responsible for solving related issues.

Q3: How many people work on each software component? Who are they?

- **Description:** The goal is to construct a graph that actually reveals the relationships between developers and the code files to which they have contributed. This graph

would help to identify how responsibilities are distributed over the community.

To answer this query an

$$interConnect(File^F, developer)$$

operation is performed. The resultant graph reveals that the distribution of the files in not uniform in the FFmpeg project. Rather, responsibilities are disseminated according to seniority and experience. For example, as shown in Figure 17, the top four developers contributed to around 550 code files of which the developer MN contributed to 227 code files alone.

Q4: Does the inclusion structure of the code base conform to the organizational structure (i.e., do Conway's law apply)?

- **Description:** The inclusion structure shows the logical relationships and interde-

Figure 17. Developer and code file relationship graph in FFMpeg

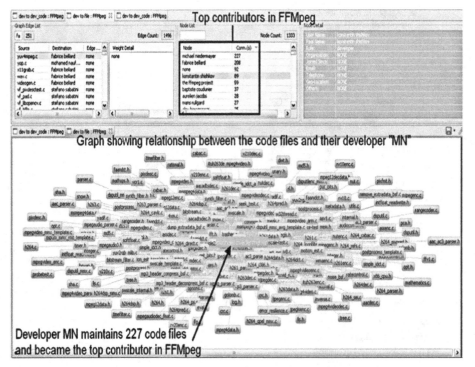

pendencies among the code files. Changes to such files might affect other related ones. Thus distribution of files among developers plays an important role in software evolution. If developers working on the same or related code files make changes to those files without the other developers involved being aware, then conflicting changes must occur. Due to this lack of communication among the developers working on such inter-related files, these conflicts are detected and resolved only during commits. But this increases the cost of resolving those conflicts.

To carry out this query, an

$$intersection(G_{File-File}, \ G_{File}^{F})$$

operation is performed. This operation takes two graphs as argument. One is a $G_{File-File}$ graph which is generated by employing the

$$interConnect(File^{F}, includeFile)$$

operation, and the other is a G_{File}^{F} graph generated by applying the

$$intraConnect \ (G_{File-Developer}, Developer)$$

operation. The resultant graph contains nodes and edges that are common to both the graphs. This graph is shown in Figure 18.

The FFMpeg project consists of 1490 code files, but the resultant graph (Figure 18) contains only 765 code files and their relationships. Thus, around 50% of the code files distributions are concerned with the organizational structure in the FFMpeg project.

Q5: What are the critical issues related to the performance of the software?

- **Description:** The main focus of this query is to categorize the issues based on a par-

Figure 18. File relationship graph generated based on common developer involvement and inclusion structure

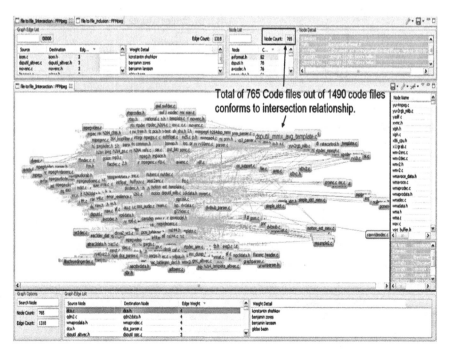

ticular condition. As an example, we categorize the issues based on the assumption that developers invest their time on those issues that are closely related to the performance of the software. It is also desirable that these issues are related to the code files for which these developers are responsible. Again, if enough information is provided by the repository, then these issues would directly lead to the sections of the code base that raise these issues.

To answer this query, an

$$intraconnect(G_{Developer-Issue}, Developer)$$

operation is performed. The resultant graph is shown in Figure 19. The edge weight in this graph shows how many developers are involved when solving two connected issues. A close look at this graph reveals that there are a few issues in the FFMpeg project that are referenced frequently by the developers with other issues. For example, *issue1322* is referenced with 258 other issues (Figure 19). Similarly, *issue763* and *issue272* are referenced with other 237 and 217 issues respectively. This wide interconnection between these issues and others reveals that they are critical for the project and have a deep impact on the performance of the software.

Case Study: 2 Eucalyptus

In this section an analysis report of the Eucalyptus community is presented. The same set of queries as in the FFMpeg project is investigated in this case as well. The contexts of the queries are the same as in the previous analysis.

Q1: Where does the expertise lay within the developer community?

- **Description:** The Eucalyptus community currently has 12 active developers, who participate in the project development.

Figure 19. Issue relationship graph generated based on common developer involvement

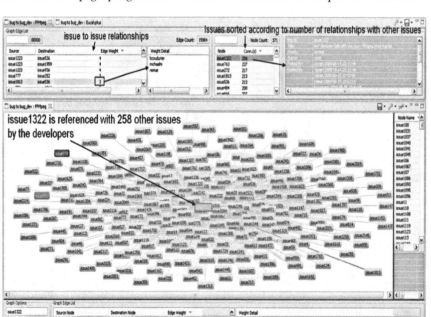

There are also other developers who contribute to the project. But, due to the fact that their contributions are not maintained properly at the code base level, the overall contribution of the developer community cannot be measured. Based on the partial information available, it is apparent that three of the developers in the Eucalyptus community have contributed more than the others.

Q2: Whom (developer) users should contact to solve an issue?

- **Description:** The outcome of this query is quite similar to that of the FFMpeg, because there is no distinct group of developers who communicate while working on the project as well as dealing with user issues. That is developers who implement certain code files are not necessarily the same ones who solve issues related to those code files.

Q3: How many people work on each software component? Who are they?

- **Description:** The result of this query is also similar to that of the FFMpeg project, where responsibilities are not evenly distributed within the developer community. For example, developer CZ alone contributed to 202 (out of 676) code files in the Eucalyptus project.

Q4: Does the inclusion structure of the code base conform to the organizational structure (i.e., do Conway's law apply)?

- **Description:** It is found that around 39% (266 out of 676) of the code files are distributed according to the communication structure of the Eucalyptus developer community. This is significantly lower than that of the FFMpeg community. This might be due to the fact that the

Eucalyptus community is a new and growing one which is still converging towards homogeneity.

Q5: What are the critical issues related to the performance of the software?

- **Description:** The result of this query in the Eucalyptus project shows that while working on one issue, developers the project consists of 402 issues, of which 350 issues are referenced with more than 50 other issues. In other words, in around 87% cases when developers show an interest in one issue they have also worked on at least 50 other issues. The graph in Figure 20 shows only those issues and their relationships that were referenced with more than 300 other issues by the developers.

This result is quite different from the FFMpeg project where the rate of this cross referencing is significantly lower.

RELATED WORK

The open source research community has proposed several techniques and tools to study open source projects. These tools, and the approaches behind them, can be classified along two main dimensions as shown in Table 2). The first dimension is the purpose of the tool (why), examples of which include social network analysis, code analysis, licensing investigation, project exploration, and conflict management. The second dimension is the data source that is used to extract information (what), examples of which include the source code, revision history, and mailing lists.

We chose to group the data sources into different categories. The software category refers to software artifacts like the source code and configuration files. Communication includes data sources such as mailing lists, and chat entries. Configuration refers to elements like revision history and bug tracks. Knowledge includes data sources

Figure 20. Issue relationship graph generated based on common developer involvement

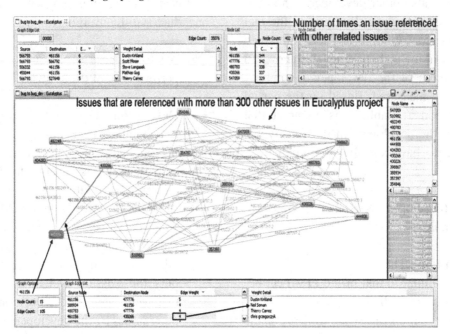

such as user forums and Wiki entries. Statistics cover data concerning the number of downloads or web hits. Finally, contribution covers patches and feature requests.

These categories are not orthogonal, for example, communication overlaps with contribution as mailing list entries are often referred to feature requests. As can be seen in Table 2, every tool focuses on a specific purpose and uses a set of data sources. For example, in Beaver, Cui, St Charles, and Potok (2009) communication and knowledge sources are used to predict the success of open source projects. Also in Mockus and Herbsleb (2002), configuration and contribution are explored to identify expertise within the project group, whereas in Biehl, Czerwinski, Smith, and Robertson (2007) and Sarma, Noroozi, and Van der Hoek (2003), source code and configuration files were mined to increase the developer' awareness of each others' contribution within the project and to effectively identify and resolve conflicts when working on shared artifacts, respectively. This gives the impression that (i) the purposes are unrelated and (ii) certain data sources are applicable for certain purposes only.

We argue that the tool purposes shown in Table 2 are in fact different functionalities of a generic OSS analysis tool. We also argue that the data sources are in fact complementary and that one data source could be relevant for several purposes. For example, source code is used to perform traditional code analysis (Knab, Pinzger, & Bernstein, 2006), social network analysis (Martinez-Romo, Robles, Ortuo-Perez, & Gonzalez-Barahona, 2008), licensing investigation (Di Penta & German, 2009) and so on.

The tool that comes closest to our approach is the Tesseract (Sarma, Maccherone, Wagstrom, & Herbsleb, 2009). This tool shows simultaneously the social and technical aspects of the relevant project, and cross links the two. It also takes into account project evolution by allowing interactive exploration of the data in a selected time period. And it highlights matches and mismatches among the technical dependencies and communication patterns of the developers. Still Tesseract has its limitations. First, the main focus of this tool the commercial software development projects and it tries to accommodate the aspects that are similar to open source software projects. Second, this tool does not consider the user base of OSS projects, which constitutes a large part of the OSS community and contributes to the project in many ways, such as bug reporting, asking for new features, feedback, mail communication and so on. Third, data collection for this tool is more manual than automated. It requires crosschecking and validation with project personnel. This process might take months to prepare data, which would hinder the usefulness of the tool.

Compared to these approaches, we proposed a compact and extensible metamodel (see section TOWARDS A GENERIC OSS ANALYSIS TOOL), since particularly at a more detailed level, the types of artifacts and their relations to be analyzed differ from project to project.

Correspondingly, support for the other dimensions discussed above can be provided either by extending the repositories or by extending the metamodel. For example, to integrate fault prediction of OSS projects, it is sufficient to incorporate the measured metrics in the corresponding repositories. On the other hand to incorporate licensing we need to extend the metamodel. It can be achieved by attaching licensing details to FileSystemItem class shown in Figure 1.

Our approach is currently aimed at the software and community sides of OSS projects. Each of these dimensions are modeled and implemented through repositories as discussed in section Repository Structure and in the appendix. As SNA traditionally employs mathematical graphs and metrics (Carrington, Scott, & Wasserman, 2005) to render and analyze relationships, we further define a set of operations (see section Graph Operations and appendix) which help support such graph construction and analysis. For example, the traditional 2-mode network in SNA can be easily constructed using the *interConnect* operation (section Graph Operations and in appendix, section The interConnect operation). This 2-mode network could then be easily transformed into two 1-mode SNA networks through the *intraConnect* operation (section Graph Operations and in appendix

section The intraConnect operation). Also for further querying, a group of set operations are defined (section Graph Operations and in appendix, section Set operations) and implemented. These operations are reusable in the sense that if other dimensions of OSS projects are mapped through repositories, then these operations can be directly applied to them as well. Thus our approach is more formal, procedural and flexible for exploring the socio-technical aspects of an OSS project while keeping perfect alignment with SNA approaches as well as reverse engineering.

DISCUSSION

Conclusion

The research problem addressed in this paper is what kind of infrastructure is needed to meet the requirements of a generic OSS analysis tool. Our approach in addressing this challenge is as follows.

First, we proposed a meta-model based approach for OSS analysis. We started the development of the metamodel, given in section II, focusing on two purposes, namely code analysis and social network analysis, and in particular combination of the two. The meta-model includes concepts for the community (Person), the software (FileSystemItem), and communication (Issue). It is not complete, as it could be augmented, for instance, with *legality* issues (like License) and *economical issues*.

Second, we formally defined graph operations (e.g., intra-Connect, interConnect, intersection, union, difference and symmetric difference), due to the fact that the abstract metamodel is a mathematical graph. These operations are discussed in section Graph Operations and in the appendix. The analysis is done by applying these operations.

Third, as a proof of the concept we developed the analysis tool Binoculars. This tool incorporates the described metamodel, and the analysis is carried out by applying the graph operations on the model. The architecture and features of this tool are discussed in TOOL SUPPORT. Binoculars were used to analyze two projects, FFMpeg and the open source version of Eucalyptus (presented in section CASE STUDY). We were able to answer questions like "Whom should a user contact to solve an issue" and "Who are the developers working on each component". During the trial the tool showed promising functionality; we were able to find answers to the enumerated questions. Despite the fact that FFMpeg can be considered as a large open source project, Binoculars worked well and smoothly. The developed metamodel proved to be excellent.

Finally, we gave a two-dimensional (purpose of the tool and used data source) classification for open source software analysis tools (section RELATED WORK). Then we argued that the tool purposes are actually different functionalities of a generic OSS tool. Moreover, the data sources are complementary and can be used for different purposes. We also discuss how our approach can be applied to fill this gap.

Ultimately, the kind of questions which the Binoculars approach addresses is not limited to open source projects. Other software development settings such as globally distributed projects may involve similar concerns such as the impact of team distribution on software architecture (Avritzer, Paulish, & Cai, 2008). The only assumption which our approach makes is that the subject project comes with relevant development data such as team communication and revision history. Even in single site development setting, the binoculars approach can be used for knowledge combination (Nonaka & Takeuchi, 1995) by combining together various elements of explicit knowledge (codified in the development artifacts) in order to build a bigger system of knowledge. A simple example of combination is the merging of the results of two developers' development history to identify overlapping efforts.

On the negative side: The GUI of Binoculars is challenging. Namely, the size of large projects tends to lead to huge graphs, which are complex and slow to render on the screen. This is a well-known challenge in the development and application of reverse engineering and program analysis tools, and is often tackled with abstraction and slicing techniques. We are studying such graph abstractions that would preserve the interesting features, but produce small enough graphs to be visualized.

Also, it is possible that two persons having the same name in a project have different responsibilities (e.g., one as a developer and the other as a user). In such case, Binoculars would not be able to distinguish between them and may lead to inconsistent result.

Future Work

The most widely accepted reverse engineering metamodel is The Dagstuhl Middle Metamodel (DMM) (Lethbridge, Tichelaar, & Ploedereder, 2004), which is illustrated in Figure 21. DMM includes various viewpoints to the system under reverse engineering. Figure 21 illustrates the file-oriented portion of the actual class diagram of DMM. The idea behind the class structure is to separate the abstract model from the concrete source code. Therefore, the model has both SourceObject and ModelObject.

Figure 21. The Dagstuhl Middle Metamodel (DMM)

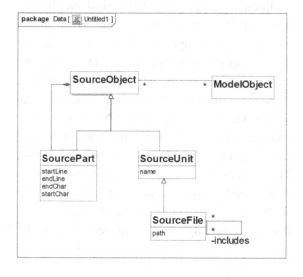

Our goal is to augment DMM with open source community related concerns. Figure 22 illustrates our current understanding of the augmentation of DMM. Remember that the Binoculars' metamodel was given in Figure 1. FileSystemItem has been left out from the Binoculars metamodel. Due to the fact that open source development is very code-oriented activity, we have chosen the subclasses of SourceObject to points of augmentation. The left-hand side of the figure shows the Binoculars metamodel and the righthand side illustrates the DMM. The four relations between the models show how they are related.

Persons are either users or developers of the system. Developers work with many SourceUnits and one SourceUnit may be coded by several developers. Therefore, Person and SourceUnit are in many-to-many relation. The SourcePart is used to model the code snippets crafted by the developers. Therefore, User and SourcePart are in a many-to-many relation. Similarly, issues are related to SourceUnits. Namely, most of the issues deal with the code-oriented questions, like bugs in the system. Therefore, Issue has a many-to-many relation with both SourcePart and SourceUnit.

The described augmentation is our next step in developing Binoculars. The relation of the current Binoculars metamodel and the more abstract parts of the DMM is worth a more comprehensive study. Is it enough just to relate our model to the code?

Current results of the tool support show very promising results and thus are subject to further study and research. As this current tool is a prototype and mainly developed to study how far it matches up to our expectations, extensions to the tool would be a topic of future work. Hence, the proposal is to develop a generic OSS analysis tool that must conform to the following:

It must support the traditional reverse engineering concept along with a community analysis mechanism.

- Customized visualization and rendering of graphs along with different levels of abstraction of data should be supported.
- From the architectural point of view: the tool should have an architecture that allows

Figure 22. The DMM augmented with the community dimension

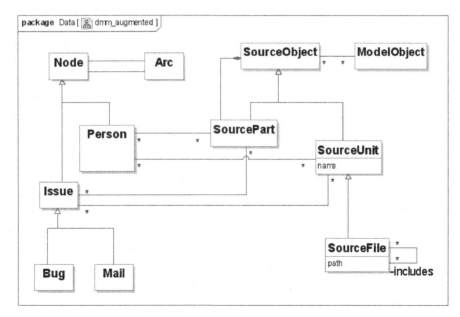

its extension, customization, and tailoring for different needs. It should be flexible enough to be tailored for other purposes relevant to the analysis of open source projects.

The tool itself will be open source, which further supports its easy customization. The use needs of the tool should facilate the following:

- Users of open source projects: the tool can be used to get an understanding of an open source project in order to assess its relevance for the needs of the user.
- Developers of open source projects: since the tool itself will be open source and customizable, the developers can publish a tailored version of the tool together with the software itself which would better serve the end users.

REFERENCES

Anvik, J., Hiew, L., & Murphy, G. (2006). *Who should fix this bug? 28th international conference on Software engineering* (pp. 361–370). New York, NY, USA: ACM.

Avritzer, A., Paulish, D., & Cai, Y. (2008). Coordination implications of software architecture in a global software development project. *Seventh Working IEEE/IFIP Conference on Software Architecture (WICSA 2008)* (pp. 107–116). Washington, DC, USA: IEEE Computer Society.

Beaver, J., Cui, X., St Charles, J., & Potok, T. (2009). Modeling success in floss project groups. *Proceedings of the 5th International Conference on Predictor Models in Software Engineering*, (pp. 1-8).

Bellard, F. (2006). *Ffmpeg naming and logo.* Retrieved from FFmpeg mailing list: lists.mplayerhq.hu/pipermail/ffmpeg-devel/2006-February/

Bellini, E., Canfora, G., Garcia, F., Piattini, M., & Visaggio, C. (2005). Pair designing as practice for enforcing and diffusion design software. *Journal of Software Maintenance and Evolution: Research and Practice*, *17*(6), 401–423. doi:10.1002/smr.322

Biehl, J., Czerwinski, M., Smith, G., & Robertson, G. (2007). Fastdash: A visual dashboard for fostering awareness in software teams. *SIGCHI conference on Human Factors in computing systems*, (pp. 1313–1322). San Jose, California, USA.

Bouktif, S., Antoniol, G., Merlo, E., & Neteler, M. (2006). A feedback based quality assessment to support open source software evolution: the grass case study. *Proceedings of the 22nd IEEE International Conference on Software Maintenance*, (pp. 155–165).

Capiluppi, A., & Fernandez-Ramil, J. (2007). A model to predict anti-regressive effort in open source software. *Proceedings of the IEEE International Conference on Software Maintenance*, (pp. 194–203).

Carrington, P., Scott, J., & Wasserman, S. (2005). *Models and methods in social network analysis.* Cambridge University press.

Cockburn, A. (2001). *Agile software development.* Indianapolis, IN: Addison-Wesley Professional.

Conway, M. E. (1968). *How do committees invent?* F. D. Thompson Publications, Inc. Reprinted by permission of Datamation magazine.

Crowston, K., & Howison, J. (2005). *The social structure of free and open source software development.* First Monday.

CYB. A., MacCormack, D., & Rusnak, J. (2008). Exploring the duality between product and organizational architectures: A test of the mirroring hypothesis. *Working Papers, Harvard Business School.*

DeLine, R., Khella, A., Czerwinski, M., & Robertson, G. (2005). Towards understanding programs through wear-based filtering. *ACM Symposium on Software Visualization*, (pp. 183–192). St. Louis, Missouri.

Deshpande, A., & Riehle, D. (2008). Continuous integration in open source software development. *Open Source Development, Communities and Quality, IFIP 20th World Computer Congress, Working Group 2.3 on Open Source Software*, (pp. 273–280).

Di Penta, & German, D. (2009). Who are source code contributors and how do they change? *Proceedings of 16th Working Conference on Reverse Engineering*, (pp. 11–20).

DOM XML parser. (2010). Retrieved from DOM XML parser: www.w3schools.com

Eclipse project. (2010). Retrieved from Eclipse project: www.eclipse.org

English, M., Exton, C., Rigon, I., & Cleary, B. (2009). Fault detection and prediction in an open-source software project. *Proceedings of the 5th International Conference on Predictor Models in Software Engineering*, (pp. 17-27).

Eucalyptus. (2011). Retrieved from The open source cloud platform: http://open.eucalyptus.com

FFmpeg. (2010). Retrieved from FFmpeg project: www.ffmpeg.org

Froehlich, J., & Dourish, P. (2004). Unifying artifacts and activities in a visual tool for distributed software development teams. *International Conference on Software Engineering*, (pp. 387–396). Edinburgh, UK. *git version control system*. (2010). Retrieved from git version control system: www.git-scm.com

Guttag, J., & Horning, J. (1993). *Larch: Languages and tools for formal specification*. New York, NY: Springer-Verlag, New york, Inc.

Herbsleb, J. (2007). *Global software engineering: The future of socio-technical coordination. Future of Software Engineering* (pp. 188–198). Washington, DC, U.S.A: IEEE Computer Society.

Herbsleb, J., Moitra, D., & Lucent Technol, I. (2001). Global software development. *IEEE Software*, *18*(2), 16–20. doi:10.1109/52.914732

Java runtime enviornment. (2011). Retrieved from Java runtime enviornment: http://www.oracle.com/

JFreeChart. (2010). Retrieved from JFreeChart: www.jfree.org

Kamei, Y., Matsumoto, S., Maeshima, H., Onishi, Y., Ohira, M., & Matsumoto, K. (2008). Analysis of coordination between developers and users in the apache community. *Proceedings of the Fourth Conference on Open Source Systems*, (pp. 81–92).

Knab, P., Pinzger, M., & Bernstein, A. (2006). Predicting defect densities in source code files with decision tree learners. *Proceedings of the International workshop on Mining software repositories*, (pp. 119–125).

Koch, S., & Stix, V. (2008). Open source project categorization based on growth rate analysis and portfolio planning methods. *Open Source Development, Communities and Quality, IFIP 20th World Computer Congress, Working Group 2.3 on Open Source Software*, (pp. 375–380).

Lethbridge, T. C., Tichelaar, S., & Ploedereder, E. (2004). The dagstuhl middle metamodel: A schema for reverse engineering. *Electronic Notes in Theoretical Computer Science*, 7–18. doi:10.1016/j.entcs.2004.01.008

Martinez-Romo, J., Robles, G., Ortuo-Perez, M., & Gonzalez-Barahona, J. M. (2008). Using social network analysis techniques to study collaboration between a floss community and a company. *Proceedings of the Fourth Conference on Open Source Systems*, (pp. 171–186).

Mller, C., Meuthrath, B., & Baumgra, A. (2008). Analyzing wiki based networks to improve knowledge processes in organizations. *Journal of Universal Computer Science, 14*(4), 526–545.

Mockus, A., & Herbsleb, J. (2002). Expertise browser: A quantitative approach to identifying expertise. *Proceedings of International Conference on Software Engineering*, (pp. 503–512). Orlando.

Mockus, A., & Herbsleb, J. (2003). An empirical study of speed and communication in globally distributed software development. *IEEE Transactions on Software Engineering, 29*(6), 481–494. doi:10.1109/TSE.2003.1205177

Nonaka, I., & Takeuchi, H. (1995). *The knowledge-creating company:How japanese companies create the dynamics of innovation.* New York: Oxford University.

Porruvecchio, G., Uras, S., & Quaresima, R. (2008). Social network analysis of communication in open source projects. *9*, pp. 220–221. Proceedings of 9th International Conference on Agile Processes in Software Engineering and Extreme Programming.

Rich Client Platform. (2010). Retrieved from Rich Client Platform: wiki.eclipse.org

Rosso, C. (2006). Continuous evolution through software architecture evaluation. *Journal of Software Maintenance and Evolution: Research and Practice, 18*(5), 351–383. doi:10.1002/smr.337

Rosso, C. (2009). Comprehend and analyze knowledge networks to improve software evolution. *Journal of Software Maintenance and Evolution: Research and Practice, 21*, 189–215. doi:10.1002/smr.408

Sarma, A. Maccherone, Wagstrom, & Herbsleb. (2009). Tesseract: Interactive visual exploration of socio-technical relationships in software development. *Proceedings of the 31st International Conference on Software Engineering*, (pp. 23–33).

Sarma, A., Noroozi, Z., & Van der Hoek, A. (2003). Palantr: Raising awareness among configuration management workspaces. *Twenty-fifth International Conference on Software Engineering*, (pp. 444–454). Portland, Oregon, USA.

Schmmer, T., & Haake, J. M. (2001). Supporting distributed software development by modes of collaboration. *Seventh European Conference on Computer Supported Cooperative Work*, (pp. 79–98).

Schwaber, K., & Beedle, M. (2001). *Agile software development with Scrum.* Englewood Cliffs, NJ: Prentice-Hall.

Souza, C. d., Quirk, S., Trainer, E., & Redmiles, D. (2007). Supporting collaborative software development through the visualization of socio-technical dependencies. *International ACM SIGGROUP Conference on Supporting Group Work*, (pp. 147–156). Sanibel Island, FL.

Tuunanen, T., Koskinen, J., & Karkkainen, T. (2006). Asla: reverse engineering approach for software license information retrieval. *Proceedings of the 10th European Conference on Software Maintenance and Reengineering*, (pp. 291–294).

Wiggins, A., Howison, J., & Crowston, K. (2009). Heartbeat: Measuring active user base and potential user interes in floss projects. [IFIP Advances in Information and Communication Technology.]. *Open Source Ecosystems: Diverse Communities Interacting., 299/2009*, 94–104. doi:10.1007/978-3-642-02032-2_10

Ye, Y. (2006). Supporting software development as knowledgeintensive and collaborative activity. *International Workshop on Interdisciplinary Software Engineering Research*, (pp. 15–22). New York NY, U.S.A.

Zhou, Y., & Davis, J. (2005). Open source software reliability model: an empirical approach. *Proceedings of the fifth workshop on Open source software engineering, 30*, pp. 1-6.

APPENDIX

Repository Structure

Let,

$$\rho = \{R^1, R^2, \cdots, R^n\}$$

be the set of repositories. Where each repository,

$$R^i = \{r_1^i, r_2^i, \cdots, r_m^i\}$$

consists of repository elements r_j^i. Each repository element

$$r_j^i = \{c_{j1}^i, c_{j2}^i, \cdots, c_{jx}^i\}$$

consists of attributes c_{jk}^i describing it. Each attribute element $c_{jk}^i = \{c_{jkp}^i\}$ consists of a number of attribute values c_{jkp}^i as shown in Figure 2.

For example, consider a set of repositories,

$$\rho = \{File^F, Person^P, Issue^I\}$$

where the $File^F$ repository contains a description of the code files, the $Person^P$ repository contains detail of each person (either user or developer) involved in the project and $Issue^I$ repository contains information about the issues (e.g., reported bugs, feature requests) raised by the project personnel. For this illustration consider only the $File^F$ repository. The repository

$$File^F = \{file_1^F, file_2^F, \cdots, file_m^F\}$$

consists of code files as repository elements. Each code file,

$$File_j^F = \{f_{name\,j1}^F, path_{j2}^F, extension_{j3}^F,$$
$$developer_{j4}^F, includes_{j5}^F, copyright_{j6}^F\}$$

consists of six attributes referring to the name of the file, its path, extension, a list of the names of developers, included files and copyright information. This repository structure is shown in Figure 3.

The InterConnect Operation

The interConnect operation denoted by

$interConnect(R^i, attributeName)$

is performed between the repository elements and corresponding attribute values. Let, $R^1 = \{r_1^1, r_2^1, \cdots, r_m^1\}$ be a repository with its repository elements r_j^1 and for each repository element r_j^1, there is an attribute $c_{j4}^1 = \{c_{j4p}^1\}$ with its attribute values c_{j4p}^1.

$interConnect\left(R^1, c_{j4}^1\right)$

results in a graph with the following vertex and edge sets.

- **Vertices:** Each r_j^1 is added to vertex list $vSetTypeA$ and each attribute value c_{j4i}^1 is added to the vertex list $vSetTypeB$ if not already added.
- **Edges:** For each r_j^1 in R^1, create edges between r_j^1 and each attribute value c_{j4i}^1. Edges are then added to edge list E.

The resultant graph will be a bipartite graph,

$G_{vSetTypeA-vSetTypeB}$
$= (vSetTypeA \bigcup vSetTypeB, E).$

For example, consider the file repository where

$File^F = \{file_1^F, file_2^F, \cdots, file_m^F\}.$

For each repository element $File_j^F$, the attribute $developer_{j4}^F$ consists of one or more developer names,

$developer_{j4}^F = \{dev_{j41}^F, dev_{j42}^F, \cdots, dev_{j4z}^F$

as attribute values.
Then

$interConnect(File^F, developer_{j4}^F)$

operation results in a graph with the following vertex and edge sets.

- **Vertices:** $file_j^F$ is added to vertex list *File* and each attribute value dev_{j4i}^F is added to the vertex list *Developer* if not already added.
- **Edges:** For each $file_j^F$ in $File^F$, create edges between $file_j^F$ and each attribute value dev_{j4i}^F. Edges are then added to edge list *E*.

The resultant bipartite graph

$$G_{File-Developer} = (File \bigcup Developer, E)$$

represents a 2-mode SNA network. It portrays the relationship between two sets of vertices *File* and *Developer*. In other words, this graph shows the relationship between the code files in the repository and the developers who are responsible for those code files. Thus, the interconnect operation can be used to generate graphs that reveal how people (i.e., developers or users) in an OSS project are related to different project artifacts (i.e., code files, issues, mail list).

The IntraConnect Operation

The intraConnect operation denoted by

$$intraConnect(G, relationship VertexSet)$$

is performed on graphs generated by the interConnect operation. Thus G is a 2-mode SNA network and is a bipartite graph. The second argument in this operation denotes one of the two vertices sets in the input bipartite graph. This operation is defined as follows.

Let

$$G_{vSetTypeA-vSetTypeB}$$
$$= \left(vSetTypeA \bigcup vSetTypeB, E\right)$$

be a graph generated by the interConnect operation. The vertex set

$$vSetTypeA = \{vA_1, vA_2, \cdots, vA_m\}$$

and vertex set

$$vSetTypeB = \{vB_1, vB_2, \cdots, vB_n\}.$$

Then,

$$intraConnect \ (G_{vSetTypeA-vSetTypeB}, \ vSetTypeA)$$

results in a graph

$$G^A_{vSetTypeB} = (V^A_{vSetTypeB}, E^A_{vSetTypeB})$$

with the following vertex and edge set,

$$V^A_{vSetTypeB} = \{vB_1, vB_2, \cdots, vB_n\}$$

And

$$E^A_{vSetTypeB} = \left\{ \begin{array}{l} (vB_j, vB_q) | (vB_j, vA_i) \in E \\ \wedge (vB_q, vA_i) \in E, \ j \neq q \end{array} \right\}$$

And the weight for each edge (vB_j, vB_q) is calculated as follows,

$$W(vB_j, vB_q) = |\{vA_i | (vB_j, vA_i)$$
$$\in E \wedge (vB_q, vA_i) \in E, j \neq q\}|,$$

that is the weight for each edge (vB_j, vB_q) is the number of nodes vA_i in $vSetTypeA$ that are common between vB_j and vB_q in the input graph.

For example, consider that the intraConnect operation will be performed on the graph

$$G_{\text{File-Developer}} = (File \bigcup Developer, E).$$

The vertex set

$$File^F = \{file^F_1, file^F_2, \cdots, file^F_m\}$$

consists of code file nodes, and vertex set

$$Developer = \{dev_1, dev_2, \cdots, dev_n\}$$

consists of developer nodes.

Then, the application of

$$intraConnect \ (G_{\text{File-Developer}} \ , File)$$

operation results in a graph

$$G^F_{developer} = (V^F_{developer}, E^F_{developer})$$

where,

$$V_{developer}^{F} = \{dev_1, dev_2, \cdots, dev_n\}$$

And

$$E_{developer}^{F} = \{(dev_j, dev_q) \mid (dev_j, file_i)$$
$$\in E \land (dev_q, file_i) \in E, j \neq q\}$$

The resultant graph $G_{developer}^{F}$ shows the relationship between developer nodes that have edges to at least one common file node in the $G_{File-Developer}$. In other words,

$$G_{developer}^{F} = (V_{developer}^{F}, E_{developer}^{F})$$

graph shows the relationship between developers who contribute or are responsible for the same code files. Hence, the intraConnect operation generates graphs that show how people (i.e., developers or users) are related to each other through project artifacts (i.e., code files, mailing list, bug repository) and vice versa.

The weight for each edge is calculated as

$$W(dev_j, dev_q) = \mid \{file_i \mid (dev_j, file_i)$$
$$\in E \land (dev_q, file_i) \in E, j \neq q\} \mid$$

Thus edge weight in the $G_{developer}^{F}$ graph shows how many code files each pair of developers share in common. This in turn reflects how strongly a group of developers are related to each other and share information and views while developing the project.

Set Operations

In this section, set operations are defined. As set operations are performed on graphs, we will use the following two graphs generated by the *intraConnect* operation,

$$G_{vSetTypeB}^{A} = (V_{vSetTypeB}^{A}, E_{vSetTypeB}^{A})$$

and

$$G_{vSetTypeB}^{C} = (V_{vSetTypeB}^{C}, E_{vSetTypeB}^{C}).$$

These graphs draw relationship among vertices in $vSetTypeB$ based on vertex sets $vSetTypeA$ and $vSetTypeC$, respectively. As an example consider the following two graphs,

$$G_{developer}^{F} = (V_{developer}^{F}, E_{developer}^{F})$$

and

$$G^I_{developer} = (V^I_{developer}, E^I_{developer}).$$

These graphs are generated by the *intraConnect* operation and show the relationships between developers based on common code file sharing and common user issues answered, respectively.

In what follows the definition of set operations is in terms of the above mentioned graphs.

- **Intersection:** The intersection operation denoted by,

$$intersection(G^A_{vSetTypeB}, G^C_{vSetTypeB})$$

keeps only those vertices and edges that are common to both $G^A_{vSetTypeB}$ and $G^C_{vSetTypeB}$ graphs. That is, the resultant graph is

$$G^{intersect}_{vSetTypeB} = (V_{vSetTypeB}, E_{vSetTypeB}),$$

where

$$V_{vSetTypeB} = V^A_{vSetTypeB} \cap V^C_{vSetTypeB}$$

$$E_{vSetTypeB} = E^A_{vSetTypeB} \cap E^C_{vSetTypeB}$$

The weights for the edges are calculated as follows: let, $W^A_{vSetTypeB}$ and $W^C_{vSetTypeB}$ be the weight sets for $G^A_{vSetTypeB}$ and $G^C_{vSetTypeB}$ respectively. Then the weight set $W_{vSetTypeB}$ for $G^{intersect}_{vSetTypeB}$ is calculated as

$$w(e_i) = \{(w(e^A_j) + w(e^C_k)), e_i = e^A_j = e^C_k\}$$

where, $w(e^A_j) \in W^A_{vSetTypeB}$, $w(e^C_k) \in W^C_{vSetTypeB}$ and $w(e_i) \in W_{vSetTypeB}$.

That is, the weight of each edge in the $G^{intersect}_{vSetTypeB}$ graph is the summation of weights of the same edge in the $G^A_{vSetTypeB}$ and $G^C_{vSetTypeB}$ graphs.

A careful look at the input graphs would show that each input graph reveals the relationships among nodes for a specific domain. Thus the weights in the input graph reflect relationship strengths for that domain. The resultant graph considers only those nodes and relationships that are present in both the input graphs (i.e., present in both domains). Thus, the edge weight in this resultant graph must show the overall impact of a relation in both the domains. This is why the weights for the edges in the resultant graph are calculated by adding up weights from both the input graphs.

For example, the

$$intersection(G^F_{developer}, G^I_{developer})$$

operation keeps only those developer vertices and edges that are common to both the $G^F_{developer}$ and $G^I_{developer}$ graphs. That is, the resultant graph is

$$G^{intersect}_{developer} = (V_{developer}, E_{developer}),$$

where

$$V_{developer} = V^F_{developer} \cap V^I_{developer}$$

$$E_{developer} = E^F_{developer} \cap E^I_{developer}.$$

The graph $G^{intersect}_{developer}$ shows those developers and their relationships that are responsible for both code files and solving user issues. Thus, an intersection operation generates graphs showing the multidimensional activities of people (i.e., users and developers) within the OSS project.

For the weight calculation, let

$$W^F_{developer} = \{w\left(e^F_1\right), w\left(e^F_2\right), \cdots, w(e^F_n)\}$$

and

$$W^I_{developer} = \{w\left(e^I_1\right), w\left(e^I_2\right), \cdots, w(e^I_m)\}$$

be the weights for $G^F_{developer}$ and $G^I_{developer}$ respectively.

Then the weight

$$W_{developer} = \{w(e_1), w(e_2), \cdots, w(e_z)\}$$

for the graph $G^{intersect}_{developer}$ is calculated as

$$w\left(e_i\right) = \{\left(w\left(e^F_j\right) + w\left(e^I_k\right)\right), e_i = e^F_j = e^I_k\}$$

Thus, the weights in $G^{intersect}_{developer}$ show the overall interactions between developers during development of the project as well as in solving issues.

- **Union:** The union operation denoted by

$$union(G^A_{vSetTypeB}, G^C_{vSetTypeB})$$

includes all the nodes and edges that are present in both input graphs. That is, the resultant graph is

$$G^{union}_{vSetTypeB} = (V_{vSetTypeB}, E_{vSetTypeB})$$

where,

$$V_{vSetTypeB} = V^A_{vSetTypeB} \bigcup V^C_{vSetTypeB},$$

$$E_{vSetTypeB} = E^A_{vSetTypeB} \bigcup E^C_{vSetTypeB}.$$

Thus this graph shows three regions, one that is common to both the input graphs and the two that are present in either one or the other of the input graphs.

To calculate the edge weights, Let $W^A_{vSetTypeB}$ and $W^C_{vSetTypeB}$ be the weight sets for $G^A_{vSetTypeB}$ and $G^C_{vSetTypeB}$ respectively. Then the weight set $W_{vSetTypeB}$ for $G^{union}_{vSetTypeB}$ is calculated as follows,

Weights for the common region of the graph are:

$$w(e_i) = \{(w(e^A_j) + w(e^C_k)), e_i = e^A_j = e^C_k\}$$

and weights for other two regions are

$$w(e_i) = \{w(e_j) \mid w(e_j) \in W^A_{vSetTypeB}$$
$$\vee w(e_j) \in W^C_{vSetTypeB}, e_i = e_j\},$$

where, $w(e^A_j) \in W^A_{vSetTypeB}$, $w(e^C_k) \in W^C_{vSetTypeB}$ and $w(e_i) \in W_{vSetTypeB}$.

Thus the weights for the common region of the graph are calculated the same way as the intersection operation and have the same rationale as the intersection operation. But the weights for the other two regions of the graph retain their source graph weights. Because each of these regions represents the relationships for a specific domain the weight should reflect the relationship strength for that domain.

Now, applying the union operation to our example graphs would generate a graph

$$G^{union}_{developer} = (V_{developer}, E_{developer}),$$

where

$$V_{developer} = V^F_{developer} \bigcup V^I_{developer},$$

$$E_{developer} = E_{developer}^{F} \bigcup E_{developer}^{I}.$$

This graph $G_{developer}^{union}$ shows three regions within the developer community. The common region shows group of developers who are interested in playing both roles (as developers and issue solvers) and the other two regions show groups of developers who either work as developers or take part only as bug or issue solvers. This graph also shows the relationships among these groups of people within the developer community. Thus, a comprehensive illustration of people's activity, interest area and contribution within the community can be visualized through this operation.

For calculating the weights, let

$$W_{developer}^{F} = \{w\left(e_{1}^{F}\right), w\left(e_{2}^{F}\right), \cdots, w(e_{n}^{F})\}$$

and

$$W_{developer}^{I} = \{w\left(e_{1}^{I}\right), w\left(e_{2}^{I}\right), \cdots, w(e_{m}^{I})\}$$

be the weights for $G_{developer}^{F}$ and $G_{developer}^{I}$ respectively.

Then the weight

$$W_{developer} = \{w(e_{1}), w(e_{2}), \cdots, w(e_{z})\}$$

for the graph $G_{developer}^{union}$ can be calculated as follows. The weights for the common region of the graph are

$$w\left(e_{i}\right) = \{\left(w\left(e_{j}^{F}\right) + w\left(e_{k}^{I}\right)\right), e_{i} = e_{j}^{F} = e_{k}^{I}\}$$

and the weights for the other regions are

$$w\left(e_{i}\right) = \{w(e_{j}) \mid w(e_{j}) \in W_{developer}^{F}$$
$$\vee w(e_{j}) \in W_{developer}^{I}, e_{i} = e_{j}\}$$

That is, the edge weight for the common region is calculated as the sum of their source weights. Therefore this would present the overall strength of the relationship between developers performing both roles (as developer and as issue solver). However, the edges that are from either of the input graphs retain their source weights, showing their communication frequency either as developers or as bug solvers.

- **Difference:** The difference operation denoted by, $difference(G_{vSetTypeB}^{A}, G_{vSetTypeB}^{C})$ results in a graph which will contain only those nodes and edges that are present in $G_{vSetTypeB}^{A}$ but not in $G_{vSetTypeB}^{C}$. That is the resultant graph is $G_{vSetTypeB}^{diff} = (V_{vSetTypeB}, E_{vSetTypeB})$, where

$$V_{vSetTypeB} = V^A_{vSetTypeB} - V^C_{vSetTypeB} = \{v_{vSetTypeB} \mid$$
$$(v_{vSetTypeB} \in V^A_{vSetTypeB}) \otimes (v_{vSetTypeB} \notin V^C_{vSetTypeB})\}$$

and

$$E_{vSetTypeB} = E^A_{vSetTypeB} - E^C_{vSetTypeB} = \{e_{vSetTypeB} \mid$$
$$(e_{vSetTypeB} \in E^A_{vSetTypeB}) \otimes (e_{vSetTypeB} \notin E^C_{vSetTypeB})\}.$$

Edge weight is calculated as follows. Let $W^A_{vSetTypeB}$ and $W^C_{vSetTypeB}$ be the weight sets for $G^A_{vSetTypeB}$ and $G^C_{vSetTypeB}$ respectively. Then the weight set $W_{vSetTypeB}$ for $G^{diff}_{vSetTypeB}$ would be,

$$w(e_i) = \{w(e_j) \mid (w(e_j) \in W^A_{vSetTypeB}), e_i = e_j\}$$

where $w(e_i) \in W_{vSetTypeB}$. That is, the weight of each edge in the $G^{diff}_{vSetTypeB}$ graph retains its source graph weight. The reason is obvious. The resultant graph contains edges from one of the input graphs which are not present in the other.

Thus they should retain their source weights.

For example, the

$$difference(G^F_{developer}, G^I_{developer})$$

operation would result in the

$$G^{diff}_{developer} = (V_{developer}, E_{developer})$$

graph, where

$$V_{developer} = V^F_{developer} - V^I_{developer} = \{v_{developer} \mid$$
$$(v_{developer} \in V^F_{developer}) \otimes (v_{developer} \notin V^I_{developer})\}$$

and

$$E_{developer} = E^F_{developer} - E^I_{developer} = \{e_{developer} \mid$$
$$(e_{developer} \in E^F_{developer}) \otimes (e_{developer} \notin E^I_{developer})\}.$$

Thus the graph $G^{diff}_{developer}$ contains only those nodes and edges that are in $G^F_{developer}$, excluding all the nodes and edges that are common between the two input graphs or in the $G^I_{developer}$ graph. In other words, this graph shows the group of people within the developer community who only concentrate on development.

For the weight calculation, let

$$W_{developer}^{F} = \{w\left(e_1^{F}\right), w\left(e_2^{F}\right), \cdots, w(e_n^{F})\}$$

and

$$W_{developer}^{I} = \{w\left(e_1^{I}\right), w\left(e_2^{I}\right), \cdots, w(e_m^{I})\}$$

be the weights for $G_{developer}^{F}$ and $G_{developer}^{I}$ respectively.

Then the weight

$$W_{developer} = \{w(e_1), w(e_2), \cdots, w(e_z)\}$$

for the graph $G_{developer}^{diff}$ can be calculated as

$$w\left(e_i\right) = \{w(e_j) \mid (w(e_j) \in W_{developer}^{F}), e_i = e_j\}.$$

That is, the weight of each edge is taken from source graph $G_{developer}^{F}$. These weights show how strongly the developers are tied together during development.

- **Symmetric Difference:** The Symmetric Difference operation denoted by

$$symmDifference(G_{vSetTypeB}^{A}, G_{vSetTypeB}^{C})$$

results in a graph which contains all the nodes and edges that are either in $G_{vSetTypeB}^{A}$ or in $G_{vSetTypeB}^{C}$, excluding the common nodes and edges. That is, the resultant graph is $G_{vSetTypeB}^{symmDiff} = (V_{vSetTypeB}, E_{vSetTypeB})$, where

$$V_{vSetTypeB} = V_{vSetTypeB}^{A} \otimes V_{vSetTypeB}^{C} = \{v_{vSetTypeB} \mid$$
$$(v_{vSetTypeB} \in V_{vSetTypeB}^{A}) \otimes (v_{vSetTypeB} \notin V_{vSetTypeB}^{C})\}$$

and

$$E_{vSetTypeB} = E_{vSetTypeB}^{A} \otimes E_{vSetTypeB}^{C} = \{e_{vSetTypeB} \mid$$
$$(e_{vSetTypeB} \in E_{vSetTypeB}^{A}) \otimes (e_{vSetTypeB} \notin E_{vSetTypeB}^{C})\}.$$

and the weights for the edges are calculated as

$$w(e_i) = \{w(e_j) \mid (w(e_j) \in W^A_{vSetTypeB})$$
$$\vee (w(e_j) \in W^C_{vSetTypeB}), e_i = e_j\}$$

where

$$w(e_i) \in W_{vSetTypeB}.$$

So, the edges in $G^{symmDiff}_{vSetTypeB}$ retain the source weights to which they actually belong because the edges in this graph are from either of the input graphs which in turn represent distinct domain of activities. Thus the edge weights should also reflect the relationship strength for that particular domain.

For example, the

$$symmDifference(G^F_{developer}, G^I_{developer})$$

operation would result in

$$G^{symmDiff}_{developer} = (V_{developer}, E_{developer})$$

graph, where

$$V_{developer} = V^F_{developer} \otimes V^I_{developer} = \{v_{developer} \mid$$
$$(v_{developer} \in V^F_{developer}) \otimes (v_{developer} \notin V^I_{developer})\}$$

and

$$E_{developer} = E^F_{developer} \otimes E^I_{developer} = \{e_{developer} \mid$$
$$(e_{developer} \in E^F_{developer}) \otimes (e_{developer} \notin E^I_{developer})\}.$$

Thus, for this example, graph $G^{symmDiff}_{developer}$ shows two groups within the developer community, one performing as developers and the other only dealing with bugs or issues. Hence, this operation can be used to find out specialized groups within the community.

For calculating the weights Let,

$$W^F_{developer} = \{w(e^F_1), w(e^F_2), \cdots, w(e^F_n)\}$$

and

$$W^I_{developer} = \{w\left(e^I_1\right), w\left(e^I_2\right), \cdots, w(e^I_m)\}$$

be the weights for $G^F_{developer}$ and $G^I_{developer}$ respectively.

Then the weight

$$W_{developer} = \{w(e_1), w(e_2), \cdots, w(e_z)\}$$

for the graph $G^{symmDiff}_{developer}$ would be,

$$w\left(e_i\right) = \{w(e_j) \mid (w(e_j) \in W^F_{vSetTypeB})$$
$$\vee (w(e_j) \in W^I_{vSetTypeB}), e_i = e_j\}.$$

That is, the edges in $G^{symmDiff}_{developer}$ retain their source weights.

This work was previously published in the International Journal of Open Source Software and Processes, Volume 3, Issue 2, edited by Stefan Koch, pp. 43-79, copyright 2011 by IGI Publishing (an imprint of IGI Global).

Chapter 7

To Fork or Not to Fork:
Fork Motivations in SourceForge Projects

Linus Nyman
Hanken School of Economics, Finland

Tommi Mikkonen
Tampere University of Technology, Finland

ABSTRACT

A project fork occurs when software developers take a copy of source code from one software package and use it to begin an independent development work that is maintained separately. Although forking in open source software does not require the permission of the original authors, the new version competes for the attention of the same developers that have worked on the original version. The motivations developers have for performing forks are many, but in general they have received little attention. The authors present the results of a study of forks performed in SourceForge (http://sourceforge.net/) and list the developers' motivations for their actions.

INTRODUCTION

A project fork takes place when software developers take a copy of the source code from one software package and use it to begin an independent development work. In general, forking results in an independent version of the system that is maintained separately from its origin. In open source software development no permission from the original authors is needed to start a fork. Therefore, if some developers are unhappy with the fashion in which the project is being managed, they can start an independent project of their own. However, since other developers must then decide which version of the project to support, forking may dilute the community as the average number of developers per system under development decreases.

Despite some high-visibility forks, such as the forking of OpenOffice (http://www.openoffice.org/) into LibreOffice (http://www.libreoffice.org/) and the creation of various projects from the code base of MySQL (http://www.mysql.com/), the whole concept of forking has seen little study. Furthermore, developers' motivations for forking are understood even less, although at times it seems

DOI: 10.4018/978-1-4666-2937-0.ch007

rational and straightforward to identify frustration with the fashion in which the main project is being managed as a core reason.

In this paper, we present the results of our investigation of SourceForge (http://sourceforge. net/) for forked projects and the motivations the authors have identified for performing a fork. Furthermore, we categorize the different motivations and identify some common misbeliefs regarding forking in general.

The rest of this paper is structured as follows: First, the paper discusses the necessary background for explaining some of the technical aspects associated with forking, and then we introduce the fashion in which the research was carried out. Next we offer insight into our most important findings, and discuss them in more detail. We then propose some directions for future research, and conclude the paper with some final remarks.

BACKGROUND

When pushed to the extreme, forks can be considered an expression of the freedom made available through free and open source software. A commonly associated downside is that forking creates the need for duplicated development efforts. In addition, it can confuse users about which forked package to use. In other words, developers have the option to collaborate and pool resources with free and open source software, but this is enforced not by free software licenses, but only by the commitment of all parties to cooperate.

There are various ways to approach forking and its study. One is to categorize the different types to differentiate between, on the one hand, forks carried out due to amicable but irreconcilable disagreements and interpersonal conflicts about the direction of the project, and on the other, forks due to both technical disagreements and interpersonal conflicts (Fogel, 2006). Still, the most obvious form of forking occurs when, due to a disagreement among developers, a program splits into two versions with the original code serving as the basis for the new version of the program.

Raymond (2001) considers the actions of the developer community as well as the compatibility of new code to be a central issue in differentiating code forking from code fragmentation. Different distributions of a program are considered 'pseudo-forks' because at first glance they appear to be forks, but in fact are not, since they can benefit enough from each others' development efforts not to be a waste, either technically or sociologically. Moody (2011) reflects Raymond's sentiments, pointing out that code fragmentation does not traditionally lead to a split in the community and is thus considered less of a concern than a fork of the same program would be. These sentiments both echo a distinction made by Fogel (2006): it is not the existence of a fork which hurts a project, but rather the loss of developers and users. Here it is worth noting, however, that forking can potentially also increase the developer community. In cases in which developers are not interested in working on the original (for instance due to frustration with the project direction, disagreements with a lead developer, or not wanting to work on a corporate sponsored project), not forking would lead to fewer developers as the developers in question would likely simply quit the project rather than continue work on the original.

Both Weber (2004) and Fogel (2006) discuss the concept of forks as being healthy for the ecosystem in a 'survival of the fittest' sense; the best code will survive. However, they also note that while a fork may benefit the ecosystem, it is likely to harm the individual project.

Another dimension to forking lies in the intention of the fork. Again, several alternatives may exist. For instance, the goal of forking can be to create different branches for stable and development versions of the same system, in which case forking is commonly considered to serve the interests of the community. At the other extreme lies the hostile takeover, which means that a commercial vendor attempts to privatize the source code (Lerner & Tirole, 2002). Perhaps somewhat paradoxically, however, the potential to fork any open source code also ensures the possibility of survival for any project. As Moody (2009) points out, the open source community and open source companies differ substantially in that companies can be bought and sold, but the community cannot. If the community disapproves of the actions of an open source company, whether due to attempts to privatize the source code or for other reasons related to an open source program, the open source community can simply fork the software from the last open version and continue working in whichever direction it chooses.

RESEARCH APPROACH

In the study, we used SourceForge (http://source-forge.net/) as the repository of open source programs from which we collected forks. SourceForge contains over 300,000 open source projects created by over three million developers. Creating new projects, participating in those that already exist, or downloading their contents is free, and developers exercise this freedom: programs are downloaded from SourceForge at a pace of more than 4,000,000 downloads daily (http://sourceforge.net/about).

SourceForge offers programmers the opportunity to briefly describe their program, and these descriptions can be searched using keywords. Using this search function, we compiled a list of all of the programs with the word "fork" – as well as dozens of intentionally misspelled variations of the word fork, none of which turned up any hits – in their description. We then analyzed all the descriptions individually to differentiate between them and to sort out programs that the developers claimed had forked their code base from another program (which we call "self-proclaimed forks") from those which included the term 'fork' for some other reason, either to describe a specific functionality of the program or as part of its name (i.e., false positives). Consequently, a program

that stated "This is a fork of …" was considered a fork, while a program which noted that it "… can be used to avoid common security problems when a process forks or is forked" was not. If it was impossible to categorize a project based on the available data, it was discarded. Our data consisted of all programs registered on SourceForge from its founding in late 1999 through 31 December 2010, resulting in a time span of slightly more than 11 years. This search yielded a total of 566 programs that developers reported to be forked.

We then analyzed the motivations stated in the descriptions of the forked programs. The coding process was done in three phases. First, we went through all of the descriptions and wrote a brief summary of the motivations, condensing the stated reasons to as few words as possible. Then, we went through all of the motivations and identified common themes, or subgroups of motivations, among them. In cases where the fork included elements from more than one theme, we placed it in the subgroup that seemed the most central to the motivation behind the fork. Finally, we examined the subgroups to identify overarching groups of themes.

To give some examples of the coding, one fork stated: "[Project name] is a fork of the [original project name] project. [The] purpose of [project name] is to add many new features like globule reproduction, text to speech, and much more." The motivation behind the fork was identified as belonging to the subgroup "add content", which in the final step was combined (with a subgroup of programs which sought to focus content) into a group called content modifications. A fork which sought to fix bugs, and a fork which was motivated by porting a program, were first put into separate subgroups, "technical: improvement" and "technical: porting," and then these subgroups were combined into the "technical modifications" group. Further examples from the data are presented in the next section.

Based on the descriptions entered by the developer, we were able to identify motivations for

381 of the forks. The group of forks which we were unable to categorize consisted of two main types of descriptions: firstly, descriptions which offered no insights as to underlying motivations, e.g., programs which simply stated which program they were forked from; secondly, cases in which it was unclear from the description if the elements described were added in the fork or if they existed in the original; in other words, one couldn't determine if the description of the program included the motivation behind the fork, for instance new technical features, or if they were describing pre-existing features common to both the original and the fork.

REASONS FOR FORKING

Based on the data obtained, developers commonly attribute their reasons for forking the code to pragmatism. For a variety of reasons, some of which were well documented and some of which were unclear, the original version of the code failed to meet developers' needs. To expand the scope of the system, the developers then decided to fork the program to a version which serves their own needs. The descriptions of the forks include programs which note that certain changes have been made to the fork, as well as those programs which discuss which changes will or should be made to the forked version. In this paper, we have not distinguished between the two: both planned and already implemented changes are treated equally, since the goal was to study motivations rather than eventual implementations. In general, the forks appear to stem from new developers rather than the original developing team splitting into two camps. In fact, the data contain almost no references to disagreements among developers that might have led to the fork. However, this does not mean that such disagreements could not have existed.

In the following section, we provide a more detailed view of the different motivations we were able to find in the data (n = 381). The main motivations fall into two large groups (content and technical modifications) which comprise nearly three quarters (72%) of all forking motivations. Four smaller groups, all of similar size, comprise an additional 23% of the motivations. These four groups included the reviving of a project, license- or Freedom of Speech (FOS)-related motivations, language- or country-related reasons, and experimental forks. The remaining motivations, grouped simply as "other," consisted of diverse yet uncommon reasons. An overview reflecting the numbers of forks appears in Figure 1.

Content Modifications

Comprising almost half of all forks, content modifications is the largest group. The two main subgroups within the content modifications category, both of which are nearly equal in size, were the adding and the focusing of content; these are briefly discussed.

Adding content is a self-explanatory reason for making a fork. The developers added new features or other content (e.g., adding better documentation, helper utilities, or larger maps to a game). Quite often, developers didn't describe additions in detail; one developer, for instance, simply noted that the program was a fork "that has the features I'm missing from [the original]." Another developer stated that the fork was "A [program name] fork with more features." In several cases, this group of forks also included bugfixes.

Focusing content implies focusing on the needs of a specific user segment. This category includes forks with both a technical and content-related focus, along with the addition of functionalities and features as well as the removal of elements or features unnecessary for a specific segment or purpose. Examples of content-related focus include programs forked in order to focus on serving the needs of dance studios, radio talk shows, catering companies, program developers, and astronomers,

Figure 1. Fork motivations in SourceForge projects

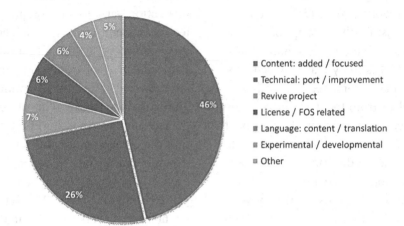

- Content: added / focused
- Technical: port / improvement
- Revive project
- License / FOS related
- Language: content / translation
- Experimental / developmental
- Other

to name but a few. Examples of technical focus include forks "aimed at higher-resolution iOS devices," a fork which "features improvements and changes that make it more oriented for use in a Plone intranet site," and a fork intended "to run on machines that have 800x600 screen resolution." In a minority of the cases in the focusing content category, the original program was forked mainly to remove elements from the original. The main goal in this group was to create a lighter or simpler version of the original, with speed and ease of use as the main focus. One developer stated that the fork was "lightweight, less bloated" and that it was forked to "make [the original] simpler, faster, more useable." Another developer noted that the fork was "Smaller, faster, easy to use."

Technical Modifications

This group, comprising just over a quarter of all forks, can be divided into two subcategories: porting and improving. A characteristic of this category was that little if anything was visibly different to the user; the forked programs simply focused on either porting or improving the original.

Porting the original code to new hardware or software was the more common of the technical motivations for forking, usually involving porting the original to fit a certain operating system,

hardware, game, plug-in, migrate to a different protocol, or other such reasons. Examples from the data for this group include a "fork of [program name] to GNU/Linux," a fork "compatible with the NT architecture," "a simple C library for communicating with the Nintendo Wii Remote [...] on a Linux system," and a program fork whose main target was to create a version "which works with ispCP." Some forks were ported to reduce dependencies; for instance, one developer who noted that the fork was "geared towards 'freeing' [the original program] from its system dependence, [thus] enabling it to run natively on e.g., Mac OS X or Cygwin." Another developer noted that the program was forked because the developer could not find a "good and recent [program type] without KDE dependency."

Improving the original program was slightly less common in the technical motivations category than porting, which focuses on improving already existing features and contains mostly bugfixes, code improvement and optimization, and security improvements. Some cases were very general in their descriptions, noting only that it was an "upgraded" or "improved" version of the original, or that the code was forked "to fix numerous problems in the code" or to "improve the quality of emulation." Others were more specific, as with the developer of one fork, who notes that "The main goal is to build a new codebase which handles bandwidth restrictions as well as upcoming security issues and other hassles which showed up [during] the last 6 months."

Reviving an Abandoned Project

The third common motivation for forking was to continue development of a project considered abandoned, deceased, stalled, retired, stagnant, inactive, or unmaintained. In several of these cases, the developers of the fork note who the original developers are and credit them. In a few cases, the developers of the fork note that they attempted (unsuccessfully) to reach the original developers; in other words, forking the code was the last available option for these developers, as the original developers could no longer be reached. One such example is a fork which the developer notes was "due to long-time inactivity" and then goes on to state "We want to thank the project founder [name] for starting this project and we intend to continue the work." In another case, also due to the inactivity of the original developer, the developer of the fork acknowledges the original author and notes that the fork "includes changes from comments made on his forum." Other examples from the data are: "This project is a fork of the excellent but dead [project name] project," "This project is a fork of the stalled [project name]," "a code fork from the (deceased) [project name] source," and, finally, "The previous maintainer is unresponsive since 2008 and the library [has] some deficiencies that need to [be] fixed. Anyway, thanks for creating this great library [name of original developer]!"

License/FOS-Related Issues

This group consists of forks which were motivated by license-related issues or a concern for the freedom of the code. Some of the forks appear to be simply a form of backup copies: stored open source versions of well-known programs. The motivation for this subgroup was a concern that

the original version might become closed source. In one case, the developer stated that the fork was due to concern about the future openness of the code. In a similar case, a developer noted about the fork that "This is a still-GPL version of [program name,] just in case." One fork simply identifies the motivation as a "license problem." In five cases, the program was forked because the original was deemed to have become either closed source or commercial, and in one case, developers noted that the fork occurred because certain bits of the original code were closed source. One fork notes that the new version removes proprietary (boot) code from the program, but that "there is no need to use this version unless you are concerned about the copyright status of the embedded boot code."

Language- and/or Country-Specific Modifications

A small group of the forks were motivated by language and country. This group could well be considered a subcategory of the "focusing content" group, but was considered separate due to its clear language- and country-related focus. The simplest, though not most common, form of forks included programs which were merely translated into one or more languages; in most cases, however, new content was also added to customize the fork for a specific country and/or group. Some examples are forks created for elections in New Zealand, the right-to-left reading of Hebrew texts, and a program "customized to meet German requirements regarding accounting and financial reporting."

Experimentation

This group consisted mostly of forks which declared that they existed for experimental purposes, with a handful citing development reasons. A feature common among many of these forks is that the developers state that the fork is temporary and that successful new features or improvements will be incorporated into the original program. Some describe the fork as simply "for testing," while others go into greater detail, noting for instance that the fork is "aimed at experimenting with a number of features turned up to maximum." One developer notes that the fork is simply "for fun," and then goes on to tell readers where they can find the original project.

Other Reasons

Of the remaining forks, a handful described it as a "community fork." In some of these cases, it was possible to identify an overarching motivation behind the community fork; in others it was not, the implications of the term in those cases remaining unclear. Two cases cite a reprogramming in a different programming language as the reason for the fork. The remaining reasons for the forks defied categorization, and included such motivations as a desire to create a study tool for the developer, as well as to test SourceForge for a different project.

Finally, the most surprising of the remaining groups was the group motivated by disagreement or breach of trust. In the beginning of the study, we assumed that a significant number of forks would stem from disagreement between developers. In reality, we were able to identify such forks, but their proportion is quite small: we identified only four cases, three of which stated that the users sought something the original developers did not intend to implement and one which noted that the fork was a reaction to a breach of trust. Furthermore, even some of these cases may be attributed to the original developers' loss of interest in the project.

DISCUSSION

The data in this paper are based on information provided by developers themselves. Many of the cases of self-proclaimed forking – such as when a developer continues an abandoned project – could arguably be defined as something other than a true fork. However, determining forks any other way

(other than through the self-proclaimed approach used here) would require a technical definition of a fork that would have to be mined from the project data. At present, no such mechanism seems to exist, and in general, differentiating between forked and fragmented code is an ambiguous practice, unless defined by elements outside of the code itself. Consequently, we have identified the developers as the most reliable source of information, at least at present.

Beyond the challenge of defining a fork, one here also needs to note two issues: how the choice of SourceForge as a sampling frame might affect the data, as well as how accurate, or complete, the descriptions offered there are. The choice of SourceForge could affect the data in several ways. The main question would seem to be whether the characteristics of the average program – or program fork – on SourceForge differ from those of programs hosted on other sites, or from independently hosted programs. For example, given that larger projects often have their own hosting, it is possible that we are seeing only a small number of forks in some categories because projects that would face such issues are not using SourceForge. As to the completeness of the motivations offered by developers, there could be a number of reasons why the information offered is incomplete. For instance, the low frequency of disagreements as a motivational factor in forking may perhaps in part be explained by either a reluctance to mention such disagreements or the limited space offered by SourceForge in which to describe the program. It is also possible that such information, while not stated on SourceForge, would be available on project homepages. Indeed, we came across a project which noted elsewhere that a disagreement among the developers of the original was a factor in the fork; however, the same project did not mention this disagreement in their description on SourceForge.

In general, the results of our study suggest that forking is not a particularly extreme situation in real-life projects. For the most part, developers' motivations are easily understandable, and forking can be considered a reasonable action. However, this does not mean that hostile takeovers are absent from high-profile projects, but simply that in the vast majority of cases, developers appear simply to seek to satisfy their own needs and to develop interesting systems. Such motivations were evident in the documentation in many ways. Furthermore, crediting the original developers was a rather common practice among those who forked a program, which further emphasizes the fact that forks sought to achieve certain goals, not to compete with existing communities. Perhaps more telling still is that a number of forks noted that they hoped to be temporary, and clearly stated their desire that the bugfixes and improvements introduced in their fork be incorporated into the original program.

FUTURE WORK

Future work regarding issues associated with forking could take numerous directions. Below we list some of the most promising directions that merit further investigation.

- **Defining a Fork:** All of the programs in the data for this article define themselves as forks. In practice, upon more careful review, many of them could perhaps more accurately be categorized as pseudo-forks, code fragmentation, or simply different distributions of a code. The creation of a commonly agreed-upon view of forking vs. fragmentation (or distributions) vs. code reuse would be a very practical step that could benefit both researchers as well as the entire open source community. It could also be possible to define a fork based on technical details, rather than depend on information provided solely by the developers.
- **Licenses Before and After Forking:** Future researchers could conduct a survey of developers who have forked a program in which they explain their choice of license in comparison to the license of the original program from which they forked.
- **Perceptions of Forking:** Another practical aspect related to forking is how programmers view it; in other words, when is it acceptable to fork, and when is it not? Furthermore, discovering whether certain behaviors make forking more acceptable among developers would be an important direction for such work.
- **Expanding the Data Set:** Performing a similar study for other sites that host open source projects would contribute to a deeper understanding of forking. Because all the data come from only one source, certain aspects may skew the results. Furthermore, it would be interesting to test if one can tie the observed categories to antecedents or consequences, e.g., are particular kinds of software more likely to fork in particular ways or are particular kinds of forks more successful?
- **Forking in Relation to Business:** A number of forks we have identified occurred because the original project became closed source. Examining what happened to these projects would deepen our understanding and view of forking in relation to business.

CONCLUSION

Forking is one of the least understood topics in open source development. While often perceived initially as something malicious, the developers who perform the actual forking cite rather straightforward reasons for their actions.

In this paper, we addressed the motivations of developers for performing a fork. The data used in the project originate from SourceForge (http://sourceforge.net/), one of the best-known hosts of open source projects, and focus on "self-proclaimed forks," or programs that the program developers themselves consider to be forks. The motivations behind forking are based on developer input, not on mining technical qualities of the project. However, using only the latter to determine forking would be difficult, as separating forking from other open source-related phenomena is problematic and inconclusive. At the very least, additional data from developers are needed to define forking.

In conclusion, while hostile takeovers and the hijacking of a project as well as a loss of developers after a fork are often associated with forking, the reality is that forks seem to be a lot less dramatic. In fact, forking appears to be more or less business as usual, and developers fork because doing so provides certain benefits for their own goals. While we were able to find forks where the rationale for forking lay in disagreement or trust issues, such cases were few in comparison to the total number of projects we studied.

REFERENCES

Fogel, K. (2006). *Producing open source software*. Sebastopol, CA: O'Reilly.

Lerner, J., & Tirole, J. (2002). Some simple economics of open source. *The Journal of Industrial Economics*, *50*(2), 197–234. doi:10.1111/1467-6451.00174

Moody, B. (2009, April 23). Who owns commercial open source and can forks work? *Linux Journal*.

Moody, B. (2011, January 28). The deeper significance of LibreOffice 3.3. *ComputerWorld UK*.

Raymond, E. S. (2001). *The Cathedral & the Bazaar: Musings on Linux and open source by an accidental revolutionary*. Sebastopol, CA: O'Reilly.

Weber, S. (2004). *The success of open source*. Cambridge, MA: Harvard University Press.

This work was previously published in the International Journal of Open Source Software and Processes, Volume 3, Issue 3, edited by Stefan Koch, pp. 1-9, copyright 2011 by IGI Publishing (an imprint of IGI Global).

Chapter 8
Software Reuse in Open Source:
A Case Study

Andrea Capiluppi
Brunel University, UK

Klaas-Jan Stol
Lero (The Irish Software Engineering Research Centre), University of Limerick, Ireland

Cornelia Boldyreff
University of East London, UK

ABSTRACT

A promising way to support software reuse is based on Component-Based Software Development (CBSD). Open Source Software (OSS) products are increasingly available that can be freely used in product development. However, OSS communities still face several challenges before taking full advantage of the "reuse mechanism": many OSS projects duplicate effort, for instance when many projects implement a similar system in the same application domain and in the same topic. One successful counter-example is the FFmpeg multimedia project; several of its components are widely and consistently reused in other OSS projects. Documented is the evolutionary history of the various libraries of components within the FFmpeg project, which presently are reused in more than 140 OSS projects. Most use them as black-box components; although a number of OSS projects keep a localized copy in their repositories, eventually modifying them as needed (white-box reuse). In both cases, the authors argue that FFmpeg is a successful project that provides an excellent exemplar of a reusable library of OSS components.

INTRODUCTION

Reuse of software components is one of the most promising practices of software engineering (Basili & Rombach, 1991). Enhanced productivity (as less code needs to be written), increased quality (since assets proven in one project can be carried through to the next) and improved business performance (lower costs, shorter time-to-market) are often pinpointed as the main benefits of developing software from a stock of reusable components (Sametinger, 1997; Sommerville, 2004).

Although much research has focused on the reuse of Off-The-Shelf (OTS) components, both Commercial OTS (COTS) and Open Source Software (OSS), in corporate software production

DOI: 10.4018/978-1-4666-2937-0.ch008

(Li *et al.*, 2009; Torchiano & Morisio, 2004), the reusability *of* OSS projects *in* other OSS projects has only recently started to draw the attention of researchers and developers in OSS communities (Lang *et al.*, 2005; Mockus, 2007; Capiluppi & Boldyreff, 2008). A vast amount of code is created daily, modified and stored in OSS repositories, and the inherent philosophy around OSS is indeed promoting reuse. Yet, software reuse in OSS projects is hindered by various factors, psychological and technical. For instance, the project to be reused could be written in a programming language that the hosting project dislikes or is incompatible with; the hosting project might not agree with the design decisions made by the project to be reused; finally, individuals in the hosting project may dislike individuals involved in the project to be reused (Senyard & Michlmayr, 2004). A search for the "*email client*" topic in the SourceForge repository (http://www.sourcforge.net) produces 128 different projects (SourceForge, 2011): this may suggest that similar features in the same domain are implemented by different projects[1], and that code and features duplication play a significant role in the production of OSS code.

The interest of practitioners and researchers in the topic of software reuse has focused on two predominant questions: (1) from the perspective of *OSS integrators* (Hauge *et al.*, 2007), how to select an OSS component to be reused in another (potentially commercial) software system, and (2) from the perspective of end-users, how to provide a level of objective "trust" in available OSS components. This interest is based on a sound reasoning; given the increasing amount of source code and documentation created and modified daily, it starts to be a (commercially) viable solution to browse for components in existing code and select existing, working resources to reuse as building blocks of new software systems, rather than building them from scratch.

Among the reported cases of successful reuse within OSS systems, components with clearly defined requirements, and hardly affecting the overall design (i.e., the "S" and "P" types of systems following the original S-P-E classification by Lehman (1980)) have often proven to be the typically reused resources by OSS projects. Reported examples include the "internationalization" (often referred to as I18N) component (which produces different output text depending on the language of the system), or the "install" module for Perl subsystems (involved in compiling the code, test and install it in the appropriate locations) (Mockus, 2007). To our best knowledge, there is no academic literature about the successful reuse of OSS, and an understanding of internal characteristics of what makes a component reusable in the OSS context is lacking.

The main focus of this paper is to report on the FFmpeg project (http://ffmpeg.org/), and its build-level components, and to show how some of these components are currently reused in other projects. This project is a cornerstone in the multimedia domain; several dozens of OSS projects reuse parts of FFmpeg, one of the most widely reused being the libavcodec component. In the domain of OSS multimedia applications, libavcodec is the most widely adopted and reused audio/video codec (**co**ding and **dec**oding) resource. Its reuse by other OSS projects is so widespread since it represents a crosscutting resource for a wide range of systems, from single-user video and audio players to converters and multimedia frameworks. As such, FFmpeg represents a unique case (Yin, 2003, p.40), which is why we selected the project for this study.

In particular, the study is an attempt to evaluate whether the reusability principle of "high cohesion and loose coupling" (Fenton, 1991; Macro & Buxton, 1987; Troy & Zweben, 1981) has an impact on the evolutionary history of the FFmpeg components.

This paper makes two contributions:

1. It studies how the *size* of FFmpeg components evolve: the empirical findings show that the libavcodec component (contained in

FFmpeg) is an "evolving and reusable" component (an "E-type" of system) (Lehman, 1980), and as such it poses several interesting challenges when other projects integrate it; and

2. It studies how the architecture of FFmpeg components evolve, and how these components evolve when separated from FFmpeg: the empirical findings show two emerging scenarios in the reuse of this resource. On the one hand, the majority of projects that reuse the FFmpeg components do so with a "black-box" strategy (Szyperski, 2002), as such incurring synchronization issues due to the independent co-evolution of the project and the component. On the other hand, a number of OSS projects apply a "white-box" reuse strategy, by maintaining a private copy of the FFmpeg components. The latter scenario is further empirically analyzed in order to obtain a better understanding of how the component is not only reused, but also integrated into a host system.

The remainder of this paper is structured following the guidelines for reporting case study research proposed by Runeson and Höst (2009). The next section provides relevant background information and an overview of related work on software components and OSS systems. This is followed by a presentation of the research design of our study. After this, the results of the empirical study are presented. Followed by threats to validity of this study. The last section concludes with the key findings and provides directions for future work.

BACKGROUND AND RELATED WORK

This section presents background and related work that is relevant for the remainder of the paper. The first subsection briefly discusses research on OSS reuse. This is followed by a discussion of Component-Based Software Development (CBSD) and the terminology used in this paper. This is followed by a brief overview of a useful and relevant categorization of components. Since this work considers the evolution of software components, a brief summary of Lehman's classification of software programs is provided. This section concludes with a brief discussion of related work regarding software decay and architectural recovery.

Component-Based Software Development and Terminology

As mentioned, Component-Based Software Development (CBSD) has been proposed as a promising approach to large-scale software reuse. It is important, however, first to define clearly what is meant by the term "component." The word "component" is often used in the context of CBSD as a reusable piece of software, either Commercial Off-The-Shelf (COTS) or Open Source. For instance, Torchiano and Morisio (2004) have derived the following definition: "*A COTS product is a commercially available or open source piece of software that other software projects can reuse and integrate into their own products.*" This definition considers a COTS or Open Source software product as an independent unit that can be reused. However, a number of authors have provided more specific definitions; a commonly cited definition can be found in Szyperski (2002, p. 41): "*A software component is a unit of composition with contractually specified interfaces and explicit context dependencies only. A software component can be deployed independently and is subject to composition by third parties.*"

As De Jonge (2005) points out, "*Component-Based Software Engineering (CBSE) is mostly concerned with execution-level components (such as COM, CCB, or EJB components).*" Szyperski (2002, p. 3) also speaks of software components as being "*excecutable units of independent pro-*

duction, acquisition, and deployment that can be composed into a functioning system."

In this paper, following De Jonge (2005) we use the term "build-level component." De Jonge speaks of build-level components as *directory hierarchies containing ingredients of an application's build process, such as source files, build and configuration files, libraries, and so on."* In an earlier paper, De Jonge (2002) uses the term "source code component." In this context, we interpret the meaning of "build-level" component to be equivalent to the term "module," as used by Clements *et al.* (2010, p. 29). They indicate that a module refers to a *unit of implementation*, and as such, can be source code or other implementation artifacts. Eick *et al.* (2001) also interpret a module to be a directory in the source code file system, which contains several files, though they note that this terminology is not standard. Tran *et al.* (1999, 2000) considered *individual* source files as modules. Clements *et al.* define a "component" to be a *runtime entity*, which is consistent with the definition by Szyperski. Although important issues are already known when incorporating and reusing whole systems into larger, overarching projects (as in the case of Linux distributions German & Hassan, 2009), in the remainder of this paper, we use the term "component" to refer to build-level component.

Components can be reused in different ways, as briefly mentioned: *black-box* reuse and *white-box* reuse (Szyperski, 2002). Black-box reuse refers to the reuse of a component as-is without any alterations. The component can only be viewed in terms of its input and output. This is typically the case when proprietary (COTS) components are used, as the source code is usually not available for proprietary software. On the other hand, when the component's source code is available, the integrator can perform *white-box* reuse. The integrator may make changes to a component to fit his or her intended purpose. Obviously, the availability of the source code makes OSS components particularly suitable for white-box reuse.

The two scenarios are summarized in Figure 1. As an example, the MPlayer project keeps a copy of the library in its repository (and it eventually modifies, or "forks," it for its own purposes, in a white-box reuse scenario), while the VLC project, at compilation time, requires the user to provide the location of an up-to-date version of the FFmpeg project (black-box reuse).

Research on Open Source Software Reuse

There is a growing body of empirical research the use of OSS components in CBSD (Ayala *et al.*, 2007; Hauge *et al.*, 2009; Capiluppi & Knowles, 2009; Li *et al.*, 2009; Ven & Mannaert, 2008). There is an increasing number of OSS products available, many of which have become viable alternatives to commercial products (Fitzgerald, 2006), and adopting OSS components to build products is a common scenario (Hauge *et al.*, 2010).

Research on OSS reuse can be classified along two dimensions. The first dimension considers the question *who* reuses the software. This can either

Figure 1. Black-box reuse (by VLC) and white-box reuse (by MPlayer)

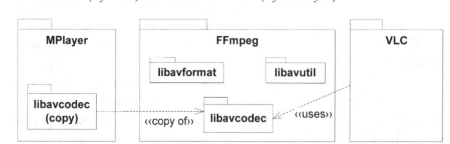

be an Independent Software Vendor (ISV), or other OSS communities. The second dimension considers the *software* that is reused, in particular the *granularity* of components. Haefliger *et al.* (2008) identified different granularities of code reuse: algorithms and methods, single lines of code, and components. Components themselves may be of a coarse granularity, i.e., complete software systems. A common example of this is the so-called "LAMP stack," (Wikipedia, n.d.) which is an "ensemble" of Linux, Apache, MySQL, and a scripting language such as Python, Perl, PHP or Ruby. Much of the literature on OSS reuse focuses such coarse grained components by ISVs, though it is noteworthy that granularity cannot be measured on a discrete scale but rather a continuous one. German *et al.* (2007) discuss dependencies between packages (which they define as an installable unit of software), such as found in Linux distributions. They define a model to represent and analyze such dependencies. Other work led by German investigated the issue of licenses when reusing different OSS components (German & Hassan, 2009; German & González-Barahona, 2009).

On the other hand, reuse can be done with components of a finer granularity. There are few studies of this, all of which focus on the reuse by other OSS projects. The study presented in this paper also considers components of relatively small granularity, which is why we discuss this related work in more detail. Table 1 provides an overview of the study objectives as well as research methods and samples.

One of the first studies that quantifies the reuse in Open Source Software is by Mockus (2007). That study focuses on reuse by identifying directories of source code files that share a number (defined by a threshold) of file names; therefore, the study only considers *white-box* reuse. Mockus studied reuse on a large sample of 38,700 unique projects with 5.3 million unique file name paths. Mockus found that approximately half of the files are used in more than one project, which indicates significant reuse among OSS projects.

Table 1. Overview of previous studies of reuse in OSS

Authors	Study objective	Method and sample
Mockus *et al.* (2007)	To identify and quantify large-scale reuse in OSS.	Survey of 38,700 projects, 13.2 MLOC
Haefliger *et al.* (2008)	Is code reuse supported in OSSD?	Multiple case study, 15 projects, in-depth analysis of 6 projects, 6MLOC
Sojer and Henkel (2010)	How important is code reuse in OSS projects? What are perceived benefits, issues and impediments of code reuse? How is code reuse affected by characteristics of developers and project?	Web-based survey, 686 responses
Heine-mann *et al.* (2011)	Do OSS projects reuse software? How much black-box/white-box?	Empirical study, 20 OSS Java projects, 3.3 MLOC

Haefliger *et al.* (2008) conducted a study of 15 OSS projects, six of which were studied in-depth. The goal of this study was an investigation of the influence of several factors identified in the literature on the support of code reuse in OSS development. Factors included standards and tools, quality ratings and certificates, and incentives as found in commercial software development firms. The study shows that all studied projects reuse software, and that black-box reuse was the predominant form.

Sojer and Henkel (2010) conducted a survey to investigate quantitatively the relationship between developer and project characteristics on the one hand and the degree of software reuse in OSS projects on the other hand. The survey among 686 OSS developers identified a number of factors, such as developers' experience in OSS projects that affect software reuse in OSS projects. Unlike other studies, such as the one by Mockus and Haefliger *et al.* mentioned, this study does not investigate actual reuse within OSS projects, but rather developers' behavior and opinions on the topic.

Heinemann *et al.* (2011) studied reuse in a sample of 20 OSS projects written in the Java programming language, using clone detection techniques complemented with manual inspection. Their study investigated whether OSS projects reuse software, and to what extent such reuse happens as white-box and black-box. They found that reuse is common in the OSS Java projects studied, in particular black-box reuse, as previously found by Haefliger *et al.* (2008). It must be noted that their measurements also counted reuse of the Java standard libraries.

Component Characterization

Components, as defined, can be characterized in different categories depending on their relationships to other components. Lungu *et al.* (2006) distinguish between four types of (Java) packages. These are:

1. **Silent Package:** No dependency relations between the package and other packages.
2. **Consumer Package:** A dependency relation from the package to other packages (that is, the package depends on, or *consumes*, functionality from other packages);
3. **Provider Package:** There is a dependency from other packages to the package (that is, the package *provides* functionality to other packages);
4. **Hybrid Package:** The package is both a consumer and provider at the same time (that is, it both *consumes* and *provides* functionality to and from other packages, respectively).

Though Lungu *et al.* refer to Java packages, which, they argue, are the main mechanism for the decomposition and modularization of a software system written in Java, we argue that the same four types listed can be used to characterize components as directories containing source code files (as defined in the previous subsection).

That is, a *provider* is a component that provides services to other components (which therefore become dependent upon the provider). Likewise, a *consumer* relies on functionality provided in other components (and is therefore dependent upon those). Incidentally, Java packages are in fact represented as directories in a source code file system.

Software Evolution and Program Classification

There is a continuous pressure on software systems to evolve in order to prevent becoming obsolete (Lehman, 1978). Lehman (1980) stated a number of "laws of software evolution". He presents a classification of programs into three classes: S, P and E, which relates to how programs evolve. The three program types are briefly summarized below.

S-Programs

Lehman (1980) described S-Programs as: "programs whose function is formally defined by and derivable from a *specification*." These are programs that solve a specific problem, which is completely defined. The specification of the problem "*directs and controls the programmer in his creation of the program that defines the desired solution*" (Lehman, 1980). Changes may of course be made to the program, for instance, to improve resource usage or improve its maintainability. However, such changes must not change the mapping between the input and output. If changes are made due to a changed specification, it is a different program that solves a new problem. Typical examples of S-type programs are library routines that implement mathematical operations, for instance the sine and cosine functions.

P-Programs

P-Programs are programs that implement a solution to a problem that is well-defined but whose implementation must be limited to an *approxima-tion* to achieve practicality. The problem statement of P-Programs *"is a model of an abstraction of a real-world situation, containing uncertainties, unknown, arbitrary criteria and continuous vari-ables"* (Lehman, 1980). Whereas the correctness of an S-Program depends on its specification, the value and validity of P-Programs is dependent on the solution acquired in a real-world environment. As the environment or world in which the program is used is changing, P-Programs themselves must also change. Examples, as suggested by Lehman, are a software program implementing the game of chess, as well as weather prediction software.

E-Programs

The defining characteristic of the third class of programs, E-Programs, is that the installation of a program itself changes the nature of the prob-lem that it is solving. As Lehman (1980) stated: *"Once the program is completed and begins to be used, questions of correctness, appropriateness and satisfaction arise [...] and inevitably lead to additional pressure for change."* In other words, the environment (or world) in which the program was originally conceived is changing due to the introduction of the program itself. Or, stated in more abstract terms, the introduction of a solu-tion (the software program) to a problem changes the nature of the problem itself. This leads to the need for continuous change to E-type programs. Lehman mentions as examples of such types of programs operating systems and air-traffic control software (Lehman, 1980).

Software Architecture, Decay and Architectural Recovery

The empirical analysis of the FFmpeg components reported below revealed several changes in the components and in their connections to the core of the system: these changes revealed (in at least one case) a decay in how some of the components are internally structured, and externally connected

to other components. Therefore this work is also related to the study of software architectures, as it relates to components, and their mutual relation-ships (Bass *et al.*, 2003).

It is now widely accepted that a system's software architecture has different *views* (IEEE, 2000); well known is the 4+1 view model of architecture (Kruchten, 1995), which defines the *logical*, *development*, *process*, *physical* views, plus a *use-case* view. As outlined, our study considers components as directories containing source code files, which would be presented in the *development* view. One related aspect that was also considered for the present study is about how such structural characteristics decay over time, how components become less cohesive and how the connections between them infringe the original design constraints.

One important aspect of software architec-tures and components is modularity (Parnas, 1972): the division of a system into modules (or components) helps in the separation of the functionality and responsibilities of the various modules. Reusability is a quality attribute that is directly related to a component's (or system's); examining the inter-component couplings (Bass *et al.*, 2003) may provide valuable insights that help to assess the reusability of a component (or system). The analysis of coupling and cohesion of object-oriented systems has also shown that a good degree of modularity is achieved by ob-serving the "loose coupling and high cohesion" principle for components (Fenton, 1991; Macro & Buxton, 1987; Troy & Zweben, 1981).

As software systems evolve over time, the soft-ware engineering literature has firmly established that software architectures and the associated code suffer from *software decay* (Eick *et al.*, 2001). Perry and Wolf (1992) speak of *architectural erosion* and *architectural drift*. The former occurs as a result of *violating* the (conceptual) software architecture. The latter is due to an *insensitivity* of stakeholders about the architecture, which may lead to an obscuration of the architecture, which in turn may cause violation of the architecture.

As a result, software systems have the progressive tendency to lose their original structure, which makes it difficult to understand and further maintain them (Schmerl *et al.*, 2006). Among the most common discrepancies between the original and the degraded structures, the phenomenon of highly coupled, and lowly cohesive, modules has already been known since 1972 (Parnas, 1972) and it is an established topic of research.

Architectural recovery is one of the recognized counter-measures to this decay (Dueñas *et al.*, 1998). Several earlier works have focused on the architectural recovery of proprietary software (Dueñas *et al.*, 1998), closed academic software (Abi-Antoun *et al.*, 2007), COTS-based systems (Avgeriou & Guelfi, 2005) and OSS (Bowman *et al.*, 1999; Godfrey & Lee, 2000; Tran *et al.*, 2000). In all of these studies, systems were selected in a specific state of evolution, and their internal structures analyzed for discrepancies between the *conceptual* and *concrete* architectures (Tran *et al.*, 2000). Researchers have proposed various approaches to address this issue by proposing frameworks (e.g., Sartipi *et al.*, 2000), methodologies (e.g., Krikhaar *et al.*, 1999) or guidelines and concrete advice to developers (e.g., Tran *et al.*, 2000).

Architectural recovery provides insights into the concrete architecture, which in turn may be of help to developers and integrators. For instance, certain architectural styles (Clements *et al.*, 2010) may be identified, which can provide valuable insights into a system's quality attributes (Bass *et al.*, 2003; Harrison & Avgeriou, 2011). Recovery is very important as well to ensure the maintainability of a software product; if the conceptual architecture is not respected, the resulting concrete architecture may become a *spaghetti* architecture, which can be an obstacle to making necessary changes to the system. In the context of software reuse, and this research in particular, components

(as defined) may be identified that can be reused in other systems (i.e., OSS projects).

RESEARCH DESIGN

The study presented in this paper is a quantitative, descriptive case study (Yin, 2003). As Easterbrook *et al.* (2008) pointed out, there exists some confusion in the software engineering literature over what constitutes a case study, distinguishing between a case study as a "worked example" and case study as an "empirical method". Case studies can also be conducted in different contexts, for instance in industry ("in vivo") or in a research/laboratory setting ("in vitro"). This study is an empirical, "in vitro" case study of one OSS project, namely FFmpeg. As such, this study presents the description and analysis of a system, and following the classification by Glass *et al.* (2002) the research approach can therefore be classified as "descriptive."

The remainder of this section proceeds as follows. First, we provide further information on the FFmpeg project. Second, we introduce the research questions that guided the research. Third, we present the definitions to operationalize this research. The section concludes with a discussion of data collection and analysis procedures.

Selection and Description of the FFmpeg System

This paper presents a case study of reuse of build-level components in the FFmpeg project. We selected this project as an example of software reuse for several reasons:

1. It has a long history of evolution as a multimedia player that has grown and refined several build-level components throughout its life cycle. Some of these components

appear like "E" type systems, instead of traditional "S" or "P" types, with lower propensity for software evolution.

2. Several of its core developers have been collaborating also in the MPlayer (http://www.mplayerhq.hu) project, one of the most commonly used multimedia players across OSS communities. Eventually, the libavcodec component has been incorporated (among others from FFmpeg) into the main development trunk of MPlayer, increasing FFmpeg's visibility and widespread usage.

3. Its components are currently reused on different platforms and architectures, both in static linking and in dynamic linking. Static linking involves the inclusion of source code files or pre-compiled libraries at compile-time, while dynamic linking involves the inclusion of a (*shared*) binary library at runtime.

4. Finally, the static-linking reuse of the FFmpeg components presents two opposite scenarios: either a *black-box* reuse strategy, with "update propagation" issues reported when the latest version of a project has to be compiled against a particular version of the FFmpeg components (Orsila *et al.*, 2008); or a *white-box* reuse strategy.

As mentioned, the FFmpeg system has successfully become a highly visible OSS project partly due to its components, libavcodec in particular, which have been integrated into a large number of OSS projects in the multimedia domain[2].

In terms of a global system's design, the FFmpeg project does not yet provide a clear description of either its internal design, or how the architecture is decoupled into components and connectors. Nonetheless, by visualizing its source tree composition (de Jonge, 2002), the folders containing the source code files appear to be semantically rich, in line with the definitions of *build-level components* (de Jonge, 2005), and *source tree composition* (de Jonge, 2002). The first column of Table 2 summarizes which fold-

ers currently contain source code and subfolders within FFmpeg.

As shown, some components act as containers for other subfolders, apart from source files, as shown in columns two and three, respectively. Typically these subfolders have the role of specifying/restricting the functionalities of the main folder in particular areas (e.g., the libavutil folder which is further divided into the various supported architectures, such as Intel x86, ARM, PPC, etc.; as mentioned, Lungu *et al.* (2006) refer to this structural "pattern" as an *Archipelago*). The fourth column describes the main functionalities of the component. It can be observed that each directory provides the build and configuration files for itself and the subfolders contained, following the definition of build-level components (de Jonge, 2005). The fifth column of Table 2 lists the month in which the component was first detected in the repository. Apart from the miscellaneous tools component, each of these are currently reused as OSS components in other multimedia projects as development libraries, for example, the libavutil component is currently redistributed as the libavutil-dev package.

Table 2 shows that the main components of this system have originated at different dates, and that the older ones (e.g., libavcodec) are typically more articulated into several directories and multiple files. The libavcodec component was created relatively early in the history of this system (08/2001), and it has now grown to some 220,000 source lines of code (SLOC) alone.

As is visible in the time-line in Figure 2, other components have coalesced since then; each component appears modularized around a specific "function," according to the "Description" column in Table 2, and as such have become more identifiable and hence reusable in other systems (and are in fact repackaged as distinct OSS projects, http://www.libav.org).

Table 2. FFmpeg build-level components

Component name	Folder count	File count	Description	First detected
libavcodec	12	625	Extensive audio/video codec library	08/2001
libpostproc	1	5	Library containing video postprocessing routines	10/2001
libavformat	1	205	Audio/video container mux and demux library	12/2002
libavutil	8	70	Shared routines and helper library	08/2005
libswscale	6	20	Video scaling library	08/2006
tools	1	4	Miscellaneous utilities	07/2007
libavdevice	1	16	Device handling library	12/2007
libavfilter	1	11	Video filtering library	02/2008

Research Questions

This research has been guided by three research questions:

RQ1: How does the *size* of FFmpeg components evolve?

- **Rationale:** at first, we were interested in how the components of FFmpeg behave in terms of their size, when they become available, and if there is a limit to growth in such components affecting their ability to be reused properly.

RQ2: How does the *architecture* of FFmpeg components evolve?

- **Rationale:** we were interested in understanding how the various FFmpeg components relate to one another in terms of coupling and cohesion. We consider these measures to be a representation of the software architecture.

RQ3: How do FFmpeg components evolve when separated from FFmpeg (e.g., in *white-box* reuse)?

- **Rationale:** as mentioned, the FFmpeg components have been reused so far in a black-box or a white-box scenario. OSS components are particularly suitable for white-box reuse due to the availability of the source code. A number of FFmpeg components have in fact been reused using a white-box reuse approach. Since in

Figure 2. Inception dates of build-level components

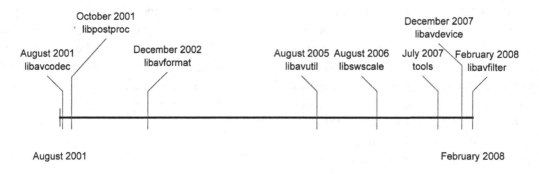

such a scenario a copy of the component is made and maintained by a new hosting project, the component is likely to evolve separately from its original host project (i.e., FFmpeg). Therefore, it is interesting to study how FFmpeg components evolve when they are reused as white-box components.

Definitions and Operationalization

This section introduces a number of definitions that are relevant to the research presented in this paper. In this paper we use terminology and definitions provided in related and previous studies.

The previous section already discussed our interpretation of the term *component*. To summarize, we consider a directory in the source code file system, containing several source code files, to be a *build-level* component (de Jonge, 2005), which are subsequently used as units of composition. Others have used the word "module" for this (e.g., Clements *et al.*, 2010).

In order to measure the evolution of components and their architectural evolution, we use a number of measurements that have been well established in software engineering measurement literature, namely coupling and cohesion. Coupling is further divided into outbound coupling (fan-out) and inbound coupling (fan-in).

Furthermore, we have considered the concept of "connection" which states whether two components are related or not.

- **Coupling:** Coupling is a measure of the degree of interdependence between modules (Fenton, 1991). There are several types of coupling, such as common coupling where modules reference a global data area, control coupling where control data is passed between modules, etc. An extensive classification of types of coupling is presented by Lethbridge and Laganiére (2001, p. 323). In this study, we define coupling as the union of "routine call" coupling and "inclusion/import" coupling. Routine call coupling refers to function calls from a component A to a component B. Inclusion/import coupling refers to dependencies expressed using the #include directive of the C preprocessor. We used the Doxygen tool (http://www.doxygen.org/) to extract this information. Since the empirical study is based on the definition of *build-level* components, two further conversions have been made:
  - ○ The *file-to-file* and the *functions-to-functions* couplings have been "lifted" (Krikhaar, 1999, p. 38, p. 85) into *folder-to-folder* couplings, as also

Figure 3. Function calls from a file in component A to a file in component B are modeled as a link between components A and B

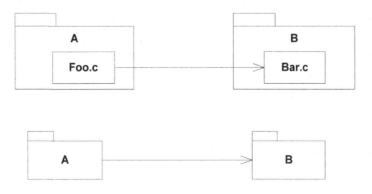

done by Tran and Holt (1999); this is graphically illustrated in Figure 3. A stronger coupling link between folder A and B will be found when many elements within A call elements of folder B.

○ Since the behavior of build-level components is studied here, the couplings to subfolders of a component have also been redirected to the component alone; hence a coupling $A{\to}B/C$ (with C being a subfolder of B) is reduced to $A{\to}B$. This is graphically illustrated in Figure 4.

- **Outbound coupling (*fan-out*):** For each component, the percentage of couplings directed from any of its elements to elements of other components, as in requests of services. A component with a large fan-out, or "controlling" many components provides an indication of poor design, since the component is probably performing more than one function.

- **Inbound coupling (*fan-in*):** For each component, the percentage of couplings directed to it from all the other components, as in "provision of services." A component with high fan-in is likely to perform often-needed tasks, invoked by many components, which is regarded as an acceptable design behavior.

- **Cohesion:** For each component, the sum of all couplings, in percentage, between its own elements (files and functions).

- **Connection:** Distilling the couplings as defined, one could say, in a Boolean manner, whether two folders are linked by a *connection* or not, disregarding the strength of the link itself[3]. The overall number of these connections for the FFmpeg project is recorded monthly in Figure 5; the connections of a folder to itself are not counted (for the encapsulation principle), while the two-way connection and is counted just once (since we are only interested in which folders are involved in a connection).

Data Collection and Analysis

The source code repository (SVN) of FFmpeg was parsed monthly, resulting in some 100 temporal points, after which the tree structures were extracted for each of these points. The monthly extraction of the raw data was achieved by downloading the repository on the first day of each month. As an example, for retrieving the snapshot for 02/2008, the following command was issued:

```
svn -r {2008-02-01} checkout svn://
svn.ffmpeg.org/ffmpeg/trunk
```

On the one hand, the number of source folders (but not yet build-level components) of the corresponding tree is recorded in Figure 5. On the other hand, in order to produce an accurate description of the tree structure as suggested by Tran *et al.* (2000), each month's data has been further parsed using Doxygen, with the aim of extracting the common coupling among the elements (i.e., source files and headers, and source functions) of the systems. Doxygen generates so-called .dot files in the process. Each of these .dot files represents a file (or a class), or a cluster of files, and its couplings towards other in the system. In order to generate the .dot files (and keep them available after the process), the Doxygen configuration file (http://mastodon.uel.ac.uk/IJOSSP2012/Doxygen_base.txt) contains these two commands:

```
"HAVE_DOT = YES"
"DOT_CLEANUP = NO"
```

Various scripts are then applied to obtain the summary of function calls (http://mastodon.uel.ac.uk/IJOSSP2012/ffmpeg-2008-02-01-summary_ALL_FUNCTION_CALLS.txt), dependencies and include relationships. The information in the summary files is at the atomic level of func-tions or files: in order to define inter-relationships between components, these relations are *lifted* (Krikhaar, 1999) to the level of the build-level components (i.e., folders) that contain them, as was mentioned.

The analysis of size growth has been performed using the SLOCCount tool (Wheeler, n.d.).

For each build-level component summarized in Table 2, a study of its relative change in terms of the contained SLOC along its lifecycle has been undertaken. In addition, a study of the architectural connections has been performed, by analyzing temporally:

1. The number of couplings that were actually involved with elements of the *same* component (as per the definition of *cohesion*);
2. The number of couplings that consisted of links *to* or *from* other components (as per the definition of *inbound* and *outbound* couplings, respectively).

Previous studies that present recovered architectures have used "box-and-line" (or box and arrow) diagrams (e.g., Bowman *et al.*, 1999). We use UML *package* diagrams (rather than *component* diagrams) to graphically visualize (build-level) components, as defined in the previous section.

Figure 5. Growth of folders and connections of the FFmpeg project

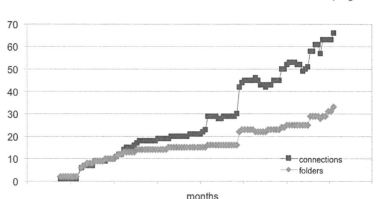

Growth of connections and folders -- FFMpeg

RESULTS AND DISCUSSION

This section provides the results of the empirical investigation, addressing the three research questions identified in the previous section. First, the size growth of the FFmpeg components is presented (see Table 2). This is followed by a presentation of an analysis of the architectural evolution of the components. This section concludes with a discussion of the deployment of libavcodec in other OSS projects.

Size Growth of FFmpeg Components

As a general result, two different evolutionary patterns can be observed, which have been clustered in the two graphs of Figure 6 and Figure 7; the measures are all relative to the highest values recorded, and they are presented as percentages on the Y-axis. In the top graph, three components (libavcodec, libavutil and libavformat in blue, yellow and red, respectively) show a linear growth as a general trend (relative to the maximum size achieved by each). In the following, these components are referred to as E-type components. On the other hand, the other components in FFmpeg (see Table 2) show a more traditional evolution that is typical for library packages, and are referred to as either "S-type" or "P-type" systems (as presented in the background section).

Size Growth in E-Type Components

Considering the top diagram in Figure 6, the libavcodec component started out as a medium-sized component (18 KSLOCs), but currently its size has reached over 220 KSLOCs, which is an increase of over 1,100%. Also, the libavformat component has moved through a comparable pattern of growth (250% increase), but with a smaller size overall (from 14 to 50 KSLOC). Although reusable resources are often regarded as "S-type" or "P-type" systems, since their evolutionary patterns manifest a reluctance to growth (as in the typical behavior of software libraries), these two components achieve an "E-type" evolutionary pattern even when heavily reused by several other projects. The studied cases appear to be driven mostly by *adaptive* maintenance (Swanson, 1976), since new audio and video formats are constantly added and refined among the functions of these components.

Using a metaphor from botany, these software components appear and grow as "fruits" from the main "plant" ("trunk" in the version control system). Furthermore, these components behave as "climacteric" fruits (such as bananas), meaning that they ripen off the parent plant (and in some cases, they must be picked in order to ripen; that is, a component needs to be separated from the parent project in order to allow it to mature and

Figure 6. Relative growth in size of E-type

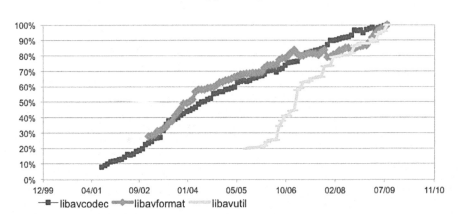

Figure 7. Relative growth in size of S- and P-type components

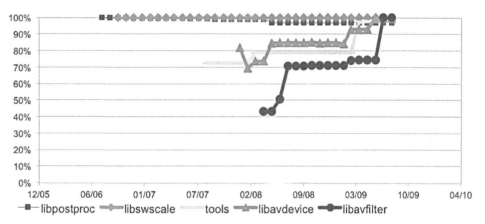

evolve). These FFmpeg components have achieved an evolution even when separated from the project they belonged to (i.e., FFmpeg), similarly to climacteric fruits.

Size Growth in S- and P-Type Components

The bottom diagram in Figure 7 details the relative growth of the remaining components. The Figures 6 and 7 show that these remaining components show a more traditional library-style type of evolution. Maintenance activities in these components are more likely to be of a *corrective* or *perfective* nature (Swanson, 1976). The components libpostproc and libswscale appear to be hardly changing at all, even though they have been formed for several years in the main project (see Figure 2). Libavdevice, when created, was already at 80% of its current state; libavfilter, in contrast, although achieving a larger growth, does so since it was created at a very small stage (600 SLOC), which has now doubled (1,400 SLOCs). These resources are effectively library-type of systems, and their reuse is simplified by the relative stability of their characteristics, meaning the type of problem they solve. Using the same metaphor as shown, the

components ("fruits") following this behavior are unlikely to ripen any further once they have been picked. Outside the main trunk of development, these components remain unchanged, even when incorporated into other OSS projects.

Architectural Evolution of FFmpeg Components

The observations related to the growth in size have been used to cluster the components based on their coupling patterns. As mentioned, each of the 100 monthly checkouts of the FFmpeg system were analyzed in order to extract the common couplings of each element (functions or files), and these common couplings were then converted (*lifted*) into connections between components.

As observed also with the growth in size, the E-type components present a steadily increasing growth of couplings compared to the more stable S-type and P-type components. In the following section, we will study whether the former also display a more modularized growth pattern, resulting in a more stable and defined behavior.

Coupling Patterns in E-Type Components

Figures 8 through 10 present the visualization of the three E-type components identified. For each component, four trends are displayed:

1. The overall amount of its common couplings;
2. The amount of couplings directed towards its elements (*cohesion*);
3. The amount of its outbound couplings (*fan-out*);
4. The amount of its inbound couplings (*fan-in*).

As seen, these trends are also measured relative to the highest values recorded in each trend, and they present the results in percentages on the Y-axis.

Each component has a continuous growth trend regarding the number of couplings affecting it. The libavutil component has one sudden discontinuity in this growth, which will be later explained. As a common trend, it is also visible that both the libavcodec and libavformat components have a strong cohesion factor, which maintains over the 75% threshold throughout their evolution. In other words, in these two components, more than 75%

of the total number of couplings are consistently between internal elements. The cohesion of libavutil, on the other hand, degrades until it becomes very low, revealing a very high fan-in. After the restructuring at around one fifth of its lifecycle (June 2006), this component becomes a *provider* (Lungu *et al.*, 2006), fully providing services to other components (more than 90% of the overall amount of its couplings – around 3,500 – are either towards its own elements or serving calls from other components).

When observing the three components as part of a common, larger system, the changes in one component become relevant to the other components as well. For example, the general trend of libavcodec is intertwined to the other two components (i.e., libavutil and libavformat) in the following ways:

1. The overall cohesion decreases during a time interval when no overall couplings (i.e., the blue trend) were added, therefore this attribute has *decayed*.
2. In parallel with the cohesion decay, the *fan-out* of libavcodec (top of Figure 5) abruptly increases, topping some 17% at the latest studied point: at a closer inspection, this

Figure 8. Coupling patterns of E-type components. Libavavcodec.

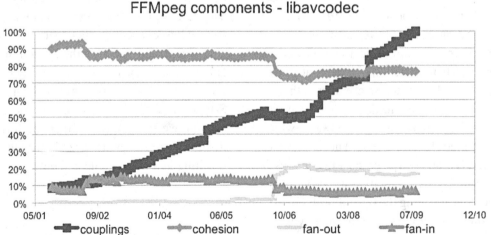

Figure 9. Coupling patterns of E-type components. Libavutil.

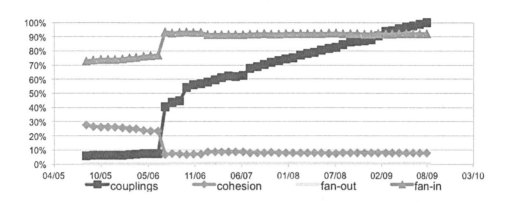

Figure 10. Coupling patterns of E-type components. Libavformat.

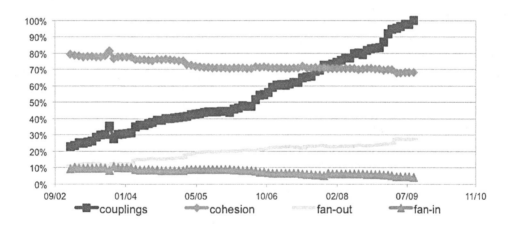

larger *fan-out* (e.g., requests of services) is increasingly directed towards the libavutil component, which around the same period (middle of Figure 5) experiences a sudden increase of its *fan-in* (i.e., provision of services).

3. Also, the *fan-in* of libavcodec decreases: in the first part of its evolution, libavcodec served numerous requests from the libavformat component; throughout the evolution, these links are converted into connections to libavutil instead, decreasing the *fan-in* of libavcodec.

4. Performing a similar analysis for libavformat, it becomes clear that its fan-out degrades, becoming gradually larger, the reason being an increasingly stronger link to the elements of both libavcodec and libavutil. This form of inter-component dependencies is a form of *architectural decay* (Eick *et al.*, 2001). This has been reproduced for the latest available data point in Figure 11: both libavformat and libavcodec depend heavily on libavutil (1,093 and 1,748 overall couplings, respectively); furthermore, the same two components are

Figure 11. High number of couplings among three components suggest that they are heavily dependent on each other

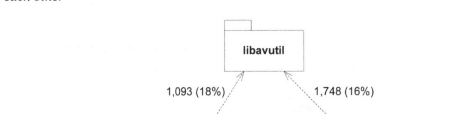

also intertwined by 523 calls by libavformat that are served by libavcodec.

Figure 11 shows that most of the couplings of these displayed components are amongst themselves; for instance, 68% of the couplings of libavformat (4,051 couplings) are couplings to itself (i.e., its cohesion); 18% (1,093) is to libavutil, and 9% is to libavcodec. Ninety-five per cent of libavformat's couplings are found within these three components; the remaining 5% are couplings to other components. When comparing these results with the plots in Figures 8 through 10 (especially the one representing the libavcodec component), it becomes clear how its architecture has decayed. In the earliest points, libavcodec represented an excellent component, with a cohesion made of 90% of all its couplings, and a fan-in of 10% of all its couplings. No fan-out was recorded, so essentially libavcodec had no need for services by other components. The latest available point, instead (see Figure 11), shows a component that has decayed, that needs more from libavutil (16% of all its couplings), and for which the fan-out has increased to some 18% of its overall couplings.

The graph in Figure 11 shows another result, representing in fact the typical trade-offs between encapsulation and decomposition: several of the common files accessed by both libavformat and libavcodec have been "relocated" (Tran & Holt, 1999) recently to a third location (libavutil), that acts as a *provider* (Lungu *et al.*, 2006) to both. This in turns has a negative effect on reusability; when trying to reuse (some of) the functionality of libavcodec, it will be necessary to include also (some of) the contents of libavutil, since a large amount of calls are issued by libavformat towards libavutil. Even worse, when trying to reuse (some of) the functionality of libavformat, it will be necessary to include also (some of the functionality of) libavutil and libavcodec, since the three components are heavily intertwined.

Coupling Patterns in S- and P-Type Components

The characteristics of the E-type components as described can be summarized as follows:

- High cohesion;
- Fan-out under a certain threshold; and
- Clear, defined behavior as a component (e.g., a "provider" as achieved by the libavutil component).

The second cluster of components identified (the "S-" and "P-type") revealed several discrepancies from the results observed previously. A list of key results is summarized here:

1. As also observed for the growth of components, the number of couplings affecting this second cluster of components reveals a difference of one (libswscale, libavdevice and libavfilter) and even two (libpostproc) orders of magnitude with respect to the E-type components.

2. Slowly growing trends in the number of couplings were observed in libavdevice and libavfilter, but their cohesion remains stable. On the other hand, a high fan-out was consistently observed in both, with values of 0.7 and 0.5, respectively. Observing more closely, these dependencies are directed towards the three E-type components defined. This suggests that these components are not yet properly designed; this may also be due to their relatively young age. Their potential reuse is subsumed to the inclusion of other FFmpeg libraries as well.

To summarize, this second type of components can be classified as slowly growing, less cohesive and more connected with other components in the same system. They can be acceptable reusable candidates, but resolving the inter-connections with other components from the same project could prove difficult.

Deployment of Libavcodec in other OSS Projects

Although identified as "E-type" components, the three components libavcodec, libavformat and libavutil have been shown as highly reusable, based on coupling patterns and size growth attributes. This is interesting, as it seems to contradict the expectation that E-type software is less reusable, due to the need to continuously evolve. In order to observe how these components are actually reused and deployed in other hosting systems, this section summarizes the study of the deployment of the libavcodec component in four OSS projects: avifile (http://avifile.sourceforge.net/), avidemux (http://fixounet.free.fr/avidemux/),

MPlayer and xine (Freitas, Roitzsch, Melanson, Mattern, Langauf, Petteno *et al.,* 2002).

The selection of these projects for the deployment study is based on their current reuse of these components. Each project hosts a copy of the libavcodec component in their code repositories, therefore implementing a *white-box* reuse strategy of this resource. In other words, these projects maintain their own copy of the libavcodec component. The issue to investigate is whether these hosting projects maintain the internal characteristics of the original libavcodec, hosted in the FFmpeg project. In order to do so, the coupling attributes of this folder have been extracted from each OSS project, and the number of connected folders has been counted, together with the total number of couplings. The results are shown in Figure 12.

Each diagram in Figure 12 represents a hosting project: the libavcodec copy presents some degree of cohesion (the re-entrant arrow), and its specific fan-in and fan-out (inwards and outwards arrows, respectively). The number of connections (i.e., distinct source folders) responsible for the fan-in and fan-out are displayed by the number in the (multi-) module diagram in the upper-left and upper-right corners. The following observations can be made:

*   The total amount of couplings in each copy is always lower than the original FFmpeg copy; this means that not the whole FFmpeg project is reused, but only some specific resources.
*   In each copy, the ratio *fan−in/fan−out* is approximately 2:1. In the xine copy, this is reversed: this is due to the fact that, apparently, xine does not host a copy of the libavformat component.
*   For each graph, the connections between libavcodec and libavutil, and between libavcodec and libavformat have been specifically detailed: the fan-in from libavformat alone has typically the same order of magnitude than all the remaining fan-in.

Figure 12. Deployment and reuse of libavcodec

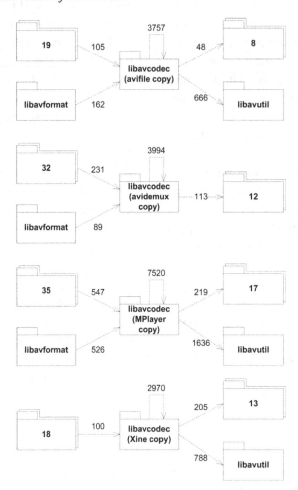

- The fan-out towards libavutil typically accounts for a much larger ratio. This is a confirmation of the presence of a consistent dependency between libavcodec and libavutil, which therefore must be reused together. The avidemux project moved the necessary dependencies to libavutil within the libavcodec component; therefore no build-level component for libavutil is detectable.

THREATS TO VALIDITY

We are aware of a few limitations of this study, which are discussed below. Threats may occur with respect to construct validity, reliability and external validity. Since we do not seek to establish any causal relationships, we do not discuss threats to internal validity.

Construct Validity

Construct validity is concerned with establishing correct operational measures for the concepts that are being studied (Yin, 2003). We used coupling and cohesion measures to represent inter-software component connections. These measures are widely used within the software engineering literature in relation to software module inter-connectivity. We interpreted the term "component" as "build-level" component, as previously done in other studies (e.g., de Jonge, 2005).

Furthermore, the build-level components presented in Table 2 (though probably accurate) are automatically assigned, but they could be only subcomponents of a larger component (e.g., composed of both libavutil and libavcodec).

Reliability

Reliability is the level to which the operational aspects of the study, such as data collection and analysis procedures, are repeatable with the same results (Yin, 2003, p. 34). At the time of our study, FFmpeg was hosted in a Subversion repository, which was parsed monthly, as discussed in the research design section. Guba (1981) states that an inquiry can be affected by "instrumental drift or decay," which may produce effects of instability. In order to guard against this, we have established an *audit trail* of the data extraction process, which is a recommended practice to establish reliability (Guba, 1981). A snapshot (of the example given in the research design section) is made publicly available (http://mastodon.uel.ac.uk/IJOSSP2012/ffmpeg-2008-02-01.tar.gz). The generated .dot files (which represent individual files, classes or clusters of files, and contain its couplings to other modules in the system) are also publicly available (http://mastodon.uel.ac.uk/IJOSSP2012/ffmpeg-2008-02-01-dots.tar).

External Validity

External validity is concerned with the extent to which the results of a study can be generalized. In our study, we have focused on one case study (FFmpeg), which is written mostly in the C programming language. Performing a similar study on a system written in, for instance, an object-oriented language (e.g., C++ or Java), the results could be quite different. However, as outlined in the introduction section, it is not our goal to present generalizations based on our results. Rather, the aim of this paper is to document a successful case of OSS reuse by other OSS projects.

CONCLUSION AND FUTURE WORK

This section presents the conclusion of this study followed by directions for future work.

Conclusion

Empirical studies of reusability of OSS resources should proceed in two strands: first, they should provide mechanisms to select the best candidate component to act as a building block in a new system; second, they should document successful cases of reuse, where an OSS component(s) has been deployed in other OSS projects. This paper contributes to the second strand by empirically analyzing the FFmpeg project, whose components are currently widely reused in several multimedia OSS applications. The empirical study was performed on project data for the last eight years of its development, studied at monthly intervals, to determine and extract the characteristics of its size, the evolutionary growth and its coupling patterns, in order to identify and understand the attributes that made its components a successful case of OSS reusable resources. After having studied these characteristics, four OSS projects were selected among the ones implementing a white-box reuse of the FFmpeg components; the deployment and the reuse of these components was studied from the perspective of their interaction with their hosting systems.

In our case study of FFmpeg, a number of findings were obtained. First, it was found that several of its build-level components make for a good start in the selection of reusable components. They coalesce, grow and become available at various points in the life cycle of this project, and all of them are currently available as building blocks for other OSS projects to use. Second, it was possible to classify (using Lehman's S-P-E program type categories) at least two types of components: one set presents the characteristics of evolutionary (E-type) systems, with a sustained growth throughout. The other set, albeit with a more recent formation, is mostly unchanged, therefore manifesting the typical attributes of software libraries.

The two clusters were compared again in the study of the connections between components. The first set showed components with either a clearly defined behavior, or an excellent cohesion of its elements. It was also found that these three components become increasingly mutually connected, which results in the formation of one single super-component. The second set appeared less stable, with accounts of a large fan-out, which suggests a poor design or immaturity of the components.

One of the reusable resources found within FFmpeg (i.e., libavcodec) was analyzed when deployed into four OSS systems that have reused it using a white-box approach. Its cohesion pattern appeared similar to the original copy of libavcodec, while it emerged with more clarity that currently its reuse is facilitated when the libavformat and libavutil components are reused, too. Given that most of the projects reusing the libavcodec library are "dynamically" linking (i.e., black box reuse) it to their code, any change made to the libavcodec library have a propagation issue (Orsila *et al.*, 2008): this means that the linking projects need to adapt their code as long as a new version of libavcodec is released; on the other hand, the projects hosting their own copy of the same library (i.e., white box reuse) will face less of the propagation issue, since the changes pushed onto the original version libavcodec will not affect their copies.

Future Work

This work has several open strands to follow: at first, it would be interesting to replicate this study to other systems that are currently widely reused. In particular, it is necessary to start defining and distinguishing the reuse of whole systems "as libraries" (such as the project zlib), from the reuse of components within larger projects (such as the component libavcodec within the FFmpeg project). In the first case, the whole project is reused as-is, and it seems likely that only a subset of functions will be reused. In the latter, the implications are more interesting; researchers and practitioners should try to extract automatically libraries that comply with reusability principles, and avoid reusing whole systems.

The second research direction that needs to be addressed is about the evolution of reusable resources. It needs to address the following questions:

- Do libraries need to remain mostly unchanged to be reusable?
- What are the main issues of forking reusable libraries to avoid the effects of "cascade updates"?

In this respect, OSS developers and interested parties have to produce a strategy for the upgrade of their resources when such resources rely heavily on external libraries.

Thirdly, the example of the components being available at different times in FFmpeg shows that other evolving projects might be able to produce a similar response to the OSS communities, by signaling the presence of reusable libraries that could benefit other projects apart from their own.

Finally, the presence of so many available OSS projects implementing similar applications (e.g., our example of over 100 projects implementing an "email client") should be analyzed further to detect how much code duplication, code cloning or components reuse is visible in these projects.

ACKNOWLEDGMENT

The authors would like to thank Dr Daniel German for the clarification on the potential conflicts of licenses in the FFmpeg project, Thomas Knowles for the insightful discussions, and Nicola Sabbi for the insider knowledge of the MPlayer system. We thank the anonymous reviewers for their constructive feedback, which has improved this paper. This work was, in part, supported by Science Foundation Ireland grant 10/CE/I1855 to Lero—The Irish Software Engineering Research Centre (www.lero. ie). This paper is a revised version of: Capiluppi, A., Boldyreff, C. & Stol, K. (2011) Successful Reuse of Software Components: A Report from the Open Source Perspective, in: Hissam, S. A., Russo, B., de Mendonça Neto, M. G. & Kon, F. (Eds.) Open Source Systems: Grounding Research, Springer, Advances in Information and Communication Technology (AICT) vol. 365, pp. 159-176.

REFERENCES

Abi-Antoun, M., Aldrich, J., & Coelho, W. (2007). A case study in re-engineering to enforce architectural control flow and data sharing. *Journal of Systems and Software*, *80*(2), 240–264. doi:10.1016/j.jss.2006.10.036

Avgeriou, P., & Guelfi, N. (2005). Resolving architectural mismatches of COTS through architectural reconciliation. In X. Franch & D. Port (Eds.), *Proceedings of the 4th International Conference on COTS-Based Software Systems* (LNCS 3412, pp. 248-257).

Ayala, C., Sørensen, C., Conradi, R., Franch, X., & Li, J. (2007). Open source collaboration for fostering off-the-shelf components selection. In Feller, J., Fitzgerald, B., Scacchi, W., & Sillitti, A. (Eds.), *Open source development, adoption, and innovation*. New York, NY: Springer. doi:10.1007/978-0-387-72486-7_2

Basili, V. R., & Rombach, H. D. (1991). Support for comprehensive reuse. *IEEE Software Engineering Journal*, *6*(5), 303–316.

Bass, L., Clements, P., & Kazman, R. (2003). *Software architecture in practice* (2nd ed.). Reading, MA: Addison-Wesley.

Bowman, I. T., Holt, R. C., & Brewster, N. V. (1999). Linux as a case study: Its extracted software architecture. In *Proceedings of the 21st International Conference on Software Engineering* (pp. 555-563).

Capiluppi, A., & Boldyreff, C. (2008). Identifying and improving reusability based on coupling patterns. In H. Mei (Ed.), *Proceedings of the 10th International Conference on Software Reuse: High Confidence Software Reuse in Large Systems* (LNCS 5030, pp. 282-293).

Capiluppi, A., & Knowles, T. (2009). Software engineering in practice: Design and architectures of FLOSS systems. In *Proceedings of the 5th IFIP WG 2.13 International Conference on Advances in Information and Communication Technology* (Vol. 299, pp. 34-46).

Clements, P., Bachmann, F., Bass, L., Garlan, D., Ivers, J., & Little, R. …Stafford, J. (2010). *Documenting software architectures: Views and beyond* (2nd ed.). Reading, MA: Addison-Wesley.

de Jonge, M. (2002). Source tree composition. In C. Gacek (Ed.), *Proceedings of the 7th International Conference on Software Reuse: Methods, Techniques, and Tools* (LNCS 2319, pp.17-32).

de Jonge, M. (2005). Build-level components. *IEEE Transactions on Software Engineering*, *31*(7), 588–600. doi:10.1109/TSE.2005.77

Dueñas, J. C., de Oliveira, W. L., & de la Puente, J. A. (1998). Architecture recovery for software evolution. In *Proceedings of the 2nd Euromicro Conference on Software Maintenance and Reengineering* (pp. 113-119).

Easterbrook, S., Singer, J., Storey, M.-A., & Damian, D. (2008). Selecting empirical methods for software engineering research. In Shull, F., Singer, J., & Sjøberg, D. I. K. (Eds.), *Guide to advanced empirical software engineering* (pp. 285–311). New York, NY: Springer. doi:10.1007/978-1-84800-044-5_11

Eick, S. G., Graves, T. L., Karr, A. F., Marron, J. S., & Mockus, A. (2001). Does code decay? Assessing the evidence from change management data. *IEEE Transactions on Software Engineering*, *27*(1), 1–12. doi:10.1109/32.895984

Fenton, N. E. (1991). *Software metrics: A rigorous approach*. London, UK: Chapman & Hall.

Fitzgerald, B. (2006). The transformation of open source software. *Management Information Systems Quarterly, 30*(3), 587–598.

Freitas, M., Roitzsch, M., Melanson, M., Mattern, T., Langauf, S., & Petteno, D. ...Lee, A. (2002). *Xine multimedia engine*. Retrieved from http://www.xine-project.org/home

German, D. M., & González-Barahona, J. M. (2009). An empirical study of the reuse of software licensed under the GNU general public license. In *Proceedings of the 5th IFIP WG 2.13 International Conference on Open Source EcoSystems: Diverse Communities Interacting* (pp. 185-198).

German, D. M., Gonzalez-Barahona, J. M., & Robles, G. (2007). A model to understand the building and running inter-dependencies of software. In *Proceedings of the 14th Working Conference on Reverse Engineering* (pp. 140-149).

German, D. M., & Hassan, A. E. (2009). License integration patterns: Addressing license mismatches in component-based development. In *Proceedings of the 31st IEEE International Conference on Software Engineering* (pp. 188-198).

Glass, R. L., Vessey, I., & Ramesh, V. (2002). Research in software engineering: An analysis of the literature. *Information and Software Technology, 44*(8), 491–506. doi:10.1016/S0950-5849(02)00049-6

Godfrey, M. W., & Lee, E. H. S. (2000). Secrets from the monster: Extracting Mozilla's software architecture. In *Proceedings of the 2nd Symposium on Constructing Software Engineering Tools* (pp. 15-23).

Guba, E. (1981). Criteria for assessing the trustworthiness of naturalistic inquiries. *Educational Communication and Technology, 29*, 75–92.

Haefliger, S., von Krogh, G., & Spaeth, S. (2008). Code reuse in open source software. *Management Science, 54*(1), 180–193. doi:10.1287/mnsc.1070.0748

Harrison, N. B., & Avgeriou, P. (2011). Pattern-based architecture reviews. *IEEE Software, 28*(6), 66–71. doi:10.1109/MS.2010.156

Hauge, Ø., Ayala, C., & Conradi, R. (2010). Adoption of open source software in software-intensive organizations - A systematic literature review. *Information and Software Technology, 52*(11), 1133–1154. doi:10.1016/j.infsof.2010.05.008

Hauge, Ø., Østerlie, T., Sørensen, C.-F., & Gerea, M. (2009, May 18). An empirical study on selection of open source software - Preliminary results. In *Proceedings of the 2nd ICSE Workshop on Emerging Trends in Free/Libre/Open Source Software Research and Development*, Vancouver, BC, Canada (pp. 42-47).

Hauge, Ø., Sørensen, C.-F., & Røsdal, A. (2007). Surveying industrial roles in open source software development. In Feller, J., Fitzgerald, B., Scacchi, W., & Sillitti, A. (Eds.), *Open source development, adoption and innovation* (pp. 259–264). New York, NY: Springer. doi:10.1007/978-0-387-72486-7_25

Heinemann, L., Deissenboeck, F., Gleirscher, M., Hummel, B., & Irlbeck, M. (2011). On the extent and nature of software reuse in open source Java projects. In K. Schmid (Ed.), *Proceedings of the 12th International Conference on Software Reuse: Top Productivity through Software Reuse* (LNCS 6727, pp. 207-222).

IEEE. (2000). *IEEE Std 1471-2000: IEEE recommended practice for architectural description of software-intensive systems*. Piscataway, NJ: IEEE.

Krikhaar, R. (1999). *Software architecture reconstruction* (Unpublished doctoral dissertation). University of Amsterdam, Amsterdam, The Netherlands.

Krikhaar, R., Postma, A., Sellink, A., Stroucken, M., & Verhoef, C. (1999). A two-phase process for software architecture improvement. In *Proceedings of the IEEE International Conference on Software Maintenance* (pp. 371-380).

Kruchten, P. B. (1995). The 4+1 view model of architecture. *IEEE Software*, *12*(5), 42–50. doi:10.1109/52.469759

Lang, B., Abramatic, J.-F., González-Barahona, J. M., Gómez, F. P., & Pedersen, M. K. (2005). Free and proprietary software in COTS-based software development. In X. Franch & D. Port (Eds.), *Proceedings of the 4th International Conference on Composition-Based Software Systems* (LNCS 3412, p. 2).

Lehman, M. M. (1978). Programs, cities, students, limits to growth? *Programming Methodology*, 42-62.

Lehman, M. M. (1980). Programs, life cycles, and laws of software evolution. *Proceedings of the IEEE*, *68*(9), 1060–1076. doi:10.1109/PROC.1980.11805

Lethbridge, T. C., & Laganière, R. (2001). *Object-oriented software engineering: Practical software development using UML and Java* (2nd ed.). London, UK: McGraw-Hill.

Li, J., Conradi, R., Bunse, C., Torchiano, M., Slyngstad, O. P. N., & Morisio, M. (2009). Development with off-the-shelf components: 10 facts. *IEEE Software*, *26*(2), 80–87. doi:10.1109/MS.2009.33

Lungu, M., Lanza, M., & Gîrba, T. (2006). Package patterns for visual architecture recovery. In *Proceedings of the 10th European Conference on Software Maintenance and Reengineering*.

Macro, A., & Buxton, J. (1987). *The craft of software engineering*. Reading, MA: Addison-Wesley.

Mockus, A. (2007). Large-scale code reuse in open source software. In *Proceedings of the First International Workshop on Emerging Trends in FLOSS Research and Development*.

Orsila, H., Geldenhuys, J., Ruokonen, A., & Hammouda, I. (2008). Update propagation practices in highly reusable open source components. In *Proceedings of the IFIP 20th World Computer Congress on Open Source Software* (Vol. 275, pp. 159-170).

Parnas, D. L. (1972). On the criteria to be used in decomposing systems into modules. *Communications of the ACM*, *15*(12), 1053–1058. doi:10.1145/361598.361623

Perry, D. E., & Wolf, A. L. (1992). Foundations for the study of software architectures. *ACM SIGSOFT Software Engineering Notes, 17*(4),

Runeson, P., & Höst, M. (2009). Guidelines for conducting and reporting case study research in software engineering. *Empirical Software Engineering, 14*(2), 131–164.

Sametinger, J. (1997). *Software engineering with reusable components*. Berlin, Germany: Springer-Verlag.

Sartipi, K., Kontogiannis, K., & Mavaddat, F. (2000). A pattern matching framework for software architecture recovery and restructuring. In *Proceedings of the 8th International Workshop on Program Comprehension* (pp. 37-47).

Schmerl, B., Aldrich, J., Garlan, D., Kazman, R., & Yan, H. (2006). Discovering architectures from running systems. *IEEE Transactions on Software Engineering, 32*(7), 454–466. doi:10.1109/TSE.2006.66

Senyard, A., & Michlmayr, M. (2004). How to have a successful free software project. In *Proceedings of the 11th Asia-Pacific Software Engineering Conference* (pp. 84-91).

Sojer, M., & Henkel, J. (2010). Code reuse in open source software development: Quantitative evidence, drivers, and impediments. *Journal of the Association for Information Systems, 11*(12), 868–901.

Sommerville, I. (2004). *Software engineering (International Computer Science Series)* (7th ed.). Reading, MA: Addison-Wesley.

SourceForge. (2011). *Email client*. Retrieved from http://sourceforge.net/directory/?q=email%20client

Swanson, E. B. (1976). The dimensions of maintenance. In *Proceedings of the 2nd International Conference on Software Engineering* (pp. 492-497).

Szyperski, C. (2002). *Component software: Beyond object-oriented programming* (2nd ed.). Reading, MA: Addison-Wesley.

Torchiano, M., & Morisio, M. (2004). Overlooked aspects of COTS-based development. *IEEE Software*, *21*(2), 88–93. doi:10.1109/MS.2004.1270770

Tran, J. B., Godfrey, M. W., Lee, E. H. S., & Holt, R. C. (2000). Architectural repair of open source software. In *Proceedings of the 8th International Workshop on Program Comprehension* (pp. 48-59).

Tran, J. B., & Holt, R. C. (1999). Forward and reverse repair of software architecture. In *Proceedings of the Conference of the Centre for Advanced Studies on Collaborative Research*.

Troy, D. A., & Zweben, S. H. (1981). Measuring the quality of structured designs. *Journal of Systems and Software*, *2*(2), 113–120. doi:10.1016/0164-1212(81)90031-5

Ven, K., & Mannaert, H. (2008). Challenges and strategies in the use of open source software by independent software vendors. *Information and Software Technology*, *50*(9-10), 991–1002. doi:10.1016/j.infsof.2007.09.001

Wheeler, D. A. (n.d.). *SLOCCount*. Retrieved from http://www.dwheeler.com/sloccount/

Wikipedia. (n.d.). *Lamp (software bundle)*. Retrieved from http://en.wikipedia.org/wiki/LAMP_(software_bundle)

Yin, R. K. (2003). *Case study research: Design and methods* (3rd ed.). Thousand Oaks, CA: Sage.

ENDNOTES

[1] Of course, a full structural evaluation of these 128 projects should be performed before arguing that no features are reused among these projects

[2] A list of OSS and commercial projects integrating the libavcodec is given and maintained under http://ffmpeg.org/projects.html

[3] The term "connection" is not intended to cover the term "dependency" between packages in a distribution, since this paper only analyses the internal architecture of components.

This work was previously published in the International Journal of Open Source Software and Processes, Volume 3, Issue 3, edited by Stefan Koch, pp. 10-35, copyright 2011 by IGI Publishing (an imprint of IGI Global).

Chapter 9

Modding as an Open Source Approach to Extending Computer Game Systems

Walt Scacchi
University of California, Irvine, USA

ABSTRACT

This paper examines what is known about the role of open source software development within the world of game mods and modding practices. Game modding has become a leading method for developing games by customizing or creating Open Source Software extensions to game software in general, and particularly to proprietary closed source software games. What, why, and how OSS and closed source software come together within an application system is the subject for this study. Observational and qualitative is used to highlight current practices and issues that can be associated with software engineering and game studies foundations with multiple examples of different game mods and modding practices are identified throughout this study.

INTRODUCTION

User modified computer games, hereafter *game mods*, are a leading form of user-led innovation that generally rely on toolkits (von Hippel, 2001) to support game design and game play experience. But modded games are not standalone systems, as they require the user to have an originally acquired or licensed copy of the unmodded game software.

Modding, the practice and process of developing game mods, is an approach to end-user

DOI: 10.4018/978-1-4666-2937-0.ch009

game software engineering (Burnett, Cook, & Rothermel, 2004) that establishes both social and technical knowledge for how to innovate by resting control over game design from their original developers. At least four types of game mods can be observed: user interface customization; game conversions; machinima; and hacking closed game systems. Each supports different kinds of open source software (OSS) extension to the base game or game run-time environment. Game modding tools and support environments that support the creation of such extensions also merit attention. Furthermore, OSS game extensions are commonly applied to either proprietary, closed source software (CSS) games, or to OSS games, but generally more so to CSS games. Why this is so also merits attention. Subsequently, we conceive of game mods as covering customizations, tailorings, remixes, or reconfigurations of game embodiments, whether in the form of game content, software, or hardware as denoting our space of interest.

The most direct way to become a game mod developer (a game *modder*) is through self-tutoring and self-organizing practices. Modding is a form of learning – learning how to mod, learning to be a game developer, learning to become a game content/software developer, learning computer game science outside or inside an academic setting, and more (El-Nasr & Smith, 2006, Scacchi, 2004). Modding is also a practice for learning how to work with others, especially on large, complex games/mods. Mod team efforts may self organize around emergent software development project leaders or "want to be" (W.T.B.) leaders, as seen for example in the *Planeshift* (http://www.planeshift.it/) OSS massively multiplayer online role-playing game (MMORPG) development and modding project (Scacchi, 2004).

Game mods, modding practices, and modders are in many ways quite similar to their counterparts in the world of OSS development, even though they are often seemingly isolated to those unaware of game software development. Modding is increasingly a part of mainstream technology development culture and practice, and especially so for games, but also for hardware-centered activities like automobile or personal computer customization. Modders are players of the games they reconfigure, just as OSS developers are also users of the systems they develop. There is no systematic distinction between developers and users in these communities, other than there are many users/players that may contribute little beyond their usage, word of mouth they share with others, and their demand for more such systems. At OSS portals like SourceForge.net, the domain

of "Games" is the second most popular project category with nearly 42K active projects, or 20% of all projects[1]. These projects develop either OSS-based games, game engines, or game development tools/SDKs, and all of the top 50 projects have each logged more than 1M downloads. So the intersection of games and OSS covers a substantial socio-technical space, as game modding and traditional OSS development are participatory, user-led modes of system development that rely on continual replenishment of new participants joining and migrating through project efforts, as well as new additions or modifications of content, functionality and end-user experience (Scacchi, 2002, 2004, 2007). Modding and OSS projects are in many ways experiments to prototype alternative visions of what innovative systems might be in the near future, and so both are widely embraced and practiced primarily as a means for learning about new technologies, new system capabilities, new working relationships with potentially unfamiliar teammates from other cultures, and more (cf. Scacchi, 2007).

Consequently, game modding appears to be (a) emerging as a leading method for developing or customizing game software; (b) primarily reliant on the development and use of OSS extensions as the ways and means for game modding; and (c) overlapping a large community of OSS projects that develop computer game software and tools that has had comparatively little study. As such, the research questions that follow then are why do these conditions exist, how have they emerged, and how are they put into practice in different game modding efforts.

This paper seeks to examine what is known so far about game mods and modding practices. The research method in this study is observational and qualitative. It seeks to snapshot and highlight current practices that can be associated with software engineering and game studies, as well as how these practice may be applied in CSS versus OSS game modding. Numerous examples of different game mods and modding practices are identified throughout to help establish an empirically grounded baseline of observations, from which further studies can build or refute. Furthermore, the four types of game mods and modding practices identified in this paper have been employed first-hand in game development projects led or produced by the author. Such observation can subsequently serve as a basis for further empirical study and technology development that ties together computer games, OSSD, software engineering, and game studies (Scacchi, 2002, 2004, 2007, 2010).

RELATED RESEARCH

Two domains of research inform the study here: software extension within the field of software engineering, and modding as cultural practice within game studies. Each is addressed in turn.

Software Extension

Game mods embody different techniques and mechanisms for software extension. However, the description of game mods and modding is often absent of its logical roots or connections back to software engineering. As suggested, mods are extensions to existing game software systems, so it is appropriate to review what we already know about software extensions and extensibility.

Parnas (1979) provides an early notion of software extension as an expression of modular software design. Accordingly, modular systems are those whose components can be added, removed, or updated while satisfying the original system functional requirements. Such concepts in turn were integrated into software architectural design language descriptions and configuration management tools (Narayanaswamy & Scacchi, 1987). But reliance on explicit software architecture descriptions is not readily found in either conventional game or mod development. Henttonnen et al. (2007) examine how software plug-ins support architectural extension, while Leveque et al. (2009) investigate how extension mechanisms like views and model-based systems support extension, also at the architectural level. Last, the modern Web architecture is itself designed according to principles of extensibility through open APIs, migration across software versions, network data content/hypertext transfer protocols, and representational state transfer (Fielding & Taylor, 2002). Mod-friendly networked multi-player games often take advantage of these software extension capabilities.

Elsewhere, Batory et al. (2002) describe how domain-specific languages (for scripting) and software product lines support software extension, and now such techniques are used in games that are open for modding. Next, OSS development as a complementary approach to software engineering, relies on OSS code and associated online artifacts that are open for extension through modification and redistribution of their source representations (Scacchi, 2007). Finally, other techniques to extend the functionality or operation of an existing CSS system may include unauthorized modifications that go beyond what the end-user license agreement might allow, and so appear to fall outside of what software engineering might anticipate or encourage. These include extensions via hacking methods like code injection or hooking, whose purpose is to gain/redirect control of normal program flow through overloading or intercepting system function calls, or provide a hidden layer of interpretation, which allow for "man in the middle" interventions. So software extensions and extensibility is a foundational concept in software engineering, as well as foundational to the development of game mods. However, the logical connections and common/uncommon legacy of game modding, OSS development, and software engineering remain under specified, which this paper begins to address.

Modding as Cultural Practice

Game modding is a practice for user content creation that creates/networks not only game mods but game modders. Within anthropological, behavioral, and sociological studies of computer game play, modding has been studied as an emerging cultural practice that mediates both game play and player interaction with other players (including the game's developers). In some early studies, modding has been designated as a form of "playbour" whereby player actions to create game extensions for use by other players is observed as a form of unpaid (or underpaid) labor that primarily benefits the financial and property interests of game development corporations or hegemonic publishers (Kucklich, 2005; Postigo, 2007; Yee, 2006).

Game modding also modifies or transforms game play experience, since what is play and what is experience(d) are culturally situated. Examples of this may include single player games being modded into multi-player games. So the experience of single player versus the game environment is transformed into other situations including player versus player, multi-player group play, or team versus team play. Similarly, the modding of games to enable experiences other than expected game play, like using a modded game for storytelling or film-making experiences is also a practice of growing interest, with the emergence of a distinguishable community of gamer-filmmakers who produce *machinima* (described later) as either a literary medium, or an art form (Kelland, 2011; Lowood & Nitsche, 2011; Marion, 2004).

Other studies have observed that user/modders also benefit from modding as a way to achieve a sense of creative ownership and meaning in the modded games they share and play with others (Postigo, 2007; Scacchi, 2002, 2004; Sotamaa, 2010), and that game mods and modding practices become central elements in what constitutes play with and through games (Taylor, 2009). Finally, as already observed, OSS project portals like Source-Forge host thousands of OSS game development projects that develop and deploy role-playing games (4.3K projects), simulation-based games (2.6K), board games (2.3K), side-scrolling/arcade

games (2K), turn-taking strategy games (1.7K), multi-user dungeons or text-based adventure/virtual worlds (1.6K), first-person shooters (1.6K), MMORPG (0.6K) and more. So development of OSS games and related game development tools can be recognized as a central element in the cultural world of computer games and game development, as well as the world of OSS development (Scacchi, 2002, 2004, 2007).

FOUR TYPES OF GAME MODS

At least four types of game mods are realized through OSS development practices. These include (i) user interface customizations and agents, (ii) game conversions, (iii) machinima, and (iv) hacking closed source game systems. Each is examined in turned, and each is facilitated (or prohibited) according to its copyright license.

User Interface Customizations and Agents

User interfaces to games embody the practice and experience of interfacing users (game players) to both the game system and the play experience designed by the game's developers. Game developers act to constrain and govern what users can do, and what kinds of experience they can realize. Some users in turn seek to achieve a form of competitive advantage during game play by modding the user interface software for their game, when so enabled by game developers. These mods acquire or reveal additional information that users believe will help their play performance and experience. User interface add-ons subsequently act as the medium through which game development studios support game product customization, which is a strategy for increasing end-user satisfaction and thus the likelihood of product success (Burnett, Cook, & Rothermel, 2004).

Four kinds of user interface customizations can be observed. First and most common, is the player's ability to select, attire or accessorize a *player's in-game identity*. Second, is for players to customize *the color palette and representational framing borders* of the their game display within the human-computer interface, much like what can also be done with Web browsers (e.g., Firefox "personas" and "themes") and other end-user software applications. Third, are *user interface add-on modules* that modify the player's in-game information management dashboard, but do not modify the underlying game play rules or functions. These add-ons provide additional information about game play state that may enhance the game play experience, as well as increasing a player's sense of immersion or omniscience within the game world through perceptual expansion. This in turn enables awareness of game events not visible in the player's pre-existing in-game view. Furthermore, some add-on facilities (e.g., those available with the proprietary *World of Warcraft* MMORPG, scripted in the LUA language) accommodate the creation of automated agent scripts that can read/parse data streamed to the UI within an existing or other add-on dashboard component, and then provide some additional value-added play experience, such as sending out messages or status reports to other players automatically. Such add-on agents thus modify or reconfigure the end-user play experience, rather than the core functionality or play mechanics available to all other of the game's players. Fourth, some add-ons allow for post-processing of the game's visual rendering or displayed appearance, by providing access to hardware specific extensions now provided by high-end graphic processor cards (e.g., FXAA routines supported by NVidia graphics). Consequently, the first two kinds of customizations result from meta-data selections within parametric system functions, while the third and fourth represent a traditional kind of user-created modular extension; one that does not affect the pre-existing game's functional requirements, nor one included in the operational source code base during subsequent system builds or releases, unless they do alter the software's requirements (e.g., by introducing a new security vulnerability or exploit that must be subsequently prevented).

Game Conversions

Game conversion mods are perhaps the most common form of game mods. Most such conversions are partial, in that they add or modify: (a) in-game characters including user-controlled character appearance or capabilities, opponent bots, cheat bots, and non-player characters; (b) play objects like weapons, potions, spells, and other resources; (c) play levels, zones, maps, terrains, or landscapes; (d) game rules; or (e) play mechanics. Some more ambitious modders go as far as to accomplish (f) total conversions that create entirely new games from existing games of a kind not easily determined from the original game. For example, one of the most widely distributed and played total game conversions is the *Counter-Strike* (CS) mod of the *Half-Life* (HL) first-person action game from Valve Software. As the success of the CS mod gave rise to millions of players preferring to play the mod over the original HL game, then other modders began to access the CS mod to further convert in part or full, to the point that Valve Software modified its game development and distribution business model to embrace game modding as part of the game play experience that is available to players who acquire a licensed copy of the HL product family. Valve has since marketed a number of CS variants that have sold over 10M copies as of 2008, thus denoting the most successful game conversion mod, as well as the most lucrative in terms of subsequent retail sales derived from a game mod.

Another example is found in games converted to serve a purpose other than entertainment, such as the development and use of games for science, technology, and engineering applications. For instance, the *FabLab* game (Scacchi, 2010) is a conversion of the *Unreal Tournament 2007* retail game, from a first-person shooter to a simulator for training semiconductor manufacturing technicians in diagnosing and treating potentially hazardous materials spills in a cleanroom environment. This conversion is not readily anticipated by knowledge of the Unreal games or underlying game engine, though it maintains operational compatibility with the Unreal game itself. So game conversions can re-purpose the look, feel, and intent of a game across application domains, while maintaining a common software product line (cf. Batory, Johnson, et al., 2002).

Finally, it is common practice that the underlying game engine has one set of license terms and conditions to protect original work (e.g., no redistribution), while game mod can have a different set of terms and conditions as a derived work (e.g., redistribution allowed only for a game mod, but not for sale). In this regard, software licenses embody the business model that the game development studio or publisher seeks to embrace, rather than just a set of property rights and constraints. For example, in *Aion*, an MMORPG from South Korean game studio NCSoft, no user created mods or user interface add-ons are allowed. Attempting to incorporate such changes would conflict with its end-user license agreement (EULA) and subsequently put such user-modders at risk of losing their access to networked *Aion* multi-player game play. In contrast, the MMORPG *World of Warcraft* allows for UI customization mods and add-ons only, but no other game conversions, no reverse engineering of the game engine, and no activity intended to bypass WoW's encryption mechanisms. And, in one more variation, for games like *Unreal Tournament*, *Half-Life*, *NeverWinter-Nights*, *Civilization* and many others, the EULAs *encourage modding and the free redistribution of mods without fee to others* who must have a licensed copy of the proprietary CSS game, but not allowing reverse engineering or redistribution of the CSS game engine required to run the OSS mods. This restriction in turns helps game companies realize the benefit of increased game sales by players who want to play with known mods, rather than with the un-modded game as sold at retail. Mods thus help improve games software sales, revenue, and profits for the game development studio, publisher, and retailer, as well as enable new modes of game play, learning, and skill development for game modders.

Machinima

Machinima can be viewed as the product of modding efforts that intend to modify the visual replay of game usage sessions. Machinima employ computer games as their creative media, such that these new media are mobilized for some other purpose (e.g., creating online cinema or interactive art exhibition). Machinima focuses attention to playing and replaying a game for the purpose of storytelling, movie making, or retelling of daunting or high efficiency game play/usage experience (Lowood & Nitsche, 2011; Marino, 204). Machinima is a form of modding the experience of playing a specific game, by recording its visual play session history, so as to achieve some other ends beyond the enjoyment (or frustration) of game play. These play-session histories can then be further modded via video editing or remixing with other media (e.g., adding music) to better enable cinematic storytelling or creative performance documentation. Machinima is a kind of play/usage history process re-enactment (cf. Scacchi, 1998) whose purpose may be documentary (replaying what the player saw or experienced during a play session) or cinematic (creatively steering a play session so as to manifest observable play process enactments that can be edited and remixed off-line to visually tell a story). Machinima mods are thus a kind of extension of game software use experience that is not bound to the architecture of the underlying game software system, except for how the game facilitates a user's ability to structure and manipulate emergent game play to realize a desired play process enactment history.

Hacking Closed Game Systems

Hacking a closed game system is a practice whose purpose oftentimes seems to be in direct challenge to the authority of commercial game developers that represent large, global corporate interests. Hacking proprietary game software is often focused not so much on how to improve competitive advantage in multi-player game play, but instead is focused on expanding the range of experiences that users may encounter through use of alternative technologies (Huang, 2003; Scacchi, 2004). For example, Huang's (2003) study instructs readers in the practice of "reverse engineering" as a hacking strategy to understand both how a game platform was designed and how it operates in fine detail. This in turn enables reconfiguration of new innovative modifications or original platform designs, such as installing and running a Linux operating system (instead of Microsoft's proprietary CSS offering), or transforming a closed arcade game into a open platform for modification and experimentation (Hertz, 2011). While many game developers seek to protect their intellectual property (IP) from reverse engineering through EULAs whose terms attempt to prohibit such action under threat of legal action, reverse engineering is not legally prohibited. Consequently, the practice of modding closed game consoles/systems is often less focused on enabling players to achieve competitive advantage when playing retail computer games, but instead may encourage those few so inclined for how to understand and ultimately create computing innovations through reverse engineering or other modifications.

Closed game system modding is a style of software extension by game modders who are willing to forego the "protections" and quality assurances that closed game system developers provide, in order to experience the liberty, skill, knowledge acquisition, conceptual appropriation ("pwned"), and potential to innovate, that mastery of reverse engineering affords. Consequently, players/modders who are willing to take responsibility for their actions (and not seek to defraud game producers due to false product warranty claims or copyright infringement), can enjoy the freedom to learn how their gaming systems work in intimate detail and to potentially learn about game system innovation through discovery and reinvention with the support of others like-minded (cf. Scacchi, 2004). Proprietary game development studios may sometimes allow for such mod-based infringement of their games. For example, the team of modders behind the hacking and conversion of the single-player CSS game, *Grand Theft Auto*, have produced an OSS (now GPL'd) game mod using code injection and hooking cheating methods to realize a networked multi-player variant called *Multi Theft Auto*, that Rockstar Games has chosen not to prosecute for potential EULA violation, but instead to embrace as GTA fan culture (Wen, 2005). Nonetheless, large corporate interests may assert that their IP rights allow them to install CSS rootkits that collect potentially private information, or that prevent the reactivation of previously available OSS (e.g., the Linux Kernel on the Sony PS3 game console) (Wikipedia, n.d.) that game system hackers seek to undo.

Finally, games are one of the most commonly modified types of proprietary CSS that are transformed into "pirated games" that are "illegally downloaded." Such game modding practice is focused on engaging a kind of meta-game that involves hacking into and modding game IP from closed to (more) open. Game piracy has thus become recognized as a collective, decentralized and placeless endeavor (i.e., not a physical organization) that relies on torrent servers as its underground distribution venue for pirated game software. As recent surveys of torrent-based downloads reveals, in 2008 the top 10 pirated games represented about 9M downloads, while in 2009 the top 5 pirated games represent more than 13M downloads, and in 2010 and 2011 the top 5 pirated PC-based games approached 18M, all suggesting a substantial growth in interest in and access to such modded game products (Ernesto, 2008, 2009, 2010, 2011). Thus, we should not be surprised by the recent efforts of game system hackers that continue to demonstrate the vulnerabilities of different hardware and software-based techniques to encrypt and secure closed game systems from would be crackers. However, it is also very instructive to learn from these exploits how difficult it is to engineer truly secure software systems, whether such systems are games or some other type of application or package. Similarly, it may also be the case that early user access to popular CSS games provides a much desired ability for a try-before-buy experience, and thus such unauthorized downloading may in fact serve to complement retail game sales and marketing, CSS version of the game, rather than reduce them (Enigmax & Ernesto, 2011).

GAME MODDING SOFTWARE TOOLS AND SUPPORT

Games are most often modded with tools providing access to unencrypted representations of game software or game platform. Such a representation is accessed and extended via a domain-specific (scripting) language. While it might seem the case that game vendors would seek to discourage users from acquiring such tools, a widespread contrary pattern is observed.

Game system developers are increasingly offering software tools for modifying the games they create or distribute, as a way to increase game sales and market share. Game/domain-specific Software Development Kits (SDKs) provided to users by game development studios represent a contemporary business strategy for engaging users to help lead product innovation from outside the studio (von Hippel, 2001). Once Id Software, maker of the *DOOM* and *Quake* game software product line, and also Epic Games, maker of the *Unreal* software game product line, started to provide prospective game players/modders with software tools that would allow them to edit game content, play mechanics, rules, or other functionality, other competing game development studios were pressured to make similar offerings or face a possible competitive disadvantage in the marketplace. However, the CSS versions of these tools do not provide access to the underlying

source code that embodies the proprietary game engine—a large software program infrastructure that coordinates computer graphics, user interface controls, networking, game audio, access to middleware libraries for game physics, and so forth. But the complexity and capabilities of such a tool suite mean that any one person, or better said, any game development or modding team, can now access modding tools or SDKs to build commercial quality CSS games through OSS extensions. But mastering these tools appears to be an undertaking likely to be only of interest to highly committed game developers who are self-supported or self-organized.

In contrast to game modding platforms provided by game development studios, there are also alternatives provided by the end-user community. One approach can be seen with facilities provided in meta-mods like *Garry's Mod* or the *AMX Mod X* mod-making package. Modders can use these packages to construct a variety of plug-ins that provide for development of in-game contraptions as game UI agents or user created art works, or to otherwise create comic books, program game conversions, and produce other kinds of user created content. But both packages require that you own a licensed CSS game like *Counter-Strike: Source*, *Half-Life 2* or *Day of Defeat: Source* from Valve Software.

A different approach to end-user game development platforms can be found arising from OSS games and game engines. The *DOOM* and *Quake* games and game engines were released as free software subject to the GPL, once they were seen by Id Software as having reached the end of their retail product cycle. Thousands of games/engines, as already observed, have been developed and released for download. Some started from the OSS that was previously the CSS platform of the original games. However, the content assets (e.g., in-game artwork) for many of these CSS-then-OSS games are not covered by the GPL, and so user-developers must still acquire a licensed copy of the original CSS game if its content is to be reused in some way (Assault Cube, n.d.).

Nonetheless, some variants of the user-created GPL'd games now feature their own content that is limited/protected by Creative Commons licenses.

OPPORTUNITIES AND CONSTRAINTS FOR MODDING

Game modding demonstrates the practical value of software extension as a user-friendly approach to customizing software. Such software can extend games open to modding into diverse product lines that flourish through reliance on domain-specific game scripting languages, and integrated SDKs. Modding also demonstrates the success of end-users learning how to extend software to create custom user interface add-ons, system conversions, replayable system usage videos, as well as to discover security vulnerabilities. Game modding therefore represents a viable form of end-user engineering of complex software that may be transferable to other domains.

Modding is a form of OSS-enabled collaboration. It is collaboration at a distance where the collaborators, including the game developers and game users, are distant in space and time from each other, yet they can interact in an open but implicitly coordinated manner through software extensions. Comparatively little explicit coordination arises, except when CSS game developers seek to embrace and encourage the creation of OSS game mods that rely on the proprietary CSS game engine (and also SDK), as a way to grow market share and mind share for the proprietary engine as a viable strategy for complementary products in the game industry (Sengupta, 1998).

However, mods are vulnerable to evolutionary system version updates that can break the functionality or interface on which the mod depends. This can be viewed as the result of inadequate software system design practice, such that existing system modularization did not adequately account for software extensions that end-users seek, or else the original developer wanted to explicitly

prohibit end-users from making modifications that transform game play mechanics/rules or unintentionally allow for modification or misappropriation of copy protected code or media assets.

Last, one the key constraints on game modding in particular, and software extension in general, are the rights and obligations that are expressed in the original software EULA. Mods tend to be licensed using OSS or freeware licenses that allow for access, study, modification, and redistribution, rather than using free software licenses (e.g., GPLv2 or GPLv3). Software extensions that might be subject to a reciprocal GPL-style license require that the base/original software system incorporate an explicit software architectural design that requires the propagation of reciprocal rights across an open interface, except through an LGPL software shim (Alspaugh, Asuncion, & Scacchi, 2009). Otherwise, the scope of effectiveness and copyright protections of either free or non-free software (or related media assets) cannot be readily determined, and thus may be subject to copyright infringement or licenses non-compliance allegations. They may also be treated as social transgressions within a community of modders whose perceived ownership of the game mods demands respect and honor of a virtual license that may or may not be legally valid (Alspaugh, Scacchi, & Asuncion, 2010). As the OSS community has long recognized, software rights and freedoms are expressed through IP licenses that insure whether or not a person has the right to access, study, modify, and redistribute the modified software, as long as the obligation to include a free software license that restates these rights in unalterable form, is included with the OSS code and its modified distributions.

CONCLUSION

Modding is emerging as a viable approach for mixing proprietary CSS systems with OSS extensions. The result is modded systems that provide the benefits of OSSD to developers of proprietary CSS systems, and to end-users who want additional functionality of their own creation, or from others they trust and seek to interact with through game play.

In contrast, modding is not so good for protecting software and media/content copyrights. Modding tests the limits of software/IP copyright practices. Some modders want to self-determine what copy/modding rights they have or not, and sometimes they act in ways that treat non-free software and related media as if it were free software. Who owns what, and which copy rights or obligations apply to that which is modded, are core socio-technical issues when engaging in modding.

This study helps to demonstrate that game modding is becoming a leading method for developing or customizing game software, whether based on proprietary CSS or OSS game systems. OSS-based software extensions are the leading ways and means for modding game-based user interfaces, converting games from one style/genre to another, for recording game play sessions for cinematic production and replay, and for hacking closed source game systems. Finally, the development of computer game software and tools itself represents a large community of OSS projects that has had comparatively little study, and thus merits further attention as its own cultural world as well as one for OSS development. This last consideration may be important as other empirical studies of OSS development that rely on data from SourceForge will increasingly include OSS game projects within large project samples. This study has therefore begun to address why and how these conditions have they emerged, and how are they put into practice in different game modding efforts. Future study should also consider whether and how modding might be applied and adopted in other application domains where CSS can be extended through OSS mods.

ACKNOWLEDGMENT

The research described in this paper has been supported by grants #0808783 and #1041918 from the National Science Foundation, and grant #N00244-10-1-0077 from the Naval Postgraduate School. No review, approval or endorsement implied. The anonymous reviewers also provided helpful suggestions for improving this paper.

REFERENCES

Alspaugh, T. A., Asuncion, H. A., & Scacchi, W. (2009, September). Intellectual property rights requirements for heterogeneously licensed systems. In *Proceedings of the 17ᵗʰ International Conference on Requirements Engineering*, Atlanta, GA (pp. 24-33).

Alspaugh, T. A., Scacchi, W., & Asuncion, H. A. (2010). Software licenses in context: The challenge of heterogeneously licensed systems. *Journal of the Association for Information Systems*, *11*(11), 730–755.

Assault Cube. (n.d.). *Licensing information*. Retrieved April 13, 2011, from from http://assault.cubers.net/docs/license.html

Batory, D., Johnson, C., MacDonald, B., & von Heeder, D. (2002). Achieving extensibility through product lines and domain specific languages: A case study. *ACM Transactions on Software Engineering and Methodology*, *11*(2), 191–214. doi:10.1145/505145.505147

Burnett, M., Cook, C., & Rothermel, G. (2004). End-user software engineering. *Communications of the ACM*, *47*(9), 53–58. doi:10.1145/1015864.1015889

El-Nasr, M. S., & Smith, B. K. (2006). Learning through game modding. *ACM Computers in Entertainment*, *4*(1), 3B. doi:10.1145/1111293.1111301

Enigmax & Ernesto. (2011). *Swiss Govt: Downloading movies and movies will stay legal.* Retrieved from http://torrentfreak.com/swiss-govt-downloading-movies-and-music-will-stay-legal-111202/

Ernesto. (2008). *Top 10 most pirated games of 2008.* Retrieved from http://torrentfreak.com/top-10-most-pirated-games-of-2008-081204/

Ernesto. (2009). *Top 10 most pirated games of 2009.* Retrieved from http://torrentfreak.com/the-most-pirated-games-of-2009-091227/

Ernesto. (2010). *Call of Duty: Black Ops most pirated game of 2010.* Retrieved from http://torrentfreak.com/call-of-duty-black-ops-most-pirated-game-of-2010-101228/

Ernesto. (2011). *Top 10 most pirated games of 2011.* Retrieved from http://torrentfreak.com/top-10-most-pirated-games-of-2011-111230/

Fielding, R. T., & Taylor, R. N. (2002). Principled design of the modern Web architecture. *ACM Transactions on Internet Technology, 2*(2), 115–150. doi:10.1145/514183.514185

Henttonen, K., Matinlassi, M., Niemela, E., & Kanstren, T. (2007). Integrability and extensibility evaluation in software architectural models—A case study. *The Open Software Engineering Journal, 1*(1), 1–20. doi:10.2174/1874107X00701010001

Hertz, G. (2011). *OutRun: Augmented reality driving video game.* Retrieved from http://www.youtube.com/watch?v=TaTB5Q11Dzc

Hertz, G. (2011). OutRun: Building the un-simulation of a driving video game. *Make, 26,* 50–53.

Huang, A. (2003). *Hacking the Xbox: An introduction to reverse engineering.* San Francisco, CA: No Starch Press.

Kelland, M. (2011). From game mod to low-budget film: The evolution of Machinima. In Lowood, H., & Nitsche, M. (Eds.), *The Machinima reader* (pp. 23–36). Cambridge, MA: MIT Press.

Kücklich, J. (2005). Precarious playbour: Modders and the digital games industry. *Fiberculture, 5.* Retrieved April 13, 2011, from http://journal.fibreculture.org/issue5/kucklich.html

Leveque, T., Estublier, J., & Vega, G. (2009). Extensibility and modularity for model-driven engineering environments. In *Proceedings of the 16th IEEE Conference on Engineering Computer-Based Systems* (pp. 305-314).

Lowood, H., & Nitsche, M. (Eds.). (2011). *The Machinima Reader.* Cambridge, MA: MIT Press.

Marino, P. (2004). *3D game-based filmmaking: The art of Machinima.* Scottsdale, AZ: Paraglyph Press.

Narayanaswamy, K., & Scacchi, W. (1987). Maintaining evolving configurations of large software systems. *IEEE Transactions on Software Engineering, 13*(3), 324–334. doi:10.1109/TSE.1987.233163

Parnas, D. L. (1979). Designing software for ease of extension and contraction. *IEEE Transactions on Software Engineering, 5*(2), 128–138. doi:10.1109/TSE.1979.234169

Postigo, H. (2007). Of mods and modders: Chasing down the value of fan-based digital game modifications. *Games and Culture, 2*(4), 300–313. doi:10.1177/1555412007307955

Postigo, H. (2008). Video game appropriation through modifications: Attitudes concerning intellectual property among modders and fans. *Convergence, 14*(1), 59–74. doi:10.1177/1354856507084419

Scacchi, W. (1998). Modeling, integrating, and enacting complex organizational processes. In Carley, K., Gasser, L., & Prietula, M. (Eds.), *Simulating organizations: Computational models of institutions and groups* (pp. 153–168). Cambridge, MA: MIT Press.

Scacchi, W. (2002). Understanding the requirements for developing open source software. *IEEE Software Engineering*, *149*(1), 24–39. doi:10.1049/ip-sen:20020202

Scacchi, W. (2004). Free/open source software development practices in the game community. *IEEE Software*, *21*(1), 59–67. doi:10.1109/MS.2004.1259221

Scacchi, W. (2007, September). Free/open source software development: Recent research results and emerging opportunities. In *Proceedings of the European Software Engineering Conference and ACM SIGSOFT Symposium on the Foundations of Software Engineering,* Dubrovnik, Croatia (pp. 459-468).

Scacchi, W. (2010). Game-based virtual worlds as decentralized virtual activity systems. In Bainbridge, W. S. (Ed.), *Online worlds: Convergence of the real and the virtual* (pp. 225–236). New York, NY: Springer. doi:10.1007/978-1-84882-825-4_18

Sengupta, S. (1998). Some approaches to complementary product strategies. *Journal of Product Innovation Management, 15*(4), 352–367. doi:10.1016/S0737-6782(97)00106-9

Sotamaa, O. (2010). When the game is not enough: Motivations and practices among computer game modding culture. *Games and Culture*, *5*(3), 239–255. doi:10.1177/1555412009359765

Taylor, T. L. (2009). The assemblage of play. *Games and Culture*, *4*(4), 331–339. doi:10.1177/1555412009343576

von Hippel, E. (2001). Perspective: User toolkits for innovation. *Journal of Product Innovation Management*, *18*(4), 247–257. doi:10.1016/S0737-6782(01)00090-X

Wen, H. (2005, May 25). Multi theft auto: Hacking multi-player into Grand Theft Auto with open source. *OSDir*. Retrieved June 1, 2011, from http://osdir.com/Article4775.phtml

Wikipedia. (n.d.). *George Hotz: Hacking the Playstation 3*. Retrieved from http://en.wikipedia.org/wiki/George_Hotz#Hacking_the_PlayStation_3

Wikipedia. (n.d.). *Multi theft auto*. Retrieved June 1, 2011, from http://www.mtavc.com/ and http://en.wikipedia.org/wiki/Multi_Theft_Auto

Yee, N. (2006). The labor of fun: How video games blur the boundaries of work and play. *Games and Culture*, *1*(1), 68–71. doi:10.1177/1555412005281819

ENDNOTES

[1]   See http://www.sourceforge.net/software-map/index.php, accessed 15 April 2011. The number one category of projects is for "Development" with more than 65K OSS projects, out of 210K projects. So OSS Development and OSS Games together represent half of the projects currently hosted on SourceForge.

This work was previously published in the International Journal of Open Source Software and Processes, Volume 3, Issue 3, edited by Stefan Koch, pp. 36-47, copyright 2011 by IGI Publishing (an imprint of IGI Global).

Chapter 10
Measuring Open Source Quality:
A Literature Review

Claudia Ruiz
Georgia State University, USA

William Robinson
Georgia State University, USA

ABSTRACT

There is an ample debate over the quality of Free/Libre Open Source Software (FLOSS) with mixed research results. The authors show that a reason for these mixed results is that quality is being defined, measured, and evaluated differently. They report the most popular approaches including software structure measures, process measures, and maturity assessment models. The way researchers have built their samples has also contributed to the mixed results with different project properties being considered and ignored. Because FLOSS projects evolve with each release, their quality does too, and it must be measured using metrics that take into account their communities' commitment to quality rather than just the structure of the resulting code. Challenges exist in defining what constitutes a defect or bug, and the role of modularity in affecting FLOSS quality. The authors suggest three considerations for future research on FLOSS quality models: (1) defect resolution rate, (2) kind of software product, and (3) modularity—both technical and organizational.

INTRODUCTION

Crowston et al. (2012) pointed out that studies that compared the quality of FLOSS with proprietary software showed mixed results. They suggested that these results vary greatly by project and proposed further research on the antecedents of quality (Crowston, Wei, Howison, & Wiggins, 2012).

This paper takes a first step towards addressing this issue by reviewing the FLOSS literature in order to answer the questions of what is quality and how is it measured. If different studies evaluate quality using different measures it will be like comparing apples and oranges. This would explain the mixed results of the FLOSS quality studies.

Because of quality's extreme subjectivity, it is not surprising that studies comparing the quality of FLOSS with proprietary in-house developed

DOI: 10.4018/978-1-4666-2937-0.ch010

software have produced mixed results (Kuan, 2003; Paulson, Succi, & Eberlein, 2004; Raghunathan, Prasad, Mishra, & Chang, 2005; Stamelos, Angelis, Oikonomou, & Bleris, 2002). The two main explanations for these results are that (1) each study has defined and measured quality differently and that (2) each study has evaluated different characteristics of FLOSS projects.

Defining quality differently will of course produce mixed results, but even when studies define quality in similar terms, they evaluate it using dissimilar criteria to select sample projects and project characteristics.

In order to understand what it is about certain FLOSS projects that lead them to produce high quality software, the antecedents of FLOSS quality must be found, and the first step to finding those antecedents is to agree on a definition and measure of quality.

The rest of the paper is organized as follows: the next two sections provide a brief background on FLOSS and Software Quality; then, we present our literature review Methodology followed by Findings and a Discussion of the implications of the findings.

FLOSS

A FLOSS project is one that offers its software under a license that is in accordance with the criteria in the Open Source Definition (OSI, 2006) providing for free redistribution of the compiled software and the openly accessible source code.

Linux, Apache, Firefox are commonly found in many computers today and were developed under open source licenses. Apache is a Web server used by 60% of Websites worldwide (von Hippel & von Krogh, 2003) and 23.2% of European and 14.5% of North American Web surfers use the Firefox Web browser (Hales, 2006).

This growing popularity begs the question: is FLOSS "better" than proprietary in-house developed software? Proprietary in-house developed software projects are considered successful if they finish on time, on budget, and meet specifications. But the same standards cannot be applied to judge the success of FLOSS projects, because they usually have minimal budgets, are always in a state of development, do not have an official end time, and do not have formal specifications (Scacchi, 2009).

This lack of objective measures of success has not deterred the adoption of FLOSS products. It even has become a common assumption that FLOSS products are of higher quality than traditionally developed software (Ajila & Wu, 2007; Stewart & Gosain, 2006) with firms entering FLOSS projects citing FLOSS's "quality and reliability" as one of the main motivating reasons for the endeavor (Bonaccorsi & Rossi, 2006).

This assumption can be traced back to Linus's law, which says that "given enough eyeballs, all bugs are shallow" (Raymond, 1999). This means that FLOSS's public peer review and frequent releases lead to fewer bugs because there are more people looking at the software, reporting errors, and fixing those errors. This assumption has a kernel of truth: it has been observed in the Apache project that most problem (bug) reports and solutions in FLOSS projects are contributed by periphery community members and less so by core developers (Rigby, German, & Storey, 2008).

Mature FLOSS projects are composed of a community, whose structure has been described as being like an "onion" with the most actively contributing members, who are the most invested in the project and have the greatest decision power in the inner part and the least contributing members with the least amount of decision power on the outside. The project leader is at the center and radiating out are the core members, the active developers, the peripheral developers, the bug fixers, the bug reporters, the readers, and the passive users (Ye & Kishida, 2003). These roles are dynamic, changing as the community evolves as the system they are building evolves (Ye & Kishida, 2003).

Each FLOSS project is different and has different development practices and processes. An example is the Apache project—it demonstrates a bazaar-style of software development. Its stages are illustrated in _Ref185587752 and described.

Identifying work to be done: Core developers look at the bug reporting database and the developer forums for change and enhancement requests. The core developers need to be persuaded of the priority of the request for it to be included in the agenda status list.

Assigning and performing development work: Core developers look for volunteers to perform the work. Priority is given to code owners (those who created or have been actively maintaining the particular module). The developer then identifies a solution and gets feedback from the rest of the developers.

Prerelease testing: Each developer performs unit testing of his/her own work. There is no integration or systems testing.

Inspections: each developer then commits his/her changes and the code is then reviewed before it is included in a stable release, while changes to development releases are reviewed after being included in the release.

Managing releases: A core team member volunteers to be the release manager and makes the decisions pertaining to the individual release. He or she delineates the scope of the release by making sure that all open requests and problems are resolved and restricts access to the code repository to avoid any more changes (Mockus, Fielding, & Herbsleb, 2002).

Modification requests submitted: After the software product is released to the public, modification requests will pour in from users and developers finding errors (defect reports) and asking for new features (enhancement requests).

These development cycle stages draw a parallel to the Scrum Agile development methodology, where a product owner creates a backlog, a prioritized list of functional and non-functional requirements for building into the product. Development is performed in sprints which are 30 day iterations of development activities, which include only the highest priority backlog requirements that can be successfully completed in the allotted time (Schwaber, 2004).

Most FLOSS development practices are very similar to Scrum Agile development methods but less structured and less *ad hoc* (see Figure 1).

SOFTWARE QUALITY

The origins of software quality can be traced back to industrial engineering and operations management and their development of product quality concepts and quality management practices. For these fields, quality is adherence to process specification (Deming, 1982, 1986) in order to produce a product that meets customer requirements with zero defects (Crosby, 1979; Juran, 1988). In order to achieve this goal, approaches such as TQM (total quality management) (Feigenbaum, 1961; Ishikawa, 1985) were developed to integrate quality into all company activities and Six Sigma to measure for quality (Tennant, 2001).

Industrial engineering and operations management's view of quality can be categorized as the manufacturing, user, and product ap-

Figure 1. FLOSS development process

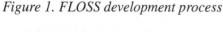
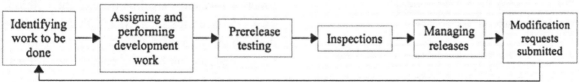

proaches to quality as described by Garvin (1984). _Ref159313461 summarizes these definitions of quality as well as others (transcendent and value). As well as categorizing definitions of quality, Garvin also categorized the eight dimensions of product quality (_Ref159330672) (Garvin, 1984) (see Table 1).

With this legacy from industrial engineering and operations management, software quality started with the product definition of quality by defining frameworks of factors. The most popular were Boehm's model of 23 factors (dimensions of quality) (Boehm, Brown, & Lipow, 1976) and McCall's with 11 factors (Cavano & McCall, 1978; McCall, Richards, & Walters, 1977) which are all listed in _Ref159330672.

Both of these frameworks of factors left out the measure (actual thing that is counted) for each factor. Each implementer and developer was left to define his or her own metrics and criteria for each factor. The ISO 9126 (ISO, 2001) Information technology – Software product evaluation: quality characteristics and guidelines for their use, which is part of the ISO 9000 set of standards by the ISO (The International Organization for Standardization) for quality management, was an attempt to standardize the quality factors to six main factors with three sub-factors under each one (see Table 2).

While the quality factor frameworks were used to assess the software product, process frameworks were developed to assess the quality of the process

Table 1. Garvin's quality definitions (1984)

Approach	Definition of Quality
Transcendent	Innate excellence that cannot be defined only recognized through experience.
Product	Discrete and measurable product characteristics.
User	Subjective consumer satisfaction.
Manufacturing	Conformance to specification.
Value	Conformance to specification at an acceptable cost or price.

producing the software and to accommodate the manufacturing definition of quality (Garvin, 1984). One such framework is the CMMI (Capability Maturity Model Integration), which is a process improvement framework that can be used to drive organizational change and to judge the process maturity of another organization. CMMI has five levels, with one being the lowest. A level five organization is one where processes are defined (level 3), quantitatively managed (level 4), and are continually being optimized (level 5). This maturity model lists the processes that an organization should have in order to be considered at a certain CMMI level but it leaves the details of how to put them into place up to the organization.

Quality factor frameworks come close to Garvin's product definition of quality because they distill quality into a set of measurable characteristics while the process maturity models most closely resemble Garvin's manufacturing definition of quality because they define quality by evaluating how close an organization's processes meet a predetermined specification. Garvin's user definition of quality, on the other hand, is hard to implement for proprietary in-house developed software because a user's satisfaction or rather dissatisfaction with a software's features or performance cannot be immediately addressed. Rather, user satisfaction must be bundled with the problem resolutions and new feature requests of all other users into a new release, patch, or service pack, which are infrequently issued due to their cost. Because of this limitation, software quality has become Garvin's value definition of quality: conformance to specification at an acceptable cost.

In contrast, FLOSS software quality most closely fits Garvin's user definition of quality. Users can directly log problem reports and new functionality requests directly into the software project's issue tracking system that is used by developers. Because FLOSS has frequent releases, those requests can become part of the software

Table 2. Quality factors

Model	Factors
McCall	Accessibility, Accountability, Accuracy, Augmentability, Communicativeness, Completeness, Conciseness, Consistency, Device-independence, Efficiency, Human engineering, Legibility, Maintainability, Modifiability, Portability, Reliability, Robustness, Self-containedness, Self-descriptiveness, Structuredness, Testability, Understandability, Usability
Boehm	Correctness, Efficiency, Flexibility, Integrity, Interoperability, Maintainability, Portability, Reliability, Reusability, Testability, Usability
ISO 9126	Efficiency, Functionality, Maintainability, Portability, Reliability, Usability
Garvin	Aesthetics, Conformance, Durability, Features, Perceived quality, Performance, Reliability, Serviceability

much more quickly than proprietary in-house developed software, thus better satisfying users.

METHODOLOGY

In order to answer the research question, how is quality defined in the FLOSS literature, we performed a literature review. We followed the guidelines for performing a systematic literature review as per Kitchenham and Charters (2007). We state the rationale for this review, the research question, the strategy used to search for primary studies, search terms, study selection criteria, data extraction strategy, and synthesis strategy (Kitchenham & Charters, 2007).

The rationale for this review is that there have been mixed results in studies looking at FLOSS quality. The probable reason is that quality is being defined and measured differently and that researchers are using different criteria to select study cases and observed characteristics.

DATA COLLECTION

The goal of this review is to answer the question of how is quality defined and measured in FLOSS literature. In order to do so we used the *EBSCO-host* online research database to search the top journals in Information Systems (*MIS Quarterly, ISR, JAIS, JMIS, ISJ,* and *EJIS*) (Association for

Information Systems, 2011) for articles matching open source software and quality between the years 1999 - 2011. We found a paper by Aksulu and Wade (2010) from a special issue on *Empirical Research on Free/Libre Open Source Software* that contained a comprehensive review of FLOSS research, categorizing it into 57 categories. Three of these categories dealt with quality: (1) *software quality*, which had 55 papers listed, (2) *software quality – testing and bug fixes*, which had 16 papers listed and (3) *software quality* – OSS security, which had nine papers listed (Aksulu & Wade, 2010). Some papers were listed under more than one category, leaving 76 unique papers.

From these papers, studies were selected based on these criteria: they had to define quality and evaluate it somehow. Papers that only mentioned quality but neither defined it nor measured it were excluded. This gave us a total of 20 papers.

To increase the number of studies in the sample, we used *Google Scholar* to search for papers that referenced the 20 papers in the original sample. We applied the same selection criteria and ended up with an extra 20 papers to add to the sample. This gave us a sample with a total of 40 papers.

To extract the data from the studies in the sample, we used grounded formal theory (Kearney, 1998, 2001). Because the definition of quality is subjective, we adopted an interpretive approach (Walsham, 1995) to this review by applying a grounded theory methodology (Strauss & Corbin, 1990). We used the Straussian type of grounded theory in order to allow previous theories and our own interpretations of quality to guide the data collection and analysis (Strauss & Corbin, 1994).

ANALYSIS

The papers of this literature review were analyzed using open, axial, and selective coding (Strauss & Corbin, 1990). As the papers were read, they were coded using open coding. Text segments from each of the papers were highlighted and labeled with a code to categorize and conceptualize the data.

The open coding phase produced 75 codes, which were used to label 637 text segments from the 40 papers gathered. The codes reflected how the authors defined quality, the measures used to operationalize it, the research methods used to analyze it, and the characteristics considered in the FLOSS projects that were used to validate their definition of quality.

The axial coding phase produced five codes which were categories containing the codes from the open coding phase. From the 75 codes from the open coding phase, four were discarded because they labeled few text segments and did not help explain how quality is interpreted in FLOSS research (see Table 3).

_Ref163888168 shows the categories produced from the axial coding phase. The categories were based on how the authors approached the research, how they analyzed the data, and how they defined quality, with the two main categories being process quality and product quality. The final category deals with the type of data sampled by the authors to validate their models, in this case, the characteristics of the FLOSS projects they examined. These categories were chosen because they follow the research process: an approach must be chosen along with an analysis method; the phenomenon of interest must be defined and finally, the data sample must be chosen.

The final phase, the selective coding phase, produced and integrated category that narrated the conceptualization of quality by FLOSS

Table 3. Categories from axial coding

Category	Description	Sample of codes within category
Research approach	Approach used to analyze quality in research study	Case study Survey Factor model Maturity model
Analysis method	Methodology used to analyze data	Regression Structural equation model Machine Learning Social Network Analysis
Process quality	Quality of development processes can be measured	Defect fixing rate Defect fixing time Definition of bug Quality assurance procedures Process metrics
Product quality	Quality of final software product.	Product metrics Number of post-release defects Cyclomatic complexity Halstead Volume CBO (coupling between objects)
Examined project representativeness	Characteristics considered of FLOSS projects used to validate operationalization of quality	Maturity Popularity Number of developers Development time examined Software type Version

researchers. The results are summarized in _Ref187246742. This phase was complete when theoretical saturation was reached—meaning, no new conceptualizations could be obtained from the data.

FINDINGS

In this section, we describe how researchers interpret quality in FLOSS publications. We consider four concepts from the literature: (1) quality as product, (2) quality as process, (3) modularity as a quality enabler, and (4) community as quality. We conclude this section with a findings summary (see Table 4).

Table 4. Categories from selective coding

Approach	Definition	Measures	Metrics Counts	Articles Mapped
Product	Software product structure and characteristics	Cohesion Complexity Size/effort Issue/bug Change/patch/version Compliance Documentation Deployment Interoperability Object coupling End user UI experience Data access Licensing Testing Maintainability Modularity	158	(Barbagallo, Francalenei, & Merlo, 2008; Capra, Francalanci, & Merlo, 2008; Conley, 2008; Koch & Neumann, 2008; Mockus, Fielding, & Herbsleb, 2000; Paulson et al., 2004; Samoladas, Gousios, Spinellis, & Stamelos, 2008; Stamelos et al., 2002; Tsantalis & Chatzigeorgiou, 2009)
Community	Developer, contributor, and user characteristics and interactions	Adoption/usage Contributions Community member activity Social network analysis Community culture Project management structure Community demographics Project distribution and inclusion Problem report activity Evolution Documentation	115	(Barbagallo et al., 2008; Kevin Crowston, Howison, & Annabi, 2006; Ghapanchi & Aurum, 2011; Koch & Neumann, 2008; Kuan, 2003; Mockus et al., 2000; Raghunathan et al., 2005; Samoladas et al., 2008; Stamelos et al., 2002)
Process	Established and repeatable procedures set in place to minimize defects and simplify work.	Testing Planning Versioning/branching Budget Bug/issue tracking Meetings Quality review Methodology/process description, execution, and compliance Consulting services Group consensus General project management Training	66	(Aberdour, 2007; K. Crowston & Scozzi, 2008; Halloran & Scherlis, 2002; Koru & Tian, 2004; Michlmayr, Hunt, & Probert, 2005; Mockus et al., 2000; Rigby et al., 2008; Zhao & Elbaum, 2003)

PRODUCT QUALITY

Studies defined quality as structural code quality (Capra et al., 2008; Conley, 2008; Gyimothy, Ferenc, & Siket, 2005; Koru & Liu, 2007; Koru & Tian, 2005; Spinellis, 2008; Stamelos et al., 2002). Metrics that are used to measure structural quality are number of statements (Spinellis, 2008; Stamelos et al., 2002), cyclomatic complexity (Capra et al., 2008; Gyimothy et al., 2005; Koch & Neumann, 2008; Koru & Tian, 2005; Spinellis, 2008; Stamelos et al., 2002; Yu, Schach, Chen, Heller, & Offutt, 2006), number of nesting levels (Barbagallo et al., 2008; Koru & Tian, 2005;

Spinellis, 2008; Stamelos et al., 2002), Halstead volume (Spinellis, 2008; Stamelos et al., 2002; Yu et al., 2006), coupling (Barbagallo et al., 2008; Capra et al., 2008; Conley, 2008; Koch & Neumann, 2008; Spinellis, 2008), coding style (Spinellis, 2008), statements per function, files per directory, percentage of numeric constants in operands (Spinellis, 2008), growth of LOC (lines of code) (Koru & Tian, 2005), modularity (Paulson et al., 2004), average coupling between objects, cohesion, number of children, depth of inheritance tree, methods inheritance factor and other internal software structure metrics (Capra et al., 2008; Conley, 2008; Gyimothy et al., 2005; Koru & Tian, 2005; Spinellis, 2008; Stamelos et al., 2002; Yu et al., 2006).

The idea behind measuring software code structure is that well-designed software is less complex, less likely to contain faults, and easier to maintain (Yu et al., 2006).

Measuring code structure left the researchers with more questions than answers. The most successful projects in terms of number of downloads and popularity were not the ones with the highest structural quality (Barbagallo et al., 2008; Yu et al., 2006). Another study found that the software modules with the highest rate of change were not the ones with the highest structural complexity (Koru & Tian, 2005). Even using machine learning algorithms with structural quality measures in order to predict faults did not produce clear results (Gyimothy et al., 2005).

Comparing structural quality between open and closed projects produced mixed results with some studies finding that FLOSS projects had quality comparable to closed projects (Samoladas, Stamelos, Angelis, & Oikonomou, 2004) while others found that open source software did not prove to have structural code quality higher than commercial software (Spinellis, 2008; Stamelos et al., 2002).

Using structural quality to define, measure, and compare FLOSS quality has not proven effec-

tive with different researchers achieving different results even when using the same metrics.

PROCESS QUALITY

Process quality is defined as in terms of defect fixing, process maturity models, and tool usage, as described in the next three subsections.

DEFECT FIXING

Defect fixing (Aberdour, 2007; Au, Carpenter, Chen, & Clark, 2009; Kevin Crowston et al., 2006; Crowston & Scozzi, 2008; Deprez & Alexandre, 2008; Ghapanchi & Aurum, 2011; Glance, 2004; Gyimothy et al., 2005; Halloran & Scherlis, 2002; Huntley, 2003; Kidane & Gloor, 2007; Koru & Tian, 2004, 2005; Kuan, 2003; Michlmayr et al., 2005; Mockus et al., 2000; Paulson et al., 2004; Samoladas et al., 2008; Sohn & Mok, 2008; Zhao & Elbaum, 2003; Zhou & Davis, 2005) is by far the most popular definition of process quality in the FLOSS quality literature. Authors have done studies defining what constitutes the process itself in order to determine how it works (Aberdour, 2007; Kevin Crowston et al., 2006; Crowston & Scozzi, 2008; Glance, 2004; Huntley, 2003; Koru & Tian, 2004, 2005; Sohn & Mok, 2008; Zhao & Elbaum, 2003; Zhou & Davis, 2005) and developed models to test its effectiveness (Ghapanchi & Aurum, 2011; Wray & Mathieu, 2008).

They have approached it in terms of total bugs fixed (Conley, 2008; Crowston et al., 2006; Crowston & Scozzi, 2008; Koru & Tian, 2004; Mockus et al., 2000; Samoladas et al., 2008) and speed of bug resolution (Au et al., 2009; Crowston et al., 2006; Huntley, 2003; Kidane & Gloor, 2007; Kuan, 2003). These approaches take into account the evolving nature of FLOSS, which is in a permanently emerging (or beta) state, different from closed software which goes through formal beta and live release cycles. It also considers that FLOSS testing and defect reporting and fixing is a community activity where developers, users, and periphery members collaborate to create the software.

However, results using this approach have been mixed. Some open source projects resolved service requests more quickly than their closed counterparts, others did not (Kuan, 2003). For other studies, software type (database, financial, game, networking) made more of a difference in determining defect resolution speed along with number of developers (groups with less than 15 developers were the most efficient) (Au et al., 2009). The main difference with closed software is that in most FLOSS projects, bugs are only addressed after feedback is received from users. There is no way to measure the quality of a release *pre hoc*, only *ad hoc* (Glance, 2004). However, this attitude is changing with projects such as GNOME, Debian, and KDE forming their own Quality Assurance teams and enforcing quality assurance tasks (Michlmayr et al., 2005).

Even though the defect fixing approach to measure FLOSS quality considers the evolving nature of its quality, research using it has not operationalized it in an evolutionary manner. Most studies have looked at the bug databases of FLOSS projects cumulatively after a certain amount of time (i.e., after six months of activity) rather than looking at defect resolution rates per release (except for Gyimothy et al., 2005; Mockus et al., 2000; Zhou & Davis, 2005) which did compare product releases), which is the evolutionary cycle of FLOSS software. The studies that looked at defects per release found that FLOSS has lower post-feature test defects than commercial software but higher post-release defects than commercial software (Mockus et al., 2000) and that release software quality is cyclical, with the Mozilla 1.2 showing a major decrease in quality, which was improved in later releases (Gyimothy et al., 2005).

Software quality in general (closed and open source) is cyclical in nature. This is illustrated in a study that showed that bug arrival rates follow a bell curve through time between releases. Whenever drastic changes were introduced to the software, the rate would also drastically change (Zhou & Davis, 2005). This would suggest that defect rates and thus defect resolution rates vary across releases depending on the changes being introduced. If the release introduces new features, or makes major changes to the architecture of the software, many defects will be introduced, while those that simply introduce defect fixes and enhancements, will introduce less.

Another issue stems from the definition of bug. Bug reports in bug databases in FLOSS project management Web sites could include anything from "failures, faults, changes, new requirements, new functionalities, ideas, and tasks" (Koru & Tian, 2004). Not to mention duplicate bug reports, poorly defined ones, and those that are out of scope with the product (Halloran & Scherlis, 2002). This happens because bug reporting systems are usually open to the public, and users without enough technical skills will make mistakes writing the bug reports (Michlmayr et al., 2005).

Measuring defect-fixing effectiveness in FLOSS projects has provided mixed results because different studies have defined and thus measured defects or bugs differently. They have also calculated defect-fixing rates by looking at bug tracking databases in the cumulative, without considering that defects are introduced and fixed cyclically in FLOSS, per release.

TOOL USAGE

FLOSS projects often rely on tools to enforce policies and standards (Halloran & Scherlis, 2002). Such tools include defect tracking systems, version control, mailing lists, automatic builds, etc. (Aberdour, 2007; Halloran & Scherlis, 2002; Michlmayr et al., 2005).

One quality assurance activity that is performed in traditional software development, peer review, is done differently in FLOSS projects with successful results. Peer reviews in open source are more efficient because there is no time wasted scheduling meeting since people work asynchronously and have more detailed discussions (Rigby et al., 2008). An example from the Apache project shows that it has three types of peer review procedures, depending on the experience and trustworthiness of the developer (Rigby et al., 2008).

Despite the successful inclusion of peer reviews into the FLOSS development process, testing procedures have not managed to make the necessary cross over into FLOSS. Most projects do not have a baseline test suite to support testing; this means regression testing cannot be performed (Zhao & Elbaum, 2003).

Developers perform their unit testing and sometimes do better than commercial software (Mockus et al., 2000), but it is up to the users to discover bugs and defects which could be eliminated with system or integrated testing.

PROCESS MATURITY MODELS

Maturity assessment models have been formulated to help users and integrators evaluate the quality of a FLOSS project versus another (del Bianco, Lavazza, Morasca, Taibi, & Tosi, 2010; Deprez & Alexandre, 2008; Deprez, Monfils, Ciolkowski, & Soto, 2007; Glott, Groven, Haaland, & Tannenberg, 2010; Groven, Haaland, Glott, & Tannenberg, 2010; Michlmayr, 2005; Samoladas et al., 2008; Soto & Ciolkowski, 2009). These models provide a set of criteria to evaluate a FLOSS project. Different models concentrate on different criteria, but they all provide a way to quantify and evaluate the quality of a FLOSS product.

Maturity models use organizational trustworthiness as a proxy for product trustworthiness and thus quality—if the product is built correctly, it will then have high quality.

The assessments are mostly for the FLOSS integrator who must assess the risk of adding the FLOSS product to his or her existing architecture.

The assessment models are not predictive (they do not evaluate the factors that lead to quality, nor do they provide a construct for quality) they simply provide a set of criteria with different scores that the integrator can then use to make the decision to adopt the FLOSS product.

MODULARITY AS THE ENABLER TO FLOSS QUALITY

FLOSS's paradox of having and adding more developers without compromising its productivity (in contrast to Brook's law that says that adding more developers increases coordination costs and decreases performance) is due to its approach to modularity. A FLOSS project is made up of many subprojects where only a few developers work together without ever having to interact with the developers in other subprojects or modules (Schweik, English, Kitsing, & Haire, 2008).

It is believed this is the reason that projects such as Linux and Apache are considered successful. They have been able to scale because of their modularity. Because of modularity, defects in one module, do not affect the rest (Mockus et al., 2000).

However, there is no single definition of modularity. The studies that have defined and measured it do quite differently. One study used "correlation between functions added and functions modified" to measure modularity. It then compared modularity across a set of open and closed projects. The open projects did not prove to be more modular than the closed ones (Paulson et al., 2004).

Another study used average component size, which was measured as program length (sum of the number of unique operands and operators) divided by number of statements. The study found that applications with smaller average component size received better user satisfaction scores (Stamelos et al., 2002).

In terms of influencing quality, modularity has produced mixed results. A study found that higher modularity does not lead to higher quality.

This study defined modularity as the distance of each package in a release from the main sequence. Because higher modularity is associated with reduced software complexity, it should result in higher structural code quality, but the authors found that the projects with higher modularity contained the greater number of defects (Conley, 2008).

Yet another study contests that it is small component design that leads to low defect density, higher user satisfaction, and easier maintenance and evolution (Aberdour, 2007).

Work distribution is another way of conceptualizing modularity. In another study, the authors found that a lower concentration of developers making changes to a module led to higher quality for the module. The authors speculated that this could explain the FLOSS paradox of many developers and high productivity: at the project level there could be many developers, but within the project, they should be organized into small teams; this would keep the concentration of authors to code low, thus fostering simpler code, higher quality and better maintainability (Koch & Neumann, 2008).

The literature has defined and operationalized modularity differently using either software structure measures (component size, distance from main sequence, *etc.*) or development organizational measures such as author concentration per class, number of authors per module, *etc.*

The development organizational measures have proven to be more effective at finding a correlation between quality and modularity, but these measures are still vaguely defined and more research needs to be performed to optimally define them and operationalize them in order to produce a universal measure of modularity.

COMMUNITY QUALITY

The researchers seem to have made arbitrary choices when it came to choosing FLOSS projects to study and in many cases did not defend their choices of software type, development time, number of projects, and project success.

By far, the most popular place to obtain data for FLOSS quality studies is the SourceForge repository maintained by Notre Dame University. But it was not the only place to find data; some case studies concentrated on popular projects that are not hosted by SourceForge such as Apache (Mockus et al., 2000; Rigby et al., 2008), Linux (Yu et al., 2006), and Eclipse (Kidane & Gloor, 2007).

Some projects considered software type a defining factor and only looked at projects of the same type (Koch & Neumann, 2008; Koru & Liu, 2007; Wray & Mathieu, 2008; Yu et al., 2006), while the rest did not consider it a factor. However one study did consider it and found that project category affects the bug resolution time (Au et al., 2009).

The development time of the projects examined by the authors was extremely variable. There were studies that examined FLOSS project data that covered development time for one week (Crowston & Scozzi, 2008), 105 weeks (Huntley, 2003), four months (Halloran & Scherlis, 2002), six months (Kidane & Gloor, 2007), *etc.* with one project capturing data from initial commit until the last commit before the stable version was released (Koch & Neumann, 2008).

Another factor that varied across the studies was the number of projects examined. From four (Crowston & Scozzi, 2008), 52 (Koru & Tian, 2004), all the way to 140 (Crowston et al., 2006), and beyond.

Another factor used to choose candidate was the success of the project measured in popularity terms such as number of downloads (Crowston et al., 2006) and SourceForge rank (Barbagallo et al., 2008; Michlmayr, 2005), which uses number of downloads and recommendations. Researchers refrained from including failed projects and only looked at those that high success measures.

The way researchers are choosing their samples is definitely a reason why there are mixed results in the FLOSS quality literature. They are looking at different types of projects, examining them for different amounts of time, and only considering popular projects.

FINDINGS SUMMARY

Quality is very subjective and hard to define absolutely. With this challenge, FLOSS researchers have used many ways to define quality. They have used product and process metrics and have found mixed results. FLOSS software is always evolving and one version might produce more defects than a previous one because of some major change in the software or the community structure.

Successful projects are those that have adopted a modular organization of their code and their community, allowing them to grow and isolate defects. They have also implemented tools to automate policy enforcement and adapted traditional software development practices to their context.

There is a need to evaluate the quality of FLOSS projects, and maturity assessment models have emerged to meet this need. However, they are hard to automate, and their scores are hard to interpret.

An important reason as to why researchers have obtained mixed results in researching FLOSS quality is that their samples have different characteristics in terms of number of projects examined, software type, time evaluated, and popularity of projects examined.

DISCUSSION

The reviewed papers show that there is a need to define and quantify quality in FLOSS development projects in order to compare them among each other and to traditionally developed software. Identifying projects that produce high quality products will lead to further research into understanding the factors that lead to higher quality and the interaction of those factors in FLOSS development projects.

The development of assessment models to ascertain quality comes from the position in traditionally developed software that established and repeatable processes lead to the development of quality products. A good example of this is the *QualiPSo* (http://www.qualipso.org) *OpenSource Maturity Model (OMM)*, is positioning itself as the CMMI for FLOSS. It allows evaluators to assess a FLOSS project on three (basic, intermediate, and advance) levels of trustworthiness based on the level of implementation of quality practices. It also provides tools for the extraction of data on FLOSS products and processes that can then be used to assess the trustworthiness of the project.

The *QualiPSo OMM* does not predict quality, however; it merely helps an evaluator assess it given his/her own criteria.

FLOSS QUALITY AS EVOLVING

With each release, the FLOSS software and its community change. Quality is not linear: the tenth release of a software product might not have fewer defects than its first. It all depends on what type of release it is; whether it is adding new features, restructuring the entire product, restructuring the way it is developed, or simply posting defect fixes. The type of release of the product is a more important determinant of its quality than its software structure, or its number of developers.

These issues could explain some of the mixed results obtained from research that only used product measures as a measure of quality – the modules with the highest change rate and the highest number of defects were not those with the lowest design quality or complexity (Koru & Tian, 2005).

DEFECT RESOLUTION RATE

Number of defects added by a release divided by the number of lines of code added by the release would seem a good measure of the quality of the software maintenance process (Mockus et al., 2000) that would allow comparison between open and closed software products. But this assumption is wrong because the release of a commercial closed software product is not the same as the one from an open source project. An open source product release resembles the commercial software after its feature test, because there is neither system nor regression testing in open source projects (Mockus et al., 2000).

These measures do not take into account FLOSS projects' community development. That is why a better measure of FLOSS quality is defect resolution rate, in terms of number of bugs resolved and average time of bug resolution. These measures not only show the quality of the code but also the community's effectiveness at achieving quality. However, these measures need to consider the priority of the bugs being resolved, the complexity of the code, and the number of people working in the bug resolution effort.

Another key issue is to define bugs as defects in the software product. Bug databases, which are used to calculate the defect resolution rates, are riddled with non-bugs, which must not be taken into account when calculating these rates.

And yet another is that the number of bugs reported depends heavily on the user population, with widely adopted projects having more bug reports. This measure is a surrogate for absolute number of bugs in the software, which is unknown and cannot be easily calculated.

MODULARITY AS DRIVER OF QUALITY

The "many eyeballs" looking at the bugs include core developers, periphery developers, sometime contributors, and users, who can easily find their way to the project's publicly available bug tracking system. This group has activity rates, contribution amounts, contributions included per release, problem reports contributed, problem reports resolved, and download statistics.

These are all metrics of the community's quality efforts. But making sure that these community members can work effectively with each other is necessary. A modular architecture of the code and the community allows a project to grow and attract new developers without having the defects of one group affect another group. Modularity should be defined in terms of technical modularity (the coupling of the modules) and organizational modularity (the coupling of the module managers/owners and the core project manager) (Tiwana, 2010).

A downside of extreme modularity, where only one developer owns a particular module is that if the module owner leaves, his or her module might become orphaned. That is why projects such as Debian are developing their own "quality assurance" groups (http://qa.debian.org), where anyone interested can join and help with mass bug filing and transitions, track orphan code, *etc*.

It seems that too much organizational modularity (how the work is divided among participants) might be bad for quality in the long run. It is important to do more research to understand what the right amount of modularity (code ownership and work distribution) looks like.

PROCESS AND PRODUCT MEASURES AS DRIVERS OF QUALITY

Product and process measures are still relevant in driving quality in FLOSS products: they are universally understood and any project community still needs to calculate and evaluate them. But they can be taken for granted and their use needs to be aided by automation tools, such as tools in the automatic build software that calculate and post correctness and reliability metrics and compare them with benchmark numbers, alerting the community members if their software product falls below the thresholds.

Relying on the "many eyeballs" to report and fix defects has helped FLOSS achieve quality, but there is something to be said for automating the process in order to produce a higher quality product before it is released.

CONCLUSION

Just like in traditionally developed software, there is little consensus in the FLOSS literature when it comes to defining quality.

Linux and Apache are by far the most studied projects in FLOSS literature. All the reviewed papers studied projects that they considered successful: they had released several versions, and had high popularity rating, and download numbers. However, failed projects also need to be studied in order to determine what led to their downfall.

FLOSS communities and their software product are emergent and need a measure of quality that will reflect their nature. Defect resolution rates (amount of defects resolved, speed of resolution) are the best way to measure a community's commitment to quality, because they recognize that FLOSS is not a static product, but ever evolving. These rates should be calculated per release, and not cumulatively, because the cycle of FLOSS evolution is the release. Researchers should be careful to only include defects and not new feature requests, duplicates, or poorly reported bugs into their calculations.

Modularity is being touted as the main driver of FLOSS quality success, but it needs to be further defined and studied in order to understand how it works.

In conclusion, from our review of the literature, we find these issues central in defining FLOSS quality:

- Product characteristics have not been a consistent basis of FLOSS quality.
- Process maturity models are not predictive (because they do not evaluate the factors that lead to quality).

- Defect-fixing effectiveness, modularity measures, and community measures have provided mixed results because each of these concepts has varied definitions.
- The release type of the product is a more important determinant of its quality than its software structure, or its number of developers.

We conclude that FLOSS quality metrics need more study in order to reach a common definition of what they measure and how they measure it.

Something else that needs to considered is the relevance of these quality measures in open source but in-house developed software such as Android (by Google), MySQL (by Oracle), which benefit from more formal testing procedures (such as beta-testing) before being released, as opposed to volunteer developed FLOSS which is released after just unit testing and moderate system testing.

REFERENCES

Aberdour, M. (2007). Achieving quality in open source software. *IEEE Software*, *24*(1), 58–64. doi:10.1109/MS.2007.2

Ajila, S. A., & Wu, D. (2007). Empirical study of the effects of open source adoption on software development economics. *Journal of Systems and Software*, *80*(9), 1517–1529. doi:10.1016/j.jss.2007.01.011

Aksulu, A., & Wade, M. (2010). A comprehensive review and synthesis of open source research. *Journal of the Association for Information Systems*, *11*, 576–656.

Association for Information Systems. (2011). *Senor scholars' basket of journals*. Retrieved from http://home.aisnet.org/displaycommon.cfm?an=1&subarticlenbr=346

Au, Y. A., Carpenter, D., Chen, X., & Clark, J. G. (2009). Virtual organizational learning in open source software development projects. *Information & Management, 46*(1), 9–15. doi:10.1016/j.im.2008.09.004

Barbagallo, D., Francalenei, C., & Merlo, F. (2008). The impact of social networking on software design quality and development effort in open source projects. In *Proceedings of the International Conference on Information Systems*.

Boehm, B. W., Brown, J. R., & Lipow, M. (1976). Quantitative evaluation of software quality. In *Proceedings of the 2nd International Conference on Software Engineering* (pp. 592-605).

Bonaccorsi, A., & Rossi, C. (2006). Comparing motivations of individual programmers and firms to take part in the open source movement. *Knowledge, Technology & Policy, 18*(4), 40–64. doi:10.1007/s12130-006-1003-9

Capra, E., Francalanci, C., & Merlo, F. (2008). An empirical study on the relationship among software design quality, development effort, and governance in open source projects. *IEEE Transactions on Software Engineering, 34*(6), 765–782. doi:10.1109/TSE.2008.68

Cavano, J. P., & McCall, J. A. (1978). A framework for the measurement of software quality. In *Proceedings of the ACM Software Quality Workshop* (pp. 133-139).

Conley, C. A. (2008). *Design for quality: The case of open source software development*. New York, NY: New York University.

Crosby, P. B. (1979). *Quality is free: The art of making quality certain*. New York, NY: McGraw-Hill.

Crowston, K., Howison, J., & Annabi, H. (2006). Information systems success in free and open source software development: Theory and measures. *Software Process Improvement and Practice, 11*(2), 123–148. doi:10.1002/spip.259

Crowston, K., & Scozzi, B. (2008). Bug fixing practices within free/libre open source software development teams. *Journal of Database Management, 19*(2), 1–30. doi:10.4018/jdm.2008040101

Crowston, K., Wei, K., Howison, J., & Wiggins, A. (2012). Free/libre open source software development: What we know and what we do not know. *ACM Computing Surveys, 44*(2). doi:10.1145/2089125.2089127

del Bianco, V., Lavazza, L., Morasca, S., Taibi, D., & Tosi, D. (2010). The QualiSPo approach to OSS product quality evaluation. In *Proceedings of the 3rd International Workshop on Emerging Trends in Free/Libre/Open Source Software Research and Development* (pp. 23-28).

Deming, W. E. (1982). *Quality, productivity, and competitive position*. Cambridge, MA: MIT Center for Advanced Engineering Study.

Deming, W. E. (1986). *Out of the crisis*. Cambridge, MA: MIT Center for Advanced Engineering Study.

Deprez, J.-C., & Alexandre, S. (2008). Comparing assessment methodologies for free/open source software: OpenBRR and QSOS. In *Proceedings of the 9th International Conference on Product-Focused Software Process Improvement* (pp. 189-203).

Deprez, J.-C., Monfils, F. F., Ciolkowski, M., & Soto, M. (2007). Defining software evolvability from a free/open-source software perspective. In *Proceedings of the Third International IEEE Workshop on Software Evolvability* (pp. 29-35).

Feigenbaum, A. (1961). *Total quality control: Engineering and management: The technical and managerial field for improving product quality, including its reliability, and for reducing operating costs and losses*. New York, NY: McGraw-Hill.

Garvin, D. A. (1984). What does 'product quality' really mean? *Sloan Management Review, 1*, 25–43.

Ghapanchi, A. H., & Aurum, A. (2011). Measuring the effectiveness of the defect-fixing process in open source software projects. In *Proceedings of the 44th Hawaii International Conference on System Sciences* (pp. 1-11).

Glance, D. G. (2004). Release criteria for the Linux Kernel. *First Monday*, *9*(4).

Glinz, M. (2007). On non-functional requirements. In *Proceedings of the 15th IEEE International Requirements Engineering Conference*.

Glott, R., Groven, A.-K., Haaland, K., & Tannenberg, A. (2010). Quality models for free/libre open source software-Towards the "silver bullet"? In *Proceedings of the 36th EUROMICRO Conference on Software Engineering and Advanced Applications* (pp. 439-446).

Groven, A.-K., Haaland, K., Glott, R., & Tannenberg, A. (2010). Security measurements within the framework of quality assessment models for free/libre open source software. In *Proceedings of the Fourth European Conference on Software Architecture: Companion Volume* (pp. 229-235).

Gyimothy, T., Ferenc, R., & Siket, I. (2005). Empirical validation of object-oriented metrics on open source software for fault prediction. *IEEE Transactions on Software Engineering*, *31*(10), 897–910. doi:10.1109/TSE.2005.112

Hales, P. (2006, December 8). Firefox use continues to rise in Europe. *The Inquirer*.

Halloran, T. J., & Scherlis, W. L. (2002). High quality and open source software practices. In *Proceedings of the 2nd Workshop on Open Source Software Engineering*.

Huntley, C. L. (2003). Organizational learning in open-source software projects: An analysis of debugging data. *IEEE Transactions on Engineering Management*, *50*(4), 485–493. doi:10.1109/TEM.2003.820136

International Organization for Standardization (ISO). (2001). *ISO 9126-1:2001, Software engineering - Product quality, Part 1: Quality model*. Geneva, Switzerland: Author.

Ishikawa, K. (1985). *What is total quality control? The Japanese way*. Upper Saddle River, NJ: Prentice Hall.

Juran, J. M. (1988). *Planning for quality*. London, UK: Collier Macmillan.

Kearney, M. H. (1998). Ready-to-wear: Discovering grounded formal theory. *Research in Nursing & Health*, *21*(2), 179–186. doi:10.1002/(SICI)1098-240X(199804)21:2<179::AID-NUR8>3.0.CO;2-G

Kearney, M. H. (2001). Enduring love: A grounded formal theory of women's experience of domestic violence. *Research in Nursing & Health*, *24*(4), 270–282. doi:10.1002/nur.1029

Kidane, Y., & Gloor, P. (2007). Correlating temporal communication patterns of the Eclipse open source community with performance and creativity. *Computational & Mathematical Organization Theory*, *13*(1), 17–27. doi:10.1007/s10588-006-9006-3

Kitchenham, B., & Charters, S. (2007). Guidelines for performing systematic literature reviews in software engineering. *Engineering, 2*.

Koch, S., & Neumann, C. (2008). Exploring the effects of process characteristics on product quality in open source software development. *Journal of Database Management*, *19*(2), 31–57. doi:10.4018/jdm.2008040102

Koru, A. G., & Liu, H. (2007). Identifying and characterizing change-prone classes in two large-scale open-source products. *Journal of Systems and Software*, *80*(1), 63–73. doi:10.1016/j.jss.2006.05.017

Koru, A. G., & Tian, J. (2004). Defect handling in medium and large open source projects. *IEEE Software, 21*(4), 54–61. doi:10.1109/MS.2004.12

Koru, A. G., & Tian, J. (2005). Comparing high-change modules and modules with the highest measurement values in two large-scale open-source products. *IEEE Transactions on Software Engineering, 31*(8), 625–642. doi:10.1109/TSE.2005.89

Kuan, J. (2003). Open source software as lead-user's make or buy decision: A study of open and closed source quality. In *Proceedings of the Second Conference on the Economics of the Software and Internet Industries.*

McCall, J. A., Richards, P. K., & Walters, G. F. (1977). Factors in software quality. *National Technology Information Service, 1-3.*

Michlmayr, M. (2005). Software process maturity and the success of free software projects. In *Proceeding of the Conference on Software Engineering: Evolution and Emerging Technologies* (pp. 3-14).

Michlmayr, M., Hunt, F., & Probert, D. (2005). Quality practices and problems in free software projects. In *Proceedings of the First International Conference on Open Source Systems.*

Mockus, A., Fielding, R. T., & Herbsleb, J. (2000). A case study of open source software development: The apache server. In *Proceedings of the 22nd International Conference on Software Engineering* (pp. 263-272).

Mockus, A., Fielding, R. T., & Herbsleb, J. D. (2002). Two case studies of open source software development: Apache and Mozilla. *ACM Transactions on Software Engineering and Methodology, 11*(3), 309–346. doi:10.1145/567793.567795

OSI. (2006). *The open source definition, version 1.9.* Retrieved August 4, 2009, from http://www.opensource.org/docs/osd

Paulson, J. W., Succi, G., & Eberlein, A. (2004). An empirical study of open-source and closed-source software products. *IEEE Transactions on Software Engineering, 30*(4), 246–256. doi:10.1109/TSE.2004.1274044

Raghunathan, S., Prasad, A., Mishra, B. K., & Chang, H. (2005). Open source versus closed source: software quality in monopoly and competitive markets. *IEEE Transactions on Systems, Man and Cybernetics. Part A, 35*(6), 903–918.

Raymond, E. (1999). The cathedral and the bazaar. *Knowledge, Technology & Policy, 12*(3), 23–49. doi:10.1007/s12130-999-1026-0

Rigby, P. C., German, D. M., & Storey, M.-A. (2008). Open source software peer review practices: a case study of the apache server. In *Proceedings of the International Conference on Software Engineering* (pp. 541-550).

Samoladas, I., Gousios, G., Spinellis, D., & Stamelos, I. (2008). The SQO-OSS quality model: Measurement based open source software evaluation. In *Proceedings of the 4th International Conference on Open Source Systems* (pp. 237-248).

Samoladas, I., Stamelos, I., Angelis, L., & Oikonomou, A. (2004). Open source software development should strive for even greater code maintainability. *Communications of the ACM, 47*(10), 83–87. doi:10.1145/1022594.1022598

Scacchi, W. (2009). Understanding requirements for open source software. In Lyytinen, K., Loucopoulos, P., Mylopoulos, J., & Robinson, W. (Eds.), *Design requirements engineering - A multi-disciplinary perspective for the next decade.* Berlin, Germany: Springer-Verlag.

Schwaber, K. (2004). *Agile project management with scrum.* Redmond, WA: Microsoft Press.

Schweik, C. M., English, R. C., Kitsing, M., & Haire, S. (2008). Brooks' versus Linus' Law: An empirical test of open source projects. In *Proceedings of the International Conference on Digital Government Research* (pp. 423-424).

Sohn, S. Y., & Mok, M. S. (2008). A strategic analysis for successful open source software utilization based on a structural equation model. *Journal of Systems and Software, 81*(6), 1014–1024. doi:10.1016/j.jss.2007.08.034

Soto, M., & Ciolkowski, M. (2009). The QualOSS open source assessment model measuring the performance of open source communities. In *Proceedings of the 3rd International Symposium on Empirical Software Engineering and Measurement* (pp. 498-501).

Spinellis, D. (2008). A tale of four kernels. In *Proceedings of the 30th International Conference on Software Engineering* (pp. 381-390).

Stamelos, I., Angelis, L., Oikonomou, A., & Bleris, G. L. (2002). Code quality analysis in open source software development. *Information Systems Journal, 12*, 43–60. doi:10.1046/j.1365-2575.2002.00117.x

Stewart, K. J., & Gosain, S. (2006). The impact of ideology on effectiveness in open source software development teams. *Management Information Systems Quarterly, 30*(2), 291–314.

Strauss, A., & Corbin, J. (1994). Grounded theory methodology - An overview. In Denzin, N. K., & Lincoln, Y. S. (Eds.), *Handbook of qualitative research* (pp. 273–285). Thousand Oaks, CA: Sage.

Strauss, A. L., & Corbin, J. M. (1990). *Basics of qualitative research: Grounded theory procedures and techniques* (1st ed.). Newbury Park, CA: Sage.

Tennant, G. (2001). *Six sigma: SPC and TQM in manufacturing and services*. Surrey, UK: Gower.

Tiwana, A. (2010). *The influence of software platform modularity on platform abandonment: An empirical study of Firefox extension developers. Unpublished Presentation*. Athens, GA: University of Georgia, Terry School of Business.

Tsantalis, N., & Chatzigeorgiou, A. (2009). Identification of move method refactoring opportunities. *IEEE Transactions on Software Engineering, 35*(3), 347–367. doi:10.1109/TSE.2009.1

von Hippel, E., & von Krogh, G. (2003). Open source software and the "private-collective" innovation model: Issues for organization science. *Organization Science, 14*(2), 209–223. doi:10.1287/orsc.14.2.209.14992

Walsham, G. (1995). The emergence of interpretivism in IS research. *Information Systems Research, 6*(4), 376–394. doi:10.1287/isre.6.4.376

Wray, B., & Mathieu, R. (2008). Evaluating the performance of open source software projects using data envelopment analysis. *Information Management & Computer Security, 16*(5), 449. doi:10.1108/09685220810920530

Ye, Y., & Kishida, K. (2003). Toward an understanding of the motivation of open source software developers. In *Proceedings of the 25th International Conference on Software Engineering* (pp. 419-429).

Yu, L., Schach, S. R., Chen, K., Heller, G. Z., & Offutt, J. (2006). Maintainability of the kernels of open-source operating systems: A comparison of Linux with FreeBSD, NetBSD, and OpenBSD. *Journal of Systems and Software, 79*(6), 807–815. doi:10.1016/j.jss.2005.08.014

Zhao, L., & Elbaum, S. (2003). Quality assurance under the open source development model. *Journal of Systems and Software, 66*(1), 65–75. doi:10.1016/S0164-1212(02)00064-X

Zhou, Y., & Davis, J. (2005). Open source software reliability model: An empirical approach. In *Proceedings of the Fifth Workshop on Open Source Software Engineering*.

This work was previously published in the International Journal of Open Source Software and Processes, Volume 3, Issue 3, edited by Stefan Koch, pp. 48-65, copyright 2011 by IGI Publishing (an imprint of IGI Global).

Chapter 11
Analyzing OSS Project Health with Heterogeneous Data Sources

Wikan Danar Sunindyo
*Vienna University of Technology, Austria &
Bandung Insitute of Technology, Indonesia*

Dietmar Winkler
Vienna University of Technology, Austria

Thomas Moser
Vienna University of Technology, Austria

Stefan Biffl
Vienna University of Technology, Austria

ABSTRACT

Stakeholders in Open Source Software (OSS) projects need to determine whether a project is likely to sustain for a sufficient period of time in order to justify their investments into this project. In an OSS project context, there are typically several data sources and OSS processes relevant for determining project health indicators. However, even within one project these data sources often are technically and/or semantically heterogeneous, which makes data collection and analysis tedious and error prone. In this paper, the authors propose and evaluate a framework for OSS data analysis (FOSSDA), which enables the efficient collection, integration, and analysis of data from heterogeneous sources. Major results of the empirical studies are: (a) the framework is useful for integrating data from heterogeneous data sources effectively and (b) project health indicators based on integrated data analyses were found to be more accurate than analyses based on individual non-integrated data sources.

INTRODUCTION

Current Open Source Software (OSS) projects involve a range of stakeholders, from core developers and co-developers to potential users and project investors. Typically, stakeholders, such as potential users or project investors need to know the status and the likely future performance of the project to determine whether the project is likely to sustain for a reasonable period of time in order to justify their investments into the project.

Recent research on using project data to support OSS health monitoring to provide immediate OSS project status, e.g., *Sourcerer* (Linstead, Bajracharya, Ngo, Rigor, Lopes, & Baldi, 2009), focus on analyzing author-topic relationships in

DOI: 10.4018/978-1-4666-2937-0.ch011

different OSS artifacts to increase understanding of the project and to raise the awareness on the health status of a project. Gall, Fluri, and Pinzger (2009) introduced the *Evolizer* approach to analyze the software evolution of OSS projects within Eclipse. This analysis is useful to investigate the current stage of OSS to be adapted continuously to changing environments, business reorientation, or modernization. Recent research on OSS project status monitoring includes participation aspects (Choi, Chengalur-Smith, & Whitmore, 2010), productivity aspects (Wahyudin & Tjoa, 2007), communication aspects (Biffl, Sunindyo, & Moser, 2010a), and community aspects (Kaltenecker, 2010). The research presented in this paper is based on the concept of project health indicators, which has been introduced by Wahyudin, Schatten, Mustofa, Biffl, and Tjoa (2006) for monitoring the health status of OSS projects during development. Example indicators that can be used by experts to assess an OSS project are: (a) service delays on open issues – the time it takes to fix bugs and issues listed in the project bug reporting system; (b) proportions of activity metrics in the community, e.g., the volume of mailing list postings, bug status changes per times slot, and updates in the SVN to learn the health of relationships between relevant activities, e.g., activities on the same bug; and (c) communication and use intensity. In a healthy project community, a reasonable relationship can be expected between measures such as the number of downloads, mailing list postings, and developer interactions in mailing lists (Wahyudin, Mustofa, Schatten, Biffl, & Tjoa, 2007).

However, challenges for monitoring the health status of OSS projects easily and frequently are: (a) manual data collection and integration from heterogeneous data sources, i.e., data sources, which represent common project-level concepts in various data formats that are non-trivial to reconcile, tend to be prone to errors and take considerable effort to integrate (Conklin, 2006); (b) the need to correlate data on different activities requires data integration; (c) manual data validation of the integrated data is hard due to different representation of common concepts, e.g., different names for one person in the data models involved; (d) data analyses of individual data sources, e.g., mailing lists, bug database (Mockus, Fielding, & Herbsleb, 2002), SVN/CVS (German, 2004), and change logs (Chen, Schach, Yu, Offutt, & Heller, 2004) have been shown to be weak to detect the health status of OSS project accurately; and (e) the large amount of data to maintain for analysis in an OSS project over time takes significant resources for storing.

In this paper, we propose and evaluate a framework for OSS data analysis, FOSSDA, which enables the efficient collection, integration, and analysis of data from heterogeneous sources. This framework provides the following contributions to address OSS project health monitoring challenges: (a) a process with semantic tool support to make data collection and integration from heterogeneous data sources more efficient; (b) adaptation of ontology-based querying techniques to OSS project monitoring, which makes data validation simpler and more effective; (c) the combination of different project metrics for analysis purposes is expected to improve project health analysis accuracy over the analysis based on individual data sources only; (d) the use of an ontology to represent OSS knowledge based on well-defined semantics and to provide extensive querying capabilities (Biffl, Sunindyo, & Moser, 2010b).

The empirical evaluation of the FOSSDA approach focuses on two research issues, namely (a) a feasibility study of FOSSDA in a pilot application with several OSS projects and (b) an integrated data model that can be used to derive a health indicator model to assess OSS project status with reasonable accuracy. Major results show that (a) the proposed framework supported efficient data collection and analysis compared to the traditional approach in the study context and (b) the integrated data model supported a more accurate analysis of OSS project health indicators.

The remainder of this paper is structured as follows. Second section discusses related work on health indicators and current frameworks on analyzing OSS project data. Third section motivates the research issues and approach; fourth section describes the empirical study. Fifth section presents results from an empirical pilot study of the framework and sixth section discusses the results based on the research issues. Finally, the seventh section concludes the paper and suggests further work.

RELATED WORK

This section summarizes related work on monitoring OSS projects, methods to collect and analyze OSS project data, and research work on defining and implementing OSS project health indicators.

OSS Project Monitoring

Von Krogh and von Hippel (2003) investigated OSS development processes and found differences between monitoring commercial software development and OSS development. In commercial software development, the project manager can apply tight management of processes and take precautions, while in OSS development software architecture and functionality are governed by a community consisting of developers, who can commit code to the authorized version of the software. Therefore, OSS project development monitoring also has to be based on the community works and agreement rather than enforced regulation as in commercial software development.

Yamauchi, Yokozawa, Shinohara, and Ishida (2000) state that in a traditional perspective, managing and leading OSS development projects seems to be impossible, because no formal quality control program exists and no authoritative leaders monitor the development project. For them it is surprising that also OSS development can achieve smooth coordination, consistency in design and continuous innovation while relying heavily on electronic environments as face-to-face supplementary; however, project monitoring for OSS projects seems still quite fragile. In addition, they discuss how OSS development avoids limitations of dispersed collaboration and addresses the sources of innovation in OSS development. Further research is needed to reveal how typical project management methodologies can be adapted to the OSS domain in order to improve the software quality, e.g., by monitoring typical OSS project product and process data.

Wahyudin and Tjoa (2007) discuss how project monitoring has traditionally been focused on human-based reporting, which is good for tightly coupled organizations to ensure the quality of project reporting. In loosely-coupled organizations like in OSS development projects, this approach does not work well, because the stakeholders typically work voluntarily and flexibly. One way to measure the performance of the project is by correlating and analyzing process event data (e.g., mailing list artifacts or bug reports) from the OSS community.

Sharma, Sugumaran, and Rajagopalan (2002) observe OSS development projects based on three aspects: structure, processes, and culture. The OSS communities can be structured along the dimensions of division of labor, coordination mechanisms, distribution of decision-making authority and organizational boundary. In OSS processes, stakeholders can have governance mechanisms, for example by applying membership management, rules and institutions, monitoring and sanctions, and reputation as one of the prime motivators for the OSS developers. Even though membership in OSS projects is open to anyone, the OSS communities manage membership effectively. They illustrate how OSS projects can be monitored via social interaction and sanctions from the communities. However, the relationships between the project data produced by the stakeholders, the activities of the stakeholders, and the quality measurement of OSS were not analyzed in their study.

To address semantic integration of data originating from heterogeneous OSS project data sources, a tool for the extraction of project data for Apache projects called *Project Data Fetcher* was initially developed and reported in Biffl, Sunindyo, and Moser (2010b). This tool allows gathering project artifacts from the mailing list, the *Bugzilla* (http://www.bugzilla.org) database, and the Subversion versioning system of Apache projects. The retrieved data allows evaluating so-called communication metrics. The *Project Data Fetcher* uses an ontology for storing extracted project data.

OSS Data Analysis Frameworks

There are several reports on tool support for a more comprehensive observation of OSS projects for data analysis. These reports involve different data sources and analysis methods as part of OSS data analysis frameworks, e.g., *Alitheia Core* (http://www.sqo-oss.org) (Gousios & Spinellis, 2009a, 2009b) and *Ohloh* (http://www.ohloh.net) (Hu & Zhao, 2008).

The *Alitheia Core* tool is an extensible platform for software quality analysis designed specifically to facilitate software engineering research on large and diverse data sources. Figure 1 shows the simplified *Alitheia Core* System Architecture, which consists of three tiers: (a) data mirroring, storage and retrieval (tier 1); (b) system core (tier 2); and (c) results presentation (tier 3). Tier 1 enables the collection of data from different data sources, e.g., subversion, mailing list, and bug

reports. However, the mirroring of the data sources tends to make data management inefficient for large projects. Tier 2 provides a range of metric plug-ins for analyzing individual OSS data to support the interpretation of the OSS project status. However, the lack of interaction and combination between these different metrics makes the conclusions on the OSS project status less strong than analyzing integrated data sources. Tier 3 provides results presentation to web interface or IDE plug-in via SQO-OSS connector library. This platform allows importing data from OSS projects into a meta-database and provides an infrastructure to run metrics on clusters of processing nodes. Currently, this tool has been applied to analyze OSS data limited to a single OSS project community, namely the Gnome ecosystem (Gousios & Spinellis, 2009b).

Ohloh is an OSS directory that anyone can edit (Hu & Zhao, 2008). *Ohloh* retrieves data from revision control repositories (such as CVS (http://savannah.nongnu.org/projects/cvs), SVN (http://tortoisesvn.net/), or Git (http://git-scm.com/)) and provides descriptive statistics about the longevity of projects, their license and metrics such as source lines of code and commit statistics. Currently, *Ohloh* provides information about 11,800 major OSS projects involving 94,330 people. However, the reports on introducing a framework for analyzing OSS project data do not report on health indicators, which allow detecting the OSS project status in a timely fashion.

Figure 1. Simplified Alitheia core system architecture (see details in Gousios & Spinellis, 2009a)

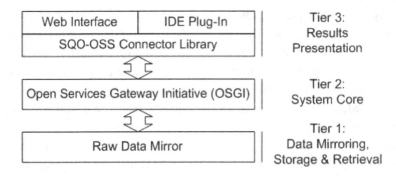

OSS Health Indicators

The term OSS project "health indicators" was introduced by Wahyudin *et al.* (2006) to help OSS stakeholders to get an overview on a large portfolio of OSS projects. Using a health indicator can be seen as analogous to measuring the temperature of the human body with respect to indicating whether a person is likely to be sick or in healthy condition (Wahyudin, 2008). This work analyzed some project metrics, e.g., open issues, proportions, and communication metrics, in four OSS Apache projects, namely *HTTPD* (http://httpd. apache.org/), *Tomcat* (http://tomcat.apache.org/), *Xindice* (http://xml.apache.org/xindice/), and *Slide* (http://jakarta.apache.org/slide/), and discussed the results with OSS experts to investigate the external validity of the indicators. Major result was that those important indicators such as developer activity or bug management performance are easy to measure but have to be augmented with other indicators, e.g., the probability of bug occurrence and/or experts' opinion, which are concealed behind the development process to determine the project health comprehensively.

In the past decade, only a limited number of studies and publication addresses communication metrics, for example Brügge and Dutoit (1997), who reported empirical evidence that metrics based on communication artifacts generate better insight into the health of application development processes than code-based metrics. Many developers ignore the fact that software code is only available late in the development process, while communication artifacts, such as e-mails, mailing list entries, or memo notes are valuable information that is available early and can be used to investigate the health of development project. To draw valid conclusions on the communication behavior of the project members and measures for improvement, a new set of metrics has to be designed. Roche (1994) showed that the results of these novel metrics may assist project managers and that their potential should not be ignored.

Early research towards OSS health indicators has been reported by Mockus, Fielding, and Herbsleb (2000, 2002) who ran an experiment on two major OSS projects, Apache Web Server (http://httpd.apache.org/) and the Mozilla browser (http://www.mozilla.org/), to investigate aspects of developer participations to compare the strengths and weaknesses of OSS projects and commercial projects. However, the focus of this work is more on the comparison of different aspects, e.g., size of the core team, productivity, and problem resolution intervals in the OSS projects than on project health. This research is a starting point to improve measurements that help the OSS developer and manager to obtain the project status faster by introducing the concept of project health indicators.

This work was continued by Wahyudin *et al.* (2007) by empirically evaluating development processes to get a status overview of OSS projects in a timely fashion and to predict project survivability based on the data available on project web repositories. However, the data collection for this approach was still done manually, by retrieving data from source code management, mailing lists, and bug reports websites. The high effort for manual data collection and for quality issues warrants the automation of data collection, integration, and quality assurance. The evaluation of the data was done separately for each data source, and did not yet discover further relationships between different sources, which could reveal further health indicators.

Bachmann and Bernstein (2009) focus on using bug tracking databases and version control system log files to support a historical view analysis for improving software process data quality. The results show that a poor correlation between linked bug reports is a strong indicator for the missing traceability and justification of source code changes. The rate of linked bug reports can be observed by linking commit messages for valid bug report numbers to the numbers of all bug reports. A poor rate is obtained when the commit messages have few connections with the bug reports. We extend the using of bug reports as health indicators by combining with other metrics in OSS projects.

RESEARCH ISSUES AND APPROACH

Building on the previous research results in Related Work Section, this Section motivates the research issues and derives the research approach.

Research Issues

The focus of this paper lies on analyzing engineering processes in OSS projects to improve the OSS project quality, e.g., by using continuous project monitoring to detect risk symptoms early. The goal of continuous project monitoring is to support informed management decisions based on the project status, e.g., whether the project is likely to be sustainable and is worth supporting. From this goal, we derived the following two research issues: (a) a framework, FOSSDA, to support efficient OSS data analysis even from heterogeneous data sources and (b) an integrated data model to support defining and investigating more accurate OSS project health indicators.

RI-1: Increasing the efficiency of data collection from heterogeneous sources in OSS projects.

The goal of this research issue is to increase data collection efficiency from heterogeneous OSS sources. Efficiency is defined as the number of units of output (e.g., data items collected and analyzed) per unit of input (e.g., personnel effort in work hours). We compare the efficiency of a traditional manual approach and the proposed automated data collection approach, FOSSDA (see Figure 2). We present a use case to measure the improvement of the automated approach over the traditional approach, especially regarding human effort, measured in person hours.

A major challenge for efficient data collection and integration is that there may exist only few information from different OSS data sources that can be connected each other. We address the research issues with the following steps: (a) literature and tool survey on data integration from heterogeneous sources, e.g., on how to analyze OSS process data, (b) identify relevant technologies to support OSS process data analysis, (c) derive OSS tools and data models to collect and analyze, (d) building FOSSDA prototypes to support structured data analysis, (e) empirical evaluation of the FOSSDA concept and prototypes for feasibility testing. The technologies used in this approach are explained further in Empirical Study Section. The OSS tools and data models are explained in Research Approach Subsection.

By following this approach, we expect to achieve more efficient data integration as tool support can reduce the manual effort for collecting and integrating data. A limitation of this approach is its dependence on the tool chain capabilities, e.g., the data collection tool only captures data from a limited scope of data sources.

RI-2: Investigate whether integrated analysis of data from heterogeneous sources can improve the accuracy of OSS project health indicators.

Different data sources, e.g., SVN, mailing list, and bug reports, can be inputs for the FOSSDA. However, the different data models used by these data sources for common project concepts, such as users and their roles (see example concepts in Figure 3), impede the data integration process. The use of different tools to collect the data also increases the complexity of integration problems. Besides, it is hard to identify the link between different data sources, e.g., names of SVN committers, which are somehow related to the names of mailing list posters. To solve these issues, we propose to design an integrated data model to support the investigation of health indicators for OSS projects.

The expected benefits of an integrated data model are: (a) that the integrated data model can provide relevant data elements to derive OSS project health indicators; and (b) the possibility to add/modify data sources for analysis with other (test) data sources that can support the integrated data model. Only related information from data sources are necessary to support the observation of health indicators, and the integrated data model contains the required information from different OSS data sources.

Inputs to the integrated data models are the knowledge and understanding of the structure of different data sources, e.g., SVN, mailing list and bug report, and the different phases of OSS development processes. The output of this approach is the integrated data model that provides all relevant information to support OSS health indicator investigations.

The process steps to derive the integrated data model can be defined as follows: (a) identify the local data models of the data sources and the tools to access the data sources; (b) identify relevant relationships and similarities between data sources and define links for those relationships; (c) derive process and product metrics from the artifacts; and (d) derive and evaluate health indicators from process and product metrics. By following these process steps, the outcome is an integrated data model for project health indicator evaluation. See details on the data model in Integrated Model Subsection.

Research Approach

This section summarizes relevant aspects of FOS-SDA and the integrated data model to address the research issues motivated in Research Issues Section. In this section we elaborate on how we addressed the process steps listed with the research issues (RI-1 and RI-2).

Framework for OSS Data Analysis

The framework for OSS data analysis is proposed to answer the first research issue (RI-1). The litera-

ture and tool survey (RI-1 step 1) and technology identification (RI-1 step 2) were the basis for the Related Work Section of this paper. FOSSDA is the result of the technology identification (RI-1 step 2) and the derivation of OSS tools and data models derivation (RI-1 step 3). This particular solution has been developed to address the basic requirement for collecting and analyzing heterogeneous OSS data systematically and can be used by different types of OSS stakeholders, e.g., project managers, investors, or developers. The FOSSDA prototypes implementation (RI-1 step 4) is the foundation for the empirical evaluation study (RI-1 step 5).

The proposed FOSSDA consists of four layers: (a) Layer 1: data sources, (b) Layer 2: core framework, (c) Layer 3: health indicators, and (d) Layer 4: presentation layer. In this paper we focus our efforts on data collection and analysis (layers 2 and 3). This framework is built based on an ontology-based knowledge representation, mapping, and reasoning and uses the *Project Data Fetcher* tool for data collection. Major novel contributions of this framework are (a) an ontology to store the integrated data collection results, (b) improvement of tools for collect data purposes, and (c) improvement of tools to analyze the collected and integrated data. Figure 2 illustrates the FOSSDA framework for analyzing OSS engineering process data using a combination of existing analysis approaches. The description of each layer is as follows.

Layer 1: Data Sources: OSS projects generate a wide range of data during development and as product application. These data can be classified as process metrics or product metrics. Process metrics can be derived from development tools that are used by the developers or other stakeholders during the development process, e.g., source code management systems, bug reporting systems, or mailing list. Product metrics can be derived from the final product, e.g., by counting the number of lines of code, the number of modules, the coupling and cohesion metrics between modules. In this layer, we provide the basis for collecting data from several types of OSS projects artifacts for further use in the next steps. Examples of common data sources for OSS process analysis and improvement are: source code management systems, bug reporting systems, and mailing lists.

Layer 2: Core Framework: The OSS data sources have heterogeneous data formats and models that impede the analysis process. Therefore, the data have to be integrated before storing and analyzing them. We applied an ontology as promising approach for data storage. The ontology consists of three heterogeneous data models (see Figure 3) derived from the tools used during software development process (i.e., versioning system, mailing list, and issue tracker). The data models of these tools contain elements which are only used in the context of the specific tool, as well as elements which are also used in context of other tools. In order to integrate the data models respectively tools, so called "common concepts" (see Figure 3 for project/process level) has to be introduced to link heterogeneous data models and tools. As a next step, the concepts of local tool data models has to be mapped to the common data model concept (mapping from data source level to project/process level in Figure 3) (Biffl, Sunindyo, & Moser, 2010a; Moser, 2009).

We apply an ontology-based tool called *Project Data Fetcher* (see Figure 2) (Biffl, Sunindyo, & Moser, 2010b) to collect data from heterogeneous

Figure 2. An analysis framework to support OSS data analysis

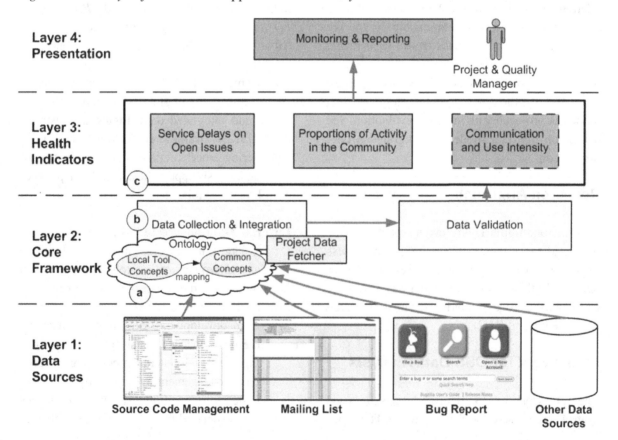

tools and store the results in an ontology. The application of an ontology allows (a) checking the data and (b) linking connected data (based on identified common concepts) from different sources, e.g., identifying that several author names in mailing list postings actually belong to the same persons who committed code to the SCM. After collecting and integrating the data, we check the validity of the data and their connections by reasoning to the ontology. The integrated and validated data are the foundation for good analysis results in the next layer. Note that the Project Data Fetcher allows data validation by using an ontology for data consistency checking.

Layer 3: Health Indicators: This layer provides approaches to derive health indicators based on the integrated and validated data. The health indicators are defined and applied in FOSSDA by analyzing the OSS project ontology as a knowledge representation of heterogeneous data sources. The related data sources are identified and then calculated to produce process metrics for health indicators. We use several OSS health indicators presented by Wahyudin *et al.* (2007): (a) service delays on open issues (indicator 1), (b) proportions of activities in the community (indicator 2), and (c) communication and use intensity (indicator 3). In this work we focus on the health indicators 1 and 2 as there is not yet sufficient valid data for analyzing indicator 3 in our study context. As there are many additional candidate indicators, we focus on these indicators because these indicators are easy to obtain and can provide the status of OSS project from different data sources faster than other indicators.

The judgment of the indicator accuracy is evaluated based on estimations of OSS experts. These experts are the members of Apache Project Management Committee (PMC) or the Apache Software Foundation's board who decide to move inactive projects to the Apache *Attic* (http://attic.apache.org/) repository. Apache *Attic* is a special repository from Apache Software Foundation to provide a process and solutions to make it clear when an Apache project has reached its end of life. Projects whose PMC are unable to muster 3 votes for a release, who have no active committers or who are unable to fulfill their reporting duties to the board are all candidates for the *Attic*.

Layer 4: Presentation Layer: This layer contains monitoring and reporting tools to provide OSS health indicators to project and quality managers. The information is provided in a textual or graphical format that is most suitable for project and quality managers to take actions based on the health indicators. One example of such tools is the Project Monitoring Cockpit (*ProMonCo*) tool (Biffl, Sunindyo, & Moser, 2010a) which can be connected to the Project Data Fetcher and provide analysis results as sample implementation of the FOSSDA presentation layer.

Integrated Data Model

To support the finding process of OSS health indicators efficiently, we propose an integrated data model based on different OSS data sources, which is illustrated in Figure 3. The integrated data model derivation is obtained by following the process steps we have mentioned in research issue 2 (RI-2). The left hand side of Figure 3 shows how to identify the local data models from different data sources, e.g., SVN, mailing list and bug tracker (RI-2 step 1) and relevant relationships of the local data sources (RI-2 step 2). The process and product level concepts ("common concepts") are obtained from these local data model as illustrated by the dashed colored lines linked to the common concepts in the top right hand side of Figure 3 (RI-2 step 3). The health indicators we derived from querying the ontology in the analysis level are shown in the bottom right hand side of Figure 3 (RI-2 step 4).

Typical efforts for collecting data from different OSS data sources have been summarized by Robles, González-Barahona, Izquierdo-Cortazar, and Herraiz (2009), who proposed to collect data from source code management, mailing list archives, and bug tracking systems. This work reports experiences on obtaining and analyzing information from rich set of development-related information in OSS projects. It gives advice for the problem that can be found when retrieving and preparing the data sources that is useful for our analysis. We follow their suggestion by capturing data from SVN, developers' mailing list, and bug report. Those data sources have similarities, e.g., the names of people involved, the time stamps when some action occurred, and names of artifacts involved that could be useful to derive the relationships between those different data sources (see Figure 3).

By identifying different data sources on the data source level we can create the integrated data model on the project/process level. We classify the data model into three parts, namely people, process, and product, based on their support for calculating the health indicators. The benefit of the integrated data model is the flexibility of the data model regarding the data sources in the data source level, i.e., we can add/introduce a new data source into the existing data sources, as long as the new data source can provide the information for the integrated data model on the project/process level. The common concepts in the integrated data model for calculating e.g., the health indicators, remain stable, even if we experiment with varying data sources to run tests or variants of empirical studies.

This integrated data model shown in Figure 3 is formulated in UML. Listing 1 shows an example of the formal representation of software developer concepts in *OWL* (Ontology Web Language, http://www.w3.org/TR/owl-features/). This example shows the project ontology including developers, deadline, name and role as representation of the data model. This example and other representation models were built with the *Protégé* (http://

protege.stanford.edu) editor that provides useful tools to generate and manage ontologies. The *Project Data Fetcher* tool (Huber, 2010) supports the storage of project data modeled in the data model using an ontological representation. The general ontology architecture consists of a set of so-called tool ontologies (one for each data source to be integrated), and a single so-called project ontology representing the common concepts as well as the mappings and required transformation between tool specific concepts and common concepts.

The *Project Data Fetcher* tool has been developed using the *Java* programming language. For accessing the ontologies, we use the ontology processing features of the *Jena* (http://jena.sourceforge.net) framework. The *Jena* framework provides an *OWL* API for programmatic access to *OWL* ontologies using *Java*. *Jena* also provides the tool "*schemagen*," which creates a *Java* class file containing an instance of the ontology model as well as the elements of the input ontology as static fields. The *Jena* Framework also contains a basic element, the *OntModel* class. The *OntModel* provides features to modify the model and persist the model into a file. Once the ontology model is accessible, the next step is to provide a way to configure the tool using "*Common Configuration.*" This configuration enables *Java* applications to read configuration data from a variety of sources, e.g., the URL of SVN, mailing list, and bug tracker data sources. For accessing the subversion repository, we used the "*SVNKit*" (http://svnkit.com) code library. This library is an OSS toolkit for Java and provides an API to access and manipulate subversion repositories online as well as local working copies. For accessing the data from the mailing list archives, we used "*mstor*" (http://mstor.sourceforge.net) library. This library provides access to email messages in *mbox* format, which is stored file-based.

Listing 2 shows an example of ontology-based querying for project monitoring to find related SVN entry from the mailing list issue.

Figure 3. Integrated data model to support OSS health indicators

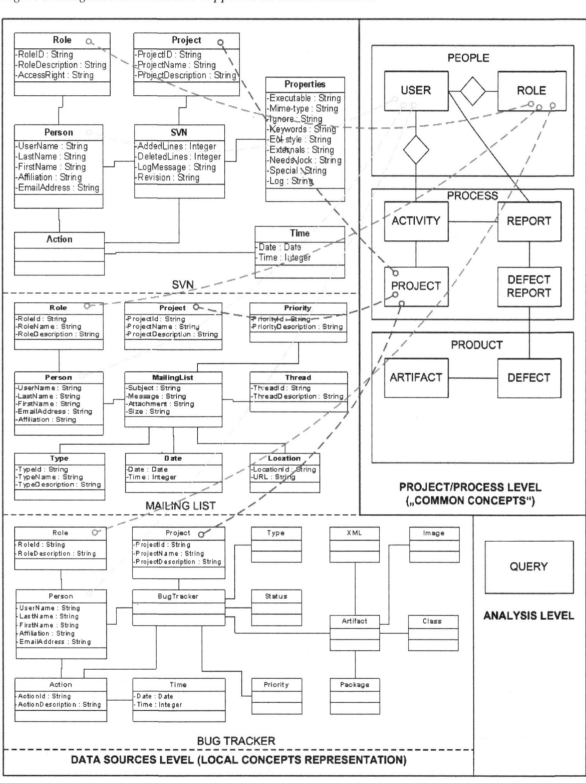

Listing 1. Excerpt of the ontology represented in OWL

```
<SubClassOf>
<Class URI="&Ontology1265201409169 ; Project" />
<ObjectMinCardinality cardinality="1">
                <ObjectProperty URI="&Ontology1265201409169; developers"/>
                <Class URI="&Ontology1265201409169; Developer"/>
</ObjectMinCardinality>
</SubClassOf>
<SubClassOf>
<Class URI="&Ontology1265201409169; Project"/>
<DataMinCardinality cardinality="1">
                <DataProperty URI="&Ontology1265201409169 ; deadline"/>
                <Datatype URI="&xsd ; dateTime"/>
</DataMinCardinality>
</SubClassOf>
<SubClassOf>
<Class URI="&Ontology1265201409169; Project"/>
<DataMinCardinality cardinality="1">
                <DataProperty URI="&Ontology1265201409169 ; name"/>
                <Datatype URI="&xsd ; string"/>
</DataMinCardinality>
</SubClassOf>
<Declaration>
<Class URI="&Ontology1265201409169; Project"/>
</Declaration>
<SubClassOf>
<Class URI="&Ontology1265201409169 ; Role"/>
<DataExactCardinality  cardinality="1">
                <DataProperty URI="&Ontology1265201409169 ; name"/>
                <Datatype URI="&xsd ; string"/>
</DataExactCardinality>
</SubClassOf>
<Declaration>
        <Class URI="&Ontology1265201409169 ; Role "/>
</Declaration>
```

EMPIRICAL STUDY

This section provides an overview of a pilot application we used to empirically investigate the feasibility of our approach, the study objects, threats to validity, and study results.

Pilot Application

To investigate the feasibility of our approach, we built a pilot application for FOSSDA. This pilot application is based on a set of tools, e.g., the *Project Data Fetcher* (Biffl, Sunindyo, & Moser,

Listing 2. Example query to find related SVN entries from a mailing list issue

```
SELECT count(?a) WHERE {domain:bug_id_17034 domain:resolvedBy ?a}
domain:bug_id_17034 owl:equalTo bugtracker:bug_id_17034
SELECT (?b) WHERE
{bugtracker:bug_id_17034 bugtracker:hasAffectedArtifact ?b}
Result: b = bugtracker:dist.xml
bugtracker:dist.xml owl:equalTo domain:dist.xml
domain:dist.xml owl:equalTo SVN:dist.xml
SELECT (?c) WHERE
{?c SVN:hasAffectedArtifact SVN:dist.xml}
Result: c = SVN:SVN_891529_dist.xml
        c = SVN:SVN_891533_dist.xml
SVN:SVN_891529_dist.xml owl:equalTo domain:SVN_891529_dist.xml
SVN:SVN_891533_dist.xml owl:equalTo domain:SVN_891533_dist.xml
Result: count(?a) = 2
```

2010b) and the *Project Monitoring Cockpit* (Biffl, Sunindyo, & Moser, 2010a). The explanation for each layer of pilot application is as follows.

Layer 1: Data Sources: In the data sources layer (FOSSDA layer 1 in Figure 2) of our pilot application, we used SVN (http://subversion. tigris.org), developers' mailing lists, and *Bugzilla* (http://www.bugzilla.org) tools. SVN is a source code management tool that is widely used to control the revision of source code during the development of OSS products. We used SVN as a data source for analysis purposes because of its popularity and ease to provide data. Developer's mailing lists allow collecting information about the activities of developers during development phase. *Bugzilla* is a bug reporting system, which can be used to monitor information on bugs and for tracking the status of the bugs.

Layer 2: Core Framework: The core framework includes the *Project Data Fetcher* (Biffl, Sunindyo, & Moser, 2010b) to collect and integrate data from the different data sources listed in layer 1. We can collect the data by defining the tool configuration, e.g., the starting number of SVN revision, starting date of mailing list posts, and the starting date of bug report collection, and then run the application. By using the ontology, we can also validate the data by using reasoning to the collected and integrated data, e.g., to identify missing or incomplete entries.

Layer 3: Health Indicators: In this pilot application, we implemented the calculation of two health indicators derived from Wahyudin *et al.* (2007).

Indicator 1: Bug delays: We measured the service delays on open issues by subtracting the closing date of issues in the bug report from the opening date of the issues. We called this service delay the "bug closure duration". We classify the bug closure duration of a project into five categories: closure duration of (a) less than 7 days, (b) between 7 and 30 days, (c) between 30 and 100 days, (d) between 100 and 365 days, and (e) more than 365 days. We use bar graphs to show the number of bugs for each category as percentage values (see Figure 5). A healthy project should provide shorter bug resolution durations with most bugs fixed in less than

7 days. We use this threshold value to see the response of developers in addressing a new bug status change within one week. We consider the developers to be fast enough to react to the bug status change within one week; otherwise they are not aware of that change.

Indicator 2: Proportion of activities: We measured the proportions by comparing the number of bug status changes per times slot and the volume of mailing list postings in the same time slots. We used a line graph to show the proportions between the bug status changes and the volume of mailing list postings per month (see Figure 6). A healthy project shows a stable proportion of activities (neither many mails nor few mails per bug). The fluctuations of activities show the imbalance between developer email submissions and bug status reports.

Layer 4: Presentation: For presenting the results of OSS health indicators analysis, we used a tool, called *Project Monitoring Cockpit* (*ProMonCo*) (Biffl, Sunindyo, & Moser, 2010a). The *ProMonCo* takes the analysis results as inputs and displays the health indicators in graphical format for the project/ quality managers.

Study Objects

We studied four projects from the Apache Software Foundation (http://www.apache.org/), namely Apache *Lenya* (http://lenya.apache.org/), Apache *Log4J* (http://logging.apache.org/log4j/1.2/), Apache *Excalibur* (http://excalibur.apache.org/) and Apache *OJB* (http://db.apache.org/ojb/). The reasons of choosing these study objects were (a) the completeness of data sources to collect, i.e., at least SVN, mailing list, and bug reports, (b) the case to collect the data and obtain information about the projects, (c) the activities of developers during development phase, (d) the maturity and lifetime of the projects are quite long for investigation, and

(e) access to OSS experts who can provide expert opinions on the actual health of these projects. According to OSS experts' opinion, *Lenya* and *Log4J* were active projects. We used *Excalibur* and *OJB*, two inactive projects that were moved to Apache Attic (http://attic.apache.org/) as counter examples for the comparison of health indicator analysis results on different project conditions.

Apache *Lenya* is a Java/XML open-source content management system based on the Apache *Cocoon* content management framework. Features include revision control, scheduling, search capabilities, workflow support, and browser-based WYSIWYG editors. *Lenya* has been an active project with around 28 developers and the latest stable release on January 20th, 2010 (version 2.0.3) regarding the time frame of data collection for this empirical study.

Apache *log4J* is a Java-based logging utility, one of the major Java Logging Framework*s*. It has been an active project with the latest stable release on April 6th, 2010 (version 1.2.16).

Apache *Excalibur* consists of a set of libraries for component-based programming in Java. Its main products include the Inversion of Control framework *Avalon*, an Avalon-based container named *Fortress*, and a set of Avalon compatible software components. Excalib*ur* is an inactive project with around 44 developers and the latest stable release on July 5th, 2007 (version 2.2.3). On December 15th, 2010 Apache *Excalibur* has been moved to Apache Attic for documentation of inactive projects.

Apache *OJB* is an Object/Relational mapping tool that allows transparent persistence for Java Objects against relational databases. *OJB* has been designed for a large range of application, from embedded systems to rich client application to multi-tier J2EE based architecture. On January 16th, 2011 Apache *OJB* has been moved to Apache Attic for documentation of inactive projects.

We collected SVN entries, mailing list, and *Bugzilla* data from four projects starting from January 1st, 2007 until December 31st, 2010 (36 months), so we have enough data for comparison of developers' activity in long period. The data set retrieved from *Lenya* consists of total 8,464 e-mail conversations (mean per month = 176.33) and 810 bug status changes (mean per month = 16.87). The data set retrieved from *Log4J* consists of total 4,605 e-mail conversations (mean per month = 95.94) and 580 bug status changes (mean per month = 12.08). The data set retrieved from *Excalibur* consists of total 886 e-mail conversations (mean per month = 18.46) and 20 bug status changes (mean per month = 0.42). The data set retrieved from *OJB* consists of total 369 e-mail conversations (mean per month = 7.68) and 18 bug status changes (mean per month = 0.38).

Threats to Validity

In this section, we discuss four types of threats to the validity of an empirical study and how we addressed these threats.

- **Conclusion validity:** Threats to conclusion validity are the reliability of treatment implementation and random heterogeneity of subjects. To deal with these threats, we use an automated tool to collect data to avoid human error during data collection. We also used limited data sources, i.e., SVN, mailing list, and *Bugzilla* instead of a bigger number of data sources to reduce the heterogeneity of our subjects.
- **Internal validity:** Threats to internal validity are the risk that the history affects the experimental results and the subjects respond differently at different time, if the test is repeated. To deal with these threats, we used a specific range of date for data collection, e.g., from January 1st, 2007 to December 31st, 2010. This date range provides stable results each time the experiment is repeated. The use of an automated tool to collect the data also makes the

subject, i.e., project data sources; respond similarly each time the test is conducted.
- **Construct validity:** Threats to construct validity are the inadequate preoperational explication of constructs and mono-method bias. To deal with these threats, we conducted a literature survey on related topics and conducted prior experiments with different methods to get experience with the OSS data analysis topic. We also used several methods for health indicator analysis.
- **External validity:** Threats to external validity are the limited number of projects we analyzed and the use of single project management standard in our experiment. Therefore, the study results have reasonable validity for OSS Apache projects but should be applied to other kinds of projects with care. To strengthen external validity in future work, we will add more projects from other project management standards, e.g., *SourceForge* and *RedHat*.

INITIAL EMPIRICAL RESULTS

In this section we show initial empirical results that illustrate the efficiency of data collection efforts using manual and automated approach and the accuracy of health indicator by using different methods on some OSS projects.

Efficiency of Data Collection

In this section, we compare the efforts to collect and process heterogeneous data for deriving OSS health indicators (see Table 1). Figure 4 illustrates the comparison of effort between two approaches: the traditional manual approach and the proposed (semi-)automated approach with FOSSDA.

The traditional manual approach follows three steps for data collection and analysis (see Figure 4, upper part):

Figure 4. Comparison of efficiency for manual and FOSSDA data collection process variants

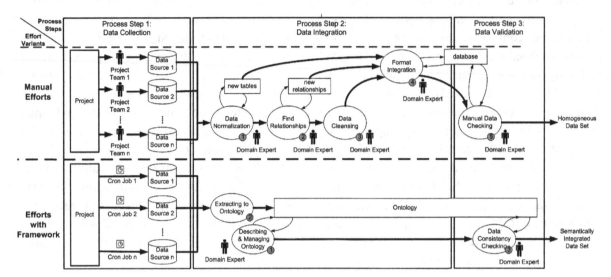

1. **Manual data collection:** The researcher chooses the projects to analyze, and then collects data directly from the project tools, e.g., by downloading the repository content from SVN, postings from developers' mailing list website, and bug reports from the *Bugzilla* website.

2. **Manual data integration:** The data from different data sources are integrated manually. The researcher has to analyze each data source and find out the structure of each data source and similarities between different data sources. This work is hard to do manually, because there are hundreds or even thousands types of data points, which may have possible relationships. The possibility to find relationships manually between different data sources is easier to be based on time aggregation (e.g., weekly, monthly, or annually), rather based on other detail information (e.g., name of authors, email address).

3. **Manual data validation:** Manual data validation is hard to do. One possible effort is to manually query the database to check the validation of data, for example, make

query on the name of developers and the name of mailing list authors and find out their relationships.

The proposed (semi-)automated approach with FOSSDA uses specific tools to automate project data collection and analysis (see Figure 4, lower part):

1. **Tool-supported data collection:** The *Project Data Fetcher* tool supports the automated collection of data from different data sources, i.e., SVN, mailing list, and bug report. The input of this tool is the configuration setting of each data source tool (i.e., SVN, mailing list, bug report) to specify scope and range of project data we want to analyze. The example configuration setting includes information of repository URL for SVN, start revision for SVN, archive URL for mailing list, starting data for mailing list, Bug List URL for Bug Report, and Starting Date for Bug Report. The configuration setting does not involve ontology setting, since the ontology setting is done automatically in the tool. This approach is suitable for normal

Table 1. Comparison of effort for manual and automated process variants (in work-hours)

Effort Variants	Process Steps	Process Items	Observed Projects			
			Lenya	Log4J	Excalibur	OJB
Traditional Manual Process Effort	Data Collection	Data coll. SVN	1.4	0.7	0.4	0.2
		Data coll. mailing list	1.0	0.5	0.3	0.2
		Data coll. bug report	0.7	0.4	0.2	0.1
	Data Integration	Normalize data	1.0	0.6	0.3	0.2
		Identify relationship	4.0	3.0	3.0	3.0
		Clean data	4.0	3.0	3.0	3.0
		Integrate format	3.0	3.0	3.0	3.0
	Data Valid.	Manual data checking	6.0	6.0	6.0	6.0
	TOTAL		**21.1**	**17.2**	**16.2**	**15.7**
Tool-Supported Process Effort	Data Collection	Run data collection tools	0.1	0.1	0.1	0.1
	Data Integration	Describe ontology	2.0	2.0	2.0	2.0
		Manage ontology	1.0	1.0	1.0	1.0
		Extract data to ontology	0.8	0.8	0.5	0.5
	Data Valid.	Data Consistency Checking	3.0	3.0	3.0	3.0
	TOTAL		**6.9**	**6.9**	**6.6**	**6.6**

developers and not necessarily a job for an ontology expert. The processes for data collection are defined as follows: (a) choose a project to analyze; (b) set the configurations of SVN, mailing list, and bug report, e.g., the revision number (for SVN) and the starting date of the data (mailing list and bug report); (c) run the *project data fetcher* to collect the required data automatically.

2. **Tool-supported data integration:** The steps of data integration are as follows: (a) inspect the structure of collected data, (b) find similarities of data attributes between different data models, e.g., name of committers in SVN and name of authors in mailing list, (c) map each data source to the ontology as data storage, (d) set the relationships between different data sources. The input to these steps is the collected data, including their structure. The output is the integrated data in the ontology.

3. **Tool-supported data validation:** The steps of the data validation are as follows: (a) take integrated data in the ontology as input, (b) use rules and restrictions to check the relationships and constraints of the data, (c) use queries to the ontology to check the consistency and integrity of the data, (d) check the data with intended data model to support the data analysis. The input to these steps is the integrated data as an ontology, including rules and relationships. The output is validated data ready for analysis.

For analyzing the data and presenting the results, we used the *Project Monitoring Cockpit* to display the health indicators to project and quality managers. This automated tool can be combined with the *Project Data Fetcher* and provides synergies of the data collection and analysis to support efficient health indicator analysis with FOSSDA for project supervisors. The analysis steps are as follows (a) handling project ontology as an input for *ProMonCo*, (b) processing this ontology and analyze into different purposes and criteria, e.g., total communication metrics, user coupling metrics, bug history metrics, (c) presenting the analysis results to the project managers. Table 1 reports the effort needed to complete the process steps using manual and tool-supported process approaches. Using the automated approach allows reducing the effort needed for operating traditional approach by up to 30%.

Accuracy of Health Indicators

This section provides results from the health indicator analysis study with two indicators, namely bug delays and proportion of activities for four OSS projects: *Lenya, Log4J, Excalibur* and *OJB*.

Indicator 1: Bug Delays: Figure 5 shows the percentage of bug delays between active projects (*Lenya, Log4J*) and inactive projects (*Excalibur, OJB*).

Most bugs get solved in less than 7 days (*Lenya*: 51%, *Log4J*: 45%, *Excalibur*: 45% and *OJB*: 50%). Further, 55% of bugs in *Excalibur* and 39% of bugs in *OJB* can be solved in less than 100 days. The conclusion of OSS health status is only based on these indicators and thus limited. The results cannot identify the current status of the OSS project.

Indicator 2: Proportion of Activities: Figure 6 shows the proportion of activities between the numbers of bug reports per number of mailing list postings each month from January 1st, 2007 until December 31st, 2010 for Lenya, Log4J, Excalibur, and OJB projects. It is assumed that in a healthy community a project should exhibit more uniform ratio among process metrics, i.e., every bug report ideally should be followed up by the devel-

Figure 5. Indicator 1: Bug fixing delays in four OSS projects

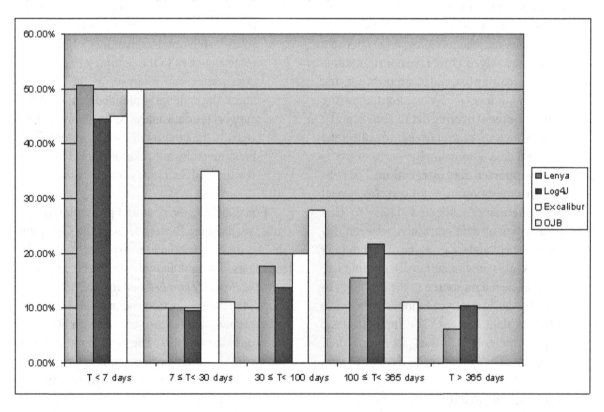

oper discussion in the mailing list. We found that the inactive projects (Excalibur and OJB) show more fluctuation and higher ratios between the number of mailing list postings and bug reports as illustrated in Figure 6. It means, the developer community retrieved more notification related to bug reports but responded less in the mailing list.

This situation may indicate illness symptoms, e.g., developers pay less attention to the project status changes and the project employs a small proportion of active developers which also signifies discouragement of developers, which need to be investigated further with OSS experts.

On the other side, the *Lenya* and *Log4J* projects show more reasonable proportions in the ratio of developer contribution. This can be interpreted as the fact that most of the changes of bug status may trigger some responses from the developers.

The accuracy of health indicator analysis depends on many factors, e.g., the number of data sources and the type of methods used. To measure the accuracy of health indicators across different projects, we compare the results of different analysis methods and data sources with the opinion of OSS experts on assessing the OSS project health status. In the context of this study we handle the OSS expert opinion as "truth" to allow assessing the quality of the results of the proposed on the health indicator approach. The experts were selected from Apache Project Management Committee (PMC) or the Apache Software Foundation (ASF). There are 10 experts selected from the projects and the foundation (4 from Lenya, 2 from Log4J, 1 from Excalibur, 1 from OJB and 2 from ASF). Their opinion was taken from observations on the OSS project development activities which are lead by the PMC. The experts decide their judgment on the status of the project based on their experiences and comparison of different project activities and their opinion was consistent during this study.

Table 2 shows the comparison between the results of the health indicator analysis and OSS expert opinion to assess the status of OSS project health. The results of using combined project metrics as health indicators (bug delays and proportion of activities) shows that the use of a single project metric (namely bug delays) provided in the empirical study context overoptimistic assessments of the OSS project health status compared to the expert opinion, which is assumed to be correct as the expert opinion uses a much wider range of input for their status assessment.

Figure 6. Indicator 2: Proportion between the number of mailing list postings and bug reports

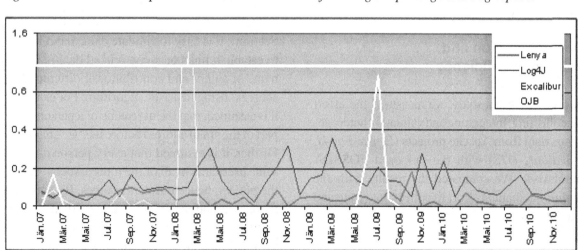

Table 2. Comparison between health indicators analysis results and OSS expert opinion

Indicators Item	Project	Indicators Result	Expert's Opinion
Bug Delays (Single Project Metric)	Lenya	Healthy	Healthy
	Log4J	Healthy	Healthy
	Excalibur	**Healthy**	**Unhealthy**
	OJB	**Healthy**	**Unhealthy**
Proportion of Activities (Combined Project Metrics)	Lenya	Healthy	Healthy
	Log4J	Healthy	Healthy
	Excalibur	Unhealthy	Unhealthy
	OJB	Unhealthy	Unhealthy

The use of multi-data sources and combination of different health indicators makes matched the expert opinion for all investigated projects and can, therefore, be considered as more accurate than using a single data source and a single health indicator analysis method in the context of this study.

DISCUSSION

In this section, we discuss the results from our research issues, namely (a) efficiency of FOS-SDA tool-supported collection, integration and validation of heterogeneous data and (b) accuracy of OSS health indicators by using multiple data sources and combined project metrics.

Data Collection and Validation Efficiency

For the empirical study, we measured the effort for collecting, integrating and validating heterogeneous data from Apache projects (*Lenya, Log4J, Excalibur, OJB*) with the proposed FOSSDA framework. We compared the results with the traditional manual effort to collect, integrate and validate data from heterogeneous data sources. The key size metrics for data collection and inte-

gration from these projects were especially based on the derivation of communication metrics and bug reporting metrics.

The design and implementation of FOSSDA is based on the needs to analyze OSS data more efficiently, based on our experience on collecting the data manually. Hence we have experience regarding measuring the effort of manual data collection and furthermore regarding the tool-supported data collection process variants. The results in Initial Empirical Results Section show that the automated approach can reduce up to 30% of the efforts required for the traditional manual approach.

The advantage of the *manual approach* is that there is no effort needed to create a new tool to collect and analyze data, i.e., the approach uses just existing tools and knowledge on the project to collect and analyze the data. Limitations of this approach are: (a) the error-proneness of the results and tediousness to repeatedly measure data from a project at different points in time, (b) need to follow similar steps each time we want to analyze a new project, (c) no use of links with similar data that could support data analysis, e.g., the name of committers and the name of mailing list post's authors.

The benefits of using the tool-supported FOS-SDA can be described as follows: (a) by using an ontology as project data storage, it is easy to maintain and query the data (see the example listings 1 and 2 in Research Issues and Approach Section); it is easy to validate data, and it is easy to establish links between related data (e.g., the name of author and contributor of different data sources) using heuristic algorithm. For example, it is assumed, that the username of a person is the part of the email address before the '@' character. Further, it is assumed that every person uses the same username in all of the tools associated with the project, hence our data sources. By applying these assumptions, it is possible to identify individuals already included in the ontology as the identical person. Even if there are variations to this rule, new rules or exceptions can be easily added to the ontology. The project manager does not have to store all project data but can focus on (the limited amount of) data needed for analysis. (b) The similarity of the Apache foundation management practices for all of their projects (e.g., all projects have a SVN, mailing list, and bug report to manage their project development) makes the configuration and the automation of data collection easy. (c) If a researcher/project and quality manager wants to analyze another project, they just have to change the configuration setting and run the tool to collect the new project data. They do not have to rebuild the tool fundamentally.

Initial extra costs of FOSSDA was the effort to use the *Project Data Fetcher* tool, the need to learn the semantic web technology to build the tool, and to learn the project tool setting before it was possible to operate and run the tool to collect data. Now, operating the *Project Data Fetcher* only needs the knowledge about running a Java application and how to set the tool and configurations, i.e., the structure of project to investigate, e.g., the location of artifacts and posting date of artifacts.

This work improved the manual data collection and validation which was proposed by Wahyudin *et al.* (2007). The usage of ontologies for data model representation and data storage is also one of FOSSDA framework benefits compared to the *Alitheia* (Gousios & Spinellis, 2009a) or the *Ohloh* (Hu & Zhao, 2008) framework.

Health Indicator Accuracy

Current using of individual health indicator methods to observe the OSS project status may raise inconsistencies on the conclusions given by those different methods. Therefore, the conclusion on the OSS project status could be different depending on the chosen indicator, e.g., one indicator may label an OSS project status healthy, while another indicator labels the same OSS project status unhealthy, which may confuse a decision maker.

In the study context, health indicators based on several project data sources have proven consistent with expert opinion to provide an overview on the status of an OSS project, i.e., whether the project is "unhealthy" or "healthy." Therefore, this information can be useful for the project manager, project investor, and other stakeholders to support decision on the OSS project, e.g., whether to add new programmers or allocate some programmers to develop some critical modules.

The combination of different indicators can strengthen the conclusion of the OSS project status compare to using the indicators separately. Adding new types of data sources is easily possible using FOSSDA and can further increase the accuracy of health indicators in varying OSS contexts.

In this research, we have compared the usage of single indicators (bug delays) and combined indicators (proportion of activities). While this study provided a promising research result, more empirical studies are needed to strengthen the external validity for a wider range of OSS projects.

In this work, we improved the health indicators notion from Wahyudin *et al.* (2007) and involving expert's opinion as one of aspects to assess the project status. The combination of different metrics, e.g., communication metrics and bug report metrics provide a new variant of data source combination, for example related to the research of Bachmann and Bernstein (2009) which focuses more on the usage of bug tracking databases and version control system log files.

CONCLUSION AND FURTHER WORK

Stakeholders in OSS projects need reliable and easy-to-determine project health indicators to predict whether the project is likely to sustain for a sufficient period of time in order to justify their investments into this project. In this paper, we have proposed FOSSDA, a framework for OSS data analysis and conducted an empirical study with four Apache projects to investigate whether using FOSSDA can support efficient data collection and analysis from heterogeneous OSS data sources. The empirical study results supported the efficiency of the tool-supported approach compared to a traditional manual approach. With the support of *Project Data Fetcher* tool in FOSSDA, project and quality manager of OSS projects can collect, integrate and validate the data easily and then use the tool *Project Monitoring Cockpit* to analyze and assess health indicators of OSS projects within hours.

The integrated data model for the Apache projects worked well to support process and project metrics for producing the health indicators and can be easily adapted to project management standards in other OSS families. The flexibility in the data sources level makes the addition and modification of the data sources easy to handle, while the integrated data model in the process and project level remains stable make the observation of OSS project health indicators more robust against changes on the data source level.

Future work will include the extension of FOSSDA with new health indicators (e.g., communication and use intensity of the developers) and additional data sources to investigate robust OSS health status indicators in several environments. For generalization of our approach, we propose to apply the framework to other OSS projects including other OSS project management standards such as *SourceForge* and *RedHat*.

ACKNOWLEDGMENT

This work has been supported by the Christian Doppler Forschungsgesellschaft, the BMWFJ, Austria and Ministry of National Education of Indonesia. We thank the reviewers for their insightful feedback to improve this paper.

REFERENCES

Bachmann, A., & Bernstein, A. (2009). Software process data quality and characteristics: A historical view on open and closed source projects. In *Proceedings of the Joint International and Annual ERCIM Workshops on Principles of Software Evolution and the Software Evolution Workshops*, Amsterdam, The Netherlands (pp. 119-128).

Biffl, S., Sunindyo, W. D., & Moser, T. (2010a). A project monitoring cockpit based on integrating data sources in open source software development. In *Proceedings of the 22nd International Conference on Software Engineering and Knowledge Engineering*, San Francisco, CA (pp. 620-627).

Biffl, S., Sunindyo, W. D., & Moser, T. (2010b). Semantic integration of heterogeneous data sources for monitoring frequent-release software projects. In *Proceedings of the 4th International Conference on Complex, Intelligent and Software Intensive Systems*, Krakow, Poland (pp. 360-367).

Brügge, B., & Dutoit, A. (1997). Communication metrics for software development. In *Proceedings of the 19th International Conference on Software Engineering* (pp. 271-281).

Chen, K., Schach, S. R., Yu, L., Offutt, J., & Heller, G. Z. (2004). Opensource change logs. *Empirical Software Engineering, 9*(3), 147–262. doi:10.1023/B:EMSE.0000027779.70556.d0

Choi, N., Chengalur-Smith, I., & Whitmore, A. (2010). Managing first impressions of new open source software projects. *IEEE Software, 27*(6), 73–77. doi:10.1109/MS.2010.26

Conklin, M. (2006). Beyond low-hanging fruit: Seeking the next generation of FLOSS data mining. In *Proceedings of the 2nd International Conference on Open Source Systems*, Como, Italy (pp. 47-56).

Gall, H. C., Fluri, B., & Pinzger, M. (2009). Change analysis with Evolizer and ChangeDistiller. *IEEE Software*, *26*(1), 26–33. doi:10.1109/MS.2009.6

German, D. M. (2004). Mining CVS repositories, the softchange experience. In *Proceedings of the 1st International Workshop on Mining Software Repositories*, Scotland, UK (pp. 17-21).

Gousios, G., & Spinellis, D. (2009a). Alitheia Core: An extensible software quality monitoring platform. In *Proceedings of the IEEE 31st International Conference on Software Engineering*, Vancouver, BC, Canada (pp. 579-582).

Gousios, G., & Spinellis, D. (2009b). A platform for software engineering research. In *Proceedings of the 6th IEEE International Working Conference on Mining Software Repositories*, Vancouver, BC, Canada (pp. 31-40).

Hu, D., & Zhao, J. L. (2008). A comparison of evaluation networks and collaboration networks in open source software communities. In *Proceedings of the 14th Americas Conference on Information Systems*, Toronto, ON, Canada (pp. 1-8).

Huber, S. (2010). *Implementation and evaluation of communication metrics for continuous software project monitoring* (Unpublished diploma thesis). Vienna University of Technology, Vienna, Austria.

Kaltenecker, A. (2010). *Deriving project health indicators of open source software projects using social network analysis* (Unpublished diploma thesis). Vienna University of Technology, Vienna, Austria.

Linstead, E., Bajracharya, S., Ngo, T., Rigor, P., Lopes, C., & Baldi, P. (2009). Sourcerer: Mining and searching internet-scale software repositories. *Data Mining and Knowledge Discovery*, *18*(2), 300–336. doi:10.1007/s10618-008-0118-x

Mockus, A., Fielding, R. T., & Herbsleb, J. (2000). A case study of open source software development: The Apache server. In *Proceedings of the International Conference on Software Engineering* (pp. 263-272).

Mockus, A., Fielding, R. T., & Herbsleb, J. D. (2002). Two case studies of open source software development: Apache and Mozilla. *ACM Transactions on Software Engineering and Methodology*, *11*(3), 309–346. doi:10.1145/567793.567795

Moser, T. (2009). *Semantic integration of engineering environments using an engineering knowledge base* (Unpublished doctoral dissertation). Vienna University of Technology, Vienna, Austria.

Robles, G., González-Barahona, J. M., Izquierdo-Cortazar, D., & Herraiz, I. (2009). Tools for the study of the usual data sources found in Libre software projects. *International Journal of Open Source Software and Processes*, *1*(1), 24–45. doi:10.4018/jossp.2009010102

Roche, J. (1994). Software metrics and measurement principles. *SIGSOFT Software Engineering Notes*, *19*(1), 77–85. doi:10.1145/181610.181625

Sharma, S., Sugumaran, V., & Rajagopalan, B. (2002). A framework for creating hybrid-open source software communities. *Information Systems Journal*, *12*(1), 7–25. doi:10.1046/j.1365-2575.2002.00116.x

von Krogh, G., & von Hippel, E. (2003). Special issue on open source software development. *Research Policy*, *32*(7), 1149–1157. doi:10.1016/S0048-7333(03)00054-4

Wahyudin, D. (2008). *Quality prediction and evaluation models for products and processes in distributed software development* (Unpublished doctoral dissertation). Vienna University of Technology, Vienna, Austria.

Wahyudin, D., Mustofa, K., Schatten, A., Biffl, S., & Tjoa, A. M. (2007). Monitoring the "health" status of open source web-engineering projects. *International Journal of Web Information Systems*, *3*(1-2), 116–139. doi:10.1108/17440080710829252

Wahyudin, D., Schatten, A., Mustofa, K., Biffl, S., & Tjoa, A. M. (2006). Introducing "health" perspective in open source Web-engineering software projects, based on project data analysis. In *Proceedings of the International Conference on Information Integration, Web-Applications and Services*, Yogyakarta, Indonesia.

Wahyudin, D., & Tjoa, A. M. (2007). Event-based monitoring of open source software projects. In *Proceedings of the Second International Conference on Availability, Reliability and Security*.

Yamauchi, Y., Yokozawa, M., Shinohara, T., & Ishida, T. (2000). Collaboration with Lean Media: How open-source software succeeds. In *Proceedings of the ACM Conference on Computer Supported Cooperative Work*, Philadelphia, PA (pp. 329-338).

This work was previously published in the International Journal of Open Source Software and Processes, Volume 3, Issue 4, edited by Stefan Koch, pp. 1-23, copyright 2011 by IGI Publishing (an imprint of IGI Global).

Chapter 12

The Influence of Open Source Software Volunteer Developers' Motivations and Attitudes on Intention to Contribute

Chorng-Guang Wu
Yuan Ze University, Taiwan

James H. Gerlach
University of Colorado at Denver, USA

Clifford E. Young
University of Colorado at Denver, USA

ABSTRACT

This study differs from previous studies on open source software (OSS) developer motivation by drawing upon theories of volunteerism and work motivation to investigate the motives and attitudes of OSS volunteer developers. The role of commitment is specifically interesting, which is well established in the volunteerism and work motivation literature as a predictor of turnover and positively related to work performance, but has been overlooked by OSS researchers. The authors have developed a research model relating motivations, commitment, satisfaction, and length of service to intention to contribute to OSS projects in the future. The research model is evaluated using data from an online survey of 181 OSS volunteer developers. The research results and more discussion of these areas of interest will be evaluated and discussed further in the chapter.

INTRODUCTION

Highly publicized corporate involvement in open source software (OSS) development creates the illusion that volunteers are no longer that important to OSS development anymore. OSS projects

such as Linux and Apache Web Server, which grew from seed planted by volunteers, are now commercialized and largely supported by business interests. These successes were followed by software donations by corporations to create new OSS projects. Sun Microsystems contributed OpenOffice, IBM open sourced Eclipse (toolkit for designing integrated development environments)

DOI: 10.4018/978-1-4666-2937-0.ch012

and Lotus Symphony (document processing applications), and Netscape released its browser suite source code to start the Mozilla project, to name a few. As a result, many OSS developers are paid by information technology vendors, OSS foundations or companies that utilize OSS to work on OSS projects. Together, these observations support the image of a highly active, highly commercialized OSS development effort that no longer relies upon volunteers who are not paid to contribute, which we refer to as 'volunteers'.

Although prominent projects such as Linux and Apache Web Server are largely sustained by commercial interests, they still benefit from volunteerism. For example, it is estimated that 18 - 25% of new Linux code still comes from volunteers (Smoker, 2010). Other less prominent OSS projects rely substantially on volunteers. Debian, a Linux distribution package, and Sahana, information management solutions for disaster response, are just two examples of the many OSS projects that rely heavily on volunteers. Drupal (content management platform) is an example of an OSS project that uses a balanced mix of volunteer developers and paid contributors.

OSS projects recruit volunteers not just for raw manpower, but more importantly, because of their remarkable skills and knowledge. Fang and Neufeld (2009) reviewed several qualitative studies on OSS project success and concluded that a lack of sustained volunteer participation is a major reason for OSS project failure. Their own qualitative study of OSS volunteers reveals that repeat volunteers make special contributions by taking on advising roles and making practical contributions such as code improvement. Consequently, there is considerable practical advantage in understanding what directs and sustains OSS developers' voluntary participation for extended periods of time.

Motivation is what draws volunteers to OSS projects. Previous studies regarding OSS developers show a variety of evidence that different types of motivations are important, but there is much less understanding of the relative importance of motivational components in different contexts (e.g., work satisfaction, performance, effort, recruitment, and retention) (Krishnamurthy, 2006). A second limitation of past research is that it mainly examined simple correlations between motivators and behavior, but research on motivational structure has shown that developers' motivations are not independent but rather are related in complex ways (Meyer et al., 2004; Roberts et al., 2006). Motivational structures need to be studied in order to better understand volunteer behavior. Thirdly, commitment, a distinguishable component of motivation, is neglected in research on OSS developers' motivation. Commitment is a predictor of employee turnover and positively related to work performance (Meyer et al., 2004). Finally, prior studies of OSS developers' motivations group volunteers and paid participants together for analysis. It is arguable that the motives of volunteers differ from those of paid participants as the involvement of volunteers is entirely discretionary.

Our work presented here advances understanding of OSS volunteerism by addressing the aforementioned limitations of past research. It investigates the role of commitment, which the work motivation literature maintains plays a key role in sustained discretionary involvement. The structural issue is addressed by adopting a comprehensive framework based specifically on goal setting, functional analysis of volunteerism and expectancy-valence theory (EVT). Functional analysis was chosen because goal-setting theory is arguably the dominant theory in the work motivation literature (Miner, 2003). EVT was chosen since it has been shown to be useful for capturing those motivational factors that are important to volunteers (Miller, 1985) and has been justified by prior research as an appropriate theory in the evaluation of OSS developer motivations (e.g., Hertel et al., 2003; Wu et al., 2007). And finally, the resulting research model is evaluated using only OSS volunteer developers as subjects, which offers an undistorted analysis of their motivational structure.

The rest of the paper is organized as follows. In the next section, we review previous research on OSS participants' motivation. Next, we develop our research model and hypotheses by applying theories of volunteerism and work motivation to the OSS volunteer context. This is followed by a section describing our research methodology consisting of instrumentation, sampling, model and hypothesis testing. The final sections are used to report and discuss our research findings.

LITERATURE AND THEORETICAL FRAMEWORK

Previous OSS Research

Initial studies on OSS developer motivation used simple analyses (e.g., rankings and correlations with effort or performance) to identify possible motivations (e.g., Hars & Ou, 2002; Lakhani & Wolf, 2005). Although these researchers allowed for multiple motives, they did not consider that OSS developers' motivations are interrelated in complex ways and different motivations impact developers differently (Roberts et al., 2006). In order to reveal these interrelationships, motivational structure would need to be studied. Thus far, there are only a few survey-based quantitative analyses based on theoretical models that have been conducted to explore motivational processes and performance of OSS developers (Hertel et al., 2003; Roberts et al., 2006; Wu et al., 2007).

Hertel et al. (2003) proposed two conceptual models, EKM (Extended Klandermans Model) and VIST (Valence, Instrumentality, Self-efficacy, Trust), for exploring the motivations of developers working on the Linux kernel project. The researchers applied theories of motivation within social movements and motivation within virtual teams to explain effort, performance and willingness to

be involved in future projects. The results showed that while some of the constructs of these theories correlated with the dependent variables, they provided negligible support when structurally tested. Identification as a Linux developer was found to be the dominant motivator of effort and engagement in OSS projects while identification, improving software for personal use and career advantages influenced willingness to be involved in future projects. Moreover, the more the developers were paid, the more time they spent on developing OSS.

Roberts et al. (2006) developed a research model relating the motivations, participation, and performance of OSS developers, and evaluated the model via an online survey and archival data collected from a longitudinal field study of software contributors to Apache projects. The study primarily examined the effects of pay, status motivation, intrinsic motivation and use-value motivation (software need) on contribution levels. Among the findings were that developers' paid participation and status motivations led to above average contribution levels, but use-value motivation led to below average contribution levels and intrinsic motivation did not significantly impact average contribution levels.

Unlike the previous studies that focused on effort or performance, Wu et al. (2007) conducted a field study of OSS developers consisting of volunteers and paid developers to identify salient determinants of open source participants' intention to continue making OSS contributions. Toward this goal, concepts from EVT have been adapted to create a theoretical model of OSS participants' intention to make future contributions. According to the findings, satisfaction with participating in OSS projects was the strongest influence on respondents' intentions to participate in future OSS projects, followed by their motivation on enhancing human capital and personal need for software. The researchers asserted that a satisfactory experience encourages sustained involvement, participants pursue instrumental behavior because of the requirement for specific software functionalities and learning by doing is of essential importance to the success of OSS projects and the sustainability of OSS communities. Helping others to develop OSS is shown to positively affect satisfaction.

In summary, empirical research on OSS developer motives has provided support for several key motivators: identification, software needs, career advancement, human capital, status and helping. We continue this investigation by associating these known motives with the elements that underlie the literature on volunteerism and work motivation.

Functional Approach to Volunteering

Motivation is defined as a psychological force inciting an individual to exert effort toward particular individual or organizational goals, and serves as a mechanism for satisfying individual needs (Robbins, 1998; George & Jones, 1999). Volunteerism is formed within an individual by a complex relationship between specific personal wants and the perceived opportunities and actual experiences provided by the volunteer context. At the heart of the motivation process is goal setting. Generally, volunteers seek out their opportunities to help and deliberate long and hard about the initiation, extent, and precise nature of their involvement (Omoto & Snyder, 1995).

Volunteering usually involves multiple motivations (Tschirhart et al., 2001). Functional analysis is a useful approach to answering why people volunteer and what sustains volunteering behavior since it implicates the importance of matching volunteer motivations to the benefits that volunteerism provides (Houle et al., 2005). The functional approach is explicitly concerned with the reasons and the purposes, the plans and the goals, that underlie and generate psychological phenomena, that is, the personal and social functions being served by an individual's thoughts, feelings, and actions (Snyder, 1993). The theory recognizes that volunteering serves different functions for different people and perhaps multiple

functions for the same person (Penner & Finkelstein, 1998). Moreover, in the same individual, different motives may be primarily engaged by different volunteer activities.

Clary et al. (1998) adopted the strategy of functional analysis to specifically identify the fundamental motivations underlying volunteerism. Using laboratory and field studies, they demonstrated predictive validity of their framework. Explicitly, the extent to which volunteers' experiences matched their motivations predicted satisfaction and intentions to volunteer in the future, in both the long and short term. Their investigation revealed six functions of volunteerism: values, understanding, social, career, protective, and enhancement. The values function refers to concerns for the welfare of others and contributions to society. This function has been likened to altruism. The understanding function served by volunteering involves the opportunity for volunteerism to permit new learning experiences and the chance to exercise knowledge, skills, and abilities that might otherwise go unpracticed. The social function designates that an individual volunteers due to strong normative or social pressure, or to get along with others in his or her reference group. The career function is concerned with increasing one's job prospects and enhancing one's career that may be obtained from participation in volunteer work. The fifth function served by volunteering is the protective function in which an individual's motivation to volunteer lies in reducing feelings of guilt about being more fortunate than others or escaping from one's personal problems. The sixth function is the enhancement function in which volunteerism serves to enhance the volunteer's self-esteem, self-confidence and self-improvement.

Functional Analysis of OSS Volunteering

The OSS literature states that OSS developers show multiple motivations to participate in open source projects (Hertel et al., 2003; Bitzer et al., 2007;

Osterloh & Rota, 2007). Their motivation may stem from within individuals and work through immediate satisfaction of needs, which is intrinsic and includes benefits gained from helping, reciprocity, enjoyment, free software ideology and so on (Dahlander & McKelvey, 2005; Stewart & Gosain, 2006). On the other hand, developers' motivation may refer to extrinsic incentives outside the individual and work through indirect satisfaction of needs, most importantly through their willingness to learn, to receive respect in their reference group or indirect financial benefits (Roberts et al., 2006; Shah, 2006). Following the tenets of functional analysis, we related those motives that have roots in the OSS volunteerism literature to the goal-driven behavior of volunteers.

Open source community is a gift culture that is motivated by altruism and reciprocity (Raymond, 2001; Bonaccorsi & Rossi, 2003). Based upon functional analysis of volunteer motivations, OSS developers' helping/reciprocity behavior is equivalent to the value function since contributions to OSS enables developers to actively show their altruistic concerns by sharing software code with others or giving it away.

In scientific societies, sharing results enables researchers both to improve their results through feedback from other members of the scientific community and to gain recognition and prestige for their work (Bonaccorsi & Rossi, 2003). The enhancement function is related to this need for peer recognition by important others dealing with similar software issues. Earning respect from fellow OSS developers satisfies the ego-driven motivation to publicly demonstrate their knowledge.

Human capital as a determinant of productivity refers to personal skills, capabilities, and knowledge (Mankiw, 2004). OSS development provides opportunities for participants to learn programming skills (Lakhani & Wolf, 2005) and communication and team management skills (Hars & Ou, 2001). Volunteer developers' motivation on enhancing human capital relates to the understanding function because individuals have the opportunity to learn new things and exercise their knowledge, skills, and abilities through code contribution.

Individuals reap professional benefits via the exchange/creation of knowledge by enhancing their professional status and establishing a reputation that is later translated into a better job. The career function works by OSS participants signaling their knowledge and skills to potential employers (Lerner & Tirole, 2002). According to Smits et al. (1993), career progression is very important to maintain the motivation of success-oriented information systems professionals with the need for achievement.

Many OSS projects start since the people promoting them have looked in vain for software to perform a particular function. They arise to satisfy a work-related demand or personal need for which there is no corresponding supply, in short to "fill an unfilled market" (Bonaccorsi & Rossi, 2003). Others seek the knowhow to modify OSS to satisfy personal or business requirements or to incorporate OSS into other products. Satisfying work-related or individual needs for software does not fall neatly under any of Clary's et al. (1998) functions of volunteering, but rather has been regarded as an instrumental avenue addressing software problems related to personal or work requirements (Wu et al., 2007). The software and the knowledge to utilize it provide use value directly to the developer and constitute another function for OSS volunteer developers. The identification of a new category is not unexpected. Clary et al. admitted they sought to identify motivations of generic relevance to volunteerism and that application of their framework to particular kinds of volunteering might reveal additional functions.

The last motivator to analyze is identification as an OSS developer. In the work motivation literature, identification is often associated with commitment (Meyer et al., 2004). Commitment has been generally treated in the motivation literature as a singular motivator and is therefore addressed separately.

The various theoretical viewpoints reviewed here are summarized by Table 1. The analysis shows that OSS volunteers reflect the general notions of what motivates volunteers, except for the addition of the instrumental need for software.

Empirical Measurement of OSS Developer Motivations

In summary, each of the motivations (except satisfying personal needs for software) espoused by the OSS literature relate well to one of Clary's six functions of common volunteerism, which are generally known to be reliable predictors of future intentions to volunteer (Clary et al., 1998). Software needs is a novel motivator for volunteers in that the outcome of volunteering provides a usable product for the volunteer. Furthermore, prior empirical research on OSS volunteerism shows an association between volunteer behavior and these motives. Therefore, we offer the following hypotheses:

H1a: Volunteer developers' motivation based on helping will have a positive influence on their intention to contribute to future OSS development.

Table 1. Motivation of volunteer developers based on functional analysis

Motivation	Descriptions	Volunteering Function
Helping	Aiding others to increase the value of OSS	Values
Peer recognition	Receiving recognition from others or reputation within the community	Enhancement
Human capital	Accumulating skills and knowledge via learning	Understanding
Career advancement	Demonstrating capacities and skillfulness to signal potential employers or to create new business opportunities	Career
Software needs	Acquiring software for use or solutions to technical problems	Use value

H1b: Volunteer developers' motivation based on peer recognition will have a positive influence on their intention to contribute to future OSS development.

H1c: Volunteer developers' motivation based on enhancing human capital will have a positive influence on their intention to contribute to future OSS development.

H1d: Volunteer developers' motivation based on career advancement will have a positive influence on their intention to contribute to future OSS development.

H1e: Volunteer developers' motivation based on satisfying personal needs for software will have a positive influence on their intention to contribute to future OSS development.

Commitment

Organizational research on volunteers shows that volunteers are important human resources and contribute significantly to the productivity of human services organizations (Johnson, 1981; Gamm & Kassab, 1983). Therefore, many organizations expect their volunteers to make defined commitments to their volunteer positions, and much organizational attention is focused on how long volunteers stay active and productive (Omoto & Snyder, 1995). Organizational commitment refers to the identification with a particular organization, the willingness to exert considerable effort on behalf of the organization, and the desire to maintain membership in the organization (Porter et al., 1974; Mowday et al., 1982). This affectively-oriented definition that forms the basis of commitment recognizes the importance of emotional attachment to the organization (Dailey, 1986).

Studies show that commitment initiates a rationalizing process through which individuals make sense of their current situation by developing attitudes that are consistent with their level of commitment (Kiesler, 1971; Salancik, 1977). Strong commitment is what makes a person assume or continue a course of action when difficulties or positive alternatives would lead them to quit

(Brickman, 1987); it represents a duty or obligation to engage in future action and arises from frequent interaction (Coleman, 1990). Prevailing research models of turnover among volunteers (Miller et al., 1990) and information technology workers (Igbaria & Greenhaus, 1992; Thatcher et al., 2002) confirm that lack of commitment affects behavioral intentions to quit, thereby affecting turnover.

Commitment is generally categorized by form: affective (result of personal involvement, identification with the organization and value congruence), normative (result of cultural and organizational socialization) and continuance (result of accumulated investments in the relationship). Previous studies on volunteers and commitment establish affective commitment as the dominant influence. In the context of OSS development, we argue that volunteer developers would form an affective commitment to the OSS project/community since the bases for the development of commitment are personal involvement with the OSS project/community, identification with the OSS project/community and shared values and ideology regarding the tenets of OSS. Hence we hypothesize:

H2: Volunteer developers' affective commitment will have a positive influence on their intention to contribute to future OSS development.

Motivation and commitment are intertwined (Meyer et al., 2004). For instance, individuals who are committed to an organization generally exhibit high levels of motivation to perform well. Yet high levels of motivation do not necessarily imply strong organizational commitment. To illustrate their point, Meyer et al. used the example of a highly motivated university professor that possessed commitment towards her profession, but not towards her university. They explain that work motivation theory separates the influences of motivation from commitment as they are theorized to work differently within an individual, each exerting its own individual force. But Meyer

et al. proposed an exception: individuals with strong affective commitment will experience greater intrinsic motivation. In the context of OSS development, volunteers with strong affective commitment to a cooperative setting of shared values may experience greater intrinsic motivation to help the community to succeed. Hence, the following hypothesis:

H3: Volunteer developers' affective commitment to their OSS community will have a positive influence on their intrinsic motivation to help.

Satisfaction

What originally motivated a volunteer to get involved may not be sufficient to sustain their involvement in the long term, unless they feel satisfied with their volunteering experience (Gidron, 1984). Satisfaction is not just a by-product for those engaged in volunteer work, but is expected by volunteers (Smith, 1981). Volunteer work is perceived as an exchange between a volunteer and her work situation (Sharp, 1978; Kemper, 1980), whereby time and effort are exchanged for satisfactions to the individual (Qureshi et al., 1979). The descriptive and prescriptive literature on volunteering suggests that volunteers should be satisfied on the job in order to persevere with it (Naylor, 1967). According to Gidron (1983), people continue to volunteer because they enjoy what they are getting from the experience; they value the rewards they are receiving and want to maintain and expand them. Volunteers' satisfaction is positively associated with taking on additional responsibilities (Miles et al., 1998).

Satisfaction increases the likelihood of predicting retention-related outcomes, namely turnover potential (Galindo–Kuhn & Guzley, 2001). Cnaan and Goldberg–Glen (1991) argued that people continue to volunteer as long as the experience, as a whole, satisfies their unique needs. Moreover, greater satisfaction is likely to mean volunteers enjoy their work, believe in its importance and will stick to it even in hard times (Gidron, 1984; Omoto & Snyder, 1995). Therefore, in the context of OSS development, we suggest that a volunteer developer's intention to make future contributions is influenced by her level of satisfaction. This leads to the following hypothesis:

H4: Volunteer developers' satisfaction with participating in OSS projects will have a positive influence on their intention to contribute to future OSS development.

Length of Service

Length of service has been identified as a potentially important correlate of intention to stay at an organization (Silcock, 1954; Price, 1981). Stoikov and Ramon (1968) pointed out that people moving to a new job obtained most of their information about the job and how it compared with their expectations within the initial employment period; as a result turnover rates were highest amongst individuals with the shortest length of service and subsequently declined with time. This is consistent with the presumption – the intrinsic difficulty of window shopping for jobs – that many of the most important features of a job cannot be appraised until one has experienced it (Reynolds, 1951). McCurley and Lynch (1996) indicated that the first six months of volunteers' experience was critical toward their retention as the greatest losses of volunteers occurred during this period. Since length of service may be an important positive correlate of turnover intention, we predict its positive influence on OSS volunteer developers' intention to contribute to future OSS development.

H5: Volunteer developers' length of service with participating in OSS projects will demonstrate a positive relationship with their intention to contribute to future OSS development.

Figure 1 demonstrates the theoretical model with indicated hypotheses. The hypothesized associations between constructs are consistent with Meyer et al.'s (2004) integrated model of work commitment and motivation. In that model, needs, values, incentives and commitment independently affect individuals' willingness to engage in work activities. Satisfaction, formed by the outcome of participation and satisfaction with the experience, causes individuals to reevaluate their intention to continue participating.

Motivation Measurement

Within the broad area of motivation research, the notion of expectancy-valence plays a central role in explaining human motivation in the workplace (Vroom, 1964; Locke & Latham, 1990; Ambrose & Kulik, 1999), which is fundamental to this study. EVT is a behavioral version of the rational choice model in economic decision making, stating that behavior is determined by conscious choices (Singer & Coffin, 1996). Its underlying premise is that behavior is a function of an individual's expectation that a response will bring reinforcement together with the perceived value of the reinforcement (Rotter, 1954). EVT is useful for evaluating the relative strength of intrinsic versus extrinsic valences in the motivational process (Mitchell, 1980).

According to Vroom (1964), an individual's work motivation is determined by the expectancies and valences associated with items currently of importance in the individual's decision space. Expectancy is interpreted as an individual's belief that a given action should lead to some certain outcome. Valence is defined as the strength of a person's positive or negative affective orientation toward the outcome. Lewin (1936) submits that valence refers to the goal properties of potential actions and outcomes as perceived by a person at a given moment. Goals desired by an individual are considered positively valent while those that the individual does not desire are negatively valent.

Figure 1. OSS volunteer developer sustained contribution model

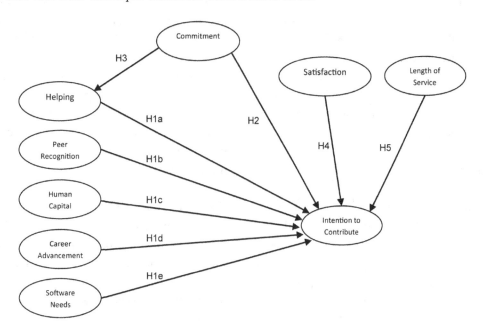

Vroom's EVT hypothesizes that the level of motivation for specific behavior is predicted by the combined strength of the individual's expectancies toward particular outcomes and the valences the individual places on those outcomes. Moreover, motivation in terms of the mathematical product of expectancy and valence can be used to predict the force on a person to perform a particular act, which has been validated experimentally (Arnold, 1981).

In this study, we propose that OSS volunteer developers' expectancies and valences can be combined in a multiplicative way to measure motivational force. Expectancy is related to volunteer developers' future expectations of OSS development, which are influenced by past experience and over time approach steady-state equilibrium as expectations become more realistic and entrenched in observed behaviors.

RESEARCH METHODOLOGY

A cross-sectional, web-based survey was performed to measure the proposed research model.

LISREL, a structural equation modeling (SEM) application, was used to validate the model and test the hypotheses. This section describes model identification, instrument construction, sampling method, construct measurement, analysis methods and final results.

Identification of the Research Model

Model identification refers to whether it is theoretically possible to derive a unique value for each and every free parameter in the research model from the observed data. If a model is not identified, then it remains so regardless of the sample size and consequently it should be re-specified (Kline, 2005). Additionally, any estimate of an unidentified parameter computed by a SEM program is arbitrary and should not be relied on (Raykov & Marcoulides, 2000). Typically, models need to be overidentified in order to be estimated and to test hypotheses about relationships among variables (Ullman, 1996). A model is called overidentified if it has fewer parameters than observations (i.e., positive degrees of freedom) and it is also identified. Our research model satisfies the necessary conditions for model identification since there are more observations than free parameters. With 21 observed variables, there are $(21 \times 22)/2 = 231$ observations available to estimate a total of 77 parameters, i.e., 9 latent variables, 20 measurement errors, 36 covariances and 12 factor loadings. Thus, our model is overidentified with 154 degrees of freedom.

Instrumentation

The instrument was developed based upon pre-validated measures. In the research model, there are five motivation constructs. Each construct item is formed by calculating the square root of the product of the motivator's expectancy and valence. Taking the square root returns the results to the same scale level as the items in the other constructs (satisfaction and commitment) in order to reflect the relationships between these constructs. Therefore, ten sets of pair-wise seven-point Likert scale items related to expectancy and valence were used to measure respondents' motivations. The expectancy and valence items were based on constructs provided by Clary et al. (1998), Ghosh et al. (2002), Hertel et al. (2003), Wasko and Faraj (2005), and Wu et al. (2007).

Developers' satisfaction was assessed using seven-point semantic differential scales from Wu et al.'s study (2007). Satisfaction with OSS development was measured with the overall perspective rather than specific facets, since empirical evidence shows that in many cases general measures of work satisfaction are as reliable as the sum of facet measures and are also more inclusive measures (Scarpello & Campbell, 1983). Commitment was operationalized using items from the Organizational Commitment Questionnaire (Mowday et al., 1982) to measure the extent to which a volunteer developer has formed an affective commitment to the OSS community based on personal involvement, community identification and value congruence. The intention to make future contributions to OSS projects was assessed using three seven-point scale items extended from Mathieson's (1991) behavioral intention construct. Length of service was defined as the number of years a developer spent participating in OSS development. Table 2 presents the operational definitions of these constructs.

The constructs were carefully written to capture the volunteer developer's motivational structure for OSS development involvement, as opposed to her interest in a specific project. Given the large

Table 2. Operationalization of constructs

Construct	Definition
Helping	Volunteer developer's valence and expectancy for helping others solve problems and sharing knowledge
Peer recognition	Volunteer developer's valence and expectancy for being recognized and respected by others within the OSS community
Human capital	Volunteer developer's valence and expectancy for improving software development skills and abilities
Career advancement	Volunteer developer's valence and expectancy for career advancement and new job opportunities
Software needs	Volunteer developer's valence and expectancy for developing software for personal use
Satisfaction	Volunteer developer's overall satisfaction with OSS development
Commitment	Volunteer developer's affective commitment to OSS community
Intention to contribute	Volunteer developer's intention to make future contributions to OSS projects

number of OSS projects, a developer would have a wide range of opportunities; moreover, in the same individual, different motives may be primarily engaged by different OSS projects.

The online survey was pre-tested with 58 OSS developers from Debian.org to verify the psychometric properties of the scales. Debian, developed by more than one thousand OSS programmers, is a free operating system that uses Linux as its kernel but most of the basic software utilities come from the GNU project (Debian, 1997). Pretest participants were requested to complete the instrument and asked to provide their comments on wording, length and structure. Respondents' remarks were used to improve the instrument's format and scale items. The resulting constructs passed the standard reliability tests. Details of the survey instrument are shown in Appendix A.

Sampling and Data Collection

The subjects chosen for this study were active and experienced developers from SourceForge.net, the largest OSS development web site in the world providing support for 2.7 million developers and 260,000 projects. The online survey was sent to 2,300 randomly selected OSS developers across a variety of open source projects: communication utilities, database, desktop, enterprise systems, networking, financial, multimedia, scientific, engineering, and format and protocol. Survey participation was solicited via an invitation email that described the purpose of the study, a request for voluntary participation and a statement of potential risk for the participant. Invitation emails for survey participation were sent through the SourceForge's email system. The survey was anonymous; a hyperlink to the online questionnaire was provided for the respondents in the email. The survey period ran one month with no follow-up.

The number of responses needed was determined by the number of constructs in the research model. According to Newton and Rudestam (1999), a rule of thumb for calculating the appropriate number of subjects in a multiple

regression analysis is to apply the formula 50 + (8 $\times$ the number of independent variables) for testing the multiple correlation (R^2). Therefore, a minimum of 114 usable responses were needed for the study. Following a single round of data collection with a response rate of 10%, 214 usable responses, consisting of 181 volunteers and 33 paid developers, were gathered. Subjects were classified as volunteers if they indicated on the survey they were not paid by their employers or other sources for their work on OSS. Since the intended research subjects of this study are strictly volunteers, our analysis was based on the data from the 181 volunteer developers. The sample contained 178 males and three females; they came from different parts of the world: 105 from North America, three from South America, 62 from Europe, eight from Oceania (Australia and New Zealand), two from Africa and one from Asia. The respondents' average age was 30 years old, with an average of five years of OSS development experience and eight years of IT experience. On average, the respondents reported prior involvement on 3.7 open source projects and spent 7.3 hours per week on OSS development.

Construct Reliability

The Cronbach's alpha was used to measure the internal consistency reliability of responses. Theory suggests that the Cronbach's alpha threshold of 0.7 is considered acceptable (Fornell & Larcker, 1981). The alpha values for peer recognition, human capital, career advancement, software needs, satisfaction, commitment and intention to contribute exceeded 0.70, indicating adequate reliability. However, the value was 0.68 for helping. Since the helping construct had two indicators, inter-item correlations were used as appropriate checks for their reliability. The correlation between the two indicators of helping was 0.516 demonstrating relatively high correlation. Thus, the construct remained unchanged in the interest of content validity. Table 3 demonstrates the descriptive statistics and the Cronbach's Alpha

Table 3. Descriptive statistics and reliability measurement

Construct	Mean	Standard Deviation	Cronbach's Alpha
Helping	5.57	0.90	0.68
Peer recognition	4.93	1.09	0.90
Human capital	5.72	0.97	0.92
Career advancement	4.51	1.27	0.87
Software needs	6.05	0.81	0.76
Satisfaction	5.36	1.09	0.84
Commitment	5.97	1.02	0.81
Intention to continue	6.25	0.87	0.86
Length of service	5.34	3.10	—

for all variables. The mean values for the five motivation constructs were all greater than four (the neutral point of the seven-point Likert scale), showing that all motivators were positively valent.

Data Analysis and Results

The research model was measured using LISREL. Based upon recommendations by Gerbing and Anderson (1988), data analysis was performed in a two-stage methodology: the first step was to evaluate the convergent and discriminant validity of the measurement model and was followed by the assessment of the structural model. This sequence permits researchers to ensure they have adequately measured constructs prior to drawing any conclusions on relationships among constructs (Bollen, 1989).

To evaluate convergent and discriminant validity for the measurement model, selected goodness-of-fit statistics related to confirmatory factor analysis (CFA), standardized indicator factor loadings and the average variance extracted (AVE) were examined. Adequate model fits, high factor loadings for each construct and the lack of

noticeable cross loadings and AVE by each construct exceeding the variance due to measurement error (i.e., greater than the generally recognized 0.50 cut-off) are required to meet construct validity for the measurement model (Fornell & Larcker, 1981; Barclay et al., 1995; Chin, 1998).

The analysis gave a chi-square (χ^2) of 273.81 with 154 degrees of freedom yielding the ratio 1.78:1 ($p < 0.00001$), which was well within the recommended range of 3:1. The goodness of fit index (GFI) was 0.91, adjusted goodness of fit index (AGFI) was 0.84, comparative fit index (CFI) was 0.95, incremental index of fit (IFI) was 0.95, normed fit index (NFI) was 0.91, root mean square residual (RMR) was 0.053 and root mean square error of approximation (RMSEA) was 0.075. Those values were within the commonly acceptable benchmarks, suggesting adequate model fit.

Each construct's indicator variable(s) and their corresponding factor loadings are listed in Appendix B. Principal components analysis with Kaiser normalization varimax rotation was used. All indicator factor loadings were significant ($p < 0.001$) and exceeded 0.70. Table 4 shows the AVE and the correlation of constructs along with significance tests. The square root of the AVE for each construct ranged from 0.72 to 1.00, which is greater than the correlation of the construct to others. Therefore, all conditions for construct validity were met.

The tests of all hypotheses were measured by examining the statistical significance of structural path. Figure 2 shows the standardized path coefficients and levels of significance for the significant associations as well as the overall fit indexes. According to the results, the R^2 value for intention to contribute is 0.67, signifying strong predictive power; moreover, the construct was well predicted by commitment ($\beta = 0.71$, $p < 0.001$), and then satisfaction ($\beta = 0.13$, $p < 0.05$), length of service ($\beta = 0.15$, $p < 0.01$), peer recognition ($\beta = 0.11$, $p < 0.05$) and human capital ($\beta = 0.18$, $p < 0.01$). Therefore, Hypotheses 1b,

Table 4. AVE and correlation of constructs

Construct (# items)		Correlation Matrix of Constructs								
		1	2	3	4	5	6	7	8	9
1	Helping (2)	**0.72**								
2	Peer recognition (2)	0.35***	**0.90**							
3	Human capital (2)	0.44***	0.26***	**0.92**						
4	Career advancement (2)	–0.07	0.25**	0.42***	**0.89**					
5	Personal needs (2)	0.12	–0.03	0.12	0.00	**0.82**				
6	Satisfaction (4)	0.11	0.12	–0.01	0.21**	–0.06	**0.75**			
7	Commitment (3)	0.44***	0.22**	0.19**	–0.03	0.16*	0.13	**0.82**		
8	Intention to contribute (3)	0.39***	0.36***	0.20*	–0.07	0.21**	0.11	0.57***	**0.80**	
9	Length of service (1)	0.23**	–0.12	0.01	–0.14	0.20**	–0.06	0.16*	0.21**	**1.00**

Diagonal elements in boldface are the square root of the average variance extracted.

*** correlation is significant at the 0.001 level.

** correlation is significant at the 0.01 level.

* correlation is significant at 0.05.

Figure 2. Standardized LISREL estimations of the structural model

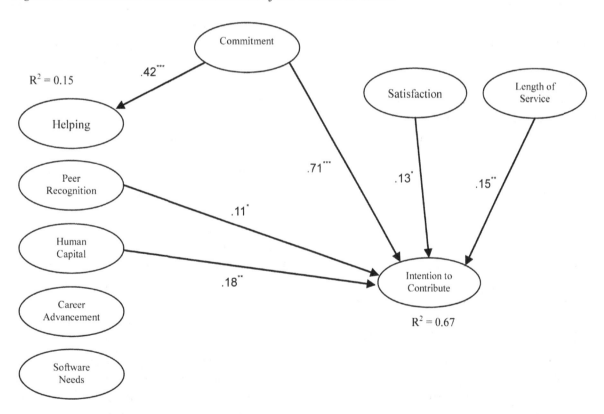

Model fit: χ^2 = 285.65 (df = 160),
GFI = 0.90, AGFI = 0.82,
CFI = 0.93, IFI = 0.93,
RMR = 0.063, RMSEA = 0.080

*** significant at p < .001
** significant at p < .01
* significant at p < .05

1c, 2, 4 and 5 were supported. OSS volunteer developers' commitment ($\beta = 0.42$, $p < 0.001$) was a strong and significant predictor of helping, thus supporting Hypothesis 3. Table 5 shows a summary of the hypotheses tested.

DISCUSSION

Although OSS development is becoming increasingly commercialized, OSS development still depends significantly on volunteers. The 181 volunteer respondents to our survey reported an average of 7.3 hours spent per week on OSS development, which is roughly the equivalent of 33 full-time developers. Unmeasured were the specialized skills, knowledge, ideas and innovations that these volunteers brought to their OSS projects. Gaining a better understanding of the reasons volunteers engage in OSS development can help project managers to leverage this valuable resource by developing practices to attract and retain volunteer developers.

Our research is best understood in the context that motivation is a resource allocation process that OSS volunteers rely on to allocate their time

Table 5. Results of hypothesis testing

Hypothesis	Result
H1a: Helping –> Intention to contribute	Not supported
H1b: Peer recognition –> Intention to contribute	Supported
H1c: Human capital –> Intention to contribute	Supported
H1d: Career advancement –> Intention to contribute	Not supported
H1e: Software needs –> Intention to contribute	Not supported
H2: Commitment–> Intention to contribute	Supported
H3: Commitment –> Helping	Supported
H4: Satisfaction –> Intention to contribute	Supported
H5: Length of service –> Intention to contribute	Supported

and energy to an array of tasks/projects that collectively satisfy their goals (Latham & Pinder, 2005). Involvement is sensitive to extraneous reasons such as personal dissatisfaction with a project manager or other social influences pertaining to a particular project or team. Hence, a strong argument can be made that motivation in the OSS context needs to be studied not within the limited confines of a single project, but in a broader community context. Also, project-level analysis is blind to the possibility that OSS volunteer developers would use multiple OSS projects to achieve their overarching goals. While it is certainly relevant to understand why individuals are involved with a specific project, looking at the project level decreases the generalizability of the assessment and likely provides an incomplete picture of motivation. In this study we focused broadly on the volunteer's overall experience with the OSS community.

This study was guided by a functional analysis of volunteerism that assessed OSS volunteer developers' motivations, attitudes related to the volunteer experience and intention to contribute to OSS development. A research framework of motivational functions formed by the combination of Clary's et al. (1998) volunteering functions with software needs provides useful categories to group motivators by goal-seeking purpose. Motivators that relate to these functions are likely to affect volunteerism, and conversely, perceived motivators that do not correspond to one of these functions are likely less effectual. For example, attitudinal factors such as enjoyment do not relate to any of the functions. Enjoyment of software development may be present in the OSS volunteer, but it is likely insufficient to sustain long-term involvement in that it does not satisfy any of her goals of volunteering. Lastly, the functions serve as categories to group like motivators, which is useful for cross-study comparison.

Given a variety of methods to study motivation, we utilized work motivation theory as it has demonstrated good explanatory power in the OSS development context (Wu et al., 2007) and EVT to develop measurements of motivational force since the theory has been justified in studying the motivations of volunteers and OSS developers (Miller, 1985; Hertel et al., 2003; Wu et al., 2007). We developed and tested a work motivation model that predicts volunteer developers' intention to participate in OSS development in the future, which is an indicator of a community's ability to retain an experienced volunteer workforce. The research model exhibited good levels of fit and strong predictive power.

The measurements of motivation for all five motivators (helping, peer recognition, increasing human capital, career advancement and software needs) are positively valent. These motivators address volunteer developers' need for values, enhancement, understanding, career and use-value functions. According to EVT, the cumulative effect of these motivators causes volunteers to act. Moreover, it is understood that motivators can have differential effects on specific volunteer behaviors. According to our results, peer recognition and enhancing human capital are the two motivators significantly influencing intention to contribute. The findings support Okoli and Oh's (2007) contention that OSS contributors often have the desire to be recognized for their contribution by means more tangible than just the satisfaction of contributing to a social good. Peer recognition is valued as it provides community validation of the contributor's worth to the project as the praise is well earned and sincere. And, OSS development provides an environment that enables developers to freely select the learning experiences that meet their needs and interests (Hars & Ou, 2002). Enhancing human capital is more than learning OSS development skills and techniques, and includes acquiring idiosyncratic knowledge and developing the ability to work with other master craftsmen.

It is surprising that no support was found in this study for the direct effect of helping on intention to contribute as altruism is commonly regarded to be the essential motivating force for OSS

volunteers. Nevertheless, volunteer developers' affective commitment was shown to be significantly associated with helping and has a positive and dominant impact on intention to contribute. The findings suggest that the motive helping is not sufficient to explain sustained involvement. Rather, it suggests that willingness to help is in part a consequence of forming an affective commitment to OSS development. This observation differs from the perspective of electronic communities of practice that asserts that individuals may contribute knowledge because they perceive that it feels good and find it interesting to help other people (Kollock, 1999). Our results indicate that helping serves the higher function of reinforcing community values and purpose. The extent a developer is willing to help co-developers reflects the level she is committed to her projects and is unwilling to leave them.

The lack of evidence for career advancement serves to emphasize the relative importance and strength of the two motivators found to significantly influence intention to contribute, peer recognition, and enhancing human capital. The likelihood of career advancement is partially dependent upon signaling (peer recognition) and enhancing human capital. Our results suggest that volunteer developers regard working on OSS as a sure way to enhance human capital (mean expectancy-valence value of 5.72) but are less certain about peer recognition (mean expectancy-valence value of 4.93) as an effective means to demonstrate (and advertise) their OSS capabilities and skillfulness publicly to potential employers, making the attainment of career advancement less certain.

No support was found for satisfying personal needs for software, yet the average expectancy-valence value for software needs (6.05) is the highest of all the motivators tested. The two results suggest that OSS volunteer developers are mostly satisfied with their quest for software, but that alone is not sufficient to hold their involvement. Hence, consistent with prior observations that numerous open source projects were initiated by the unmet need that the founders had for specialized software or software patches (von Hippel, 1988; Raymond, 2001; Lerner & Tirole, 2002), our results show that participants in OSS development efforts directly benefit from the software they help to develop because they have a personal or job related use for it. However, this benefit is not a determining factor in their decision to make contributions in the future.

The study findings identify volunteer developers' affective commitment as the strongest predictor of their intention to make future contributions, followed by satisfaction with participating in open source projects and length of service. Commitment and satisfaction both occupy pivotal positions in the volunteerism literature. For example, Chacon et al. (2007) found that commitment is the fundamental variable to predict greater volunteer involvement. Also, volunteerism theory suggests that individuals who believe that they have satisfied their motivations for volunteering are more likely to form an intention to continue to volunteer. Our results indicate that satisfaction is a result of having had prior expectations met and consequently satisfied developers would be more likely to continue participating in OSS development.

With respect to length of service, studies suggest that it is a good predictor of turnover (Price, 1981). Mowday et al. (1982) argued that individuals with longer service are expected to have a greater involvement in the organization and its goals. Our finding is consistent with these observations that the degree of intention to contribute increases as length of service increases.

Research Limitations

There are several limitations to this study requiring further investigation. First, the cross-sectional nature of our survey design may confine our ability to prove causal inferences. Cross-sectional design is useful for identifying relationships among constructs, but it does not address why the relationships should be presented. Nor does it enable us to analyze the process by which motivation and attitude form and change over time. Therefore, further research targeted on specific OSS projects may help to expand our understanding of the discriminating effects of motivation and attitudes on volunteer developers' intention to contribute to future OSS projects.

In addition, our response rate of 10% may raise concerns about possible response bias. The low response rate may be attributed to our decision not to send follow-up requests at the risk of being perceived as a spammer; nor did we offer our sample any incentive (e.g., lottery) to respond to the survey. Moreover, online survey by nature may present potential problems with respect to security and confidentiality that discourage participation (Smith, 1997). Finally, technical issues associated with incompatibilities between browsers may have precluded some from accessing the survey as its appearance may have been different from one respondent to another (Dillman, 2000).

However, low response rate alone does not necessarily mean bias if survey respondent characteristics are representative of non-respondents (Krosnick, 1999; Dillman, 2000). In reality, the measurement of non-response bias in web survey is a challenge since in most cases the identity of non-respondents is unknown (Dey, 1997). To address this problem, we measured early and late respondents for systematic differences, similar to the analysis performed by Hutchinson et al. (1987) and Johnson et al. (2000). In comparing the data from the earliest 30% of respondents with that of the last 30%, we found that there were no significant mean or correlation differences in the attitudinal variables across the respondents. This provides reasonable evidence that response bias was not a problem.

There are two other possible response biases present in our study. Our survey showed that female respondents did not make up a significant percentage (1.6%) of the sample, which seems to be a particular OSS phenomenon in regards to gender. Other OSS studies reported similar low response rates (e.g., Ghosh et al., 2002, 1.1%), suggesting that women do not play a sizable role in the development of open source and free software. Alternatively, literature suggests that males tend to respond to web surveys at higher rates than do females (Smith & Leigh, 1997; Tomsic et al., 2000; Carini et al., 2001). Therefore, this may have contributed to the low response rate for females. The other possible bias relates to the average of five years of OSS development experience reported by our respondents, which suggests a bias towards the engaged. In this study, we suggest that expectancy is related to volunteer developers' future expectations of OSS development that are generally heavily influenced by past experience and over time approach steady-state equilibrium as expectations become more realistic and entrenched in observed behaviors. This interpretation is reasonable since our research subjects are experienced, and their expectations are supposedly aligned with their past experiences.

GENERAL IMPLICATIONS AND CONCLUSION

Our research indicates that OSS project managers cannot assume that OSS volunteer developers will continue to work on a project simply because they have a need for their software. Rather, project managers will have to respond to their motives for volunteering and their attitudes towards OSS. Motivational issues will likely increase in importance as OSS communities face new challenges regarding project management, governance, licensing and productivity. OSS project managers will need to be careful not to overemphasize the priorities of the OSS project at the risk of discouraging its volunteers. For instance, seeking more time

and more work from a volunteer is usually not a welcome request (Galindo–Kuhn & Guzley, 2001) and changing organizational values may lead to volunteer turnover (McCurley & Lynch, 1996) as the new values may be incongruent with volunteers' values. The latter might very well relate to the special case of OSS commercialization since changes in project values might erode volunteers' commitment to OSS development. OSS project leaders could use our research model to study the needs of their volunteer developers and use that information to strategically promote their organizations in ways that speak to the abiding concerns of the volunteers they seek to recruit and retain.

One area of weakness that our study revealed is career advancement. While it is unrealistic for OSS projects to run placement centers, they can facilitate advancement by improving peer recognition. Most employers look for candidates with accomplishments, which exemplify the quality of work or reflect positive attributes of the worker. The most convincing accomplishments are measurable. One example of measured recognition used by some OSS projects is meritocracy, which assigns greater responsibility (status) based upon prior accomplishments. Special designations such as certification might be another approach.

The results of our study also suggest that steps taken by project leaders to strengthen affective commitment within volunteers are likely to be effective. Boezeman and Ellemers (2008) identified ways to strengthen affective commitment in volunteer organizations that should be directly applicable to OSS projects: demonstrations of the importance of the organization's work, respect and pride for volunteers and task-oriented support. They contend that for volunteer workers the focus of their commitment is not likely to be on their team or organization but is more likely focused on the plight of the people the organization is serving. Hence, OSS project leaders should consider using testimonials or other evidence of how the beneficiaries are served by the OSS project to strengthen OSS developer's affective commitment. This reinforces within the volunteer the importance of her work and communicates a sense of emotion-support for her. Also, acts of appreciation for OSS developers' donations of time and effort could be used to show respect and pride in the accomplishments of their volunteers. The other method of instilling affective commitment in volunteers is task-oriented support. Task-oriented support could be as simple as compiling a manual that provides guidelines for carrying out activities within the OSS project. Others suggest that mentors can be used for the purpose of task-oriented support, especially if the mentor's abilities match the goal-oriented needs of the volunteer (Joo & Park, 2009). For instance, an OSS volunteer developer whose goal is to become a core developer would benefit more from a mentor who is a core developer than one who is just familiar with the project. Development feedback can also be used to strengthen commitment and enhance the motive to learn. Engaging in this practice in OSS development, team leaders would provide volunteer developers with behaviorally relevant information on how to improve their performance without exerting pressure for a particular outcome. Constructive development feedback is known to boost motivation, enhance interest in the task itself and create an orientation towards learning and improvement. In summary, volunteers who feel supported and respected by their OSS project will attempt to reciprocate through affective commitment toward the organization.

Volunteer developers' satisfaction with OSS development is another significant determinant of their intention to contribute. Consequently, OSS project managers can enhance volunteers' intention level by properly identifying and managing the factors underlying their satisfaction. Project managers should consistently examine volunteer developers' attitudes on an ongoing basis by conducting periodic surveys on volunteers' current satisfaction level and track any changes in their attitudes over time. Areas of concern should include: work experience, attainment of rewards and growth and development. Managers should specifically attempt to discover factors that negatively impact satisfaction.

The finding also reveals that length of service and intention to contribute are correlated in a positive way. Volunteer developers, unlike paid workers, can quit the OSS project at their own discretion as they are not controlled by employment contracts and/or relationships. While some attrition is expected due to age, untypically high levels of attrition, particularly in the first months of service, are usually associated with negative work experiences or unrealistic expectations on the part of the volunteer. Therefore, project managers should monitor attrition rates and take corrective actions as deemed necessary.

This research also has implications for information systems researchers. Our research focused on five functions of volunteering. One particular function, social, does not appear in our model. Although a prior study by Hertel et al. (2003) was relatively unsuccessful at demonstrating its relevance, it could easily be retested using our research model. The protection function remains unexplored by OSS researchers as well.

Our research model is an excellent starting point from which to build more elaborate models. One empirical design for testing OSS volunteer developers' intention to continue would include observing novice developers' initial motivations and post-expectations in order to faithfully capture the complex, dynamic interrelationships between involvement and continuance decision. Knowledge of volunteer developers' initial expectancies and valences are useful to understanding why some participants quit. It may be the case that discontinuers start with a set of expectancies and valences that are different from continuers. Another possibility is that discontinuers may be uncertain about the realization of delayed benefits such as career advancement, as our findings show that career advancement is not a significant influential factor on continuance. Additionally, antecedents need to be incorporated into the model in order to better understand how affective commitment is formed and strengthened. Studies investigating this relationship might provide greater understanding of the full implications of affective commitment and motivation on OSS volunteer developer involvement.

REFERENCES

Ambrose, M. L., & Kulik, C. T. (1999). Old friends, new faces: Motivation research in the 1990s. *Journal of Management, 25*(3), 231–292. doi:10.1177/014920639902500302

Arnold, H. J. (1981). A test of the validity of the multiplicative hypothesis of expectancy-valence theories of work motivation. *Academy of Management Journal, 24*(1), 128–141. doi:10.2307/255828

Barclay, D., Thompson, R., & Higgins, C. (1995). The partial least square approach to causal modeling: Personal computer adoption and use as an illustration. *Technology Studies, 2*(2), 285–309.

Bitzer, J., Schrettl, W., & Schroder, P. J. H. (2007). Intrinsic motivation in open source software development. *Journal of Comparative Economics, 35*(1), 160–169. doi:10.1016/j.jce.2006.10.001

Boezeman, E. J., & Ellemers, N. (2008). Pride and respect in volunteers' organizational commitment. *European Journal of Social Psychology, 38*, 159–172. doi:10.1002/ejsp.415

Bollen, K. A. (1989). *Structural equations with latent variables*. New York, NY: John Wiley & Sons.

Bonaccorsi, A., & Rossi, C. (2003). Why open source software can succeed. *Research Policy, 32*(7), 1243–1258. doi:10.1016/S0048-7333(03)00051-9

Brickman, P. (1987). *Commitment, conflict, and caring*. Upper Saddle River, NJ: Prentice Hall.

Carini, R. M., Hayek, J. C., Kuh, G. D., Kennedy, J. M., & Ouimet, J. A. (2001). *College student responses to web and paper surveys: Does mode matter?* Paper presented at the 41st Annual Forum of the Association for Institutional Research, Long Beach, CA.

Chacon, F., Vecina, M. L., & Davila, M. C. (2007). The three-stage model of volunteers' duration of service. *Social Behavior and Personality, 35*(5), 627–642. doi:10.2224/sbp.2007.35.5.627

Chin, W. W. (1998). The partial least squares approach to structural equation modeling. In Marcoulides, G. A. (Ed.), *Modern methods for business research* (pp. 295–336). Mahwah, NJ: Lawrence Erlbaum.

Clary, E. G., Snyder, M., Ridge, R. D., Copeland, J., Stukas, A. A., Haugen, J., & Miene, P. (1998). Understanding and assessing the motivations of volunteers: A functional approach. *Journal of Personality and Social Psychology, 74*(6), 1516–1530. doi:10.1037/0022-3514.74.6.1516

Cnaan, A. R., & Goldberg–Glen, R. S. (1991). Measuring motivation to volunteer in human services. *The Journal of Applied Behavioral Science, 27*(3), 269–284. doi:10.1177/0021886391273003

Coleman, J. S. (1990). *Foundations of social theory*. Cambridge, MA: Belknap Press.

Dahlander, L., & McKelvey, M. (2005). Who is not developing open source software? Non-users, users, and developers. *Economics of Innovation and New Technology, 14*(7), 617–635. doi:10.1080/1043859052000344705

Dailey, R. C. (1986). Understanding organizational commitment for volunteers: Empirical and managerial implications. *Journal of Voluntary Action Research, 15*(1), 19–31.

Debian. (1997). *A brief history of Debian: Debian Documentation Team*. Retrieved November 16, 2011, from http://www.debian.org/doc/manuals/project-history/

Dey, E. L. (1997). Working with low survey response rates: The efficacy of weighing adjustments. *Research in Higher Education, 38*(2), 215–227. doi:10.1023/A:1024985704202

Dillman, D. (2000). *Mail and Internet surveys: The total design method* (2nd ed.). New York, NY: John Wiley & Sons.

Fang, Y., & Neufeld, D. (2009). Understanding sustained participation in open source software projects. *Journal of Management Information Systems, 25*(4), 9–50. doi:10.2753/MIS0742-1222250401

Fornell, C., & Larcker, D. F. (1981). Evaluating structural equations with unobservable variables and measurement error. *JMR, Journal of Marketing Research, 18*(1), 39–50. doi:10.2307/3151312

Galindo–Kuhn, R., & Guzley, R. M. (2001). The volunteer satisfaction index: Construct definition, measurement, development, and validation. *Journal of Social Service Research, 28*(1), 45–68. doi:10.1300/J079v28n01_03

Gamm, L., & Kassab, C. (1983). Productivity assessment of volunteer programs in not–for–profit human services organizations. *Journal of Voluntary Action Research, 12*(3), 23–38.

George, J., & Jones, G. (1999). *Understanding and managing organizational behavior* (2nd ed.). Reading, MA: Addison-Wesley.

Gerbing, D. W., & Anderson, J. C. (1988). An updated paradigm for scale development incorporating unidimensionality and its assessment. *JMR, Journal of Marketing Research, 25*(2), 186–192. doi:10.2307/3172650

Ghosh, R. A., Glott, R., Krieger, B., & Robles, G. (2002). *Free/libre and open source software: Survey and study, FLOSS final report*. Maastricht, The Netherlands: International Institute of Infonomics, University of Maastricht. Retrieved January 16, 2008, from http://www.infonomics.nl/FLOSS/report/Final4.htm

Gidron, B. (1983). Source of job satisfaction among service volunteers. *Journal of Voluntary Action Research, 12*(1), 20–35.

Gidron, B. (1984). Predictors of retention and turnover among service volunteer workers. *Journal of Social Service Research, 8*(1), 1–16. doi:10.1300/J079v08n01_01

Hars, A., & Ou, S. (2002). Working for free? – Motivations of participating in open source projects. *International Journal of Electronic Commerce, 6*(3), 25–39.

Hertel, G., Niedner, S., & Hermann, S. (2003). Motivation of software developers in the open source projects: An Internet–based survey of contributors to the Linux kernel. *Research Policy, 32*(7), 1159–1177. doi:10.1016/S0048-7333(03)00047-7

Houle, B. J., Sagarin, B. J., & Kaplan, M. F. (2005). A functional approach to volunteerism: Do volunteer motives predict task preference? *Basic and Applied Social Psychology, 27*(4), 337–344. doi:10.1207/s15324834basp2704_6

Hutchison, J., Tollefson, N., & Wigington, H. (1987). Response bias in college freshman's responses to mail surveys. *Research in Higher Education, 26*(1), 99–106. doi:10.1007/BF00991936

Igbaria, M., & Greenhaus, J. H. (1992). Determinants of MIS employees' turnover intentions: A structural equation model. *Communications of the ACM, 35*(2), 34–49. doi:10.1145/129630.129631

Johnson, L. C., Beaton, R., Murphy, S., & Pike, K. (2000). Sampling bias and other methodological threats to the validity of health survey research. *International Journal of Stress Management, 7*(4), 247–267. doi:10.1023/A:1009589812697

Johnson, M. (1981). *Voluntary social services.* Oxford, UK: Basil Blackwell and Martin Robertson.

Joo, B. K., & Park, S. (2009). Career satisfaction, organizational commitment, and turnover intention. *Leadership and Organization Development Journal, 31*(6), 482–500. doi:10.1108/01437731011069999

Kemper, T. D. (1980). Altruism and voluntary action. In Smith, D. H., & Macaulay, J., & Associates. (Eds.), *Participation in social and political activities* (pp. 306–338). San Francisco, CA: Jossey-Bass.

Kiesler, C. A. (1971). *The psychology of commitment: Experiments linking behavior to belief.* New York, NY: Academic Press.

Kline, R. B. (2005). *Principles and practices of structural equation modeling* (2nd ed.). New York, NY: Guilford Press.

Kollock, P. (1999). The economies of online cooperation: Gifts, and public goods in cyberspace. In Smith, M. A., & Kollock, P. (Eds.), *Communities in cyberspace* (pp. 220–239). New York, NY: Routledge.

Krishnamurthy, S. (2006). On the intrinsic and extrinsic motivation of free/libre/open source (FLOSS) developers. *Knowledge, Technology & Policy, 18*(4), 17–39. doi:10.1007/s12130-006-1002-x

Krosnick, J. (1999). Survey research. *Annual Review of Psychology, 50,* 537–567. doi:10.1146/annurev.psych.50.1.537

Lakhani, K. R., & Wolf, R. G. (2005). Why hackers do what they do: Understanding motivation effort in free/open source software projects. In Feller, J., Fitzgerald, B., Hissam, S. A., & Lakhani, K. R. (Eds.), *Perspectives on free and open source software* (pp. 3–23). Cambridge, MA: MIT Press. doi:10.2139/ssrn.443040

Latham, G. P., & Pinder, C. C. (2005). Work motivation theory and research at the dawn of the twenty–first century. *Annual Review of Psychology, 56,* 485–516. doi:10.1146/annurev.psych.55.090902.142105

Lerner, J., & Tirole, J. (2002). Some simple economics of open source. *The Journal of Industrial Economics, 50*(2), 197–234. doi:10.1111/1467-6451.00174

Lewin, K. (1936). *Principles of topological psychology.* New York, NY: McGraw-Hill. doi:10.1037/10019-000

Locke, E. A., & Latham, G. P. (1990). Work motivation and satisfaction: Light at the end of the tunnel. *Psychological Science, 1*(4), 240–246. doi:10.1111/j.1467-9280.1990.tb00207.x

Mankiw, G. N. (2004). *Principles of economics* (3rd ed.). Mason, OH: Thomson South–Western Press.

Mathieson, K. (1991). Predicting user intentions: Comparing the technology acceptance model with the theory of planned behavior. *Information Systems Research, 2*(3), 173–191. doi:10.1287/isre.2.3.173

McCurley, S., & Lynch, R. (1996). *Volunteer management: Mobilizing all the resources of the community.* Downers Grove, IL: Heritage Arts.

Meyer, J. P., Becker, T. E., & Vandenberghe, C. (2004). Employee commitment and motivation: A conceptual analysis and integrative model. *The Journal of Applied Psychology, 89*(6), 991–1007. doi:10.1037/0021-9010.89.6.991

Miles, I., Sullivan, W., & Kuo, E. (1998). Ecological restoration volunteers: The benefits of participation. *Urban Ecosystems*, 2(1), 27–41. doi:10.1023/A:1009501515335

Miller, L. E. (1985). Understanding the motivation of volunteers: An examination of personality differences and characteristics of volunteers' paid employment. *Journal of Voluntary Action Research*, 14(2-3), 112–122.

Miller, L. E., Powell, G. N., & Seltzer, J. (1990). Determinants of turnover among volunteers. *Human Relations*, 43(9), 901–917. doi:10.1177/001872679004300906

Miner, J. B. (2003). The rated importance, scientific validity, and practical usefulness of organizational behavior theories: A quantitative review. *Academy of Management Learning & Education*, 2(3), 250–268. doi:10.5465/AMLE.2003.10932132

Mitchell, T. R. (1980). Expectancy–value models in organizational psychology. In Feather, N. T. (Ed.), *Expectations and actions* (pp. 293–311). Mahwah, NJ: Lawrence Erlbaum.

Mowday, R. T., Porter, L. W., & Steers, R. M. (1982). *Employee–organization linkages: The psychology of commitment and absenteeism and turnover*. New York, NY: Academic Press.

Naylor, H. (1967). *Volunteers today: Finding, training and working with them*. New York, NY: Association Press.

Newton, R. R., & Rudestam, K. E. (1999). *Your statistical consultant: Answers to your data analysis questions*. Thousand Oaks, CA: Sage.

Okoli, C., & Oh, W. (2007). Investigating recognition–based performance in an open content community: A social capital perspective. *Information & Management*, 44(3), 240–252. doi:10.1016/j.im.2006.12.007

Omoto, A. M., & Snyder, M. (1995). Sustained helping without obligation: Motivation, longevity of service, and perceived attitude change among AIDS volunteers. *Journal of Personality and Social Psychology*, 68(4), 671–686. doi:10.1037/0022-3514.68.4.671

Osterloh, M., & Rota, S. (2007). Open source software development – Just another case of collective invention? *Research Policy*, 36(2), 157–171. doi:10.1016/j.respol.2006.10.004

Penner, L. A., & Finkelstein, M. A. (1998). Dispositional and structural determinants of volunteerism. *Journal of Personality and Social Psychology*, 74(2), 525–537. doi:10.1037/0022-3514.74.2.525

Porter, L. W., Steers, R. M., Mowday, R. T., & Boulian, P. V. (1974). Organizational commitment, job satisfaction and turnover among psychiatric technicians. *The Journal of Applied Psychology*, 59(5), 603–609. doi:10.1037/h0037335

Price, J. L. (1981). A causal model of turnover for nurses. *Academy of Management Journal*, 24(3), 543–565. doi:10.2307/255574

Qureshi, H., Davies, B., & Challis, D. (1979). Motivations and rewards of volunteers and informal care givers. *Journal of Voluntary Action Research*, 8(1-2), 47–55.

Raykov, T., & Marcoulides, G. A. (2000). *A first course in structural equation modeling*. Mahwah, NJ: Lawrence Erlbaum.

Raymond, E. S. (2001). *The cathedral and the bazaar: Musings on Linux and open source by an accidental revolutionary*. Sebastopol, CA: O'Reilly.

Reynolds, L. G. (1951). *The structure of labor markets: Wages and labor mobility in theory and practice* (4th ed.). Westport, CT: Greenwood Press.

Robbins, S. P. (1998). *Organizational behavior* (8th ed.). Upper Saddle River, NJ: Prentice Hall.

Roberts, J. A., Hann, I. H., & Slaughter, S. A. (2006). Understanding the motivations, participation, and performance of open source software developers: A longitudinal study of the Apache project. *Management Science, 52*(7), 984–999. doi:10.1287/mnsc.1060.0554

Rotter, J. B. (1954). *Social learning and clinical psychology*. Upper Saddle River, NJ: Prentice Hall. doi:10.1037/10788-000

Salancik, G. R. (1977). Commitment and control of organizational behavior and belief. In Staw, B., & Salancik, G. R. (Eds.), *New directions in organizational behavior* (pp. 1–54). Chicago, IL: St. Clair Press.

Scarpello, V., & Campbell, J. P. (1983). Job satisfaction: Are all the parts there? *Personnel Psychology, 36*(3), 577–600. doi:10.1111/j.1744-6570.1983.tb02236.x

Shah, S. K. (2006). Motivation, governance, and the viability of hybrid forms in open source software development. *Management Science, 52*(7), 1000–1014. doi:10.1287/mnsc.1060.0553

Sharp, E. G. (1978). Citizen organization in policing issues and crime prevention: Incentives for participation. *Journal of Voluntary Action Research, 7*(1-2), 45–58.

Silcock, H. (1954). The phenomenon of labour turnover. *Journal of the Royal Statistical Society. Series A (General), 117*(4), 429–440. doi:10.2307/2342680

Singer, M. S., & Coffin, T. K. (1996). Cognitive and volitional determinants of job attitudes in a voluntary organization. *Journal of Social Behavior and Personality, 11*(2), 313–328.

Smith, C. B. (1997). Casting the net: Surveying an Internet population. *Journal of Computer Mediated Communication, 3*(1). Retrieved November 27, 2011, from http://www.ascusc.org/jcmc/vol3/issue1/smith.html

Smith, D. H. (1981). Altruism, volunteers, and volunteerism. *Journal of Voluntary Action Research, 10*(1), 21–36.

Smith, M. A., & Leigh, B. (1997). Virtual subjects: Using the Internet as an alternative source of subjects and research environment. *Behavior Research Methods, Instruments, & Computers, 29*(4), 469–505. doi:10.3758/BF03210601

Smits, S. J., Mclean, E. R., & Tanner, J. R. (1993). Managing high-achieving information systems professionals. *Journal of Management Information Systems, 9*(4), 103–120.

Smoker, D. (2010). *75% of Linux code written by paid developers*. Retrieved November 18, 2011, from http://www.osnews.com/story/22786/75_of_Linux_Code_Written_by_Paid_Developers

Snyder, M. (1993). Basic research and practical problems: The promise of a 'functional' personality and social psychology. *Personality and Social Psychology Bulletin, 19*(3), 251–264. doi:10.1177/0146167293193001

Stewart, K. J., & Gosain, S. (2006). The impact of ideology on effectiveness in open source software development teams. *Management Information Systems Quarterly, 30*(2), 291–314.

Stoikov, V., & Raimon, R. L. (1968). Determinants of differences in the quit rate among industries. *The American Economic Review, 58*(5), 1283–1298.

Thatcher, J. B., Stepina, L. P., & Boyle, R. J. (2002). Turnover of information technology workers: Examining empirically the influence of attitudes, job characteristics, and external markets. *Journal of Management Information Systems, 19*(3), 231–261.

Tomsic, M. L., Hendel, D. D., & Matross, R. P. (2000). *A World Wide Web response to student satisfaction surveys: Comparisons using paper and Internet formats*. Paper presented at the 40th Annual Meeting of the Association for Institutional Research, Cincinnati, OH.

Tschirhart, M., Mesch, D. J., Perry, J. L., Miller, T. K., & Lee, G. (2001). Stipended volunteers: their goals, experiences, satisfaction, and likelihood of future service. *Nonprofit and Voluntary Sector Quarterly*, *30*(3), 422–443. doi:10.1177/0899764001303002

Ullman, J. B. (1996). Structural equation modeling. In Tabachnick, B. G., & Fidell, L. S. (Eds.), *Using multivariate statistics* (3rd ed., pp. 709–819). New York, NY: Harper Collins College.

von Hippel, E. (1988). *The sources of innovation*. New York, NY: Oxford University Press.

Vroom, V. H. (1964). *Work and motivation*. New York, NY: John Wiley & Sons.

Wasko, M. M., & Faraj, S. (2005). Why should I share? Examining social capital and knowledge contribution in electronic networks of practice. *Management Information Systems Quarterly*, *29*(1), 35–57.

Wu, C. G., Gerlach, J. H., & Young, C. E. (2007). An empirical analysis of open source software developers' motivations and continuance intentions. *Information & Management*, *44*(3), 253–262. doi:10.1016/j.im.2006.12.006

APPENDIX A

Survey Items

Table 6. Attitude

Construct	Item Wording
Intention to Contribute	1. I intend to continue participating in OSS projects rather than discontinue my involvement. 2. I expect to engage in OSS projects in the future. 3. I would be willing to make future contributions to OSS projects.
Commitment	1. I am willing to put in a great deal of effort beyond that normally expected in order to help the community be successful. 2. I support the community's value. 3. I really care about the fate of the community.
Satisfaction	How do you feel about your overall experience of participating in OSS projects: 1. Very dissatisfied ● ● ● Very satisfied 2. Very displeased ● ● ● Very pleased 3. Very frustrated ● ● ● Very contented 4. Very terrible ● ● ● Very delighted

Intention to contribute and commitment using the following scale:

1 = strongly disagree; 2 = disagree; 3 = somewhat disagree; 4 = neutral;

5 = somewhat agree; 6 = agree; 7 = strongly agree

Table 7. Motivations

Construct		Item Wording
Helping	1	● Being able to help other OSS developers is to me. (Valence) ● Participating in OSS projects will give me an opportunity to help others solve their problems. (Expectancy)
	2	● Sharing code and programming practice in an OSS community is to me. (Valence) ● Participating in OSS projects will give me an opportunity to share my knowledge about programming. (Expectancy)
Peer Recognition	1	● Gaining peer recognition in the open source community is to me. (Valence) ● I will gain recognition from others in the open source community through my contributions. (Expectancy)
	2	● Earning respect from other developers in the open source community is to me. (Valence) ● By my OSS contributions, I will earn the respect of other developers in the community. (Expectancy)
Human Capital	1	● Improving my performance at software development is to me. (Valence) ● Participating in OSS projects will improve my software development performance. (Expectancy)
	2	● Advancing my skills at software development is to me. (Valence) ● Participating in OSS projects will advance my skills in developing software. (Expectancy)
Career Advancement	1	● Improving my job opportunities is to me. (Valence) ● Participating in OSS projects will get me a better job. (Expectancy)
	2	● Advancing my career is to me. (Valence) ● Participating in OSS projects will aid in advancing my career. (Expectancy)

continued on following page

Table 7. Continued

Construct		Item Wording
Software Needs	1	• Developing software that corresponds to my needs is to me. (Valence) • Writing open source code will produce software tailored to my needs. (Expectancy)
	2	• I engage in OSS products that I intend to use. (Valence) • I will use the OSS products that I helped develop. (Expectancy)

Valence items using the following scale:
1 = very unimportant; 2 = unimportant; 3 = somewhat unimportant;
4 = neutral; 5 = somewhat important; 6 = important; 7 = very important
Expectancy items using the following scale:
1 = strongly disagree; 2 = disagree; 3 = somewhat disagree; 4 = neutral;
5 = somewhat agree; 6 = agree; 7 = strongly agree

APPENDIX B

Table 8. Factor Loadings

Items	1	2	3	4	5	6	7	8	9
Helping 1	**.757**	.192	.068	−.216	.036	.119	.189	.143	.060
Helping 2	**.820**	.061	.263	.078	.073	.011	.124	.057	−.085
Peer Recognition 1	.083	**.919**	.074	.100	.044	.057	.104	.139	−.041
Peer Recognition 2	.138	**.894**	.083	.145	−.026	.001	.097	.166	−.074
Human Capital 1	.087	.079	**.943**	.179	.015	−.076	.069	−.021	−.015
Human Capital 2	.242	.086	**.878**	.239	.037	.011	.090	.117	−.011
Career Advancement 1	−.036	.124	.229	**.868**	−.044	.189	−.065	−.038	−.015
Career Advancement 2	−.056	.123	.175	**.915**	.038	.063	.065	−.040	−.057
Software Needs 1	.054	−.083	.058	.081	**.874**	−.090	.044	.139	.091
Software Needs 2	.039	.101	−.012	−.081	**.888**	.103	.067	.067	.012
Satisfaction 1	.214	.064	.016	.047	.038	**.849**	.107	.032	−.016
Satisfaction 2	.069	−.042	.000	.073	.155	**.861**	.064	.059	−.168
Satisfaction 3	−.043	.050	−.004	.036	−.149	**.769**	−.074	−.122	.216
Satisfaction 4	.326	.007	−.093	.123	−.031	**.770**	.007	.068	−.120
Commitment 1	.013	.239	.122	.087	.077	.051	**.769**	.191	−.027
Commitment 2	.152	.026	.029	−.017	−.001	.022	**.886**	.191	.039
Commitment 3	.202	−.015	.028	−.069	.075	.033	**.801**	.326	.081
Intention to Contribute 1	.153	.129	.075	−.070	−.008	.038	.170	**.880**	.022
Intention to Contribute 2	−.034	.027	−.007	.044	.191	.027	.258	**.793**	.069
Intention to Contribute 3	.093	.203	.022	−.057	.082	.014	.245	**.798**	.066
Length of Service	.118	−.107	−.022	−.065	.105	−.064	.073	.134	**.939**

Each indicator variable of motivation constructs was calculated as the product of the valence value and the expectancy value.

This work was previously published in the International Journal of Open Source Software and Processes, Volume 3, Issue 4, edited by Stefan Koch, pp. 24-48, copyright 2011 by IGI Publishing (an imprint of IGI Global).

Chapter 13
Framework for Graphical User Interfaces of Geospatial Early Warning Systems

Martin Hammitzsch
Helmholtz Centre Potsdam, GFZ German Research Centre for Geosciences, Germany

ABSTRACT

An important component of Early Warning Systems (EWS) for man-made and natural hazards is the command and control unit's Graphical User Interface (GUI). All relevant information of an EWS is concentrated in this GUI and offered to human operators. However, when designing the GUI, not only the user experience and the GUI's screens are relevant, but also the frameworks and technologies that the GUI is built on and the implementation of the GUI itself are of great importance. Implementations differ based on their applications in different domains but the design and approaches to implement the GUIs of different EWS often show analogies. The design and development of such GUIs are performed repeatedly on some parts of the system for each EWS. Thus, the generic GUI framework of a geospatial EWS for tsunamis is introduced to enable possible synergistic effects on the development of other new related technology. The results presented here could be adopted and reused in other EWS for man-made and natural hazards.

INTRODUCTION

As part of an Early Warning and Mitigation System (EWMS), the Decision Support System (DSS) provides processing, assessment, visualization, decision support, analysis, warning and management functions for the purpose of supporting

disaster management related activities regarding threats (Raape et al., 2010) of natural or man-made hazards such as tsunamis. Thus, the DSS is intended to help the officer on duty to become aware of a current situation, to assess incoming information, to exploit synergies of information fusion and analysis, to assess the impact and consequences and to make informed decisions (Raape et al., 2010). As a result, the DSS and especially its user interface are taken into account for a tsunami

DOI: 10.4018/978-1-4666-2937-0.ch013

EWMS initially designed and implemented in the project Distant Early Warning System (DEWS). Hammitzsch et al. (2010) outline that the DEWS project has the objective of creating a new generation of interoperable early warning systems based on an open sensor platform. This platform integrates Open Geospatial Consortium (OGC) Sensor Web Enablement (SWE) compliant sensor systems for the rapid detection of hazardous events, such as earthquakes, sea level anomalies, ocean floor occurrences and ground displacements for the case of tsunami early warnings. Based on the upstream information flow, DEWS focuses on the improvement of downstream capacities for warning centers, especially by improving information logistics for effective and targeted warning message aggregation for a multilingual environment. Even though DEWS was primarily focused on tsunami early warning in the Indian Ocean region, Lendholt and Hammitzsch (2011) explain that the system offers a modular design that serves as a reference architecture for early warning systems independent of the hazard type and region. A generic reference architecture for early warning systems should have components designed for serving in new deployments and new sites without re-programming or compilation procedures. Instead, deployment-specific add-ons or plug-ins should be easy to add in a configurable system based on the needs of a specific scenario. This means, also, that the user interface has to be not bound to specific hazard characteristics and must be developed and implemented independently from specific infrastructure characteristics. Wächter et al. (2011) report that these developments are resumed and continued by the project Collaborative, Complex, and Critical Decision-Support in Evolving Crises (TRIDEC, TRIDEC 2010) focusing on real-time intelligent information management and including the design and implementation of a robust and scalable service infrastructure supporting the integration and utilization of existing resources with accelerated generation of large volumes of data.

METHODOLOGY

After providing the motivation for the presented results and the application of free and open source software (FOSS), the technological framework for a command and control unit's GUI to be applied in each EWS for man-made and natural hazards is introduced with a simplified architecture for the Command and Control User Interface (CCUI) used in natural crisis management (NCM) for tsunamis developed in DEWS and TRIDEC. In this context, the selected GUI frameworks and geo frameworks are introduced together with an application oriented Geographic Information System (GIS) and the relevant standards and technologies.

MOTIVATION AND PRECONDITIONS

In 'The Global Survey Of Early Warning Systems,' Annan (2006) concludes that considerable shortcomings and gaps remain, especially in developing countries, where basic capacities, equipment and resources are often not available. The UN (2006) reports that systems for some hazards, such as tsunamis, are often absent. In this regard, Löwe et al. (2011) summarize that the Boxing Day Tsunami of 2004 killed over 240,000 people in 14 countries and inundated the affected shorelines with waves reaching heights of up to 30 m. Whereas tsunami early warning capabilities have improved in the meantime by continuing the development of modular Tsunami Early Warning Systems (TEWS), recent tsunami events, such as the Chile 2010 and the Honshu 2011 tsunami, demonstrate that there are still shortcomings in the systems. Furthermore, most of the disaster management systems currently in place are proprietary systems (Chen et al., 2010). These proprietary systems are, however, challenged by limitations such as high cost, low flexibility, and constrained compatibility (Ashcroft et al., 2002; Burghardt, 2006). For example, Chen et al. (2010) exemplify adopting the FOSS concept due to following reasons: to evade many of the existing challenges, such as a lack of funds to generate proprietary software; to endorse greater flexibility, wealth of knowledge, and improved compatibility; and to make widespread deployment and customization a reality.

In this regard, Steiniger and Bocher (2009) argue that the development of FOSS has experienced a boost over the last few years. The variety of FOSS that can be found on desktop computers ranges from word processors and web browsers to drawing and scientific applications. In the GIS domain, the widespread use of FOSS is apparent as well. This rise in popularity of free GIS tools can be measured using four indicators. The first indicator is the number of projects started in the last few years. The second indicator is the increasing financial support by governmental organizations for the foundation of FOSS GIS projects. The third indicator is the download rates of free desktop GIS software. Finally, a fourth indicator is an increasing number of cases of using open source GIS software. Along with this trend towards the application of FOSS goes the number of research publications that mentions the use of open source software tools and libraries (i.e., Mitasova & Neteler, 2004). Moreover, software and algorithms developed in research projects are increasingly published under open source licenses (e.g., Badard & Braun, 2003, Pebesma, 2004, Burghardt et al., 2005, Buliung & Remmel, 2008). As such, it is important to note that the FOSS movement that postulates freedom of use and modification for software is not restricted to software only. Rather, one regards free software as 'the foundation of a learning society where we share our knowledge in a way that others can build upon' (Lee, 2011). Hence, this movement also includes the free availability of data that forms a basis for our knowledge. Reid and Martin (2001) discussed the potential of open source software for implementing spatial data infrastructures (SDIs). They conclude that 'open-source software provides great potential to make available components for SDI implementations that are affordable by resource poor organizations'

and add that 'many building blocks for SDIs are already available.' Ramsey (2007) remarks that 'existing [FOSS GIS] products are now entering a phase of rapid refinement and enhancement'. He further emphasizes that 'open source [GIS] software can provide a feature-complete alternative to proprietary software in most system designs.'

Thus, a FOSS concept is followed to increase the utility of the CCUI and to leverage benefits such as low cost, flexibility, and improved compatibility. Furthermore, the presented framework based on FOSS tries to fill the gaps outlined partially by providing an approach to copy findings and development to implement a CCUI for natural and man-made hazards.

COMMAND AND CONTROL USER INTERFACE

Based on profound FOSS community activities and results described hereinafter, the CCUI will be based on the Eclipse Rich Client Platform (RCP) and the User-friendly Desktop Internet GIS (uDig) Software Development Kit (SDK), with their behind frameworks and standards. Hammitzsch et al. (2010) summarize that existing standards have been integrated, wherever possible. The CCUI integrates various services standardized by OGC. Using the Web Map Service (WMS) and Web Feature Service (WFS) specifications, spatial data are utilized to present the situation picture and to integrate a simulation system via the Web Processing Service (WPS), to identify the affected areas. Warning messages are compiled and transmitted using the Common Alerting Protocol (CAP) for the content together with addressing information using the Emergency Data Exchange Language – Distribution Element (EDXL-DE). Both standards are specified by the Organization for the Advancement of Structured Information Standards (OASIS). Internal interfaces are realized with SOAP web services. Standards and functionalities are implemented mainly via plug-ins, a central concept of the Eclipse RCP that enables the building of platform applications with user interfaces. Figure 1 depicts the stack of frameworks, libraries, technologies and plug-ins adopted and realized in the CCUI.

Atop of various library and functionality plug-ins, the CCUI reveals its functionalities to the operator via a GUI assembled by so-called perspectives (see Figure 1, Element 1). Each perspective determines visible actions and provides views within a window that regard the dedicated major tasks of the operator. The composition of the GUI's graphical part (i.e., the perspectives) is described in Hammitzsch et al. (2012) and forms the basis for the technological approach presented in this paper. Hammitzsch et al. (2012) explain that the following main perspectives support operators doing their tasks with EWSs for man-made and natural hazards. The Monitoring Perspective (see Figure 1, Element 2), exemplar-

ily shown in Figure 2, provides a survey of a specific area and contributes an overall situation picture to the operator, with geo-spatial information to track running events. The Forecasting Perspective (see Figure 1, Element 3), exemplarily shown in Figure 3, supports the operator in analyzing different probable forecasts provided by the simulation system. The Message Composition Perspective (see Figure 1, Element 4), exemplarily shown in Figure 4, facilitates the operator to prepare and send warning messages or system messages. The Dissemination Perspective (see Figure 1, Element 5) provides a comprehensive overview of the status of disseminated messages sent through the different dissemination channels and allows observation of all disseminations initiated for specific user groups. The Situation Picture Perspective (see Figure 1, Element 6) also known as the Map Perspective is included via uDig and provides a set of preconfigured and

Figure 1. CCUI framework stack

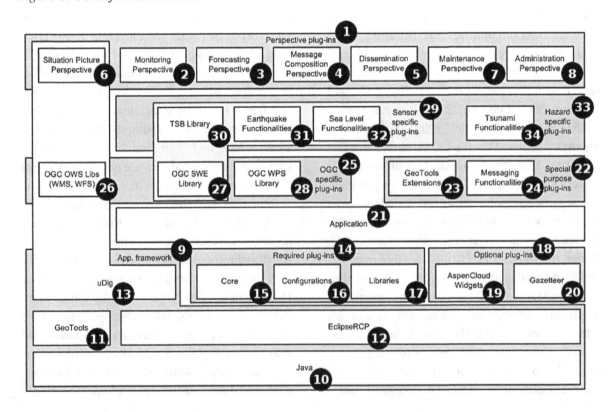

Figure 2. CCUI monitoring perspective with exemplary setup for Thailand developed in DEWS

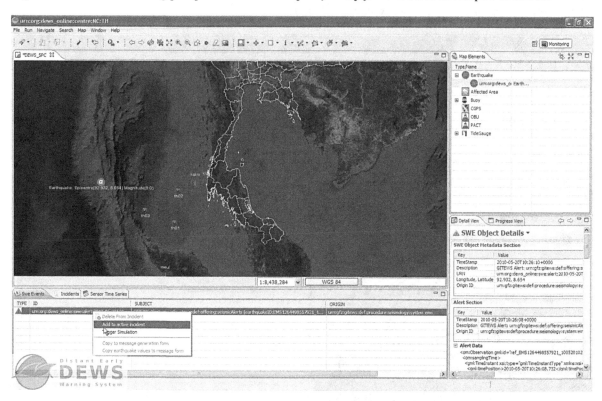

Figure 3. CCUI forecasting perspective with evaluation setup for Turkey developed in TRIDEC (Ozel et al., forthcoming)

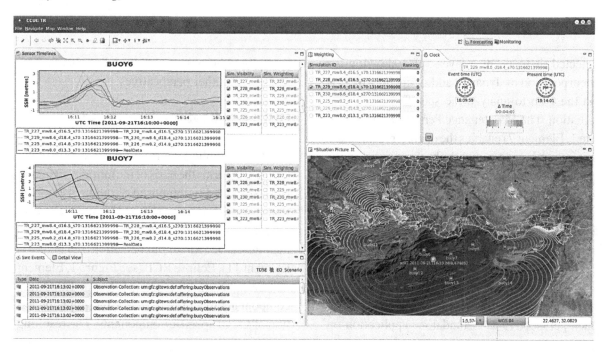

Figure 4. CCUI message composition perspective with validation setup for Indonesia developed in continued DEWS activities (Hammitzsch et al., 2012)

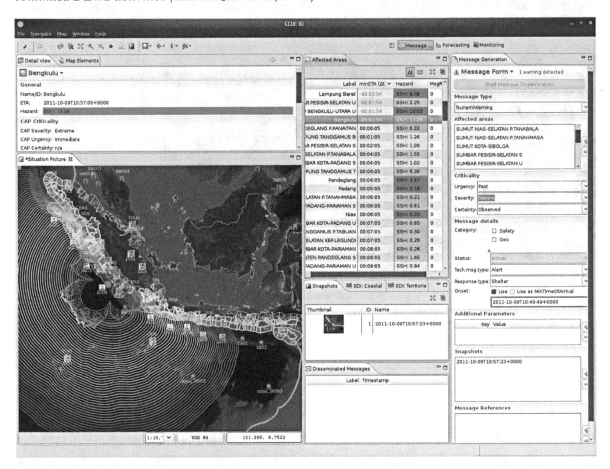

selected thematic map layers, also allowing the incorporation of dynamic additional information on the map to analyze the specifics of a given situation. The Maintenance Perspective (see Figure 1, Element 7) enables the operator to maintain sensors and sensor networks by means of requesting sensor observations and planning services as well as rebinding and disconnecting them. The Administration Perspective (see Figure 1, Element 8) allows the administration of configurations and settings needed for information logistics. Additionally, each of the perspectives ships its own libraries, employed solely by the relevant perspective. This distribution allows the deployment of each perspective as a standalone application or,

as outlined here, in a compound application together with other perspectives.

CCUI Application Framework

The CCUI application framework (see Figure 1, Element 9) forms the basis of the introduced framework stack and is composed of the Java Platform Enterprise Edition (Java EE; see Figure 1, Element 10) together with components built upon GeoTools including a GeoAPI implementation (see Figure 1, Element 11), Eclipse RCP (see Figure 1, Element 12) and uDIG (see Figure 1, Element 13). These components form the basis for the implementation of CCUI specific components. The resulting platform that is employed to build the CCUI on top is introduced briefly in this section.

Eclipse and Eclipse Rich Client Platform

Aniszczyk (2010) describes Eclipse as an open source community focused on providing an extensible development platform for building software and developing a universal platform for application frameworks and exemplary tools that make it easy and cost-effective to build and deploy software. There is a large consortium of major software vendors, solution providers, corporations, educational and research institutions, and individuals working cohesively to create an ecosystem that enhances and cultivates the Eclipse platform with complementary products, capabilities, and services.

While the Eclipse platform is designed to serve as an open tools platform, it is architected so that its components could be used to build almost any client application. The minimal set of plug-ins needed to build a rich client application is collectively known as the Eclipse RCP. Applications can be built using a subset of this platform. This rich set of applications is still based on the dynamic plug-in model, and the user interface is built using the same toolkits and extension points. The layout and function of the workbench is under the fine-grained control of the plug-in developer, in this case (Irawan, 2009).

With regard to Eclipse RCP, Irawan et al. (2010) comments that many people that have built, or are building RCP applications state that the main value they get from using the RCP is that it allows them to build a professional-looking application quickly, with a native look-and-feel, on multiple platforms, allowing them to focus on their value added. They appreciate that the components that form the RCP are of high quality, are actively maintained, and are open source. They often discover, after the initial adoption of RCP, that there are many other Eclipse components available.

Several individuals have also discovered that the inherent extensibility of Eclipse allows them to build not only a closed-form product but also an open-ended platform in their own domain.

User-Friendly Desktop Internet GIS 'uDig,' its Software Development Kit and the Eclipse RCP Target Platform

uDig is an open source desktop application framework, built with RCP technology. uDig can be used as a stand-alone application, can be extended with RCP plug-ins and can be used as a plug-in for an existing RCP application (Refractions, 2010a). Thus, uDig is used as an off-the-shelf product, and it also provides an environment to implement solutions for domain specific applications (WhereGroup, 2010). Refractions (2010a) reports that the goal of uDig is to provide a complete Java solution for Desktop GIS data access, editing, and viewing. uDig aims to be the following: user-friendly, providing a familiar graphical environment for GIS users; desktop located, running as a thick client, natively on Windows, Mac OS/X and Linux; Internet oriented, adhering to standards such as OGC WMS, WFS, Web Coverage Service (WCS) and de facto geospatial web services such as GeoRSS, Keyhole Markup Language (KML) and tiles; and GIS ready, providing the framework on which complex analytical capabilities can be built and gradually subsuming those capabilities into the main application.

Thus, the integration of uDig as an open source GIS framework in Eclipse RCP based applications saves efforts on developing necessary GIS functionality and leverages the flexibility of the underlying Eclipse framework. However, Steiniger and Bocher (2009) also point out that there are two perceived disadvantages that result from the use of Eclipse RCP as the core component: The first disadvantage is the size of the application, and the second disadvantage is that the GUI is quite similar to the development environment for programming and thus, may be too complex for end users. On the positive side, the user and the developer documentation are very good, and the project management and software development processes are outlined and documented.

Using Eclipse RCP, the development of uDig started between 2004 and 2005 and has been initiated by Refractions Research Inc. in Canada, which also develops the spatial extension PostGIS for the PostgreSQL database (Steiniger & Bocher, 2009). Based on Eclipse RCP, uDig is developed in Java and was initially focused on the editing of vector data. However, since 2007 the uDig team has been joined by the JGrass team, which works on raster analysis functionality (Antonello & Francheschi, 2007). Besides JGrass, further projects are involved in the development. Because of the joint work of these projects and the possibility of using uDig as a frontend for the PostGIS database (which has already a very wide user base), the user and developer community grows consistently (Steiniger & Bocher, 2009). uDig is further developed and maintained at the present time under the Refraction Research and uDig user community to make it a better and more powerful application. This activity follows the vision to fill in functional gaps in the two technology communities: the open source geospatial community and the open standards geospatial community, as represented by OGC (Tress & Moestofa, 2009). To perform standardized operations for core GIS functionality such as data reading, coordinate re-projection, and rendering, uDig uses the well-established GeoTools library (Refractions, 2010b).

Open Source Java GIS Toolkit 'GeoTools'

GeoTools is a free, open source Java geospatial toolkit for working with both vector and raster data (GeoTools, 2010) and is a library that provides classes, objects, and methods required to implement standards conformant to geospatial applications (Santokhee, 2008). The library con-

sists of a large number of various modules that can be combined according to programmer needs (Santokhee, 2008) and that allow you to do the following: access GIS data in many file formats and spatial databases; work with an extensive range of map projections; filter and analyze data in terms of spatial and non-spatial attributes; compose and display maps with complex styling; and create and analyze graphs and networks (GeoTools, 2010). Santokhee (2008) reports that GeoTools can be readily extended by adding new modules, either for custom applications or as contributions to the library. GeoTools supports additional formats through the use of plug-ins. A developer can control the formats supported by the application by only including the plug-ins required. Thus, GeoTools can be used to build applications of many different types covering most processes of GISs, including network server applications and desktop clients. GeoTools leverages a modern, object oriented structure and uses common, well documented computational design patterns. The library consists of loosely dependent modules to present third party programmers with a coherent, easily usable code base. GeoTools implements the core global geospatial standards of the International Organization for Standardization (ISO) and of the OGC to ensure maximal interoperability with other geospatial software. GeoTools is a project that is growing continuously and breaking new grounds by implementing untested standards. The library is therefore still evolving to address weaknesses in certain areas, to implement new functionality, to work around defects in existing standards and to embrace newer standards when proposed. GeoTools provides almost no graphical user interface functionality. Thus developers planning applications that will depend on the library should carefully assess the relevant strengths and weaknesses of GeoTools.

Importantly, not only is GeoTools an open source Java GIS toolkit providing implementations of many OGC specifications as they are developed, but it also is associated with the GeoAPI project that creates geospatial Java interfaces (OSGEO, 2010).

GeoAPI's Java Language Programming Interfaces for Geospatial Applications

In 2003 the GeoTools project started an outreach program in the form of the GeoAPI project as an effort to collaborate with other projects working in the same domain and as a line of communication to the standards community (GeoTools, 2011). The GeoAPI provides a set of Java language programming interfaces which include many of the data structures and manipulation methods needed for GIS applications (OGC, 2011). It provides neutral, interface-only APIs derived from OGC and ISO standards to reduce duplication and to increase interoperability (Desruisseaux & Garnett, 2010). The need for a standardized set of programming interfaces that remains constant across different toolkits is reflected in GeoAPI's history, which includes an attempt for GeoAPI to become a standard. Desruisseaux et al. (2010) recollects that the GeoAPI project was initially an initiative of various open source communities wanting to reduce work duplication. The goal was to make it easier to exchange pieces of software between independent projects, so that a project does not need to reinvent functions already provided by another project. In 2004, GeoAPI merged with the GO-1 initiative from OGC. In September 2004, the creation of a GeoAPI working group has been approved by OGC voting members. In May 2005, the GO-1 final specification, which includes GeoAPI interfaces, finally, has been accepted as an OGC standard. Discussing why a standardized set of programming interfaces is required instead of the standardized OGC web services, Desruisseaux et al. (2010) proposes that web services are efficient ways to publish geographic information using existing software. However, some users need to build their own solution, for example as a wrapper on top of their own numerical model. Many

existing software packages provide sophisticated developer toolkits, but each toolkit has its own learning curve, and one cannot easily switch from one toolkit to another or mix components from different toolkits. Using standardized interfaces, a significant part of the API can remain constant across different toolkits, thus reducing both the learning curve and the interoperability challenges.

OGC (2011) summarizes that the GeoAPI interfaces closely follow the abstract model and concrete specifications published collaboratively by the ISO in its 19100 series of documents and the OGC in its abstract and implementation specifications. GeoAPI provides an interpretation and adaptation of these standards to match the expectations of Java programmers. These standards provide GeoAPI with the richness which comes from the expertise of the specification writers. Clients benefit from the potential for interoperability which comes from using a well-defined, standardized data model. Implementors benefit from having a pre-defined set of well-considered, formal boundaries to modularize their development work. So the GeoAPI interfaces provide a layer which separates client code, which would call the API, from library code, which implements the API. These interfaces are not an implementation. Clients can use the API without concern for the particular implementation which they will use. One of various groups, that have implemented different subsets of GeoAPI, is GeoTools introduced.

Java Programming Language and Computing Platform

Based on the use of available frameworks and libraries, the characteristics of the underlying technology used (i.e., Java) will be summarized, to outline the potentials of this technology for the future adoption of the CCUI in related EWS application domains.

Jendrock et al. (2006) argue that developers today increasingly recognize the need for distributed, transactional, and portable applications that leverage the speed, security, and reliability of server-side technology. In the world of information technology, enterprise applications must be designed, built, and produced for less money, with greater speed, and with fewer resources. With the Java EE platform, development of enterprise applications is easy and fast. The aim of the Java EE platform is to provide developers with a powerful set of APIs while reducing the development time, reducing the application complexity, and improving the application performance. Furthermore, Jendrock et al. (2010) adds that the Java EE platform is developed through the Java Community Process (JCP), which is responsible for all Java technologies. Expert groups, composed of interested parties, have created Java Specification Requests (JSRs) to define the various Java EE technologies. The work of the Java community under the JCP program helps to ensure Java technology's standard of stability and cross-platform compatibility.

Importantly, Java EE is platform independent and supports applications on various computing platforms ranging from super computers and enterprise servers on the one end to mobile and embedded devices on the other end. It is a de-facto industry standard for developing applications. Java EE is one of the most widely used technologies in its field. Finally, Java EE is free and supported by a large worldwide community and with lots of vendors in the information technology (IT) domain.

Generic CCUI Plug-Ins

The CCUI application framework introduced in Figure 1 is supplemented with required plug-ins (see Figure 1, Element 14). The core plug-in (see Figure 1, Element 15) provides core functionality for graphical parts of the application such as perspectives, views, and internal events. The configurations plug-in (see Figure 1, Element 16) contains the central configurations and settings

used to store all of the plug-in preferences, e.g., region and hazard dependent configurations for the different setups depicted in Figures 2 through 4. The libraries plug-in (see Figure 1, Element 17) contains the libraries accessed by other plug-ins, e.g., to work with standards such as CAP, EDXL-DE and SOAP. Further plug-ins provide functionalities to be used optionally (see Figure 1, Element 18) by other plug-ins built on top. For example, the AspenCloud widgets (see Figure 1, Element 19) extend the available Standard Widget Toolkit (SWT) widgets integrated in Eclipse RCP and thus form a new widget with an entirely new capacity, meeting the specific requirements of the CCUI, which are related to time management. Another optional plug-in named gazetteer (see Figure 1, Element 20) contributes to the main application by providing access to a gazetteer service to assist the operator in the task of navigating around the map by typing a location name and centering the map on its coordinates. Other optional plug-ins might be integrated if desired.

EWS Specific CCUI Plug-Ins

The application plug-in (see Figure 1, Element 21) is based on the introduced application framework, the required plug-ins and the optional plug-ins. The application plug-in is the plug-in from which the application is started and which forms the basis for specific EWS implementation. On the basis of the described layers of the CCUI framework, EWS specifics are implemented by further plug-ins. Special purpose plug-ins (see Figure 1, Element 22) extend functionality, for example, with extensions to the GeoTools library (see Figure 1, Element 23) and required messaging functionality for communication (see Figure 1, Element 24). Standards defined by the OGC are covered by OGC specific plug-ins (see Figure 1, Element 25). uDig already provides the required functionality to communicate via WMS and WFS (see Figure 1, Element 26). However, other functionalities to access sensors via SWE (see Figure 1, Element 27) and to instruct geospatial processing via WPS (see Figure 1, Element 28) are added by further plug-ins.

Hazard Specific CCUI Plug-Ins

Additional sensor specific plug-ins (see Figure 1, Element 29) such as the Tsunami Service Bus (TSB) plug-in (see Figure 1, Element 30) and the earthquake (see Figure 1, Element 31) and sea level (see Figure 1, Element 32) plug-ins extend the generic and standardized access covering system and hazard specifics (see Figure 1, Element 33), in this case for earthquake and sea level monitoring. Further hazard specifics and convenience functionality might be provided by other plug-ins such as the tsunami functionalities plug-in (see Figure 1, Element 34), which provides specific functionality to deal with aspects related to tsunami risks in a geospatial EWS for tsunami warning and mitigation. Also, the already introduced perspectives that reveal the functionality of one or more operators on duty are hazard specific plug-ins that expose graphically the required and implemented functionality.

Realization as Desktop GIS Preferred to WebGIS

The CCUI is developed as a Desktop GIS utilizing an open standards based Service Oriented Architecture (SOA) with the adoption of free and open source technologies, software and frameworks, as discussed earlier. This section outlines briefly why the Desktop GIS approach has been applied.

Nalani (2009) explains that the rapid growth of the Internet has led to an increasing concern over the WebGIS approach, with the World Wide Web (WWW) offering new application areas. This approach provides access to geographic information via the WWW and is used to distribute information to potentially numerous users. Because of the considerable interest in geospatial data visu-

alization through web services that employ GIS the widespread availability of internet and related services such as WWW technology have been widely applied in geospatial data visualization and in providing the infrastructure to allow wide access to geo-referenced data or GIS services. Further, these technologies provide an advanced means to assist with visual data exploration and spatial decision making systems in the context of landslides, earthquakes, flood modeling and debris flow.

Additionally, Siddiquee et al. (2009) state that the WebGIS is comparatively new but is a very fast growing sub-set of GIS. WebGIS is achieving particular significance for spatial data handling over the web. In other words, WebGIS are used for distributing and processing geographic information via the Internet and the WWW. It is attaining increasing momentum and acceptability for different levels of users, such as geospatial data handlers and producers as well as governmental and non-governmental agencies. Because the WebGIS is platform independent, this capability reduces the necessity for purchasing costly Desktop GIS software. WebGIS then refers to GIS that uses web technologies as a method for communication between the elements of a GIS (Avraam, 2009).

However, the WhereGroup (2010) argues that Desktop GIS enables a wide range of users to process geospatial data and to utilize a wealth of geospatial functionality based on comparatively cheap and readily available Personal Computers (PCs). Over time, Desktop GIS has become a typical example that represents a tendency to move from powerful centralized computing hardware to decentralized networks of PCs for geo-data processing. With the introduction of distributed architectures and web based processing services, the use of geospatial data has moved from its limited traditional application areas to a mainstream source of information. At the same time, the relevance of stand-alone Desktop GIS products is steadily declining. While the total number of installed seats is more or less stable, most Desktop GIS now plug into service oriented SDIs as data sources and thus combine the advantages of local processing capabilities with distributed architectures. In this regard, Avraam (2009) summarizes that the interaction between the components is usually very direct in Desktop GIS. Data, maps and analysis happen on the same computer, so communication is done internally. Enterprise Desktop GIS often allows the user to communicate with data remotely, and sometimes even analysis is performed remotely. WebGIS enables the communication of all components to happen through the web, enabling diverse data, analysis algorithms, users and visualization techniques that may be hosted at any location on the web.

Summarizing the WebGIS approach, there is a major focus on cloud computing (Armbrust et al., 2009) in which the Desktop GIS approach changes dramatically from a traditional monolithic desktop application, accessing a few remote services only, to a desktop application that provides access to both integrated functionality and distributed services on servers and the cloud. With the increasing performance of accessing network nodes in the WWW and the growing availability of widespread services in the cloud, a modern GIS has to support the access and usage of distributed services to be suitable for the future. However, cloud computing is still an emerging approach in its current state, and does not cover professional requirements that need to be met to be implemented in (enterprise) Desktop GIS. Apparently, WebGIS solutions do not provide the large amount of professional functionalities today provided by Desktop GIS solutions. Also, Web-GIS solutions are often specialized applications with single components in what is termed GIS, providing limited functionality tailored to specific and not extensive application fields. Moreover, limited web mapping applications accessing the so-called GeoWeb (Leclerc et al., 2001) are often misleadingly described as WebGIS. Finally, a major drawback of the cloud dependent WebGIS is that the response time can be long, depending on a number of factors, such as connection capacity, data volume, network traffic, and processor power (Bonnici, 2005). Thus, an application specific GIS such as an EWS for tsunamis should implement a Desktop GIS approach based on a geo framework that provides both access to distributed services and access to integrated functionality, allowing utilization of the appropriate functionality based on the required needs.

DEVELOPMENT AND RESEARCH CONTINUED AS FOSS INITIATIVE

Löwe et al. (2011) summarize that all developments of the CCUI are based to the largest extent on FOSS components and industry standards. They announce that emphasis has been and will be made on leveraging open source technologies that support mature system architecture models wherever appropriate. All open source software produced is foreseen to be published on FOSSLAB, a publicly available software repository provided by the Centre for GeoInformation Technology (CeGIT) of the GFZ German Research Centre for Geosciences. FOSSLAB is a platform for the development of FOSS projects in a geospatial context, allowing users to save, advance and reuse results achieved in previous and on-going project activities and enabling further development and collaboration with a wide community including scientists, developers, users and stakeholders. Furthermore, FOSSLAB constitutes an umbrella encompassing a number of related geoinformatic activities, such as the documentation of best practices for working experiences and results with SDIs, GIS, spatial processing on clusters and in clouds, and geomatics related topics.

APPLICATIONS

In this regard, readers interested in the ideas covered in this paper and readers who want to make use of those ideas in constructive ways are enabled to act on or apply those ideas by firstly visiting the related FOSSLAB sub-projects at www.fosslab. org. Secondly, using the products and results offered by the FOSSLAB sub-projects, asking and answering questions, reporting bugs and making feature requests are critical parts of the projects' communities. Still only a few key persons represent the communities in small, gradually evolving groups and provide instructions successively and on request. It is the user feedback which can strongly drive the projects and the technologies. Beyond the user activities, it would be greatly appreciated getting help with the development of the projects. This can mean getting involved with the discussions on the development mailing lists, answering user questions, providing patches for bug-fixes or features, and helping to improve the documentation.

In this context it is important to mention that behind the work presented here various software components form the overall system by providing the required data and services, which finally expose their information and functionality to an operator on duty (OOD) with the CCUI. These required software components have to be built, deployed and configured appropriately on an operating system (OS) with other suitably installed FOSS before the CCUI can be used. Based on activities in the DEWS successor TRIDEC stable versions of these components, used in the problem domain of natural crisis management for tsunamis, are bundled irregularly together with the pre-installed OS on a raw disk image to be used with many virtualization software packages. Alternatively, there is the opportunity to download these components, publicly shared on the FOSSLAB sub-projects one by one, and to install them with the help of available instructions.

and exposes the generic framework designed and developed in conjunction with the realization of the CCUI. Specifically, the user interface framework presented for early warning systems is an attempt to provide an appropriate and useful concept for the business of public safety, emergency management and homeland security. The concept presented is independent of a specific hazard domain, thus provides a generic solution for specific applications in the area of EWS and might be adopted in other systems for managing natural and man-made hazards. Within DEWS and TRIDEC, the designed concepts have been realized and implemented as generic software components validated and approved by different interest groups in several project-internal and public live-demonstrations, demonstrating the complete early warning system prototype including the CCUI as a concept for an adaptable and extensible user interface for early warning systems (Lendholt & Hammitzsch, 2011). In this regard, Hammitzsch et al. (2012) assert that the overall system, including the CCUI and its framework, has received preliminary evaluation by the stakeholders and domain experts and is currently under further development. More extensive evaluation and revision of this system is expected to be completed in the future with multiple experts from research and government agencies offering their opinions on the system. Through open-ended survey questions, the requirements of the system have to be controlled and successively refined. In addition, the unique benefits of the system in providing a FOSS multi hazard framework concept implementation, and the relevance of the approach followed here should be affirmed by the respective stakeholders. Finally, decision-makers in local and regional authorities already have expressed interest in the system (ICT, 2010).

CONCLUSION

This paper covers the investigation and results of selecting the appropriate GUI and geospatial frameworks for the implementation of the CCUI

ACKNOWLEDGMENT

The work presented in this paper is part of the research and development in the DEWS project (contract no. 045453), partially funded by the 6th

Framework Program of the European Commission. DEWS is based on the collective creativity, idealism and optimism of a global community sharing achievements of performed work and findings with free and open source licenses. Thus, it is not possible to acknowledge all of the individuals and institutions that have contributed. The author would like to express his sincere thanks to all of those who contributed towards the development of DEWS and its CCUI by providing the vital foundations with their efforts and collectively shared results. Further findings and developments are conducted within the TRIDEC project (contract no. 258723), partially supported by the 7th Framework Program of the European Commission. The author is grateful to the anonymous reviewers for their comments, which have helped to improve the earlier version of this paper.

REFERENCES

Aniszczyk, C. (2010). *Eclipse IDE project resources*. Retrieved October 31, 2010, from http://www.ibm.com/developerworks/opensource/top-projects/eclipse/eclipse-starthere.html

Annan, K. A. (2006). Foreword to the global survey of early warning systems. In *Proceedings of the Third International Conference on Global Survey of Early Warning Systems*, Bonn, Germany.

Armbrust, M., Fox, A., Griffith, R., Joseph, A. D., Katz, R. H., & Konwinski, A. …Zaharia, M. (2009). *Above the clouds: A Berkeley view of cloud computing*. Retrieved December 27, 2011, from http://www.eecs.berkeley.edu/Pubs/TechRpts/2009/EECS-2009-28.html

Ashcroft, J., Daniels, D. J., & Hart, S. V. (2002). *Crisis Information Management Software (CIMS) feature comparison report*. Washington, DC: National Institute of Justice.

Avraam, M. (2009). *Geoweb: Web mapping and web GIS*. Retrieved November 3, 2010, from http://michalisavraam.org/2009/03/geoweb-web-mapping-and-web-gis/

Badard, T., & Braun, A. (2003). OXYGENE: An open framework for the deployment of geographic web services. In *Proceedings of the 21st International Cartographic Conference*, Durban, South Africa.

Bonnici, A. M. (2005). *Web GIS software comparison framework*. Retrieved November 8, 2010, from http://www.webgisdev.com/webgis_framework.pdf

Buliung, R. N., & Remmel, T. K. (2008). Open source, spatial analysis, and activity-travel behaviour research: Capabilities of the aspace package. *Journal of Geographical Systems*, *10*(2), 191–216. doi:10.1007/s10109-008-0063-7

Burghardt, D., Neun, M., & Weibel, R. (2005). Generalization services on the web – classification and an initial prototype implementation. *Cartography and Geographic Information Science*, *32*(4), 257–268. doi:10.1559/152304005775194665

Chen, R., Thiyagarajan, T., Rao, R. H., & Lee, J. K. (2010). Design of a FOSS system for flood disaster management. In *Proceedings of the 7th International Conference on Information Systems for Crisis Response and Management*, Seattle, WA.

Desruisseaux, M., & Garnett, J. (2010). *Home*. Retrieved October 31, 2010, from http://docs.codehaus.org/display/GEO/Home

Desruisseaux, M., Garnett, J., et al. (2010). *FAQ*. Retrieved October 31, 2010, from http://docs.codehaus.org/display/GEO/FAQ

DEWS. (2010). *Distant early warning system*. Retrieved December 17, 2011, from http://www.dews-online.org

GeoTools. (2010). *GeoTools user guide frequently asked questions*. Retrieved October 29, 2010, from http://docs.geotools.org/stable/userguide/faq.html

GeoTools. (2011). *End of GeoAPI involvement*. Retrieved December 18, 2011, from http://geotoolsnews.blogspot.com/2011/01/end-of-geoapi-involvement.html

Hammitzsch, M., Lendholt, M., & Esbrí, M. A. (2012). User interface prototype for geospatial early warning systems – a tsunami showcase. *Natural Hazards and Earth System Sciences*, *12*, 555–573. doi:10.5194/nhess-12-555-2012

Hammitzsch, M., Lendholt, M., & Wächter, J. (2010). Distant early warning system for tsunamis – A wide-area and multi-hazard approach. In *Proceedings of the Conference of the European Geosciences Union: Vol. 12. Geophysical Research Abstracts*. Retrieved August 17, 2010, from http://meetingorganizer.copernicus.org/EGU2010/EGU2010-4496.pdf

Irawan, H., McCrary, T., Barbareau, L., et al. (2010). *RCP FAQ*. Retrieved October 31, 2010, from http://wiki.eclipse.org/index.php/RCP_FAQ#Why_should_I_build_my_application_on_the_Eclipse_Rich_Client_Platform.3F

Irawan, H., Vogel, L., Ebert, R., et al. (2009). *Rich client platform*. Retrieved October 31, 2010, from http://wiki.eclipse.org/index.php/Rich_Client_Platform

Jendrock, E., Ball, J., Carson, D., Evans, I., Fordin, S., & Haase, K. (2006). *The Java EE 5 tutorial: For Sun Java System Application Server Platform Edition 9* (Java Series). Upper Saddle River, NJ: Prentice Hall.

Jendrock, E., Evans, I., Gollapudi, D., Haase, K., & Srivathsa, C. (2010). *The Java EE 6 tutorial 1: Basic concepts (Java Series)*. Upper Saddle River, NJ: Prentice Hall.

Leclerc, Y., Reddy, M., Iverson, L., & Heller, A. (2001). The GeoWeb - A new paradigm for finding data on the Web. In *Proceedings of the International Cartographic Conference*, Beijing, China.

Lee, M. (2011). *What is free software and why is it so important for society?* Retrieved June 13, 2011, from http://www.fsf.org/about/what-is-free-software

Lendholt, M., & Hammitzsch, M. (2011). Generic information logistics for early warning systems. In *Proceedings of the 8th International Conference on Information Systems for Crisis Response and Management*, Lisbon, Portugal.

Löwe, P., Hammitzsch, M., & Lendholt, M. (2011, May 19-20). *Significance of FOSSGIS in the TRIDEC Project*. Paper presented at the Conference of Geoinformatics, Prague, Czech Republic. Retrieved June 11, 2011, from http://geoinformatics.fsv.cvut.cz/gwiki/Significance_of_FOSSGIS_in_the_TRIDEC_Project

Mitasova, H., & Neteler, M. (2004). GRASS as an open source free software GIS: Accomplishments and perspectives. *Transactions in GIS*, *8*(2), 145–154. doi:10.1111/j.1467-9671.2004.00172.x

Nalani, H. A. (2009). WebGIS based 3D visualization of geospatial data. In *Proceedings of the Applied Geoinformatics for Society and Environment Conference*, Stuttgart, Germany (pp. 212-215). Retrieved November 3, 2010, from http://www.gis-news.de/papers/AGSE_Proceedings_2009_07_01_1025.pdf

OGC. (2011). *GeoAPI*. Retrieved December 18, 2011, from http://www.geoapi.org

OSGEO. (2010). *GeoTools InfoSheet*. Retrieved October 31, 2010, from http://www.osgeo.org/geotools

Ozel, N. M., Necmioglu, O., Yalciner, A. C., Kalafat, D., Yilmazer, M., & Comoglu, M. ... Erdik, M. (forthcoming, June 17-22). *Tsunami early warning in the Eastern Mediterranean, Aegean and Black Sea*. Paper to be presented at the 22nd International Ocean and Polar Engineering Conference, Rhodes (Rodos), Greece.

Pebesma, E. J. (2004). Multivariable geostatistics in S: The gstat package. *Computers & Geosciences*, *30*(7), 683–691. doi:10.1016/j.cageo.2004.03.012

Raape, U., Teßmann, S., Wytzisk, A., Steinmetz, T., Wnuk, M., & Hunold, M. ...Jirka, S. (2010). Decision support for tsunami early warning in Indonesia: The role of OGC standards. In M. Konecny, T. L. Bandrova, & S. Zlatanova (Eds.), *Geographic information and cartography for risk and crisis management* (Vol. 2, pp. 233-247). Berlin, Germany: Springer-Verlag.

Ramsey, P. (2007). *The state of open source GIS*. Paper presented at the annual Free and Open Source Software for Geospatial Conference, Vancouver, BC, Canada.

Refractions Research. (2010a). *A GIS framework for eclipse*. Retrieved October 31, 2010, from http://udig.refractions.net/

Refractions Research. (2010b). *Developing with uDig*. Retrieved October 31, 2010, from http://udig.refractions.net/developers/

Reid, J., & Martin, F. (2001). *The open source movement and its potential in implementing spatial data infrastructures*. Paper presented at the International Symposium on Spatial Data Infrastructure, Melbourne, Australia.

Results, I. C. T. (2010). *New tsunami early warning system stands guard*. Retrieved August 17, 2010, from http://cordis.europa.eu/ictresults/index.cfm?tpl=article&ID=91371

Santokhee, A. (2008). *GeoTools*. Retrieved June 13, 2011, from http://www.resc.rdg.ac.uk/twiki/bin/view/Resc/GeoTools

Siddiquee, Z. H., Strzalka, A., & Eicker, U. (2009). Publication of energy consumption data of Scharnhauser Park via Web GIS. In *Proceedings of the Conference of the Applied Geoinformatics for Society and Environment*, Stuttgart, Germany (pp. 186-190). Retrieved November 3, 2010, from http://www.gis-news.de/papers/AGSE_Proceedings_2009_07_01_1025.pdf

Steiniger, S., & Bocher, E. (2009). An overview on current free and open source desktop GIS developments. *International Journal of Geographical Information Science*, *23*(10), 1345–1370. doi:10.1080/13658810802634956

Tress, S., & Moestofa, A. (2009). uDig – An overview of open source desktop GIS application. In *Proceedings of the Conference of the Applied Geoinformatics for Society and Environment*, Stuttgart, Germany.

TRIDEC. (2010). *Collaborative, complex, and critical decision processes in evolving crises*. Retrieved December 17, 2011, from http://www.tridec-online.eu

UN. (2006). Global survey of early warning systems. In *Proceedings of the Third International Conference on Early Warning*, Bonn, Germany.

Wächter, J., Fleischer, J., Häner, R., Küppers, A., Lendholt, M., & Hammitzsch, M. (2011). Development of tsunami early warning systems and future challenges. In *Proceedings of the Conference of the European Geosciences Union: Vol. 13. Geophysical Research Abstracts*. Retrieved December 17, 2011, from http://meetingorganizer.copernicus.org/EGU2011/EGU2011-11015-2.pdf

WhereGroup. (2010). *Desktop GIS*. Retrieved November 3, 2010, from http://www.wheregroup.com/en/desktop_gis

Compilation of References

Aberdour, M. (2007). Achieving quality in open source software. *IEEE Software*, *24*(1), 58–64. doi:10.1109/MS.2007.2

Abi-Antoun, M., Aldrich, J., & Coelho, W. (2007). A case study in re-engineering to enforce architectural control flow and data sharing. *Journal of Systems and Software*, *80*(2), 240–264. doi:10.1016/j.jss.2006.10.036

Adams, P. J., Capiluppi, A., & Boldyreff, C. (2009). Coordination and productivity issues in free software: The role of brooks' law. In *Proceedings of the International Conference on Software Maintenance* (pp. 319-328). Washington, DC: IEEE Computer Society.

Ågerfalk, P. J., Deverell, A., Fitzgerald, B., & Morgan, L. (2005). Assessing the role of open source software in the European secondary software sector: A voice from industry. In *Proceedings of the First International Conference on Open Source Systems*, Genova, Italy.

Agruss, C. (2000). Software installation testing - how to automate tests for smooth system installation. *Software Testing & Quality Engineering*, 32-37.

Ahmed, S. M. Z. (2008). A comparison of usability techniques for evaluating information retrieval system interfaces. *Performance Measurement and Metrics*, *9*(1), 48–58. doi:10.1108/14678040810869422

Ajila, S. A., & Wu, D. (2007). Empirical study of the effects of open source adoption on software development economics. *Journal of Systems and Software*, *80*(9), 1517–1529. doi:10.1016/j.jss.2007.01.011

Aksulu, A., & Wade, M. (2010). A comprehensive review and synthesis of open source research. *Journal of the Association for Information Systems*, *11*, 576–656.

Alspaugh, T. A., Asuncion, H. A., & Scacchi, W. (2009, September). Intellectual property rights requirements for heterogeneously licensed systems. In *Proceedings of the 17th International Conference on Requirements Engineering*, Atlanta, GA (pp. 24-33).

Alspaugh, T. A., Scacchi, W., & Asuncion, H. A. (2010). Software licenses in context: The challenge of heterogeneously licensed systems. *Journal of the Association for Information Systems*, *11*(11), 730–755.

Ambrose, M. L., & Kulik, C. T. (1999). Old friends, new faces: Motivation research in the 1990s. *Journal of Management*, *25*(3), 231–292. doi:10.1177/014920639902500302

Amit, R., & Zott, C. (2001). Value creation in e-business. *Strategic Management Journal*, *22*(6-7), 493–520. doi:10.1002/smj.187

Andreasen, M., Nielsen, H., Schrøder, S., & Stage, J. (2006). Usability in open source software development: Opinions and practice. *Information Technology and Control*, *5*(3A), 303–312.

Aniszczyk, C. (2010). *Eclipse IDE project resources*. Retrieved October 31, 2010, from http://www.ibm.com/developerworks/opensource/top-projects/eclipse/eclipse-starthere.html

Annan, K. A. (2006). Foreword to the global survey of early warning systems. In *Proceedings of the Third International Conference on Global Survey of Early Warning Systems*, Bonn, Germany.

Anvik, J., Hiew, L., & Murphy, G. (2006). *Who should fix this bug? 28th international conference on Software engineering* (pp. 361–370). New York, NY, USA: ACM.

Arkin, B., Stender, S., & McGraw, G. (2005). Software penetration testing. *IEEE Security and Privacy*, *3*(1), 84–87. doi:10.1109/MSP.2005.23

Armbrust, M., Fox, A., Griffith, R., Joseph, A. D., Katz, R. H., & Konwinski, A. ...Zaharia, M. (2009). *Above the clouds: A Berkeley view of cloud computing*. Retrieved December 27, 2011, from http://www.eecs.berkeley.edu/Pubs/TechRpts/2009/EECS-2009-28.html

Arnold, H. J. (1981). A test of the validity of the multiplicative hypothesis of expectancy-valence theories of work motivation. *Academy of Management Journal*, *24*(1), 128–141. doi:10.2307/255828

Ashcroft, J., Daniels, D. J., & Hart, S. V. (2002). *Crisis Information Management Software (CIMS) feature comparison report*. Washington, DC: National Institute of Justice.

Assault Cube. (n.d.). *Licensing information*. Retrieved April 13, 2011, from from http://assault.cubers.net/docs/license.html

Association for Information Systems. (2011). *Senor scholars' basket of journals*. Retrieved from http://home.aisnet.org/displaycommon.cfm?an=1&subarticlenbr=346

Attewell, P. (1992). Technology diffusion and organizational learning: The case of business computing. *Organization Science*, *3*(1), 1–19. doi:10.1287/orsc.3.1.1

Au, Y. A., Carpenter, D., Chen, X., & Clark, J. G. (2009). Virtual organizational learning in open source software development projects. *Information & Management*, *46*(1), 9–15. doi:10.1016/j.im.2008.09.004

Avgeriou, P., & Guelfi, N. (2005). Resolving architectural mismatches of COTS through architectural reconciliation. In X. Franch & D. Port (Eds.), *Proceedings of the 4th International Conference on COTS-Based Software Systems* (LNCS 3412, pp. 248-257).

Avraam, M. (2009). *Geoweb: Web mapping and web GIS*. Retrieved November 3, 2010, from http://michalisavraam.org/2009/03/geoweb-web-mapping-and-web-gis/

Avritzer, A., Paulish, D., & Cai, Y. (2008). Coordination implications of software architecture in a global software development project. *Seventh Working IEEE/IFIP Conference on Software Architecture (WICSA 2008)* (pp. 107–116). Washington, DC, USA: IEEE Computer Society.

Ayala, C., Sørensen, C., Conradi, R., Franch, X., & Li, J. (2007). Open source collaboration for fostering off-the-shelf components selection . In Feller, J., Fitzgerald, B., Scacchi, W., & Sillitti, A. (Eds.), *Open source development, adoption, and innovation*. New York, NY: Springer. doi:10.1007/978-0-387-72486-7_2

Bachmann, A., & Bernstein, A. (2009). Software process data quality and characteristics: A historical view on open and closed source projects. In *Proceedings of the Joint International and Annual ERCIM Workshops on Principles of Software Evolution and the Software Evolution Workshops*, Amsterdam, The Netherlands (pp. 119-128).

Badard, T., & Braun, A. (2003). OXYGENE: An open framework for the deployment of geographic web services. In *Proceedings of the 21st International Cartographic Conference*, Durban, South Africa.

Baldwin, C. Y., & Clark, K. B. (2006). The architecture of participation: Does code architecture mitigate free riding in the open source development model? *Management Science*, *52*(7), 1116–1127. doi:10.1287/mnsc.1060.0546

Barbagallo, D., Francalenei, C., & Merlo, F. (2008). The impact of social networking on software design quality and development effort in open source projects. In *Proceedings of the International Conference on Information Systems*.

Barclay, D., Thompson, R., & Higgins, C. (1995). The partial least square approach to causal modeling: Personal computer adoption and use as an illustration. *Technology Studies*, *2*(2), 285–309.

Basili, V. R., & Rombach, H. D. (1991). Support for comprehensive reuse. *IEEE Software Engineering Journal*, *6*(5), 303–316.

Bass, L., Clements, P., & Kazman, R. (2003). *Software architecture in practice* (2nd ed.). Reading, MA: Addison-Wesley.

Batory, D., Johnson, C., MacDonald, B., & von Heeder, D. (2002). Achieving extensibility through product lines and domain specific languages: A case study. *ACM Transactions on Software Engineering and Methodology, 11*(2), 191–214. doi:10.1145/505145.505147

Beaver, J., Cui, X., St Charles, J., & Potok, T. (2009). Modeling success in floss project groups. *Proceedings of the 5th International Conference on Predictor Models in Software Engineering*, (pp. 1-8).

Bellard, F. (2006). *Ffmpeg naming and logo*. Retrieved from FFmpeg mailing list: lists.mplayerhq.hu/pipermail/ffmpeg-devel/2006-February/

Bellini, E., Canfora, G., Garcia, F., Piattini, M., & Visaggio, C. (2005). Pair designing as practice for enforcing and diffusion design software. *Journal of Software Maintenance and Evolution: Research and Practice, 17*(6), 401–423. doi:10.1002/smr.322

Benbasat, I., Goldstein, D. K., & Mead, M. (1987). The case research strategy in studies of information systems. *Management Information Systems Quarterly, 11*(3), 368–386. doi:10.2307/248684

Benlian, A., & Hess, T. (2010). Comparing the relative importance of evaluation criteria in proprietary and open-source enterprise application software selection a conjoint study of ERP and office systems. *Information Systems Journal*.

Bernhard, P. J. (1994). A reduced test suite for protocol conformance testing. *ACM Transactions on Software Engineering and Methodology, 3*(3), 201–220. doi:10.1145/196092.196088

Biehl, J., Czerwinski, M., Smith, G., & Robertson, G. (2007). Fastdash: A visual dashboard for fostering awareness in software teams. *SIGCHI conference on Human Factors in computing systems*, (pp. 1313–1322). San Jose, California, USA.

Biffl, S., Sunindyo, W. D., & Moser, T. (2010a). A project monitoring cockpit based on integrating data sources in open source software development. In *Proceedings of the 22nd International Conference on Software Engineering and Knowledge Engineering*, San Francisco, CA (pp. 620-627).

Biffl, S., Sunindyo, W. D., & Moser, T. (2010b). Semantic integration of heterogeneous data sources for monitoring frequent-release software projects. In *Proceedings of the 4th International Conference on Complex, Intelligent and Software Intensive Systems*, Krakow, Poland (pp. 360-367).

Bitzer, J., Schrettl, W., & Schroder, P. J. H. (2007). Intrinsic motivation in open source software development. *Journal of Comparative Economics, 35*(1), 160–169. doi:10.1016/j.jce.2006.10.001

Bodker, M., Nielsen, L., & Orngreen, R. N. (2007). Enabling user centered design processes in open source communities, usability and internationalization, HCI and culture. In *Proceedings of the 2nd International Conference on Usability and Internationalization held as part of the HCI International Conference Part I* (pp. 10-18).

Boehm, B. W., Brown, J. R., & Lipow, M. (1976). Quantitative evaluation of software quality. In *Proceedings of the 2nd International Conference on Software Engineering* (pp. 592-605).

Boezeman, E. J., & Ellemers, N. (2008). Pride and respect in volunteers' organizational commitment. *European Journal of Social Psychology, 38*, 159–172. doi:10.1002/ejsp.415

Bollen, K. A. (1989). *Structural equations with latent variables*. New York, NY: John Wiley & Sons.

Bonaccorsi, A., & Rossi, C. (2003). Why open source software can succeed. *Research Policy, 32*(7), 1243–1258. doi:10.1016/S0048-7333(03)00051-9

Bonaccorsi, A., & Rossi, C. (2006). Comparing motivations of individual programmers and firms to take part in the open source movement. *Knowledge, Technology & Policy, 18*(4), 40–64. doi:10.1007/s12130-006-1003-9

Bonaccorsi, A., Rossi, C., & Giannangeli, S. (2006). Adaptive entry strategies under dominant standards: Hybrid business models in the Open Source Software Industry. *Management Science, 52*, 1085–1098. doi:10.1287/mnsc.1060.0547

Bonnici, A. M. (2005). *Web GIS software comparison framework*. Retrieved November 8, 2010, from http://www.webgisdev.com/webgis_framework.pdf

Bouktif, S., Antoniol, G., Merlo, E., & Neteler, M. (2006). A feedback based quality assessment to support open source software evolution: the grass case study. *Proceedings of the 22nd IEEE International Conference on Software Maintenance*, (pp. 155–165).

Bowman, I. T., Holt, R. C., & Brewster, N. V. (1999). Linux as a case study: Its extracted software architecture. In *Proceedings of the 21st International Conference on Software Engineering* (pp. 555-563).

Boynton, A. C., Zmud, R. W., & Jacobs, G. C. (1994). The influence of IT management practice on IT use in large corporations. *Management Information Systems Quarterly*, *18*(3), 299–318. doi:10.2307/249620

Brickman, P. (1987). *Commitment, conflict, and caring*. Upper Saddle River, NJ: Prentice Hall.

Brügge, B., & Dutoit, A. (1997). Communication metrics for software development. In *Proceedings of the 19th International Conference on Software Engineering* (pp. 271-281).

Buliung, R. N., & Remmel, T. K. (2008). Open source, spatial analysis, and activity-travel behaviour research: Capabilities of the aspace package. *Journal of Geographical Systems*, *10*(2), 191–216. doi:10.1007/s10109-008-0063-7

Burghardt, D., Neun, M., & Weibel, R. (2005). Generalization services on the web – classification and an initial prototype implementation. *Cartography and Geographic Information Science*, *32*(4), 257–268. doi:10.1559/152304005775194665

Burnett, M., Cook, C., & Rothermel, G. (2004). End-user software engineering. *Communications of the ACM*, *47*(9), 53–58. doi:10.1145/1015864.1015889

Burnstein, I., Suwanassart, T., & Carlson, R. (1996). Developing a Testing Maturity Model for software test process evaluation and improvement. In *Proceedings of the IEEE International Test Conference* (pp. 581-589).

Canfora, G., Cerulo, L., & Penta, M. D. (2007). Identifying changed source code lines from version repositories. In *Proceedings of the Fourth International Workshop on Mining Software Repositories* (p. 14). Washington, DC: IEEE Computer Society.

Capiluppi, A., & Boldyreff, C. (2008). Identifying and improving reusability based on coupling patterns. In H. Mei (Ed.), *Proceedings of the 10th International Conference on Software Reuse: High Confidence Software Reuse in Large Systems* (LNCS 5030, pp. 282-293).

Capiluppi, A., & Fernandez-Ramil, J. (2007). A model to predict anti-regressive effort in open source software. *Proceedings of the IEEE International Conference on Software Maintenance*, (pp. 194–203).

Capiluppi, A., & Knowles, T. (2009). Software engineering in practice: Design and architectures of FLOSS systems. In *Proceedings of the 5th IFIP WG 2.13 International Conference on Advances in Information and Communication Technology* (Vol. 299, pp. 34-46).

Capiluppi, A., Baravalle, A., & Heap, N. (2010). Open standards and e-learning: the role of open source software. In *Proceedings of the 6th International Conference on Open Source Systems,* Notre Dame, IN.

Capra, E., Francalanci, C., & Merlo, F. (2008). An empirical study on the relationship among software design quality, development effort, and governance in open source projects. *IEEE Transactions on Software Engineering*, *34*(6), 765–782. doi:10.1109/TSE.2008.68

Capra, E., & Wasserman, A. I. (2008). A framework for evaluating managerial styles in open source projects. *IFIP International Federation for Information Processing*, *275*, 1–14. doi:10.1007/978-0-387-09684-1_1

Carini, R. M., Hayek, J. C., Kuh, G. D., Kennedy, J. M., & Ouimet, J. A. (2001). *College student responses to web and paper surveys: Does mode matter?* Paper presented at the 41st Annual Forum of the Association for Institutional Research, Long Beach, CA.

Carrington, P., Scott, J., & Wasserman, S. (2005). *Models and methods in social network analysis*. Cambridge University press.

Carroll, J., & Swatman, P. (2000). Structured-case: A methodological framework for building theory in information systems research. *European Journal of Information Systems*, *9*, 235–242. doi:10.1057/palgrave/ejis/3000374

Cavano, J. P., & McCall, J. A. (1978). A framework for the measurement of software quality. In *Proceedings of the ACM Software Quality Workshop* (pp. 133-139).

Çetin, G., & Göktürk, M. (2008). A measurement based framework for assessment of usability-centricness of open source software projects. In *Proceedings of the IEEE International Conference on Signal Image Technology and Internet Based Systems* (pp. 585-592).

Chacon, F., Vecina, M. L., & Davila, M. C. (2007). The three-stage model of volunteers' duration of service. *Social Behavior and Personality*, *35*(5), 627–642. doi:10.2224/sbp.2007.35.5.627

Chen, R., Thiyagarajan, T., Rao, R. H., & Lee, J. K. (2010). Design of a FOSS system for flood disaster management. In *Proceedings of the 7th International Conference on Information Systems for Crisis Response and Management*, Seattle, WA.

Chen, K., Schach, S. R., Yu, L., Offutt, J., & Heller, G. Z. (2004). Opensource change logs. *Empirical Software Engineering*, *9*(3), 147–262. doi:10.1023/B:EMSE.0000027779.70556.d0

Chesbrough, H., & Rosenbloom, R. S. (2002). The role of the business model in capturing value from innovation: Evidence from Xerox Corporation's technology spin-off companies. *Industrial and Corporate Change*, *11*(3), 529–555. doi:10.1093/icc/11.3.529

Chin, W. W. (1998). The partial least squares approach to structural equation modeling. In Marcoulides, G. A. (Ed.), *Modern methods for business research* (pp. 295–336). Mahwah, NJ: Lawrence Erlbaum.

Choi, N., Chengalur-Smith, I., & Whitmore, A. (2010). Managing first impressions of new open source software projects. *IEEE Software*, *27*(6), 73–77. doi:10.1109/MS.2010.26

Chrusch, M. (2000). The whiteboard: Seven great myths of usability. *Interaction*, *7*(5), 13–16. doi:10.1145/345242.345251

Clary, E. G., Snyder, M., Ridge, R. D., Copeland, J., Stukas, A. A., Haugen, J., & Miene, P. (1998). Understanding and assessing the motivations of volunteers: A functional approach. *Journal of Personality and Social Psychology*, *74*(6), 1516–1530. doi:10.1037/0022-3514.74.6.1516

Clements, P., Bachmann, F., Bass, L., Garlan, D., Ivers, J., & Little, R. …Stafford, J. (2010). *Documenting software architectures: Views and beyond* (2nd ed.). Reading, MA: Addison-Wesley.

Cnaan, A. R., & Goldberg–Glen, R. S. (1991). Measuring motivation to volunteer in human services. *The Journal of Applied Behavioral Science*, *27*(3), 269–284. doi:10.1177/0021886391273003

Cockburn, A. (2001). *Agile software development*. Indianapolis, IN: Addison-Wesley Professional.

Cohen, W. M., & Levinthal, D. A. (1989). Innovation and learning: The two faces of R & D. *The Economic Journal*, *99*(397), 569–596. doi:10.2307/2233763

Cohen, W. M., & Levinthal, D. A. (1990). Absorptive capacity: A new perspective on learning and innovation. *Administrative Science Quarterly*, *35*(1), 128–152. doi:10.2307/2393553

Coleman, J. S. (1990). *Foundations of social theory*. Cambridge, MA: Belknap Press.

Comrey, A. L., & Lee, H. B. (1992). *A first course on factor analysis* (2nd ed.). Mahwah, NJ: Lawrence Erlbaum.

Conklin, M. (2006). Beyond low-hanging fruit: Seeking the next generation of FLOSS data mining. In *Proceedings of the 2nd International Conference on Open Source Systems*, Como, Italy (pp. 47-56).

Conley, C. A. (2008). *Design for quality: The case of open source software development*. New York, NY: New York University.

Conway, M. E. (1968). *How do committees invent?* F. D. Thompson Publications, Inc. Reprinted by permission of Datamation magazine.

Cox, D. (2005). A pragmatic HCI approach: Engagement by reinforcing perception with functional design and programming. *SIGCSE Bulletin*, *37*(3), 39–43. doi:10.1145/1151954.1067459

Cronbach, L. J. (1951). Coefficient alpha and the internal consistency of tests. *Psychometrica*, *16*, 297–334. doi:10.1007/BF02310555

Crosby, P. B. (1979). *Quality is free: The art of making quality certain*. New York, NY: McGraw-Hill.

Crowston, K., & Howison, J. (2005). *The social structure of free and open source software development.* First Monday.

Crowston, K., Annabi, H., & Howison, J. (2003). Defining open source software project success. In *Proceedings of the 24th International Conference on Information Systems,* Seattle, WA.

Crowston, K., Howison, J., & Annabi, H. (2006). Information systems success in free and open source software development: Theory and measures. *Software Process Improvement and Practice, 11*(2), 123–148. doi:10.1002/spip.259

Crowston, K., & Scozzi, B. (2008). Bug fixing practices within free/libre open source software development teams. *Journal of Database Management, 19*(2), 1–30. doi:10.4018/jdm.2008040101

Crowston, K., Wei, K., Howison, J., & Wiggins, A. (2012). Free/libre open source software development: What we know and what we do not know. *ACM Computing Surveys, 44*(2). doi:10.1145/2089125.2089127

CYB. A., MacCormack, D., & Rusnak, J. (2008). Exploring the duality between product and organizational architectures: A test of the mirroring hypothesis. *Working Papers, Harvard Business School.*

Daffara, C., & Gonzalez-Barahona, J. M. (2007). *Guide for SMEs (No. Deliverable D8.1.1).* Retrieved from http://www.flossmetrics.org/sections/deliverables/docs/deliverables/WP8/D8.1.1-SMEs_Guide.pdf

Dahlander, L. (2007). Penguin in a new suit: A tale of how de novo entrants emerged to harness free and open source software communities. *Industrial and Corporate Change, 16*(5), 913–943. doi:10.1093/icc/dtm026

Dahlander, L., & McKelvey, M. (2005). Who is not developing open source software? Non-users, users, and developers. *Economics of Innovation and New Technology, 14*(7), 617–635. doi:10.1080/1043859052000344705

Dailey, R. C. (1986). Understanding organizational commitment for volunteers: Empirical and managerial implications. *Journal of Voluntary Action Research, 15*(1), 19–31.

Dannenberg, R. B., & Ernst, G. W. (1982). Formal program verification using symbolic execution. *IEEE Transactions on Software Engineering, 8*(1), 43–52. doi:10.1109/TSE.1982.234773

de Groot, A., Kiigler, S., Adams, P. J., & Gousios, G. (2006). Call for quality: Open source software quality observation. *IFIP International Federation for Information Processing, 203,* 57–62. doi:10.1007/0-387-34226-5_6

de Jonge, M. (2002). Source tree composition. In C. Gacek (Ed.), *Proceedings of the 7th International Conference on Software Reuse: Methods, Techniques, and Tools* (LNCS 2319, pp.17-32).

de Jonge, M. (2005). Build-level components. *IEEE Transactions on Software Engineering, 31*(7), 588–600. doi:10.1109/TSE.2005.77

Debian. (1997). *A brief history of Debian: Debian Documentation Team.* Retrieved November 16, 2011, from http://www.debian.org/doc/manuals/project-history/

Dedrick, J., & West, J. (2003, December 12-14). Why firms adopt open source platforms: A grounded theory of innovation and standards adoption. In *Proceedings of the Workshop on Standard Making: A Critical Research Frontier for Information Systems,* Seattle, WA (pp. 236-257).

del Bianco, V., Lavazza, L., Morasca, S., Taibi, D., & Tosi, D. (2010). The QualiSPo approach to OSS product quality evaluation. In *Proceedings of the 3rd International Workshop on Emerging Trends in Free/Libre/Open Source Software Research and Development* (pp. 23-28).

DeLine, R., Khella, A., Czerwinski, M., & Robertson, G. (2005). Towards understanding programs through wear-based filtering. *ACM Symposium on Software Visualization,* (pp. 183–192). St. Louis, Missouri.

Deming, W. E. (1982). *Quality, productivity, and competitive position.* Cambridge, MA: MIT Center for Advanced Engineering Study.

Deming, W. E. (1986). *Out of the crisis.* Cambridge, MA: MIT Center for Advanced Engineering Study.

Deprez, J.-C., & Alexandre, S. (2008). Comparing assessment methodologies for free/open source software: OpenBRR and QSOS. In *Proceedings of the 9th International Conference on Product-Focused Software Process Improvement* (pp. 189-203).

Deprez, J.-C., Monfils, F. F., Ciolkowski, M., & Soto, M. (2007). Defining software evolvability from a free/open-source software perspective. In *Proceedings of the Third International IEEE Workshop on Software Evolvability* (pp. 29-35).

Deshpande, A., & Riehle, D. (2008). Continuous integration in open source software development. *Open Source Development, Communities and Quality, IFIP 20th World Computer Congress, Working Group 2.3 on Open Source Software*, (pp. 273–280).

Desruisseaux, M., & Garnett, J. (2010). *Home*. Retrieved October 31, 2010, from http://docs.codehaus.org/display/GEO/Home

Desruisseaux, M., Garnett, J., et al. (2010). *FAQ*. Retrieved October 31, 2010, from http://docs.codehaus.org/display/GEO/FAQ

DEWS. (2010). *Distant early warning system*. Retrieved December 17, 2011, from http://www.dews-online.org

Dey, E. L. (1997). Working with low survey response rates: The efficacy of weighing adjustments. *Research in Higher Education*, 38(2), 215–227. doi:10.1023/A:1024985704202

Di Penta, & German, D. (2009). Who are source code contributors and how do they change? *Proceedings of 16th Working Conference on Reverse Engineering*, (pp. 11–20).

Dillman, D. (2000). *Mail and Internet surveys: The total design method* (2nd ed.). New York, NY: John Wiley & Sons.

DOM XML parser. (2010). Retrieved from DOM XML parser: www.w3schools.com

Dubé, L., & Paré, G. (2003). Rigor in information systems positivist case research: Current practices, trends, and recommendations. *Management Information Systems Quarterly*, 27(4), 597–635.

Dueñas, J. C., de Oliveira, W. L., & de la Puente, J. A. (1998). Architecture recovery for software evolution. In *Proceedings of the 2nd Euromicro Conference on Software Maintenance and Reengineering* (pp. 113-119).

Duijnhouwer, F. W., & Widdows, C. (2010). *Open Source Maturity Model*. Retrieved from http://www.osspartner.com

Easterbrook, S., Singer, J., Storey, M.-A., & Damian, D. (2008). Selecting empirical methods for software engineering research . In Shull, F., Singer, J., & Sjøberg, D. I. K. (Eds.), *Guide to advanced empirical software engineering* (pp. 285–311). New York, NY: Springer. doi:10.1007/978-1-84800-044-5_11

Eclipse project. (2010). Retrieved from Eclipse project: www.eclipse.org

Eick, S. G., Graves, T. L., Karr, A. F., Marron, J. S., & Mockus, A. (2001). Does code decay? Assessing the evidence from change management data. *IEEE Transactions on Software Engineering*, 27(1), 1–12. doi:10.1109/32.895984

El Emam, K. (1997). *Spice: The Theory and Practice of Software Process Improvement and Capability determination*. Washington, DC: IEEE Computer Society.

El-Nasr, M. S., & Smith, B. K. (2006). Learning through game modding. *ACM Computers in Entertainment*, 4(1), 3B. doi:10.1145/1111293.1111301

English, M., Exton, C., Rigon, I., & Cleary, B. (2009). Fault detection and prediction in an open-source software project. *Proceedings of the 5th International Conference on Predictor Models in Software Engineering*, (pp. 17-27).

Enigmax & Ernesto. (2011). *Swiss Govt: Downloading movies and movies will stay legal*. Retrieved from http://torrentfreak.com/swiss-govt-downloading-movies-and-music-will-stay-legal-111202/

Ericson, T., Subotic, A., & Ursing, S. (1997). TIM - a Test Improvement Model. *International Journal on Software Testing . Verification and Reliability*, 7(4), 229–246. doi:10.1002/(SICI)1099-1689(199712)7:4<229::AID-STVR149>3.0.CO;2-M

Ernesto. (2008). *Top 10 most pirated games of 2008*. Retrieved from http://torrentfreak.com/top-10-most-pirated-games-of-2008-081204/

Ernesto. (2009). *Top 10 most pirated games of 2009*. Retrieved from http://torrentfreak.com/the-most-pirated-games-of-2009-091227/

Ernesto. (2010). *Call of Duty: Black Ops most pirated game of 2010*. Retrieved from http://torrentfreak.com/call-of-duty-black-ops-most-pirated-game-of-2010-101228/

Ernesto. (2011). *Top 10 most pirated games of 2011.* Retrieved from http://torrentfreak.com/top-10-most-pirated-games-of-2011-111230/

Ernst, M. D., Cockrell, J., Griswold, W. G., & Notkin, D. (2001). Dynamically discovering likely program invariants to support program evolution. *IEEE Transactions on Software Engineering, 27*(2), 99–123. doi:10.1109/32.908957

Eucalyptus. (2011). Retrieved from The open source cloud platform: http://open.eucalyptus.com

Faden, R. R., Beauchamp, T. L., & King, N. M. P. (1986). *A history and theory of informed consent.* Oxford, UK: Oxford University Press.

Fagan, M. E. (1986). Advances in Software Inspections. *IEEE Transactions on Software Engineering, 12*(7), 744–751.

Fang, Y., & Neufeld, D. (2009). Understanding sustained participation in open source software projects. *Journal of Management Information Systems, 25*(4), 9–50. doi:10.2753/MIS0742-1222250401

Feigenbaum, A. (1961). *Total quality control: Engineering and management: The technical and managerial field for improving product quality, including its reliability, and for reducing operating costs and losses.* New York, NY: McGraw-Hill.

Feller, J., Finnegan, P., & Hayes, J. (2008). Delivering the 'whole product': Business model impacts and agility challenges in a network of open source firms. *Journal of Database Management, 19*(2), 95–108. doi:10.4018/jdm.2008040105

Fenton, N. E. (1991). *Software metrics: A rigorous approach.* London, UK: Chapman & Hall.

Fernández-Ramil, J., Izquierdo-Cortazar, D., & Mens, T. (2009). What does it take to develop a million lines of open source code? In *Proceedings of the 5ᵗʰ International Conference on Open Source Systems* (pp. 170-184).

Fernandez-Ramil, J., Lozano, A., Wermelinger, M., & Capiluppi, A. (2008). Empirical studies of open source evolution . In Mens, T., & Demeyer, S. (Eds.), *Software evolution: State-of-the-art and research advances* (pp. 263–288). Berlin, Germany: Springer-Verlag.

FFmpeg. (2010). Retrieved from FFmpeg project: www.ffmpeg.org

Fichman, R. G., & Kemerer, C. F. (1997). The assimilation of software process innovations: An organizational learning perspective. *Management Science, 43*(10), 1345–1363. doi:10.1287/mnsc.43.10.1345

Fielding, R. T., & Taylor, R. N. (2002). Principled design of the modern Web architecture. *ACM Transactions on Internet Technology, 2*(2), 115–150. doi:10.1145/514183.514185

Fitzgerald, B., & Kenny, T. (2003, December 14-17). Open source software in the trenches: Lessons from a large scale implementation. In *Proceedings of 24th International Conference on Information Systems*, Seattle, WA (pp. 316-326).

Fitzgerald, B. (2006). The transformation of open source software. *Management Information Systems Quarterly, 30*(3), 587–598.

Fitzgerald, B. (2009). Open source software adoption: Anatomy of success and failure. *International Journal of Open Source Software and Processes, 1*(1), 1–23. doi:10.4018/jossp.2009010101

Fitzpatrick, R., & Higgins, C. (1998). Usable software and its attributes: A synthesis of software quality. In *Proceedings of the European, Community Law and Human-Computer Interaction in People and Computers XIII Conference*, London, UK (pp. 3-21).

Fleming, L., & David, M. W. (2007). Brokerage, boundary spanning and leadership in open innovation communities. *Organization Science, 18*(2), 165–180. doi:10.1287/orsc.1060.0242

Fogel, K. (2006). *Producing open source software.* Sebastopol, CA: O'Reilly.

Fornell, C., & Bookstein, F. L. (1982). Two structural equation models: LISREL and PLS applied to consumer exit voice theory. *JMR, Journal of Marketing Research, 19*, 440–452. doi:10.2307/3151718

Fornell, C., & Larcker, D. F. (1981). Evaluating structural equations with unobservable variables and measurement error. *JMR, Journal of Marketing Research, 18*(1), 39–50. doi:10.2307/3151312

Freitas, M., Roitzsch, M., Melanson, M., Mattern, T., Langauf, S., & Petteno, D. …Lee, A. (2002). *Xine multimedia engine.* Retrieved from http://www.xine-project.org/home

Froehlich, J., & Dourish, P. (2004). Unifying artifacts and activities in a visual tool for distributed software development teams. *International Conference on Software Engineering,* (pp. 387–396). Edinburgh, UK. *git version control system.* (2010). Retrieved from git version control system: www.git-scm.com

Galindo–Kuhn, R., & Guzley, R. M. (2001). The volunteer satisfaction index: Construct definition, measurement, development, and validation. *Journal of Social Service Research, 28*(1), 45–68. doi:10.1300/J079v28n01_03

Gall, H. C., Fluri, B., & Pinzger, M. (2009). Change analysis with Evolizer and ChangeDistiller. *IEEE Software, 26*(1), 26–33. doi:10.1109/MS.2009.6

Gamm, L., & Kassab, C. (1983). Productivity assessment of volunteer programs in not–for–profit human services organizations. *Journal of Voluntary Action Research, 12*(3), 23–38.

Garmus, D., & Herron, D. (2001). *Function point analysis: measurement practices for successful software projects.* Reading, MA: Addison-Wesley.

Garvin, D. A. (1984). What does 'product quality' really mean? *Sloan Management Review, 1,* 25–43.

George, J., & Jones, G. (1999). *Understanding and managing organizational behavior* (2nd ed.). Reading, MA: Addison-Wesley.

GeoTools. (2010). *GeoTools user guide frequently asked questions.* Retrieved October 29, 2010, from http://docs.geotools.org/stable/userguide/faq.html

GeoTools. (2011). *End of GeoAPI involvement.* Retrieved December 18, 2011, from http://geotoolsnews.blogspot.com/2011/01/end-of-geoapi-involvement.html

Gerbing, D. W., & Anderson, J. C. (1988). An updated paradigm for scale development incorporating unidimensionality and its assessment. *JMR, Journal of Marketing Research, 25*(2), 186–192. doi:10.2307/3172650

German, D. M. (2004). Mining CVS repositories, the softchange experience. In *Proceedings of the 1st International Workshop on Mining Software Repositories,* Scotland, UK (pp. 17-21).

German, D. M. (2004). Using software trails to reconstruct the evolution of software: Research articles. *Journal of Software Maintenance and Evolution: Research and Practice—Analyzing the Evolution of Large-Scale Software, 16*(6), 367-384.

German, D. M., & González-Barahona, J. M. (2009). An empirical study of the reuse of software licensed under the GNU general public license. In *Proceedings of the 5th IFIP WG 2.13 International Conference on Open Source EcoSystems: Diverse Communities Interacting* (pp. 185-198).

German, D. M., & Hassan, A. E. (2009). License integration patterns: Addressing license mismatches in component-based development. In *Proceedings of the 31st IEEE International Conference on Software Engineering* (pp. 188-198).

German, D. M., Gonzalez-Barahona, J. M., & Robles, G. (2007). A model to understand the building and running inter-dependencies of software. In *Proceedings of the 14th Working Conference on Reverse Engineering* (pp. 140-149).

Ghapanchi, A. H., & Aurum, A. (2011). Measuring the effectiveness of the defect-fixing process in open source software projects. In *Proceedings of the 44th Hawaii International Conference on System Sciences* (pp. 1-11).

Ghosh, R. A. (2006). *Economic impact of open source software on innovation and the competitiveness of the information and communication technologies (ICT) sector in the EU.* Maastricht, The Netherlands: United Nations University (UNU) MERIT.

Ghosh, R. A., Glott, R., Krieger, B., & Robles, G. (2002). *Free/libre and open source software: Survey and study, FLOSS final report.* Maastricht, The Netherlands: International Institute of Infonomics, University of Maastricht. Retrieved January 16, 2008, from http://www.infonomics.nl/FLOSS/report/Final4.htm

Gidron, B. (1983). Source of job satisfaction among service volunteers. *Journal of Voluntary Action Research, 12*(1), 20–35.

Gidron, B. (1984). Predictors of retention and turnover among service volunteer workers. *Journal of Social Service Research*, 8(1), 1–16. doi:10.1300/J079v08n01_01

Glance, D. G. (2004). Release criteria for the Linux Kernel. *First Monday*, 9(4).

Glass, R. L., Vessey, I., & Ramesh, V. (2002). Research in software engineering: An analysis of the literature. *Information and Software Technology*, 44(8), 491–506. doi:10.1016/S0950-5849(02)00049-6

Glinz, M. (2007). On non-functional requirements. In *Proceedings of the 15th IEEE International Requirements Engineering Conference*.

Glott, R., Groven, A.-K., Haaland, K., & Tannenberg, A. (2010). Quality models for free/libre open source software-Towards the "silver bullet"? In *Proceedings of the 36th EUROMICRO Conference on Software Engineering and Advanced Applications* (pp. 439-446).

Godfrey, M. W., & Lee, E. H. S. (2000). Secrets from the monster: Extracting Mozilla's software architecture. In *Proceedings of the 2nd Symposium on Constructing Software Engineering Tools* (pp. 15-23).

Golden, E. (2009). Early-stage software design for usability. In *Proceedings of the 31ˢᵗ International Conference on Software Engineering*, Vancouver, BC, Canada.

Goldman, R., & Gabriel, R. (2004). *Innovation happens elsewhere: How and why a company should participate in open source*. San Francisco, CA: Morgan Kaufmann.

Goode, S. (2005). Something for nothing: Management rejection of open source software in Australia's top firms. *Information & Management*, 42(5), 669–681. doi:10.1016/j.im.2004.01.011

Gordijn, J., & Akkermans, H. (2003). Value-based requirements engineering: Exploring innovative e-commerce ideas. *Requirements Engineering*, 8(2), 114–134. doi:10.1007/s00766-003-0169-x

Gousios, G., & Spinellis, D. (2009a). Alitheia Core: An extensible software quality monitoring platform. In *Proceedings of the IEEE 31st International Conference on Software Engineering*, Vancouver, BC, Canada (pp. 579-582).

Gousios, G., & Spinellis, D. (2009b). A platform for software engineering research. In *Proceedings of the 6th IEEE International Working Conference on Mining Software Repositories*, Vancouver, BC, Canada (pp. 31-40).

Groven, A.-K., Haaland, K., Glott, R., & Tannenberg, A. (2010). Security measurements within the framework of quality assessment models for free/libre open source software. In *Proceedings of the Fourth European Conference on Software Architecture: Companion Volume* (pp. 229-235).

Gruber, M., & Henkel, J. (2004). New ventures based on open innovation –an empirical analysis of start-up firms in embedded Linux. *International Journal of Technology Management*, 33(4), 356–372. doi:10.1504/IJTM.2006.009249

Guba, E. (1981). Criteria for assessing the trustworthiness of naturalistic inquiries. *Educational Communication and Technology*, 29, 75–92.

Gummerson, E. (1998). *Qualitative methods in management research*. Newbury Park, CA: Sage.

Guo, P. J., Zimmermann, T., Nagappan, N., & Murphy, B. (2010). Characterizing and predicting which bugs get fixed: an empirical study of Microsoft windows. In *Proceedings of the 32nd ACM/IEEE International Conference on Software Engineering* (pp. 495-504). New York, NY: ACM.

Guttag, J., & Horning, J. (1993). *Larch: Languages and tools for formal specification*. New York, NY: Springer-Verlag, New york, Inc.

Gyimothy, T., Ferenc, R., & Siket, I. (2005). Empirical validation of object-oriented metrics on open source software for fault prediction. *IEEE Transactions on Software Engineering*, 31(10), 897–910. doi:10.1109/TSE.2005.112

Haefliger, S., von Krogh, G., & Spaeth, S. (2008). Code reuse in open source software. *Management Science*, 54(1), 180–193. doi:10.1287/mnsc.1070.0748

Hales, P. (2006, December 8). Firefox use continues to rise in Europe. *The Inquirer*.

Halloran, T. J., & Scherlis, W. L. (2002). High quality and open source software practices. In *Proceedings of the 2nd Workshop on Open Source Software Engineering*.

Hammitzsch, M., Lendholt, M., & Wächter, J. (2010). Distant early warning system for tsunamis – A wide-area and multi-hazard approach. In *Proceedings of the Conference of the European Geosciences Union: Vol. 12. Geophysical Research Abstracts*. Retrieved August 17, 2010, from http://meetingorganizer.copernicus.org/EGU2010/EGU2010-4496.pdf

Hammitzsch, M., Lendholt, M., & Esbrí, M. A. (2012). User interface prototype for geospatial early warning systems – a tsunami showcase. *Natural Hazards and Earth System Sciences*, *12*, 555–573. doi:10.5194/nhess-12-555-2012

Hao-Yun Huang, Q. L., & Panchal, J. H. (2010). Analysis of the structure and evolution of an open-source community. In *Proceedings of the ASME International Design Engineering Technical Conferences & Computers and Information in Engineering Conference*.

Harrington, S., & Guimaraes, T. (2005). Corporate culture, absorptive capacity and IT success. *Information and Organization*, *15*(1), 39–63. doi:10.1016/j.infoandorg.2004.10.002

Harrison, N. B., & Avgeriou, P. (2011). Pattern-based architecture reviews. *IEEE Software*, *28*(6), 66–71. doi:10.1109/MS.2010.156

Hars, A., & Ou, S. (2002). Working for free? – Motivations of participating in open source projects. *International Journal of Electronic Commerce*, *6*(3), 25–39.

Hauge, Ø., Østerlie, T., Sørensen, C.-F., & Gerea, M. (2009, May 18). An empirical study on selection of open source software - Preliminary results. In *Proceedings of the 2nd ICSE Workshop on Emerging Trends in Free/Libre/Open Source Software Research and Development*, Vancouver, BC, Canada (pp. 42-47).

Hauge, O., Ayala, C., & Conradi, R. (2010). Adoption of open source software in software-intensive organizations - a systematic literature review. *Information and Software Technology*, *52*(11), 1133–1154. doi:10.1016/j.infsof.2010.05.008

Hauge, Ø., Sørensen, C.-F., & Røsdal, A. (2007). Surveying industrial roles in open source software development . In Feller, J., Fitzgerald, B., Scacchi, W., & Sillitti, A. (Eds.), *Open source development, adoption and innovation* (pp. 259–264). New York, NY: Springer. doi:10.1007/978-0-387-72486-7_25

Hecker, F. (1999). Setting up a shop: The business of open source software. *IEEE Software*, *16*(1), 45–51. doi:10.1109/52.744568

Hedberg, H., Iivari, N., Rajanen, M., & Harjumaa, L. (2007). Assuring quality and usability in open source software development. In *Proceedings of the 1st International Workshop on Emerging Trends in FLOSS Research and Development* (p. 2).

Heinemann, L., Deissenboeck, F., Gleirscher, M., Hummel, B., & Irlbeck, M. (2011). On the extent and nature of software reuse in open source Java projects. In K. Schmid (Ed.), *Proceedings of the 12th International Conference on Software Reuse: Top Productivity through Software Reuse* (LNCS 6727, pp. 207-222).

Henderson, A. (2005). The innovation pipeline: Design collaborations between research and development. *Interaction*, *12*(1), 24–29. doi:10.1145/1041280.1041295

Henttonen, K., Matinlassi, M., Niemela, E., & Kanstren, T. (2007). Integrability and extensibility evaluation in software architectural models—A case study. *The Open Software Engineering Journal*, *1*(1), 1–20. doi:10.2174/1874107X00701010001

Herbsleb, J. (2007). *Global software engineering: The future of socio-technical coordination. Future of Software Engineering* (pp. 188–198). Washington, DC, U.S.A: IEEE Computer Society.

Herbsleb, J., Moitra, D., & Lucent Technol, I. (2001). Global software development. *IEEE Software*, *18*(2), 16–20. doi:10.1109/52.914732

Herbsleb, J., Zubrow, D., Goldenson, D., Hayes, W., & Paulk, M. (1997). Software quality and the Capability Maturity Model. *Communications of the ACM*, *40*(6), 30–40. doi:10.1145/255656.255692

Hertel, G., Niedner, S., & Hermann, S. (2003). Motivation of software developers in the open source projects: An Internet–based survey of contributors to the Linux kernel. *Research Policy*, *32*(7), 1159–1177. doi:10.1016/S0048-7333(03)00047-7

Hertz, G. (2011). *OutRun: Augmented reality driving video game*. Retrieved from http://www.youtube.com/watch?v=TaTB5Q11Dzc

Hertz, G. (2011). OutRun: Building the un-simulation of a driving video game. *Make*, *26*, 50–53.

Hindle, A., German, D. M., & Holt, R. (2008). What do large commits tell us? A taxonomical study of large commits. In *Proceedings of the International Working Conference on Mining Software Repositories* (pp. 99-108). New York, NY: ACM.

Houle, B. J., Sagarin, B. J., & Kaplan, M. F. (2005). A functional approach to volunteerism: Do volunteer motives predict task preference? *Basic and Applied Social Psychology*, *27*(4), 337–344. doi:10.1207/s15324834basp2704_6

Howard, M. (2006). A process for performing security code reviews. *IEEE Security and Privacy*, *4*(4), 74–79. doi:10.1109/MSP.2006.84

Hu, D., & Zhao, J. L. (2008). A comparison of evaluation networks and collaboration networks in open source software communities. In *Proceedings of the 14th Americas Conference on Information Systems*, Toronto, ON, Canada (pp. 1-8).

Huang, A. (2003). *Hacking the Xbox: An introduction to reverse engineering*. San Francisco, CA: No Starch Press.

Huber, S. (2010). *Implementation and evaluation of communication metrics for continuous software project monitoring* (Unpublished diploma thesis). Vienna University of Technology, Vienna, Austria.

Huntley, C. L. (2003). Organizational learning in open-source software projects: An analysis of debugging data. *IEEE Transactions on Engineering Management*, *50*(4), 485–493. doi:10.1109/TEM.2003.820136

Hussey, J., & Hussey, R. (1997). *Business research: A practical guide for undergraduate and postgraduate students*. Basingstoke, UK: Macmillan Business.

Hutchison, J., Tollefson, N., & Wigington, H. (1987). Response bias in college freshman's responses to mail surveys. *Research in Higher Education*, *26*(1), 99–106. doi:10.1007/BF00991936

IEEE. (1986). *Std 1008-1987: IEEE standard for Software Unit Testing*. Washington, DC: IEEE Computer Society.

IEEE. (2000). *IEEE Std 1471-2000: IEEE recommended practice for architectural description of software-intensive systems*. Piscataway, NJ: IEEE.

IEEE. (2008). *Std 829-2008: IEEE Standard for Software and System Test Documentation*. Washington, DC: IEEE Computer Society.

Igbaria, M., & Greenhaus, J. H. (1992). Determinants of MIS employees' turnover intentions: A structural equation model. *Communications of the ACM*, *35*(2), 34–49. doi:10.1145/129630.129631

Iivari, J., & Iivari, N. (2006). Varieties of user-centeredness. In *Proceedings of the 39th Annual Hawaii International Conference on System Sciences* (p. 8).

Iivari, N. (2009a). Empowering the users? A critical textual analysis of the role of users in open source software development. *AI & Society*, *23*(4), 511–528. doi:10.1007/s00146-008-0182-1

Iivari, N. (2009b). Constructing the users in open source software development: An interpretive case study of user participation. *Information Technology & People*, *22*(2), 132–156. doi:10.1108/09593840910962203

International Organization for Standardization (ISO). (2001). *ISO 9126-1:2001, Software engineering - Product quality, Part 1: Quality model*. Geneva, Switzerland: Author.

International Organization for Standardization (ISO). (2001). *ISO/IEC 14598-1 Information technology - software product evaluation. Part 1: General overview*. Geneva, Switzerland: ISO.

International Organization for Standardization (ISO). (2001). *ISO/IEC 9126-1 Software engineering - product quality. Part 1: Quality model*. Geneva, Switzerland: ISO.

International Organization for Standardization. (1997). *ISO 9241: Ergonomics requirements for office with visual display terminals (VDTs)*. Geneva, Switzerland: ISO/IEC.

International Organization for Standardization. (2001). *ISO/IEC 9126-1: Software engineering – product quality – Part 1: Quality model* (1st ed., pp. 9–10). Geneva, Switzerland: ISO/IEC.

International Organization for Standardization. (2004). *ISO/IEC 15504-1 Information technology process assessment. Part 1: Concepts and vocabulary.* Geneva, Switzerland: ISO.

Irawan, H., McCrary, T., Barbareau, L., et al. (2010). *RCP FAQ.* Retrieved October 31, 2010, from http://wiki.eclipse.org/index.php/RCP_FAQ#Why_should_I_build_my_application_on_the_Eclipse_Rich_Client_Platform.3F

Irawan, H., Vogel, L., Ebert, R., et al. (2009). *Rich client platform.* Retrieved October 31, 2010, from http://wiki.eclipse.org/index.php/Rich_Client_Platform

Ishikawa, K. (1985). *What is total quality control? The Japanese way.* Upper Saddle River, NJ: Prentice Hall.

Izquierdo-Cortazar, D., Robles, G., Ortega, F., & Gonzalez-Barahona, J. M. (2009). Using software archaeology to measure knowledge loss in software projects due to developer turnover. In *Proceedings of the Hawaii International Conference on System Sciences* (pp. 1-10). Washington, DC: IEEE Computer Society.

Java runtime enviornment. (2011). Retrieved from Java runtime enviornment: http://www.oracle.com/

Jendrock, E., Ball, J., Carson, D., Evans, I., Fordin, S., & Haase, K. (2006). *The Java EE 5 tutorial: For Sun Java System Application Server Platform Edition 9* (Java Series). Upper Saddle River, NJ: Prentice Hall.

Jendrock, E., Evans, I., Gollapudi, D., Haase, K., & Srivathsa, C. (2010). *The Java EE 6 tutorial 1: Basic concepts (Java Series).* Upper Saddle River, NJ: Prentice Hall.

JFreeChart. (2010). Retrieved from JFreeChart: www.jfree.org

Johnson, L. C., Beaton, R., Murphy, S., & Pike, K. (2000). Sampling bias and other methodological threats to the validity of health survey research. *International Journal of Stress Management, 7*(4), 247–267. doi:10.1023/A:1009589812697

Johnson, M. (1981). *Voluntary social services.* Oxford, UK: Basil Blackwell and Martin Robertson.

Joo, B. K., & Park, S. (2009). Career satisfaction, organizational commitment, and turnover intention. *Leadership and Organization Development Journal, 31*(6), 482–500. doi:10.1108/01437731011069999

Joreskog, K., & Wold, H. (1982). *Systems under indirect observation: causality, structure and prediction.* Amsterdam, The Netherlands: North-Holland.

Juran, J. M. (1988). *Planning for quality.* London, UK: Collier Macmillan.

Juristo, N. (2009). Impact of usability on software requirements and design. In A. De Lucia & F. Ferrucci (Eds.), *Proceedings of the International Summer Schools Tutorial on Software Engineering* (LNCS 5413, pp. 55-77).

Kagdi, H. H., Hammad, M., & Maletic, J. I. (2008). Who can help me with this source code change? In *Proceedings of the 24th IEEE International Conference on Software Maintenance* (pp. 157-166). Washington, DC: IEEE Computer Society.

Kaiser, H. F. (1960). The application of electronic computers to factor analysis. *Educational and Psychological Measurement, 20,* 141–151. doi:10.1177/001316446002000116

Kaiser, H. F. (1970). A second generation little jiffy. *Psychometrika, 35,* 401–417. doi:10.1007/BF02291817

Kaltenecker, A. (2010). *Deriving project health indicators of open source software projects using social network analysis* (Unpublished diploma thesis). Vienna University of Technology, Vienna, Austria.

Kamei, Y., Matsumoto, S., Maeshima, H., Onishi, Y., Ohira, M., & Matsumoto, K. (2008). Analysis of coordination between developers and users in the apache community. *Proceedings of the Fourth Conference on Open Source Systems,* (pp. 81–92).

Katz, J. (1972). *Experimentation with human beings.* New York, NY: Russell Sage Foundation.

Kearney, M. H. (1998). Ready-to-wear: Discovering grounded formal theory. *Research in Nursing & Health, 21*(2), 179–186. doi:10.1002/(SICI)1098-240X(199804)21:2<179::AID-NUR8>3.0.CO;2-G

Kearney, M. H. (2001). Enduring love: A grounded formal theory of women's experience of domestic violence. *Research in Nursing & Health*, *24*(4), 270–282. doi:10.1002/nur.1029

Kelland, M. (2011). From game mod to low-budget film: The evolution of Machinima . In Lowood, H., & Nitsche, M. (Eds.), *The Machinima reader* (pp. 23–36). Cambridge, MA: MIT Press.

Kemper, T. D. (1980). Altruism and voluntary action . In Smith, D. H., & Macaulay, J., & Associates. (Eds.), *Participation in social and political activities* (pp. 306–338). San Francisco, CA: Jossey-Bass.

Kidane, Y., & Gloor, P. (2007). Correlating temporal communication patterns of the Eclipse open source community with performance and creativity. *Computational & Mathematical Organization Theory*, *13*(1), 17–27. doi:10.1007/s10588-006-9006-3

Kiesler, C. A. (1971). *The psychology of commitment: Experiments linking behavior to belief*. New York, NY: Academic Press.

Kim, L. (1998). Crisis construction and organizational learning: Capability building in catching-up at Hyundai motor. *Organization Science*, *9*(4), 506–521. doi:10.1287/orsc.9.4.506

Kim, S., Whitehead, E. J., & Zhang, Y. (2008). Classifying software changes: Clean or buggy? *IEEE Transactions on Software Engineering*, *34*(2), 181–196. doi:10.1109/TSE.2007.70773

Kitchenham, B., & Charters, S. (2007). Guidelines for performing systematic literature reviews in software engineering. *Engineering, 2*.

Kline, R. B. (2005). *Principles and practices of structural equation modeling* (2nd ed.). New York, NY: Guilford Press.

Knab, P., Pinzger, M., & Bernstein, A. (2006). Predicting defect densities in source code files with decision tree learners. *Proceedings of the International workshop on Mining software repositories*, (pp. 119–125).

Koch, S., & Stix, V. (2008). Open source project categorization based on growth rate analysis and portfolio planning methods. *Open Source Development, Communities and Quality, IFIP 20th World Computer Congress, Working Group 2.3 on Open Source Software*, (pp. 375–380).

Koch, S. (2009). Exploring the effects of sourceforge.net coordination and communication tools on the efficiency of open source projects using data envelopment analysis. *Empirical Software Engineering*, *14*(4), 397–417. doi:10.1007/s10664-008-9086-4

Koch, S., & Neumann, C. (2008). Exploring the effects of process characteristics on product quality in open source software development. *Journal of Database Management*, *19*(2), 31–57. doi:10.4018/jdm.2008040102

Koch, S., & Schneider, G. (2002). Effort, co-operation and co-ordination in an open source software project: GNOME. *Information Systems Journal*, *12*, 27–42. doi:10.1046/j.1365-2575.2002.00110.x

Koenig, J. (2004). *Seven open source business strategies for competitive advantage*. Half Moon Bay, CA: Riseforth, Inc.

Kollock, P. (1999). The economies of online cooperation: Gifts, and public goods in cyberspace . In Smith, M. A., & Kollock, P. (Eds.), *Communities in cyberspace* (pp. 220–239). New York, NY: Routledge.

Koomen, T., & Pol, M. (1999). *Test Process Improvement: a practical step-by-step guide to structured testing*. Reading, MA: Addison-Wesley.

Kooths, S., Langenfurth, M., & Kalwey, N. (2003). Open-source software: An economic assessment. *MICE Economic Research Studies*, *4*, 59.

Koppelman, H., & Van Dijk, B. (2006). Creating a realistic context for team projects in HCI. *SIGCSE Bulletin*, *38*(3), 58–62. doi:10.1145/1140123.1140142

Koru, A. G., & Liu, H. (2007). Identifying and characterizing change-prone classes in two large-scale open-source products. *Journal of Systems and Software*, *80*(1), 63–73. doi:10.1016/j.jss.2006.05.017

Koru, A. G., & Tian, J. (2004). Defect handling in medium and large open source projects. *IEEE Software*, *21*(4), 54–61. doi:10.1109/MS.2004.12

Koru, A. G., & Tian, J. (2005). Comparing high-change modules and modules with the highest measurement values in two large-scale open-source products. *IEEE Transactions on Software Engineering, 31*(8), 625–642. doi:10.1109/TSE.2005.89

Krikhaar, R. (1999). *Software architecture reconstruction* (Unpublished doctoral dissertation). University of Amsterdam, Amsterdam, The Netherlands.

Krikhaar, R., Postma, A., Sellink, A., Stroucken, M., & Verhoef, C. (1999). A two-phase process for software architecture improvement. In *Proceedings of the IEEE International Conference on Software Maintenance* (pp. 371-380).

Krishnamurthy, S. (2003). An analysis of open source business models . In Feller, J., Fitzgerald, B., Hissam, S. A., & Lakhani, K. (Eds.), *Perspectives on open source and free software*. Cambridge, MA: MIT Press.

Krishnamurthy, S. (2006). On the intrinsic and extrinsic motivation of free/libre/open source (FLOSS) developers. *Knowledge, Technology & Policy, 18*(4), 17–39. doi:10.1007/s12130-006-1002-x

Krosnick, J. (1999). Survey research. *Annual Review of Psychology, 50*, 537–567. doi:10.1146/annurev.psych.50.1.537

Kruchten, P. B. (1995). The 4+1 view model of architecture. *IEEE Software, 12*(5), 42–50. doi:10.1109/52.469759

Kuan, J. (2003). Open source software as lead-user's make or buy decision: A study of open and closed source quality. In *Proceedings of the Second Conference on the Economics of the Software and Internet Industries*.

Kücklich, J. (2005). Precarious playbour: Modders and the digital games industry. *Fiberculture, 5*. Retrieved April 13, 2011, from http://journal.fibreculture.org/issue5/kucklich.html

Lakhani, K. R., & Wolf, R. G. (2005). Why hackers do what they do: Understanding motivation effort in free/open source software projects . In Feller, J., Fitzgerald, B., Hissam, S. A., & Lakhani, K. R. (Eds.), *Perspectives on free and open source software* (pp. 3–23). Cambridge, MA: MIT Press. doi:10.2139/ssrn.443040

Lakhani, K., & Von Hippel, E. (2003). How open source software works: "Free" user-to-user assistance. *Research Policy, 32*(6), 923–943. doi:10.1016/S0048-7333(02)00095-1

Lane, P. J., Koka, B. R., & Pathak, S. (2006). The reification of absorptive capacity: A critical review and rejuvenation of the construct. *Academy of Management Review, 31*(4), 833–863. doi:10.5465/AMR.2006.22527456

Lang, B., Abramatic, J.-F., González-Barahona, J. M., Gómez, F. P., & Pedersen, M. K. (2005). Free and proprietary software in COTS-based software development. In X. Franch & D. Port (Eds.), *Proceedings of the 4th International Conference on Composition-Based Software Systems* (LNCS 3412, p. 2).

Laplante, P., Gold, A., & Costello, T. (2007). Open source software: Is it worth converting? *IT Professional, 9*(4), 28–33. doi:10.1109/MITP.2007.72

Latham, G. P., & Pinder, C. C. (2005). Work motivation theory and research at the dawn of the twenty–first century. *Annual Review of Psychology, 56*, 485–516. doi:10.1146/annurev.psych.55.090902.142105

Leclerc, Y., Reddy, M., Iverson, L., & Heller, A. (2001). The GeoWeb - A new paradigm for finding data on the Web. In *Proceedings of the International Cartographic Conference*, Beijing, China.

Lee, M. (2011). *What is free software and why is it so important for society?* Retrieved June 13, 2011, from http://www.fsf.org/about/what-is-free-software

Lee, A., & Baskerville, R. (2003). Generalizing in information systems research. *Information Systems Research, 14*(3), 221–243. doi:10.1287/isre.14.3.221.16560

Lee, S. Y. T., Kim, H. W., & Gupta, S. (2009). Measuring open source software success. *Omega, 37*(2), 426–438. doi:10.1016/j.omega.2007.05.005

Lehman, M. M. (1978). Programs, cities, students, limits to growth? *Programming Methodology*, 42-62.

Lehman, M. M. (1980). Programs, life cycles, and laws of software evolution. *Proceedings of the IEEE, 68*(9), 1060–1076. doi:10.1109/PROC.1980.11805

Lendholt, M., & Hammitzsch, M. (2011). Generic information logistics for early warning systems. In *Proceedings of the 8th International Conference on Information Systems for Crisis Response and Management*, Lisbon, Portugal.

Lerner, J., & Tirole, J. (2000). The simple economics of the open source. *The Journal of Industrial Economics, 52*(2), 197–234.

Lerner, J., & Tirole, J. (2002). Some simple economics of open source. *The Journal of Industrial Economics, 50*(2), 197–234. doi:10.1111/1467-6451.00174

Lerner, J., & Tirole, J. (2005). The scope of open source licensing. *Journal of Law Economics and Organization, 21*(1), 20–56. doi:10.1093/jleo/ewi002

Lethbridge, T. C., & Laganière, R. (2001). *Object-oriented software engineering: Practical software development using UML and Java* (2nd ed.). London, UK: McGraw-Hill.

Lethbridge, T. C., Tichelaar, S., & Ploedereder, E. (2004). The dagstuhl middle metamodel: A schema for reverse engineering. *Electronic Notes in Theoretical Computer Science*, 7–18. doi:10.1016/j.entcs.2004.01.008

Leung, H. K. N., & White, L. (1990). A study of integration testing and software regression at the integration level. In *Proceedings of the Conference on Software Maintenance* (pp. 290-301).

Leveque, T., Estublier, J., & Vega, G. (2009). Extensibility and modularity for model-driven engineering environments. In *Proceedings of the 16th IEEE Conference on Engineering Computer-Based Systems* (pp. 305-314).

Levitt, B., & March, J. G. (1988). Organizational learning. *Annual Review of Sociology, 14*, 319–340. doi:10.1146/annurev.so.14.080188.001535

Lewin, K. (1936). *Principles of topological psychology*. New York, NY: McGraw-Hill. doi:10.1037/10019-000

Lewis, C. (2006). HCI and cognitive disabilities. *Interaction, 13*(3), 14–15. doi:10.1145/1125864.1125880

Li, J., Conradi, R., Bunse, C., Torchiano, M., Slyngstad, O. P. N., & Morisio, M. (2009). Development with off-the-shelf components: 10 facts. *IEEE Software, 26*(2), 80–87. doi:10.1109/MS.2009.33

Linder, J., & Cantrell, S. (2000). Changing business models: Surveying the landscape. *Accenture*, 1-13.

Lindgaard, G. (2006). Notions of thoroughness, efficiency, and validity: Are they valid in HCI practice? *International Journal of Industrial Ergonomics, 36*, 1069–1074. doi:10.1016/j.ergon.2006.09.007

Linstead, E., Bajracharya, S., Ngo, T., Rigor, P., Lopes, C., & Baldi, P. (2009). Sourcerer: Mining and searching internet-scale software repositories. *Data Mining and Knowledge Discovery, 18*(2), 300–336. doi:10.1007/s10618-008-0118-x

Locke, E. A., & Latham, G. P. (1990). Work motivation and satisfaction: Light at the end of the tunnel. *Psychological Science, 1*(4), 240–246. doi:10.1111/j.1467-9280.1990.tb00207.x

Löwe, P., Hammitzsch, M., & Lendholt, M. (2011, May 19-20). *Significance of FOSSGIS in the TRIDEC Project*. Paper presented at the Conference of Geoinformatics, Prague, Czech Republic. Retrieved June 11, 2011, from http://geoinformatics.fsv.cvut.cz/gwiki/Significance_of_FOSSGIS_in_the_TRIDEC_Project

Lowood, H., & Nitsche, M. (Eds.). (2011). *The Machinima Reader*. Cambridge, MA: MIT Press.

Lundell, B., Lings, B., & Lindqvist, E. (2010). Open source in Swedish companies: Where are we? *Information Systems Journal, 20*(6), 519–535. doi:10.1111/j.1365-2575.2010.00348.x

Lungu, M., Lanza, M., & Gîrba, T. (2006). Package patterns for visual architecture recovery. In *Proceedings of the 10th European Conference on Software Maintenance and Reengineering*.

Ma, D., Schuler, D., Zimmermann, T., & Sillito, J. (2009). Expert recommendation with usage expertise. In *Proceedings of the International Conference on Software Maintenance* (pp. 535-538). Washington, DC: IEEE Computer Society.

MacKenzie, D., Eggert, P., & Stallman, R. (2002). *Comparing and merging files with GNU diff and patch*. London, UK: Network Theory.

MacLean, A. C., Pratt, L. J., Krein, J. L., & Knutson, C. D. (2010). Trends that affect temporal analysis using sourceforge data. In *Proceedings of the 5th International Workshop on Public Data about Software Development* (p. 6).

Macro, A., & Buxton, J. (1987). *The craft of software engineering*. Reading, MA: Addison-Wesley.

Malone, T. W., Weill, P., Lai, R. K., D'Urso, V. T., Herman, G., Apel, T. G., & Woerner, S. (2006). *Do some business models perform better than others?* SSRN eLibrary.

Mankiw, G. N. (2004). *Principles of economics* (3rd ed.). Mason, OH: Thomson South–Western Press.

Mao, C., Lu, Y., & Zhang, J. (2007). Regression testing for component-based software via built-in test design. In *Proceedings of the ACM Symposium on Applied Computing* (pp. 1416-1421).

Marino, P. (2004). *3D game-based filmmaking: The art of Machinima*. Scottsdale, AZ: Paraglyph Press.

Markov, N. (2003). *An introduction to the UCD methodology in the current environment.* Paper presented at the CASCON Workshop.

Marshall, C., & Rossman, G. B. (2006). *Designing qualitative research* (4th ed.). Thousand Oaks, CA: Sage.

Martinez-Romo, J., Robles, G., Ortuo-Perez, M., & Gonzalez-Barahona, J. M. (2008). Using social network analysis techniques to study collaboration between a floss community and a company. *Proceedings of the Fourth Conference on Open Source Systems,* (pp. 171–186).

Mathieson, K. (1991). Predicting user intentions: Comparing the technology acceptance model with the theory of planned behavior. *Information Systems Research, 2*(3), 173–191. doi:10.1287/isre.2.3.173

McCall, J. A., Richards, P. K., & Walters, G. F. (1977). Factors in software quality. *National Technology Information Service, 1-3.*

McCurley, S., & Lynch, R. (1996). *Volunteer management: Mobilizing all the resources of the community.* Downers Grove, IL: Heritage Arts.

Meyer, J. P., Becker, T. E., & Vandenberghe, C. (2004). Employee commitment and motivation: A conceptual analysis and integrative model. *The Journal of Applied Psychology, 89*(6), 991–1007. doi:10.1037/0021-9010.89.6.991

Michlmayr, M. (2005). Software process maturity and the success of free software projects. In *Proceeding of the Conference on Software Engineering: Evolution and Emerging Technologies* (pp. 3-14).

Michlmayr, M., Hunt, F., & Probert, D. (2005). Quality practices and problems in free software projects. In *Proceedings of the First International Conference on Open Source Systems.*

Miles, I., Sullivan, W., & Kuo, E. (1998). Ecological restoration volunteers: The benefits of participation. *Urban Ecosystems, 2*(1), 27–41. doi:10.1023/A:1009501515335

Miles, M. B., & Huberman, A. M. (1994). *Qualitative data analysis: An expanded sourcebook* (2nd ed.). Thousand Oaks, CA: Sage.

Miller, L. E. (1985). Understanding the motivation of volunteers: An examination of personality differences and characteristics of volunteers' paid employment. *Journal of Voluntary Action Research, 14*(2-3), 112–122.

Miller, L. E., Powell, G. N., & Seltzer, J. (1990). Determinants of turnover among volunteers. *Human Relations, 43*(9), 901–917. doi:10.1177/001872679004300906

Miller, W., & Myers, E. W. (1985). A file comparison program. *Software, Practice & Experience, 15*(11), 1025–1040. doi:10.1002/spe.4380151102

Minbaeva, D., Pedersen, T., Bjorkman, I., Fey, C., & Park, H. (2003). MNC knowledge transfer, subsidiary absorptive capacity, and HRM. *Journal of International Business Studies, 34*(6), 586–599. doi:10.1057/palgrave.jibs.8400056

Miner, J. B. (2003). The rated importance, scientific validity, and practical usefulness of organizational behavior theories: A quantitative review. *Academy of Management Learning & Education, 2*(3), 250–268. doi:10.5465/AMLE.2003.10932132

Mishra, P., & Hershey, K. A. (2004). Etiquette and the design of educational technology. *Communications of the ACM, 47*(4), 45–49. doi:10.1145/975817.975843

Mitasova, H., & Neteler, M. (2004). GRASS as an open source free software GIS: Accomplishments and perspectives. *Transactions in GIS*, 8(2), 145–154. doi:10.1111/j.1467-9671.2004.00172.x

Mitchell, T. R. (1980). Expectancy–value models in organizational psychology . In Feather, N. T. (Ed.), *Expectations and actions* (pp. 293–311). Mahwah, NJ: Lawrence Erlbaum.

Mller, C., Meuthrath, B., & Baumgra, A. (2008). Analyzing wiki based networks to improve knowledge processes in organizations. *Journal of Universal Computer Science*, 14(4), 526–545.

Mockus, A. (2007). Large-scale code reuse in open source software. In *Proceedings of the First International Workshop on Emerging Trends in FLOSS Research and Development.*

Mockus, A., & Herbsleb, J. (2002). Expertise browser: A quantitative approach to identifying expertise. *Proceedings of International Conference on Software Engineering*, (pp. 503–512). Orlando.

Mockus, A., Fielding, R. T., & Herbsleb, J. (2000). A case study of open source software development: The apache server. In *Proceedings of the 22nd International Conference on Software Engineering* (pp. 263-272).

Mockus, A., Fielding, R. T., & Herbsleb, J. D. (2002). Two case studies of open source software development: Apache and Mozilla. *ACM Transactions on Software Engineering and Methodology*, 11(3), 309–346. doi:10.1145/567793.567795

Mockus, A., & Herbsleb, J. (2003). An empirical study of speed and communication in globally distributed software development. *IEEE Transactions on Software Engineering*, 29(6), 481–494. doi:10.1109/TSE.2003.1205177

Moody, B. (2009, April 23). Who owns commercial open source and can forks work? *Linux Journal*.

Moody, B. (2011, January 28). The deeper significance of LibreOffice 3.3. *ComputerWorld UK*.

Morasca, S., Taibi, D., & Tosi, D. (2010). T-DOC: a Tool for the Automatic Generation of Testing Documentation for OSS Products. In *Proceedings of the IFIP International Conference on Open Source Software.*

Morasca, S., Taibi, T., & Tosi, D. (2009). Certifying the testing process of open source software: New challenges or old methodologies? In *Proceedings of the IEEE International Workshop on Free/Libre/Open Source Software Research and Development* (pp. 25-30).

Mørch, A. I., Stevens, G., Won, M., Klann, M., Dittrich, Y., & Wulf, V. (2004). Component-based technologies for end-user development. *Communications of the ACM*, 47(9), 59–62. doi:10.1145/1015864.1015890

Morell, L. J. (1990). A theory of fault-based testing. *IEEE Transactions on Software Engineering*, 16(8), 844–857. doi:10.1109/32.57623

Morgan, L., & Finnegan, P. (2010). Open innovation in secondary software firms: An exploration of managers' perceptions of open source software. *SIGMIS Database*, 41(1), 76–95.

Morris, M., Schindehutte, M., & Allen, J. (2005). The entrepreneurs business model: Toward a unified perspective. *Journal of Business Research*, 58, 725–735. doi:10.1016/j.jbusres.2003.11.001

Moser, T. (2009). *Semantic integration of engineering environments using an engineering knowledge base* (Unpublished doctoral dissertation). Vienna University of Technology, Vienna, Austria.

Mowday, R. T., Porter, L. W., & Steers, R. M. (1982). *Employee–organization linkages: The psychology of commitment and absenteeism and turnover*. New York, NY: Academic Press.

Myers, E. W. (1986). An o(nd) difference algorithm and its variations. *Algorithmica*, 1, 251–266. doi:10.1007/BF01840446

Myers, M. D. (1997). Qualitative research in information systems. *Management Information Systems Quarterly*, 21(2), 241–242. doi:10.2307/249422

Nalani, H. A. (2009). WebGIS based 3D visualization of geospatial data. In *Proceedings of the Applied Geoinformatics for Society and Environment Conference*, Stuttgart, Germany (pp. 212-215). Retrieved November 3, 2010, from http://www.gis-news.de/papers/AGSE_Proceedings_2009_07_01_1025.pdf

Narayanaswamy, K., & Scacchi, W. (1987). Maintaining evolving configurations of large software systems. *IEEE Transactions on Software Engineering*, *13*(3), 324–334. doi:10.1109/TSE.1987.233163

Naylor, H. (1967). *Volunteers today: Finding, training and working with them*. New York, NY: Association Press.

Neuman, W. L. (1991). *Social research methods: Qualitative and quantitative approaches*. Boston, MA: Allyn and Bacon.

Newton, R. R., & Rudestam, K. E. (1999). *Your statistical consultant: Answers to your data analysis questions*. Thousand Oaks, CA: Sage.

Nichols, D. M., Thomson, K., & Yeates, S. A. (2001). Usability and open-source software development. In *Proceedings of the ACM SIGCHI Symposium on Computer Human Interaction*, Palmerston North, New Zealand (pp. 49-54).

Nichols, D. M., & Twidale, M. B. (2006). Usability processes in open source projects. *Software Process Improvement and Practice*, *11*(2), 149–162. doi:10.1002/spip.256

Nielsen, J. (1999). User Interface Directions for the Web. *Communications of the ACM*, *42*(1), 65–72. doi:10.1145/291469.291470

Nonaka, I., & Takeuchi, H. (1995). *The knowledge-creating company: How japanese companies create the dynamics of innovation*. New York: Oxford University.

Nunnally, J. C., & Bernste, I. A. (1994). *Psychometric theory* (3rd ed.). New York, NY: McGraw-Hill.

O' Mahony, S., & Ferraro, F. (2007). The emergence of governance in an open source community. *Academy of Management Journal*, *50*(5), 1079–1106. doi:10.5465/AMJ.2007.27169153

OGC. (2011). *GeoAPI*. Retrieved December 18, 2011, from http://www.geoapi.org

Okoli, C., & Oh, W. (2007). Investigating recognition–based performance in an open content community: A social capital perspective. *Information & Management*, *44*(3), 240–252. doi:10.1016/j.im.2006.12.007

Oksanen, V., & Kupsu, M. (2008). *OSLC Open Source License Checker V3*. Retrieved from http://forge.ow2.org/projects/oslcv3/

Omoto, A. M., & Snyder, M. (1995). Sustained helping without obligation: Motivation, longevity of service, and perceived attitude change among AIDS volunteers. *Journal of Personality and Social Psychology*, *68*(4), 671–686. doi:10.1037/0022-3514.68.4.671

Orlikowksi, W. J., & Baroudi, J. (1991). Studying information technology in organizations: Research approaches and assumptions. *Information Systems Research*, *2*(1), 1–28. doi:10.1287/isre.2.1.1

Orsila, H., Geldenhuys, J., Ruokonen, A., & Hammouda, I. (2008). Update propagation practices in highly reusable open source components. In *Proceedings of the IFIP 20th World Computer Congress on Open Source Software* (Vol. 275, pp. 159-170).

Orso, A. (2010). Monitoring, analysis, and testing of deployed software. In *Proceedings of the FSE/SDP Workshop on Future of Software Engineering Research* (pp. 263-268).

OSGEO. (2010). *GeoTools InfoSheet*. Retrieved October 31, 2010, from http://www.osgeo.org/geotools

OSI. (2006). *The open source definition, version 1.9*. Retrieved August 4, 2009, from http://www.opensource.org/docs/osd

Osterhof, A. (2001). *Classroom applications of educational measurement*. Upper Saddle River, NJ: Prentice Hall.

Osterloh, M., & Rota, S. (2007). Open source software development – Just another case of collective invention? *Research Policy*, *36*(2), 157–171. doi:10.1016/j.respol.2006.10.004

Osterwalder, A. (2004). *The business model ontology - a proposition in a design science approach*. Lausanne, Switzerland: University of Lausanne.

Osterwalder, A., Pigneur, Y., & Tucci, C. L. (2005). Clarifying business models: Origins, present, and future of the concept. *Communications of the Association for Information Systems*, *15*, 2–40.

Ostrand, T. J., & Balcer, M. J. (1988). The category-partition method for specifying and generating functional tests. *Communications of the ACM, 31*(6), 676–686. doi:10.1145/62959.62964

Otte, T., Moreton, R., & Knoell, H. D. (2008). Applied quality assurance methods under the open source development model. In *Proceedings of the IEEE 32nd International Computer Software and Applications Conference* (pp. 1247-1252).

Ozel, N. M., Necmioglu, O., Yalciner, A. C., Kalafat, D., Yilmazer, M., & Comoglu, M. …Erdik, M. (forthcoming, June 17-22). *Tsunami early warning in the Eastern Mediterranean, Aegean and Black Sea*. Paper to be presented at the 22nd International Ocean and Polar Engineering Conference, Rhodes (Rodos), Greece.

Pan, K., Kim, S., & Whitehead, E. J. Jr. (2009). Toward an understanding of bug fix patterns. *Empirical Software Engineering, 14*(3), 286–315. doi:10.1007/s10664-008-9077-5

Parnas, D. L. (1972). On the criteria to be used in decomposing systems into modules. *Communications of the ACM, 15*(12), 1053–1058. doi:10.1145/361598.361623

Parnas, D. L. (1979). Designing software for ease of extension and contraction. *IEEE Transactions on Software Engineering, 5*(2), 128–138. doi:10.1109/TSE.1979.234169

Paulson, J. W., Succi, G., & Eberlein, A. (2004). An empirical study of open-source and closed-source software products. *IEEE Transactions on Software Engineering, 30*(4), 246–256. doi:10.1109/TSE.2004.1274044

Pebesma, E. J. (2004). Multivariable geostatistics in S: The gstat package. *Computers & Geosciences, 30*(7), 683–691. doi:10.1016/j.cageo.2004.03.012

Penner, L. A., & Finkelstein, M. A. (1998). Dispositional and structural determinants of volunteerism. *Journal of Personality and Social Psychology, 74*(2), 525–537. doi:10.1037/0022-3514.74.2.525

Perry, D. E., & Wolf, A. L. (1992). Foundations for the study of software architectures. *ACM SIGSOFT Software Engineering Notes, 17*(4), Runeson, P., & Höst, M. (2009). Guidelines for conducting and reporting case study research in software engineering. *Empirical Software Engineering, 14*(2), 131–164.

Petrinja, E., Nambakam, R., & Sillitti, A. (2009). Introducing the OpenSource Maturity Model. In *Proceedings of the IEEE International Workshop on Free/Libre/Open Source Software Research and Development*.

Pezzè, M., & Young, M. (2007). *Software Testing and Analysis. Process, Principles, and Techniques*. New York, NY: John Wiley & Sons.

Porruvecchio, G., Uras, S., & Quaresima, R. (2008). Social network analysis of communication in open source projects. *9*, pp. 220–221. Proceedings of 9th International Conference on Agile Processes in Software Engineering and Extreme Programming.

Porter, L. W., Steers, R. M., Mowday, R. T., & Boulian, P. V. (1974). Organizational commitment, job satisfaction and turnover among psychiatric technicians. *The Journal of Applied Psychology, 59*(5), 603–609. doi:10.1037/h0037335

Postigo, H. (2007). Of mods and modders: Chasing down the value of fan-based digital game modifications. *Games and Culture, 2*(4), 300–313. doi:10.1177/1555412007307955

Postigo, H. (2008). Video game appropriation through modifications: Attitudes concerning intellectual property among modders and fans. *Convergence, 14*(1), 59–74. doi:10.1177/1354856507084419

Pretschner, A., Prenninger, W., Wagner, S., Kuhnel, C., Baumgartner, M., Sostawa, B., & Zolch, R. (2005). One evaluation of model-based testing and its automation. In *Proceedings of the 27th International Conference on Software Engineering* (pp. 392-401).

Price, J. L. (1981). A causal model of turnover for nurses. *Academy of Management Journal, 24*(3), 543–565. doi:10.2307/255574

Qureshi, H., Davies, B., & Challis, D. (1979). Motivations and rewards of volunteers and informal care givers. *Journal of Voluntary Action Research, 8*(1-2), 47–55.

Raape, U., Teßmann, S., Wytzisk, A., Steinmetz, T., Wnuk, M., & Hunold, M. …Jirka, S. (2010). Decision support for tsunami early warning in Indonesia: The role of OGC standards. In M. Konecny, T. L. Bandrova, & S. Zlatanova (Eds.), *Geographic information and cartography for risk and crisis management* (Vol. 2, pp. 233-247). Berlin, Germany: Springer-Verlag.

Raghunathan, S., Prasad, A., Mishra, B. K., & Chang, H. (2005). Open source versus closed source: software quality in monopoly and competitive markets. *IEEE Transactions on Systems, Man and Cybernetics . Part A*, *35*(6), 903–918.

Rajala, R., Nissila, J., & Westerlund, M. (2006). Determinants of OSS revenue model choices. In *Proceedings of the 14th European Conference of Information Systems*, Gothenburg, Sweden.

Ramsey, P. (2007). *The state of open source GIS*. Paper presented at the annual Free and Open Source Software for Geospatial Conference, Vancouver, BC, Canada.

Raykov, T., & Marcoulides, G. A. (2000). *A first course in structural equation modeling*. Mahwah, NJ: Lawrence Erlbaum.

Raymond, E. (1999). The cathedral and the bazaar. *Knowledge, Technology & Policy*, *12*(3), 23–49. doi:10.1007/s12130-999-1026-0

Raymond, E. S. (1999). *The magic cauldron*. Sebastopol, CA: O'Reilly Media.

Raymond, E. S. (2001). *The cathedral and the bazaar: Musings on Linux and open source by an accidental revolutionary*. Sebastopol, CA: O'Reilly.

Refractions Research. (2010a). *A GIS framework for eclipse*. Retrieved October 31, 2010, from http://udig.refractions.net/

Refractions Research. (2010b). *Developing with uDig*. Retrieved October 31, 2010, from http://udig.refractions.net/developers/

Reid, J., & Martin, F. (2001). *The open source movement and its potential in implementing spatial data infrastructures*. Paper presented at the International Symposium on Spatial Data Infrastructure, Melbourne, Australia.

Remenyi, D. (1998). *Doing research in business and management: An introduction to process and method*. Thousand Oaks, CA: Sage.

Results, I. C. T. (2010). *New tsunami early warning system stands guard*. Retrieved August 17, 2010, from http://cordis.europa.eu/ictresults/index.cfm?tpl=article&ID=91371

Reynolds, L. G. (1951). *The structure of labor markets: Wages and labor mobility in theory and practice* (4th ed.). Westport, CT: Greenwood Press.

Rich Client Platform. (2010). Retrieved from Rich Client Platform: wiki.eclipse.org

Riehle, D. (2009). *The commercial OSS business model*. Paper presented at the Americas Conference of Information Systems, San Francisco, CA.

Rigby, P. C., German, D. M., & Storey, M.-A. (2008). Open source software peer review practices: a case study of the apache server. In *Proceedings of the International Conference on Software Engineering* (pp. 541-550).

Robbins, S. P. (1998). *Organizational behavior* (8th ed.). Upper Saddle River, NJ: Prentice Hall.

Roberts, J. A., Hann, I. H., & Slaughter, S. A. (2006). Understanding the motivations, participation, and performance of open source software developers: A longitudinal study of the Apache project. *Management Science*, *52*(7), 984–999. doi:10.1287/mnsc.1060.0554

Robles, G., & González-Barahona, J. M. (2006). Contributor turnover in libre software projects. In *Proceedings of the IFIP Open Source Software Conference* (Vol. 203, pp. 273-286).

Robles, G., González-Barahona, J. M., & Guervós, J. J. M. (2006). Beyond source code: The importance of other artifacts in software development (a case study). *Journal of Systems and Software*, *79*(9), 1233–1248. doi:10.1016/j.jss.2006.02.048

Robles, G., González-Barahona, J. M., Izquierdo-Cortazar, D., & Herraiz, I. (2009). Tools for the study of the usual data sources found in Libre software projects. *International Journal of Open Source Software and Processes*, *1*(1), 24–45. doi:10.4018/jossp.2009010102

Roche, J. (1994). Software metrics and measurement principles. *SIGSOFT Software Engineering Notes, 19*(1), 77–85. doi:10.1145/181610.181625

Rosen, L. U. (2004). *Open source licensing: Software freedom and intellectual property law.* Upper Saddle River, NJ: Prentice Hall.

Rosso, C. (2006). Continuous evolution through software architecture evaluation. *Journal of Software Maintenance and Evolution: Research and Practice, 18*(5), 351–383. doi:10.1002/smr.337

Rosso, C. (2009). Comprehend and analyze knowledge networks to improve software evolution. *Journal of Software Maintenance and Evolution: Research and Practice, 21*, 189–215. doi:10.1002/smr.408

Rotter, J. B. (1954). *Social learning and clinical psychology.* Upper Saddle River, NJ: Prentice Hall. doi:10.1037/10788-000

Salancik, G. R. (1977). Commitment and control of organizational behavior and belief . In Staw, B., & Salancik, G. R. (Eds.), *New directions in organizational behavior* (pp. 1–54). Chicago, IL: St. Clair Press.

Sametinger, J. (1997). *Software engineering with reusable components.* Berlin, Germany: Springer-Verlag.

Samoladas, I., Gousios, G., Spinellis, D., & Stamelos, I. (2008). The SQO-OSS quality model: Measurement based open source software evaluation. In *Proceedings of the 4th International Conference on Open Source Systems* (pp. 237-248).

Samoladas, I., Stamelos, I., Angelis, L., & Oikonomou, A. (2004). Open source software development should strive for even greater code maintainability. *Communications of the ACM, 47*(10), 83–87. doi:10.1145/1022594.1022598

Santelices, R. A., Chittimalli, P. K., Apiwattanapong, T., Orso, A., & Harrold, M. J. (2008). Test-suite augmentation for evolving software. In *Proceedings of the IEEE International Conference on Automated Software Engineering* (pp. 218-227).

Santokhee, A. (2008). *GeoTools.* Retrieved June 13, 2011, from http://www.resc.rdg.ac.uk/twiki/bin/view/Resc/GeoTools

Sarma, A. Maccherone, Wagstrom, & Herbsleb. (2009). Tesseract: Interactive visual exploration of socio-technical relationships in software development. *Proceedings of the 31st International Conference on Software Engineering,* (pp. 23–33).

Sarma, A., Noroozi, Z., & Van der Hoek, A. (2003). Palantr: Raising awareness among configuration management workspaces. *Twenty-fifth International Conference on Software Engineering,* (pp. 444–454). Portland, Oregon, USA.

Sartipi, K., Kontogiannis, K., & Mavaddat, F. (2000). A pattern matching framework for software architecture recovery and restructuring. In *Proceedings of the 8th International Workshop on Program Comprehension* (pp. 37-47).

Scacchi, W. (2007, September). Free/open source software development: Recent research results and emerging opportunities. In *Proceedings of the European Software Engineering Conference and ACM SIGSOFT Symposium on the Foundations of Software Engineering,* Dubrovnik, Croatia (pp. 459-468).

Scacchi, W. (1998). Modeling, integrating, and enacting complex organizational processes . In Carley, K., Gasser, L., & Prietula, M. (Eds.), *Simulating organizations: Computational models of institutions and groups* (pp. 153–168). Cambridge, MA: MIT Press.

Scacchi, W. (2002). Understanding the requirements for developing open source software. *IEEE Software Engineering, 149*(1), 24–39. doi:10.1049/ip-sen:20020202

Scacchi, W. (2004). Free/open source software development practices in the game community. *IEEE Software, 21*(1), 59–67. doi:10.1109/MS.2004.1259221

Scacchi, W. (2009). Understanding requirements for open source software . In Lyytinen, K., Loucopoulos, P., Mylopoulos, J., & Robinson, W. (Eds.), *Design requirements engineering - A multi-disciplinary perspective for the next decade.* Berlin, Germany: Springer-Verlag.

Scacchi, W. (2010). Game-based virtual worlds as decentralized virtual activity systems . In Bainbridge, W. S. (Ed.), *Online worlds: Convergence of the real and the virtual* (pp. 225–236). New York, NY: Springer. doi:10.1007/978-1-84882-825-4_18

Scarpello, V., & Campbell, J. P. (1983). Job satisfaction: Are all the parts there? *Personnel Psychology*, *36*(3), 577–600. doi:10.1111/j.1744-6570.1983.tb02236.x

Schmerl, B., Aldrich, J., Garlan, D., Kazman, R., & Yan, H. (2006). Discovering architectures from running systems. *IEEE Transactions on Software Engineering*, *32*(7), 454–466. doi:10.1109/TSE.2006.66

Schmmer, T., & Haake, J. M. (2001). Supporting distributed software development by modes of collaboration. *Seventh European Conference on Computer Supported Cooperative Work*, (pp. 79–98).

Schwaber, K. (2004). *Agile project management with scrum*. Redmond, WA: Microsoft Press.

Schwaber, K., & Beedle, M. (2001). *Agile software development with Scrum*. Englewood Cliffs, NJ: Prentice-Hall.

Schweik, C. M., English, R. C., Kitsing, M., & Haire, S. (2008). Brooks' versus Linus' Law: An empirical test of open source projects. In *Proceedings of the International Conference on Digital Government Research* (pp. 423-424).

Seffah, A. (2003). Learning the ropes: Human-centered design skills and patterns for software engineers' education. *Interaction*, *10*(5), 36–45. doi:10.1145/889692.889693

Seffah, A., Donyaee, M., Kline, R. B., & Padda, H. K. (2006). Usability measurement and metrics: A consolidated model. *Software Quality Journal*, *14*, 159–178. doi:10.1007/s11219-006-7600-8

Seffah, A., & Metzker, E. (2004). The obstacles and myths of usability and software engineering. *Communications of the ACM*, *47*(12), 71–76. doi:10.1145/1035134.1035136

Sengupta, S. (1998). Some approaches to complementary product strategies. *Journal of Product Innovation Management*, *15*(4), 352–367. doi:10.1016/S0737-6782(97)00106-9

Senyard, A., & Michlmayr, M. (2004). How to have a successful free software project. In *Proceedings of the 11th Asia-Pacific Software Engineering Conference* (pp. 84-91).

Shah, S. K. (2006). Motivation, governance, and the viability of hybrid forms in open source software development. *Management Science*, *52*(7), 1000–1014. doi:10.1287/mnsc.1060.0553

Sharma, S., Sugumaran, V., & Rajagopalan, B. (2002). A framework for creating hybrid-open source software communities. *Information Systems Journal*, *12*(1), 7–25. doi:10.1046/j.1365-2575.2002.00116.x

Sharp, E. G. (1978). Citizen organization in policing issues and crime prevention: Incentives for participation. *Journal of Voluntary Action Research*, *7*(1-2), 45–58.

Shneiderman, B. (2000). Universal usability. *Communications of the ACM*, *43*(5), 84–91. doi:10.1145/332833.332843

Siddiquee, Z. H., Strzalka, A., & Eicker, U. (2009). Publication of energy consumption data of Scharnhauser Park via Web GIS. In *Proceedings of the Conference of the Applied Geoinformatics for Society and Environment*, Stuttgart, Germany (pp. 186-190). Retrieved November 3, 2010, from http://www.gis-news.de/papers/AGSE_Proceedings_2009_07_01_1025.pdf

Silcock, H. (1954). The phenomenon of labour turnover. *Journal of the Royal Statistical Society. Series A (General)*, *117*(4), 429–440. doi:10.2307/2342680

Singer, J., & Vinson, N. G. (2002). Ethical issues in empirical studies of software engineering. *IEEE Transactions on Software Engineering*, *28*(12), 1171–1180. doi:10.1109/TSE.2002.1158289

Singer, M. S., & Coffin, T. K. (1996). Cognitive and volitional determinants of job attitudes in a voluntary organization. *Journal of Social Behavior and Personality*, *11*(2), 313–328.

Śliwerski, J., Zimmermann, T., & Zeller, A. (2005). When do changes induce fixes? In *Proceedings of the International Workshop on Mining Software Repositories* (pp. 1-5). New York, NY: ACM.

Smith, C. B. (1997). Casting the net: Surveying an Internet population. *Journal of Computer Mediated Communication*, *3*(1). Retrieved November 27, 2011, from http://www.ascusc.org/jcmc/vol3/issue1/smith.html

Smith, D. H. (1981). Altruism, volunteers, and volunteerism. *Journal of Voluntary Action Research*, *10*(1), 21–36.

Smith, M. A., & Leigh, B. (1997). Virtual subjects: Using the Internet as an alternative source of subjects and research environment. *Behavior Research Methods, Instruments, & Computers, 29*(4), 469–505. doi:10.3758/BF03210601

Smits, S. J., Mclean, E. R., & Tanner, J. R. (1993). Managing high-achieving information systems professionals. *Journal of Management Information Systems, 9*(4), 103–120.

Smoker, D. (2010). *75% of Linux code written by paid developers*. Retrieved November 18, 2011, from http://www.osnews.com/story/22786/75_of_Linux_Code_Written_by_Paid_Developers

Snyder, M. (1993). Basic research and practical problems: The promise of a 'functional' personality and social psychology. *Personality and Social Psychology Bulletin, 19*(3), 251–264. doi:10.1177/0146167293193001

Sohn, S. Y., & Mok, M. S. (2008). A strategic analysis for successful open source software utilization based on a structural equation model. *Journal of Systems and Software, 81*(6), 1014–1024. doi:10.1016/j.jss.2007.08.034

Sojer, M., & Henkel, J. (2010). Code reuse in open source software development: Quantitative evidence, drivers, and impediments. *Journal of the Association for Information Systems, 11*(12), 868–901.

Sommerville, I. (2004). *Software engineering (International Computer Science Series)* (7th ed.). Reading, MA: Addison-Wesley.

Sotamaa, O. (2010). When the game is not enough: Motivations and practices among computer game modding culture. *Games and Culture, 5*(3), 239–255. doi:10.1177/1555412009359765

Soto, M., & Ciolkowski, M. (2009). The QualOSS open source assessment model measuring the performance of open source communities. In *Proceedings of the 3rd International Symposium on Empirical Software Engineering and Measurement* (pp. 498-501).

SourceForge. (2011). *Email client*. Retrieved from http://sourceforge.net/directory/?q=email%20client

Souza, C. d., Quirk, S., Trainer, E., & Redmiles, D. (2007). Supporting collaborative software development through the visualization of socio-technical dependencies. *International ACM SIGGROUP Conference on Supporting Group Work*, (pp. 147–156). Sanibel Island, FL.

Spinellis, D. (2008). A tale of four kernels. In *Proceedings of the 30th International Conference on Software Engineering* (pp. 381-390).

Stallman, R. (2002). *Free software, free society: Selected essays of Richard M. Stallman*. Boston, MA: GNU Press.

Stamelos, I., Angelis, L., Oikonomou, A., & Bleris, G. L. (2002). Code quality analysis in open source software development. *Information Systems Journal, 12*, 43–60. doi:10.1046/j.1365-2575.2002.00117.x

Steiniger, S., & Bocher, E. (2009). An overview on current free and open source desktop GIS developments. *International Journal of Geographical Information Science, 23*(10), 1345–1370. doi:10.1080/13658810802634956

Stevens, J. (1986). *Applied multivariate statistics for the social sciences*. Mahwah, NJ: Lawrence Erlbaum.

Stewart, K. J., & Gosain, S. (2006). The impact of ideology on effectiveness in open source software development teams. *Management Information Systems Quarterly, 30*(2), 291–314.

Stoikov, V., & Raimon, R. L. (1968). Determinants of differences in the quit rate among industries. *The American Economic Review, 58*(5), 1283–1298.

Strauss, A. L., & Corbin, J. M. (1990). *Basics of qualitative research: Grounded theory procedures and techniques* (1st ed.). Newbury Park, CA: Sage.

Strauss, A., & Corbin, J. (1994). Grounded theory methodology - An overview . In Denzin, N. K., & Lincoln, Y. S. (Eds.), *Handbook of qualitative research* (pp. 273–285). Thousand Oaks, CA: Sage.

Swanson, E. B. (1976). The dimensions of maintenance. In *Proceedings of the 2nd International Conference on Software Engineering* (pp. 492-497).

Szyperski, C. (2002). *Component software: Beyond object-oriented programming* (2nd ed.). Reading, MA: Addison-Wesley.

Taibi, D., Lavazza, L., & Morasca, S. (2007). OpenBQR: a framework for the assessment of OSS. *International Journal on Open Source Development, Adoption and Innovation*, 173-186.

Taylor, T. L. (2009). The assemblage of play. *Games and Culture*, *4*(4), 331–339. doi:10.1177/1555412009343576

Te'eni, D. (2007). HCI is in business---focusing on organizational tasks and management. *Interaction*, *14*(4), 16–19. doi:10.1145/1273961.1273975

Tennant, G. (2001). *Six sigma: SPC and TQM in manufacturing and services*. Surrey, UK: Gower.

Thatcher, J. B., Stepina, L. P., & Boyle, R. J. (2002). Turnover of information technology workers: Examining empirically the influence of attitudes, job characteristics, and external markets. *Journal of Management Information Systems*, *19*(3), 231–261.

The Qualipso Project 1. (2010). *How European software industry perceives OSS trustworthiness and what are the specific criteria to establish trust in OSS*. Retrieved from http://www.qualipso.eu/node/45

Tiwana, A. (2010). *The influence of software platform modularity on platform abandonment: An empirical study of Firefox extension developers. Unpublished Presentation*. Athens, GA: University of Georgia, Terry School of Business.

Todorova, G., & Durisin, B. (2007). Absorptive capacity: Valuing a reconceptualization. *Academy of Management Review*, *32*(3), 774–786. doi:10.5465/AMR.2007.25275513

Tomsic, M. L., Hendel, D. D., & Matross, R. P. (2000). *A World Wide Web response to student satisfaction surveys: Comparisons using paper and Internet formats*. Paper presented at the 40th Annual Meeting of the Association for Institutional Research, Cincinnati, OH.

Torchiano, M., & Morisio, M. (2004). Overlooked aspects of COTS-based development. *IEEE Software*, *21*(2), 88–93. doi:10.1109/MS.2004.1270770

Tosi, D., & Tahir, A. (2010). How developers test their Open Source Software Products. A survey of well-known OSS projects. In *Proceedings of the 5th International Conference on Software and Data Technologies*.

Tran, J. B., & Holt, R. C. (1999). Forward and reverse repair of software architecture. In *Proceedings of the Conference of the Centre for Advanced Studies on Collaborative Research*.

Tran, J. B., Godfrey, M. W., Lee, E. H. S., & Holt, R. C. (2000). Architectural repair of open source software. In *Proceedings of the 8th International Workshop on Program Comprehension* (pp. 48-59).

Tress, S., & Moestofa, A. (2009). uDig – An overview of open source desktop GIS application. In *Proceedings of the Conference of the Applied Geoinformatics for Society and Environment*, Stuttgart, Germany.

TRIDEC. (2010). *Collaborative, complex, and critical decision processes in evolving crises*. Retrieved December 17, 2011, from http://www.tridec-online.eu

Troy, D. A., & Zweben, S. H. (1981). Measuring the quality of structured designs. *Journal of Systems and Software*, *2*(2), 113–120. doi:10.1016/0164-1212(81)90031-5

Tsantalis, N., & Chatzigeorgiou, A. (2009). Identification of move method refactoring opportunities. *IEEE Transactions on Software Engineering*, *35*(3), 347–367. doi:10.1109/TSE.2009.1

Tschirhart, M., Mesch, D. J., Perry, J. L., Miller, T. K., & Lee, G. (2001). Stipended volunteers: their goals, experiences, satisfaction, and likelihood of future service. *Nonprofit and Voluntary Sector Quarterly*, *30*(3), 422–443. doi:10.1177/0899764001303002

Tushman, M. L. (1977). Special boundary roles in the innovation process. *Administrative Science Quarterly*, *22*(4), 587–605. doi:10.2307/2392402

Tushman, M. L., & Nadler, D. (1986). Organizing for innovation. *California Management Review*, *28*(3), 74–92.

Tuunanen, T., Koskinen, J., & Karkkainen, T. (2006). Asla: reverse engineering approach for software license information retrieval. *Proceedings of the 10th European Conference on Software Maintenance and Reengineering*, (pp. 291–294).

Tuunanen, T., Koskinen, J., & Kärkkäinen, T. (2009). Automated software license analysis. *International Journal on Automated Software Engineering*, *16*(3), 455–490. doi:10.1007/s10515-009-0054-z

Ukkonen, E. (1985). Algorithms for approximate string matching. *Information and Control*, *64*(1-3), 100–118. doi:10.1016/S0019-9958(85)80046-2

Ullman, J. B. (1996). Structural equation modeling . In Tabachnick, B. G., & Fidell, L. S. (Eds.), *Using multivariate statistics* (3rd ed., pp. 709–819). New York, NY: Harper Collins College.

UN. (2006). Global survey of early warning systems. In *Proceedings of the Third International Conference on Early Warning*, Bonn, Germany.

van de Ven, A. H., & Ferry, D. L. (1980). *Measuring and assessing organizations*. New York, NY: John Wiley & Sons.

Van Den Bosch, F. A. J., Volberda, H. W., & De Boer, M. (1999). Coevolution of firm absorptive capacity and knowledge environment: Organizational forms and combinative capabilities. *Organization Science*, *10*(5), 551–568. doi:10.1287/orsc.10.5.551

Ven, K., & Verelst, J. (2008, June 9-11). The organizational adoption of open source server software: A quantitative study. In *Proceedings of the 16th European Conference on Information Systems*, Galway, Ireland (pp. 1430-1441).

Ven, K., & Mannaert, H. (2008). Challenges and strategies in the use of open source software by independent software vendors. *Information and Software Technology*, *50*(9-10), 991–1002. doi:10.1016/j.infsof.2007.09.001

Ven, K., & Verelst, J. (2010). Determinants of the use of knowledge sources in the adoption of open source server software: An absorptive capacity perspective. *International Journal of Technology Diffusion*, *1*(4), 53–70. doi:10.4018/jtd.2010100105

Ven, K., & Verelst, J. (2011). An empirical investigation into the assimilation of open source server software. *Communications of the Association for Information Systems*, *28*(1), 117–140.

Ven, K., & Verelst, J. (in press). A qualitative study on the organizational adoption of open source server software. *Information Systems Management*.

Ven, K., Verelst, J., & Mannaert, H. (2008). Should you adopt open source software. *IEEE Software*, *25*(3), 54–59. doi:10.1109/MS.2008.73

Viorres, N., Xenofon, P., Stavrakis, M., Vlachogiannis, E., Koutsabasis, P., & Darzentas, J. (2007). Major HCI challenges for open source software adoption and development online communities and social computing. In *Proceedings of the 2nd International Conference OCSC held as part of HCI International* (pp. 455-464).

von Hippel, E. (1988). *The sources of innovation*. New York, NY: Oxford University Press.

von Hippel, E. (2001). Perspective: User toolkits for innovation. *Journal of Product Innovation Management*, *18*(4), 247–257. doi:10.1016/S0737-6782(01)00090-X

Von Hippel, E., & Von Krogh, G. (2003). Open source software and the "private-collective" innovation model: Issues for organization science. *Organization Science*, *14*(2), 209–223. doi:10.1287/orsc.14.2.209.14992

von Krogh, G., & von Hippel, E. (2003). Special issue on open source software development. *Research Policy*, *32*(7), 1149–1157. doi:10.1016/S0048-7333(03)00054-4

Vroom, V. H. (1964). *Work and motivation*. New York, NY: John Wiley & Sons.

Wächter, J., Fleischer, J., Häner, R., Küppers, A., Lendholt, M., & Hammitzsch, M. (2011). Development of tsunami early warning systems and future challenges. In *Proceedings of the Conference of the European Geosciences Union: Vol. 13. Geophysical Research Abstracts*. Retrieved December 17, 2011, from http://meetingorganizer.copernicus.org/EGU2011/EGU2011-11015-2.pdf

Wahyudin, D. (2008). *Quality prediction and evaluation models for products and processes in distributed software development* (Unpublished doctoral dissertation). Vienna University of Technology, Vienna, Austria.

Wahyudin, D., & Tjoa, A. M. (2007). Event-based monitoring of open source software projects. In *Proceedings of the Second International Conference on Availability, Reliability and Security*.

Wahyudin, D., Schatten, A., Mustofa, K., Biffl, S., & Tjoa, A. M. (2006). Introducing "health" perspective in open source Web-engineering software projects, based on project data analysis. In *Proceedings of the International Conference on Information Integration, Web-Applications and Services*, Yogyakarta, Indonesia.

Wahyudin, D., Mustofa, K., Schatten, A., Biffl, S., & Tjoa, A. M. (2007). Monitoring the "health" status of open source web-engineering projects. *International Journal of Web Information Systems*, 3(1-2), 116–139. doi:10.1108/17440080710829252

Walsham, G. (1995). The emergence of interpretivism in IS research. *Information Systems Research*, 6(4), 376–394. doi:10.1287/isre.6.4.376

Wang, Y., Guo, D., & Shi, H. (2007). Measuring the evolution of open source software systems with their communities. *SIGSOFT Software Engineering Notes*, 32(6), 7. doi:10.1145/1317471.1317479

Wasko, M. M., & Faraj, S. (2005). Why should I share? Examining social capital and knowledge contribution in electronic networks of practice. *Management Information Systems Quarterly*, 29(1), 35–57.

Weber, S. (2004). *The success of open source*. Cambridge, MA: Harvard University Press.

Wen, H. (2005, May 25). Multi theft auto: Hacking multi-player into Grand Theft Auto with open source. *OSDir*. Retrieved June 1, 2011, from http://osdir.com/Article4775.phtml

West, J., & O' Mahony, S. (2008). The role of participation architecture in growing sponsored open source communities. *Industry and Innovation*, 15(2), 145–168. doi:10.1080/13662710801970142

Weyuker, E. J., & Vokolos, F. I. (2000). Experience with performance testing of software systems: issues, an approach, and case study. *IEEE Transactions on Software Engineering*, 26(12), 1147–1156. doi:10.1109/32.888628

Wheeler, D. A. (n.d.). *SLOCCount*. Retrieved from http://www.dwheeler.com/sloccount/

WhereGroup. (2010). *Desktop GIS*. Retrieved November 3, 2010, from http://www.wheregroup.com/en/desktop_gis

Whetten, D. A. (1987). Organizational growth and decline processes. *Annual Review of Sociology*, 13, 335–358. doi:10.1146/annurev.so.13.080187.002003

Wiggins, A., Howison, J., & Crowston, K. (2009). Heartbeat: Measuring active user base and potential user interes in floss projects. [IFIP Advances in Information and Communication Technology.]. *Open Source Ecosystems: Diverse Communities Interacting.*, 299/2009, 94–104. doi:10.1007/978-3-642-02032-2_10

Wikipedia. (n.d.). *George Hotz: Hacking the Playstation 3*. Retrieved from http://en.wikipedia.org/wiki/George_Hotz#Hacking_the_PlayStation_3

Wikipedia. (n.d.). *Lamp (software bundle)*. Retrieved from http://en.wikipedia.org/wiki/LAMP_(software_bundle)

Wikipedia. (n.d.). *Multi theft auto*. Retrieved June 1, 2011, from http://www.mtavc.com/ and http://en.wikipedia.org/wiki/Multi_Theft_Auto

Winter, S., Wagner, S., & Deissenboeck, F. (2007). A comprehensive model of usability. In J. Gulliksen, M. Borup Harning, P. Palanque, G. C. van der Veer, & J. Wesson (Eds.), *Proceedings of the EIS Joint Working Conferences on Engineering Interactive Systems* (LNCS 4940, pp. 106-122).

Wohlin, C., Runeson, P., Host, M., Ohlsson, M. C., Regnell, B., & Wesslen, A. (2000). *Experimentation in software engineering*. Boston, MA: Kluwer Academic.

Wray, B., & Mathieu, R. (2008). Evaluating the performance of open source software projects using data envelopment analysis. *Information Management & Computer Security*, 16(5), 449. doi:10.1108/09685220810920530

Wu, C. G., Gerlach, J. H., & Young, C. E. (2007). An empirical analysis of open source software developers' motivations and continuance intentions. *Information & Management*, 44(3), 253–262. doi:10.1016/j.im.2006.12.006

Yamauchi, Y., Yokozawa, M., Shinohara, T., & Ishida, T. (2000). Collaboration with Lean Media: How open-source software succeeds. In *Proceedings of the ACM Conference on Computer Supported Cooperative Work*, Philadelphia, PA (pp. 329-338).

Ye, Y. (2006). Supporting software development as knowledge-intensive and collaborative activity. *International Workshop on Interdisciplinary Software Engineering Research*, (pp. 15–22). New York NY, U.S.A.

Ye, Y., & Kishida, K. (2003). Toward an understanding of the motivation of open source software developers. In *Proceedings of the 25th International Conference on Software Engineering* (pp. 419-429).

Yee, N. (2006). The labor of fun: How video games blur the boundaries of work and play. *Games and Culture*, *1*(1), 68–71. doi:10.1177/1555412005281819

Ye, Y., Nakakoji, K., Yamamoto, Y., & Kishida, K. (2004). The co-evolution of systems and communities in Free and Open Source software development . In Koch, S. (Ed.), *Free/Open Source software development* (pp. 59–82). Hershey, PA: Idea Group. doi:10.4018/978-1-59140-369-2.ch003

Yin, R. K. (2003). *Case study research: Design and methods* (3rd ed.). Newbury Park, CA: Sage.

Yu, L., Schach, S. R., Chen, K., Heller, G. Z., & Offutt, J. (2006). Maintainability of the kernels of open-source operating systems: A comparison of Linux with FreeBSD, NetBSD, and OpenBSD. *Journal of Systems and Software*, *79*(6), 807–815. doi:10.1016/j.jss.2005.08.014

Yunwen, Y., & Kishida, K. (2003). Toward an understanding of the motivation of open source software developers. In *Proceedings of the 25th International Conference on Software Engineering* (pp. 419-429).

Zaharias, P., & Poylymenakou, A. (2009). Developing a usability evaluation method for e-learning applications: Beyond functional usability. *International Journal of Human-Computer Interaction*, *25*(1), 75–98. doi:10.1080/10447310802546716

Zahra, S. A., & George, G. (2002). Absorptive capacity: A review, reconceptualization, and extension. *Academy of Management Review*, *27*(2), 185–203.

Zhao, L., & Elbaum, S. (2003). Quality assurance under the open source development model. *International Journal of Systems and Software*, *66*(1), 65–75.

Zhou, Y., & Davis, J. (2005). Open source software reliability model: An empirical approach. In *Proceedings of the Fifth Workshop on Open Source Software Engineering*.

Zimmermann, T., Kim, S., Zeller, A., & Whitehead, E. J., Jr. (2006). Mining version archives for co-changed lines. In *Proceedings of the International Workshop on Mining Software Repositories* (pp. 72-75). New York, NY: ACM.

About the Contributors

Stefan Koch is Professor and Chair at Bogazici University, Department of Management. His research interests include user innovation, cost estimation for software projects, the open source development model, the evaluation of benefits from information systems, and ERP systems. He has published over 20 papers in peer-reviewed journals, including *Information Systems Journal, Information Economics and Policy, Decision Support Systems, Empirical Software Engineering, Electronic Markets, Information Systems Management, Journal of Database Management, Journal of Software Maintenance and Evolution, Enterprise Information Systems,* and *Wirtschaftsinformatik,* and over 30 in international conference proceedings and book collections. He has also edited a book titled "Free/Open Source Software Development" for an international publisher in 2004, and serves as Editor-in-Chief of the *International Journal on Open Source Software & Processes.*

* * *

Timo Aaltonen is a principal researcher in Nokia Research Center. He got the doctoral degree in 2005 while studying formal methods. After the dissertation he initiated the open source research in the department of software systems at Tampere University of Technology together with Imed Hammouda. Aaltonen managed several open source related research projects during the years. In 2010 Aaltonen left the university and joined Nokia Research Center.

Faheem Ahmed received his M.E.Sc. (2004) and Ph.D. (2006) in Electrical Engineering from the University of Western Ontario, London, Canada. Currently he is an assistant professor at College of Information Technology, UAE University, Al Ain, United Arab Emirates. Ahmed had many years of industrial experience holding various technical positions in software development organizations. During his professional career he has been actively involved in the life cycle of software development process including requirements management, system analysis and design, implementation, testing, delivery and maintenance. Dr. Ahmed has authored and co-authored many peer-reviewed research articles in leading journals and conference proceedings in the area of software engineering; His current research interests are Software Product Line, Software Process Modeling, Software Process Assessment, and Empirical Software Engineering. He is a member of IEEE.

Stefan Biffl is an associate professor of software engineering at the Institute of Software Technology and Interactive Systems, TU Vienna (http://qse.ifs.tuwien.ac.at/~biffl). He received MS and PhD degrees in computer science from TU Vienna and an MS degree in social and economic sciences from the University of Vienna in 2001. He received an Erwin-Schrödinger research scholarship and spent one year as researcher at the Fraunhofer IESE, focusing on quality management and empirical software engineering. Also, in 2001 he received the Habilitation degree Venia Docendi for his work on empirical software engineering in project management and quality management. In 2006 he worked as guest researcher at Czech Technical University, Department of Cybernetics. Since 2010 Stefan Biffl is the head of the Christian Doppler research laboratory "CDL-Flex."

Cornelia Boldyreff is the Associate Dean (Research and Enterprise) at the School of Architecture, Computing and Engineering at the University of East London. She gained her PhD in Software Engineering from the University of Durham. In 2004 she moved to the University of Lincoln to become the first Professor of Software Engineering at the university, where she co-founded and directed the Centre for Research in Open Source Software. She has over 25 years experience in software engineering research and has published extensively on her research in the field. She is a Fellow of the British Computer Society and a founding committee member of the BCSWomen Specialist Group. She has been actively campaigning for more women in SET throughout her career.

Andrea Capiluppi is a Lecturer in Software Engineering at University Brunel since May 2012. Before that, he was a Senior Lecturer at the University of East London, from February 2009 to April 2012, and a Senior Lecturer at University of Lincoln, UK, for three years, from January 2006 to February 2009. He has gained a PhD from Politecnico di Torino, Italy, in May 2005, and has held a Researcher position and a Consultant position at the Open University in UK. In November 2003 he was a Visiting Researcher in the GSyC group at the University of Rey Juan Carlos de Madrid, Spain, one of the partners of the project proposal. His publications include some 50 papers, published in leading international conferences and journals, mostly devoted to the Open Source Software topic. He has been a consultant to several industrial companies and has published works where results on FLOSS research have been disseminated in commercial sites. He has taken part in one of the packages of the CALIBRE project, a €1.5 million pan-European EU research project focused on the use of FLOSS in industry.

Luiz Fernando Capretz has almost 30 years of international experience in the software engineering field as a practitioner, manager and educator. Having worked in Brazil, Argentina, U.K., Japan, Italy and the UAE, he is currently an Associate Professor and the Director of the Software Engineering Program at the University of Western Ontario, Canada. He has published over 100 peer-reviewed research papers on software engineering in leading international journals and conference proceedings, and he has co-authored two books in the field. His present research interests include software engineering (SE), human factors in SE, software estimation, software product lines, and software engineering education. Dr. Capretz received his Ph.D. in Computing Science from the University of Newcastle upon Tyne (U.K.), his M.Sc. in Applied Computing from the National Institute for Space Research (INPE, Brazil), and his B.Sc. in Computer Science from State University of Campinas (UNICAMP, Brazil). He is an IEEE senior member, ACM member, MBTI certified practitioner, Professional Engineer in Ontario (Canada).

Peter De Bruyn obtained a Master's degree Business Engineering in Management Information Systems from the Faculty of Applied Economics at the University of Antwerp in 2010. Currently, he is working as a doctoral researcher at the Department of Management Information Systems of the University of Antwerp. His main research topics include the organizational adoption of IT and the extension of Normalized Systems theory into the domain of Business Process Modeling and Enterprise Architectures. As of January 2011, he has been granted a Ph.D. research fellowship from the Agency for Innovation by Science and Technology in Flanders (IWT).

James H. Gerlach is a Professor of Information Systems at the The Business School, University of Colorado at Denver. He holds a M.S. in Computer Science and a Ph.D. in Management, both from Purdue University. His research interests include open source software and management of information systems technology. His work appears in such notable journals as *Management Information Systems Quarterly, IEEE Computer, IEEE Software, Communications of the ACM, Information & Management, Decision Support Systems* and *The Accounting Review*. He currently serves on the editorial boards of *International Journal of Information Systems in the Service Sector* and *International Journal of Information and Decision Sciences*.

Jesus M. Gonzalez-Barahona teaches and researches in Universidad Rey Juan Carlos, Móstoles (Spain). He started to be involved in the promotion of libre software in 1991. Since then, he has carried on several activities in this area, including the organization of seminars and courses, and the participation in working groups on libre software, both at the Spanish and European levels. Currently he collaborates with several libre software projects (including Debian) and associations, writes in several media about topics related to libre software, and consults for companies and public administrations on issues related to their strategy on these topics. His research interests include understanding libre software development, where he has published several papers, and is participating in some international research projects. He is also one of the promoters of the idea of an European master program on libre software, and has specific interest in the education in that area.

Martin Hammitzsch is a researcher at the CeGIT Center for GeoInformation Technology of the GFZ German Research Centre for Geosciences. He received his MSc in Software Systems Engineering at the Hasso-Plattner-Institute at the University of Potsdam. His research activities include the system design and development of early warning systems for natural and man-made hazards and the applicability of emerging technologies in geoinformatics.

Imed Hammouda is currently an adjunct professor at Tampere University of Technology (TUT) where he is heading the international master's programme at the department of software systems. He got his PhD in software engineering from TUT in 2005. Dr. Hammouda's research interests include open source software, community-driven software development, and software architecture. He is co-leading TUTOpen - TUT research group on open source software. He has been leading and involved in several research projects related to various open initiatives.

Daniel Izquierdo-Cortazar is a PhD student at the Universidad Rey Juan Carlos in Móstoles, Spain. He earned a degree in computer science from the same university and obtained his master degree in computer networks and computer science systems in 2006. His research work is centered in the assessment of libre software communities from an engineering point of view and especially with regard to quantitative and empirical issues. Right now he holds a grant from the Universidad Rey Juan Carlos to dedicate part of his time to his PhD's thesis. He was also involved in European-funded projects such as QualOSS or FLOSSWorld. He also teaches at Universidad Rey Juan Carlos, Móstoles (Spain) in the Master on Free Software.

Spyridoula Lakka holds a Degree in Mathematics from the University of Athens (Greece) and an M.Sc. degree in Computer Science from the University of Liverpool (UK). She has a working experience in management position at the Managing Authority of the Greek Ministry of Education and a teaching experience in Information Technology in secondary education and vocational training. She is currently a PhD candidate and is conducting research in the field of Management of Information Systems with a focus on the managerial implications of Open Source Software (OSS). Topics of research interest include OSS business models, factors affecting diffusion of OSS and impact of OSS on software market structures and competition.

Dracoulis Martakos is an Associate Professor at the Department of Informatics and Telecommunications at the National and Kapodistrian University of Athens. He received his B.Sc. in Physics, M.Sc. in Electronics and Radio Communications and Ph.D. in Real-Time Computing from the same university. He is a consultant to public and private organizations and a project leader in numerous national and international projects. He serves on the Board of the Hellenic Chapter of the Association of Information Systems (AIS) and he is the author or co-author of more than 70 scientific publications and a number of technical reports and studies.

Christos Michalakelis holds a Mathematics degree from the University of Athens, Greece, an M.Sc. degree in Software Engineering (The University of Liverpool, UK). He also holds an M.Sc. degree in "Administration and Economics of Telecommunication Networks" and a PhD from the University of Athens (Department of Informatics and Telecommunications), in the area of techno-economics and forecasting of new products growth in high technology markets. He has been working for 7 years with the Greek Ministry of Education, as an IT manager. He specializes in demand estimation and forecasting of high technology products, market competition, price modeling and the application of economic theories over the information and telecommunication technologies.

Tommi Mikkonen is a Professor of Computer Science at Tampere University of Technology in Finland. Tommi has pioneered the research and education on open source software development in Finland. Tommi's current research interests include open source software development, cloud computing, web programming, mashup development, and community creation.

Sandro Morasca is a professor of computer science at the Università degli Studi dell'Insubria in Como and Varese, Italy, and he is the president of OpenSoftEngineering. In the past, he was an associate professor and assistant professor at the Politecnico di Milano in Milano, Italy. He was a faculty research assistant and later a visiting scientist at the department of computer science of the University of Maryland at College Park. Sandro Morasca has been actively carrying out research in the software engineering field in empirical software engineering, specification of concurrent and real-time software systems, software verification, and open source software, and has published about 20 journal papers and 70 conference papers. Sandro Morasca has been involved in a number of national and international projects. He was the Leader of the activity related to the trustworthiness of open source software in the QualiPSo project, financed by the European Union. Sandro Morasca has served on the PC of a number of international software engineering conferences and i currently on the editorial board of "Empirical Software Engineering: An International Journal," published by Springer-Verlag.

Thomas Moser is postdoctoral researcher of software and knowledge engineering at the Institute of Software Technology and Interactive Systems, TU Vienna, Austria. He received his MSc and PhD degrees in business informatics from TU Vienna in 2006 and 2010, respectively, and works as a post-doc researcher in the research area "Semantic Integration" in the Christian Doppler Laboratory "CDL-Flex" since 2010. His research areas include data modeling and semantic web technologies for modeling engineering knowledge and the connection of design-time and runtime engineering processes, as well as practical and business applications of semantic web technologies.

Linus Nyman is a doctoral student at the Hanken School of Economics in Finland. His primary research focus is on code forking in open source software. When not working on his PhD, Linus can be found teaching classes on corporate strategy as well as guest lecturing on open source software. He has a master's degree in Economics and Business Administration, also from the Hanken School of Economics.

Arif Raza received his M.Sc. (1994) in Computing Science from University of London, U.K. and Ph.D. (2011) in Software Engineering from the University of Western Ontario, Canada. Dr. Raza has several years of teaching experience in Computer Science and Software Engineering. He has authored and co-authored several research articles in many peer-reviewed journals and conference proceedings in the area of software engineering. His current research interests include empirical investigation regarding usability improvement and assessment of open source software projects. Currently he is serving as postdoctoral research fellow at the University of Western Ontario, Canada.

William N. Robinson is an associate professor in the Department of Computer Information Systems at Georgia State University. His research interests include requirements engineering, model-driven systems development, and e-commerce. He received his PhD in computer science from the University of Oregon. He is a member of the IEEE, the ACM, and the Association for Information Systems.

Claudia Ruiz is a PhD candidate in the Computer Information Systems Department at Georgia State University. Her research interests include open source software development, social computing, and data mining. She received her MS in computer information systems from Georgia State University.

Walt Scacchi is senior research scientist and research faculty member in the Institute for Software Research, and also Director of Research at the Center for Computer Games and Virtual Worlds, both at University of California, Irvine. He received a PhD in Information and Computer Science at UC Irvine in 1981. From 1981-1998, he was a professor at the University of Southern California. Dr. Scacchi returned to UC Irvine in 1999 to join ISR. His research interests include open source software development, computer game culture and technology, virtual worlds for modeling and simulating complex engineering and business processes, developing decentralized heterogeneous information systems, software acquisition, and organizational analysis of system development projects. Dr. Scacchi is an active researcher with more than 150 research publications, and has directed more than 60 externally funded research projects. He also has had numerous consulting and visiting scientist positions with more than 25 firms or institutes, including four start-up ventures.

Teta Stamati has obtained a Degree in Computer Science from National and Kapodistrian University of Athens (Greece) in 1998. She also holds an MPhil Degree in Information Systems from University of Manchester (UMIST) (UK), an MBA Degree from Lancaster University Business School (UK) and a Phd in Information Systems from the Informatics and Telecommunication Department from National and Kapodistrian University of Athens (Greece). She has extensive experience in top management positions in leading ICT companies of the Greek and European private sector. She is currently Research Associate at the Department of Informatics and Telecommunications of National and Kapodistrian University of Athens. Her current research interests include information systems, business models, electronic and mobile government, service science, e/m-commerce, SOA and cloud computing.

Klaas-Jan Stol is a researcher at Lero, the Irish Software Engineering Research Centre, where he has worked since 2008. He holds a PhD in Software Engineering from the University of Limerick, Ireland, and a MSc in Software Engineering from the University of Groningen, the Netherlands. His research interests are in Open Source Software (OSS), software development methods (including OSS development practices), software architecture, component-based software development, software reuse and empirical software engineering.

Wikan Danar Sunindyo received his master degree in computational logic at the Dresden University of Technology, Germany in 2007. Since 2008 he works as a PhD researcher at TU Vienna, Austria in the research area "Complex Systems". His main research areas include Open Source Software, automation systems, process observation and analysis, and semantic web technologies to better integrate heterogeneous engineering environments.

M. M. Mahbubul Syeed is a PhD student and working as a researcher in the department of Software Systems, Tampere University of Technology. He obtained M.Sc degree in Information Technology from the same department in 2010. His research area includes analysis of open source systems and projects.

Tarja Systä is a professor at Tampere University of Technology, department of software systems. Her current research interests include software maintenance and analysis, software architectures, model-driven software development, and development and management of service-oriented systems.

Davide Taibi is a post doc researcher at the Università degli Studi dell'Insubria's department of computer science and consultant at OpenSoftEngineering. His research interests include empirical software engineering and measurement, especially concerning OSS quality evaluation; OSS business models; and OSS Marketing. Taibi is involved in several OSS projects and serves as the sales director of the Italian Open Source Competence Center (www.ccos.it).

Davide Tosi received his BS in telecommunication engineering (2000) at the Polytechnic of Milano, a MS in computer science (2002) and his PhD in computer science (2007) at the University of Milano Bicocca. After two years as a post-doc at the department of computer science at the University of Milano Bicocca, currently Davide Tosi is a research fellow at the Università degli Studi dell'Insubria and charter member of OpenSoftEngineering. His research interests include software testing and analysis, mobile agent systems, component based systems, self-managed systems and services, and open source quality and testing. He has published about 25 research papers in international journals, conferences and workshops. Davide Tosi has been involved in several national and international projects, including EU-funded projects such as SHADOWS and QUALIPSO. Davide Tosi has served on the PC of a number of international software conferences.

Kris Ven received his Ph.D. in Applied Economics from the Faculty of Applied Economics of the University of Antwerp, Belgium, in 2008. He is currently a postdoctoral researcher at the Department of Management Information Systems of the University of Antwerp. His research interests include the organizational adoption of IT and the link between innovation in organizations and the use of information technology. He has performed several studies on the organizational adoption of open source software. He has authored and presented several papers at international conferences on open source software, and has published in several academic journals, including the Journal of Database Management, Communications of the Association for Information Systems, IEEE Software and Information and Software Technology.

Dietmar Winkler received an MS in computer science from TU Vienna, Austria, in 2003. He worked as a guest researcher at the Czech Technical University, Department of Cybernetics in 2007 and received a PhD research scholarship at Fraunhofer IESE in Kaiserslautern, Germany, in 2008. Since 2010 he is researcher for quality management and software process improvement in the Christian Doppler Laboratory for "Software Engineering Integration for Flexible Automation Systems" (CDL-Flex). Moreover, he works as software engineering and process management consultant. His research interests include Software Engineering, Engineering Processes, Quality Management, and Empirical Software Engineering.

Chorng-Guang Wu is an Assistant Professor of Information Systems at College of Management, Yuan Ze University, Taiwan. He received his PhD in Information Systems from the University of Colorado at Denver. He also holds an MS degree in Computer Based Systems from the State University of New York at Binghamton and a B.B.A. degree from National Cheng Kung University in Taiwan. He worked previously as a software engineer and system analyst with several years of industry experience in the area of enterprise systems. His current research interests include open source software development, e-business, enterprise resource planning, customer relationship management and cloud computing. His research was published in several conference proceedings and peer-reviewed journals in the fields of information systems, computer science and technology management.

Clifford E. Young is Professor of Marketing and Associate Dean of Faculty at The Business School, University of Colorado at Denver. He received his BS in Physics from Colorado State University and his MBA and PhD in Business from University of Utah. Dr. Young's primary thrust is in the area of marketing research methodology, survey development and research analysis. He also has experience in selling and sales deployment analysis. Dr. Young has authored or coauthored over 60 articles in journals and national proceedings of marketing and management. In addition he has consulted for companies in the areas of marketing forecasting, sales deployment analysis, service quality assessment and management vision and values analysis.

Index